The Barn

ALSO BY WRIGHT THOMPSON

The Cost of These Dreams

Pappyland

The Barn

The Secret History
of a Murder in Mississippi

—

WRIGHT THOMPSON

PENGUIN PRESS

NEW YORK

2024

PENGUIN PRESS
An imprint of Penguin Random House LLC
penguinrandomhouse.com

LIBRARY OF CONGRESS CATALOGING-IN-PUBLICATION DATA

Names: Thompson, Wright, author.
Title: The barn : the secret history of a
murder in Mississippi / Wright Thompson.
Description: New York : Penguin Press, 2024. |
Includes bibliographical references and index. |
Identifiers: LCCN 2024010566 (print) | LCCN 2024010567 (ebook) |
ISBN 9780593299821 (hardcover) | ISBN 9780593299838 (ebook)
Subjects: LCSH: Till, Emmett, 1941-1955. |
Lynching—Mississippi—History—20th century. | Murder—Social
aspects—Mississippi—Delta (Region) | African American teenage
boys—Crimes against—Mississippi. | African Americans—Civil
rights—Mississippi—Delta (Region) | Racism against Black
people—Government policy—Mississippi. | Collective
memory—Mississippi—Delta (Region) | Delta (Miss. : Region)—Race
relations—History—20th century.
Classification: LCC HV6465.M7 T54 2024 (print) |
LCC HV6465.M7 (ebook) | DDC 364.1/34—dc23/eng/20240515
LC record available at https://lccn.loc.gov/2024010566
LC ebook record available at https://lccn.loc.gov/2024010567

Printed in the United States of America
1st Printing

Book design and family trees by Christina Nguyen

Map illustrations by Daniel Lagin

For Wheeler and Marvel

CONTENTS

I

The Barn *1*

II

Destinies *75*

III

1955 *195*

IV

Tomorrow *307*

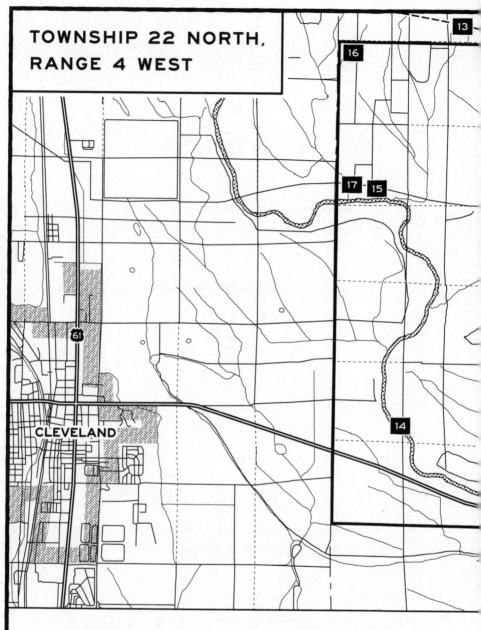

TOWNSHIP 22 NORTH, RANGE 4 WEST

13

16

17 15

61

14

CLEVELAND

1. Fannie Lou Hamer's home
2. Roy Bryant's store in Ruleville
3. Clint Shurden's home
4. Luster Bayless's home
5. Roy Bryant's grave
6. Peavine railroad
7. Robert Johnson's crossroads
8. Dockery Plantation
9. Dougherty Bayou
10. Drew-Ruleville Road
11. The Barn
12. Willie Reed's home
13. Drew-Merigold Road

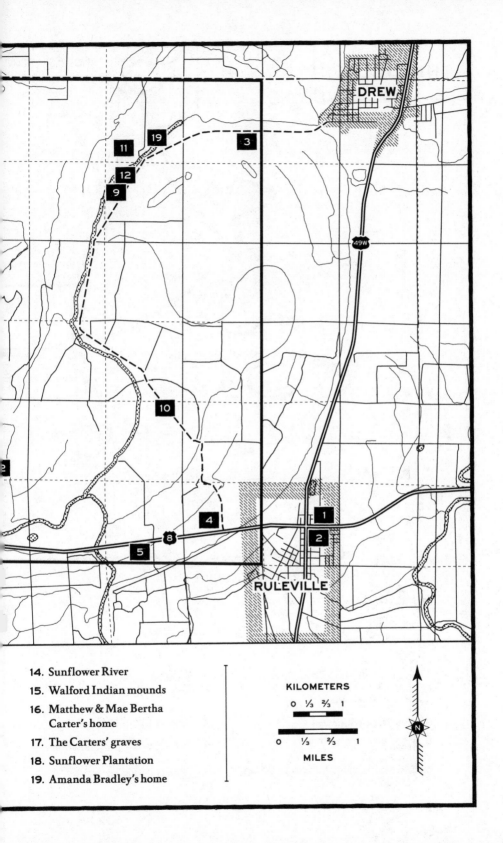

DREW

49W

10

19
11
12
9
3

4
8
5
1
2

RULEVILLE

KILOMETERS

0   ⅓   ⅔   1

0   ⅓   ⅔   1

MILES

N

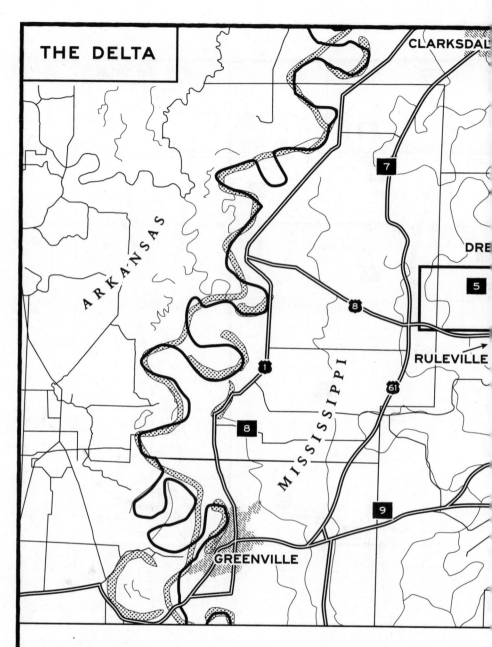

THE DELTA

CLARKSDAL[E]

ARKANSAS

MISSISSIPPI

DRE[W]

RULEVILLE

GREENVILLE

1. Emmett Till's body found here

2. Moses Wright's home

3. New Hope community

4. Duck Hill

5. Township 22 North, Range 4 West

6. Location of Joe Pullum's lynching

7. Allendale (author's farm)

8. Delta Pine & Land plantation

9. Charley Patton's grave

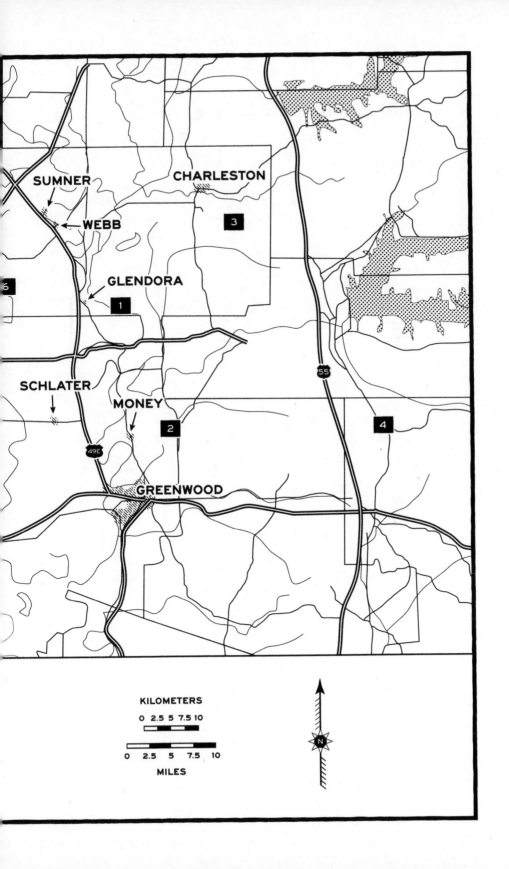

Emmett Till's Family Tree

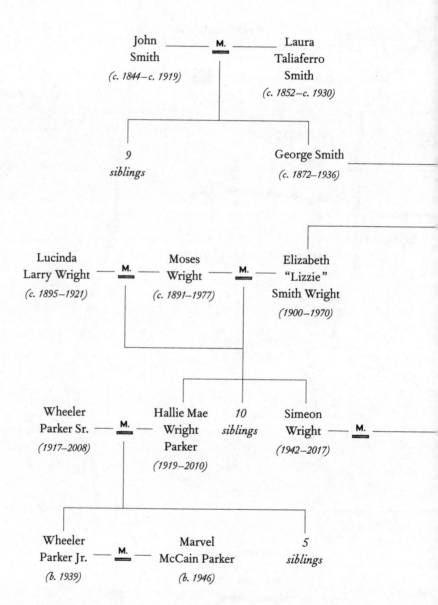

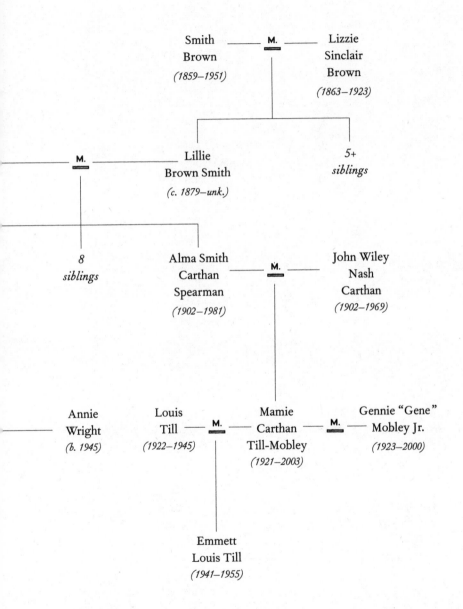

Smith
Brown
(1859–1951)

M.

Lizzie
Sinclair
Brown
(1863–1923)

M.

Lillie
Brown Smith
(c. 1879–unk.)

5+
siblings

8
siblings

Alma Smith
Carthan
Spearman
(1902–1981)

M.

John Wiley
Nash
Carthan
(1902–1969)

Annie
Wright
(b. 1945)

Louis
Till
(1922–1945)

M.

Mamie
Carthan
Till-Mobley
(1921–2003)

M.

Gennie "Gene"
Mobley Jr.
(1923–2000)

Emmett
Louis Till
(1941–1955)

Milam–Bryant Family Tree

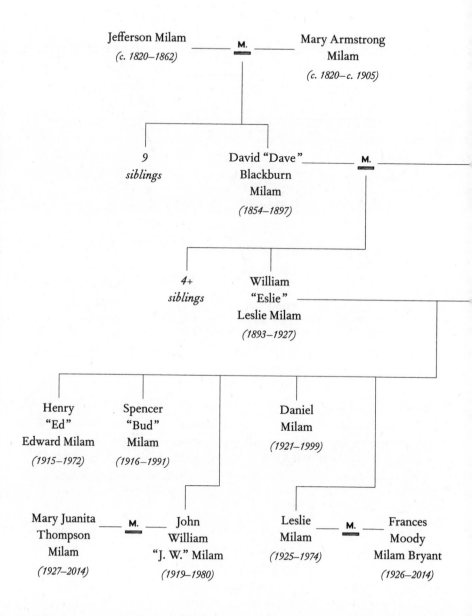

Jefferson Milam
(c. 1820–1862)

M.

Mary Armstrong
Milam
(c. 1820–c. 1905)

9
siblings

David "Dave"
Blackburn
Milam
(1854–1897)

M.

4+
siblings

William
"Eslie"
Leslie Milam
(1893–1927)

Henry
"Ed"
Edward Milam
(1915–1972)

Spencer
"Bud"
Milam
(1916–1991)

Daniel
Milam
(1921–1999)

Mary Juanita
Thompson
Milam
(1927–2014)

M.

John
William
"J. W." Milam
(1919–1980)

Leslie
Milam
(1925–1974)

M.

Frances
Moody
Milam Bryant
(1926–2014)

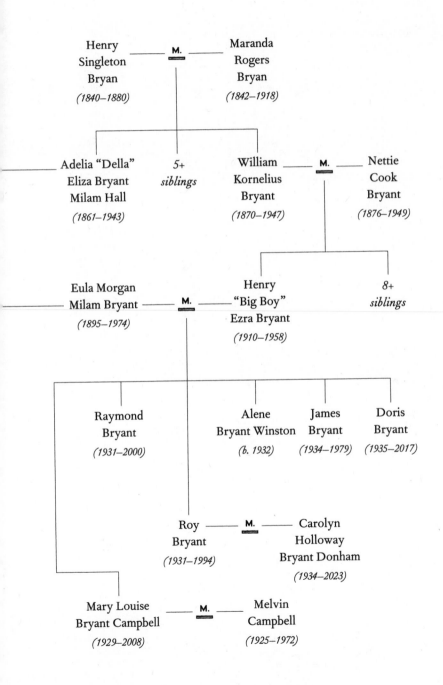

Henry Singleton Bryan
(1840–1880)

M.

Maranda Rogers Bryan
(1842–1918)

Adelia "Della" Eliza Bryant Milam Hall
(1861–1943)

5+ siblings

William Kornelius Bryant
(1870–1947)

M.

Nettie Cook Bryant
(1876–1949)

Eula Morgan Milam Bryant
(1895–1974)

M.

Henry "Big Boy" Ezra Bryant
(1910–1958)

8+ siblings

Raymond Bryant
(1931–2000)

Alene Bryant Winston
(b. 1932)

James Bryant
(1934–1979)

Doris Bryant
(1935–2017)

Roy Bryant
(1931–1994)

M.

Carolyn Holloway Bryant Donham
(1934–2023)

Mary Louise Bryant Campbell
(1929–2008)

M.

Melvin Campbell
(1925–1972)

I

The Barn

W illie Reed awoke early Sunday morning to the sound of mockingbirds. Mosquitoes hovered and darted on the bayou behind his house. The cypress floorboards creaked beneath his feet as he stepped outside into a wall of humidity. Local kids like Willie had a name for the little riffles rising from the dirt: heat monkeys, animated like a living thing. A Mississippi Delta sunrise is feral and predatory; even at 6:00 a.m., the air feels hot on the way in and stagnant on the way out. Daylight had broken an hour before Reed started his short walk to Patterson's country store, one of the many little places out in the country that sold rag bologna and hoop cheese. It was August 28, 1955. His grandfather wanted fresh meat to cook for breakfast. Willie was eighteen years old, with a boyish face that made him look at least three or four years younger. Delicate lashes framed his almond-shaped eyes. His girlfriend, Ella Mae, lived a few miles south on Roy Clark's plantation.

Late August meant they were a week into cotton-picking season. In a few hours, after church ended, hundreds of men, women, and children would be pulling nine-foot sacks through the rows of cotton on the other side of the road. The past few growing seasons had been hard on everyone but for the first time in two or three years the price looked good enough for farmers to clear a little profit, depending on the whim of the landlord. Reed and his family worked for Clint Shurden, one of eighteen siblings who'd all left sharecropping behind to form a little empire around the Delta town of Drew. The Reeds usually made money for a year of work, and Clint also paid Willie three dollars a day to help him out around the place.

The people on the other side of the narrow dirt road never made a dime working for their landlord, Leslie Milam, who'd moved into the old Kimbriel place a few years back. Milam was the first member of his hardscrabble family to gain a toehold in the cloistered world of Delta landowners. Bald like his brother J.W., with sagging jowls and a double chin, Leslie was renting to own from the kind of family his had aspired for generations to become, the Ivy League–educated Sturdivants, whose empire included at least twelve thousand acres and a sizable investment in a three-year-old business named Holiday Inn. Leslie's thick brows rose in a perpetual look of surprise above his eyes, which were just a little too close together.

The Black folks who lived in the country between Ruleville and Drew had quickly come to hate Leslie. They had a word for men like him, a whispered sarcastic curse. Leslie Milam was a *striver.* The year before he'd told Alonzo and Amanda Bradley that they owed him eleven dollars, which he'd forgive if they stayed another season. They'd also learned to recognize the mean, cigar-chewing J. W. Milam, who came around from time to time.

When old Dr. Kimbriel had farmed the place, the local sharecropper kids like Willie's uncle James would play in the long, narrow cypress barn just off from the white gabled house. Willie had been inside it once, too. The neighborhood children liked to chase the pigeons that flew through the cobwebbed rafters. Nobody chased pigeons once Leslie moved in.

That Sunday morning Willie turned left on the dirt road mirroring Dougherty Bayou and its knobby bald cypress trees. Five million years ago the range of these trees had stretched far to the north of Mississippi, but the Ice Age had reduced them to a narrow band around the Gulf of Mexico. Cypresses, sequoias, and redwoods are some of the oldest trees on the planet. Reed walked past the trees, down to the New Hope Missionary Baptist Church, which sat between the road and the bayou.

Dougherty Bayou was the name of the water that drained this part of the Delta into the Sunflower River. Mostly the bayou was known locally for its connection to the Confederate cavalry general Nathan Bedford Forrest, whose postwar extracurriculars included a turn as the first grand wizard of the Ku Klux Klan, which had originally been led by his former staff officers. The old white folks loved to talk about the Wizard of the Saddle, about how he led his cavalry along the Dougherty Bayou as he moved quietly toward Yazoo City. Forrest Trail, they called the old Indian hunting path that would become the Drew-Cleveland Road, which would later be renamed the Drew-Ruleville Road, which had originally been built in the first place by General Forrest's brother. The Confederate army once moved down this road to the beat of horse hooves and animal breath. Reed walked the same ground with the quiet shuffle of shoe soles on dirt. The sun had been up for an hour already, and the outline of rows emerged from the darkness.

Abandoned shacks dotted the countryside around Reed's home. There weren't as many people around as there had been just a few years before. Many of his neighbors had already left the Mississippi Delta. These were the last days of a way of life. With each passing year more and more sharecropper houses sat empty as machines replaced people. Modern civilization spun just a few hours north, connected by family ties and railroads and telephones but separated by what Black expats in Chicago called the Cotton Curtain. Local high schools would soon start scheduling reunions in Chicago, since that's where all the graduates were living anyway.

Reed took a left to cut through Leslie Milam's farm, aiming to cross over the dark, slow-moving Dougherty Bayou, full of crappie and bream the perfect size for a cast-iron skillet. That's when he heard the pickup truck. He turned and looked down the road and saw a two-tone Chevrolet kicking up dirt. A white cab with a green body. The truck turned directly in front of him. The driver pulled up to the long cypress barn. Four white men sat shoulder to shoulder in the cab. In the back, three Black men sat with a terrified Black child.

The child was fourteen-year-old Emmett Till. He had two terrible hours left to live.

I FIRST HEARD ABOUT THE BARN four years ago. A community organizer named Patrick Weems said we needed to take a drive through the Mississippi Delta during one of those endless days of the early pandemic. I'd been driving a lot during lockdown. My response to the world ending was to go home. I am from Clarksdale, Mississippi, one of those faded Delta farm towns built to support the sharecropper South that emerged after the Civil War. My family farms the same land we farmed in 1913, just twenty-three miles northwest of the barn Weems insisted I see. I'd been almost completely separated from the agricultural part of my history as a child. My family's farm had seemed like a past I wanted to leave behind. Then being back home forced me to consider where and how I'd grown up. What I found as I drove was that all that running hadn't really taken me anywhere at all. I remained a child of the Delta. I'd stop on the levee, a bandanna tight around my mouth and nose to keep out the trailing wake of dust, looking out at the land. I'd let the red dirt settle and I'd stare out at the endless, flat farms. This was some of the most fertile ground in the world—an alluvial plain and not an actual river delta—made rich from nutrients deposited by a million years of flooding rivers. If you could fly into the air like one of the extinct songbirds that once called this land home, you would see fingers of water stretching out like a hand from the wide, violent Mississippi into the flatland, rivers like the Yazoo, Sunflower, and Tallahatchie, bayous like Dougherty and Hushpuckena and the Bogue Phalia. Black citizens called the Tallahatchie the Singing River because of all the lynching victims who'd been thrown into its dark water. Their souls sang out from the water, a wellspring of Black death and white wealth.

Farming at its essence is just the practice of getting water onto land and then getting it off again, and the eighteen-county teardrop of the Mississippi Delta does this as well as anywhere on earth. On the eastern boundary between the flatland and hill country a series of reservoirs trapped the runoff and on the western edge levees kept the big river from flooding out crops and people. Humans had stopped the natural order of things, halting the patterns that created their fertile home, working with puritanical resolve to harvest the bounty that had taken a million years to create. Nothing about the physical appearance or ecosystem of the Delta carries any of the Creator's fingerprints. This land is man-made. Not until learning about the barn had I considered the idea that removing God's dominion from his creation might also remove his protection, leaving this corner of the world undefended from the impulses and desires of man, and the demands of commerce.

When I was growing up, the seasons still dominated life. Little towns came alive with planting and harvest festivals. The romantic smell of my childhood world is that sweet, decaying blanket of defoliant that still settles on my hometown in the last days of summer. Little yellow airplanes streak across the sky leaving wakes of billowing poison. My mother walks into our front yard when picking season begins and breathes deeply. She's a child again and her father is coming home for dinner, the big midday meal, hanging his fedora by the front door and talking with pride about his stand of cotton. The house is alive again with the shuffle of cards and the pop of grease and understated Methodist prayers for themselves and their neighbors. Her dad got his ship shot out from beneath him in the Pacific Ocean during World War II and every morning when he drank his glass of cold milk he quietly went back to the rattling thirst he felt holding on to a piece of decking and looking to the blinding horizon for help. Every Sunday he'd take his family for a drive around the farm, steering his station wagon through the fields, proud there were no weeds around his cotton plants. My grandmother and mother loved to make fun of his meticulousness. He'd been a dentist before the war, and they joked that Doc McKenzie wanted more than anything to floss his rows.

I can draw from memory a detailed road map of the Delta. At Tutwiler, Highway 49 forks, the west route going near where Willie Reed walked in 1955 and the east route cutting down to Greenwood, where Reed was born. Highway 1 follows the river, through Gunnison, and runs parallel to Highway 61. Highway 61, where Bob Dylan sang about God wanting his killing done, connects Clarksdale and Cleveland. Little dying farm communities cling to the roadside between the two old railroad towns. Shelby, home of my family, where my grandparents are buried on the outskirts of town. Winstonville, where Ray Charles and B. B. King played to sharecropper crowds at the Harlem Inn, which fire took down to a grassy spot on the east side of the road. Mound Bayou, the famous all-Black town founded by freed enslaved people. And Merigold, ten miles west of the land Willie Reed and his family farmed. All of these places, and the history buried around them, aren't disparate dots on a map but threads in a tapestry, woven together, so that the defining idea of the Delta is to me one of overlap, of echo, from the graves of bluesmen to the famous highways. Many times I've sketched these mother roads on a bar napkin. Which is to say that the Delta is my home, my family's home, for generations now. I know it well, and I'd never heard about the barn until Patrick Weems told me I needed to take a ride, just as I had somehow never heard the story of Emmett Till until I went to college out of state.

The barn where Till was murdered, Patrick said, was just *some guy's barn*, full of decorative Christmas angels and duck-hunting gear, sitting there in Sunflower County without a marker or any sort of memorial, hiding in plain sight, haunting the land. The current owner was a dentist. He grew up around the barn. When he bought it, he didn't know its history. Till's murder, a brutal window into the truth of a place and its people, had been pushed almost completely from the local collective memory, not unlike the floodwaters kept at bay by carefully engineered reservoirs and levee walls.

PATRICK WEEMS RUNS THE Emmett Till Interpretative Center, or ETIC, in Sumner, Mississippi. His job is to make sure people never forget about Emmett Till's murder. We set a time to spend a day following the Till trail that his organization was working to establish and protect; it is his goal to preserve all the places associated with Emmett's murder, with the hope that these places might teach future generations to be better than their ancestors. Weems is skinny, with hair nearly to his shoulders and a dark sense of humor. A local Black political leader said he decided to trust Weems because only progressive white boys wore their hair like that. Patrick climbed into the passenger seat of my truck holding his breakfast: an ice-cold can of Coca-Cola.

We agreed to start in Money.

Money, Mississippi, was once home to the Money Planting Company, owned by Charles Merrill of Merrill Lynch, whose grandsons now donate to Weems's ETIC, perhaps in hopes of settling some cosmic debt. Follow Grand Boulevard in Greenwood past all the cotton mansions, and cross over the Yalobusha River bridge, and the boulevard name changes to Money Road. That's the road where Emmett Till whistled at Carolyn Bryant and three days later got kidnapped and murdered by her husband and his brothers.

"I just can't imagine the dark of night being in the back of that truck," Weems says quietly. "He just turned fourteen."

Till's murder gave powerful fuel to the civil rights movement in 1955, and his symbolic importance has only grown since. When Americans gather to protest racial violence, someone almost certainly carries his picture, held high like a cross, no name needed. His innocent, hopeful face delivers the message. But the way Till exists in the firmament of American history stands in startling opposition to the gaps in what we know about his killing. No one knows for certain how many people were involved. Most historians think at least six were present. There's a small orbit of researchers who have made this murder their life's work, filmmakers like Keith

Beauchamp and Fatima Curry, authors like Devery Anderson and Chris Benson, retired law enforcement officers like Dale Killinger, journalists like Jerry Mitchell, academics like Dave Tell at Kansas and Davis Houck at Florida State. These folks mostly agree on all the details but argue over how many people were present at the barn. After four years of reporting, I think the number is probably eight.

Following the trial, protected by double-jeopardy laws, the acquitted killers got paid to give a confession to a national magazine—a heavily fictionalized account written by their lawyers and author William Bradford Huie—and Leslie Milam and his barn were written out of the story for his protection. That story allowed Leslie Milam and several others to get away with murder. Huie's phony history did its job. Ask most people where Emmett Till died and they'll say Money, the town where he whistled. The Equal Justice Initiative in Montgomery says Money. Wikipedia does, too. The Library of Congress website skips entirely over the barn, which is located just outside Drew, hometown of musician Pops Staples and football star Archie Manning. "If you go through Drew," Weems says, "and stop and ask somebody, 'Do you know where Emmett Till was murdered?' I think nine out of ten people will say, 'What are you talking about?'"

What does it matter whether there were two people or eight on hand for the torture and murder of a child in Mississippi in 1955, or whether it took place in Sunflower County or the next county over? I've come to believe these details mean everything. There are many well-known facts about the murder, confirmed by multiple sources over decades, but still there remains a deep vein of mystery. This book is my attempt to go beyond what is known and explore the unknown registers of a killing that, when seen clearly, illuminates the true history of our country. The covering up of Till's murder was not something that was perpetrated by a few bad apples. It couldn't have been. The erasure was a collective effort, one that continues to this day. This isn't comfortable history to face. The more I looked at the story of the barn and came to understand the forces that moved everyone involved into the Mississippi Delta in 1955, the more I understood that the tragedy of humankind isn't that sometimes a few depraved individuals do what the rest of us could never do. It's that the rest of us hide those hateful things from view, never learning the lesson that hate grows stronger and more resistant when it's pushed underground. There lies the true horror of Emmett Till's murder and the undeserved gift of his martyrdom. Empathy only lives at the intersection of facts and imagination, and once you know his story, you can't unknow it. Once you connect all the dots, there's almost nowhere they don't lead. Which is why so many have fought literally and figuratively for so long to keep the reality from view.

That's Weems's job, then, to help the ETIC board find and broadcast the truth about an actual human being whose name has become so symbolic. It's unpopular work in certain corners of the Delta. As we drove, I asked Patrick if he was armed.

"I'm naive enough to not carry a gun," he said.

He laughed and said not all of his team agreed.

We talked as we drove down into the flatlands. The dividing line between the Hills and the Delta is stark, marked by an actual descent. The landscape changes, quickly and dramatically, and the horizon feels unreachable. Following Highway 6 toward Clarksdale, we took the left at Marks, a town Martin Luther King Jr. visited the spring he was assassinated in Memphis. He'd chosen the Delta as the best place to launch his efforts to unite poor white and poor Black people. That terrified the men who worked the levers of capitalism. My friend Curtis Wilkie, a celebrated journalist, was with King in Marks that day. Curtis walked out of a local church and saw King sitting in a running car. The window was rolled down and they chatted. King ate a piece of cold fried chicken. He had two weeks to live. Curtis asked him if he was afraid. "No," King told him.

Weems and I left Marks in the rearview mirror and cut south on Highway 3, through Lambert and then Vance, the birthplace of John Lee Hooker. This land remains some of the most valuable in the world, snapped up at eight thousand dollars an acre by private wealth managers and pension funds. Bill Gates is the third-largest landowner in the state of Mississippi. But collapsed houses and barns, too many to count, mark the Delta roadside. About the only way to tell which houses are occupied and which are empty is by looking for a satellite dish. We drove past the shell of an abandoned elementary school. Trees and vines grew inside the building, nature reclaiming it season by season. Graffiti in the entrance hall read "You're already dead."

Not long ago I walked into an abandoned house on a farm and found the calendar still turned to some distant past harvest. Vinyl records were scattered in the other room. The O'Jays' *Identify Yourself* and *In the Mood with Tyrone Davis*. Pay stubs. An overdue bill from Ferretti's hardware store in Shelby with a handwritten note on the bottom, almost apologizing for the ask, the fraying ends of a working community. I tried hard to find the people who'd lived here. They had vanished. I sat down and flipped through old notebooks marked with page after page of addition, subtraction, long division, a family trying to make the math change a finite and insufficient amount of money. Phone numbers for Clara in Chicago and Julia in Indianapolis had been scribbled in the margins. A shopping list: Half a pint of E&J. Two six-packs of Southpaw. One bottle of Wild Irish Rose. One pack of menthol cigarettes. Shorts. A speeding ticket. An unopened summons.

"This is a dying region," Weems said. "It's been dying since August 28, 1955."

WILLIE REED HID BETWEEN the road and the barn as he heard Emmett Till cry out in pain. Emmett didn't make words, just noises, grunts, wild cries. Reed saw the green-and-white truck parked in front of the barn, which was also painted green. He listened. Then, helpless, he kept walking to the store. But he stopped at the sharecropper house a hundred yards away. Family friends Alonzo and Amanda Bradley lived there. They were the people Leslie Milam said owed him eleven dollars after a whole year of work. Amanda was awake and working on breakfast.

"Mandy," Reed asked, "who they beating to death down there?"

She looked out the window toward the barn but didn't leave the house. It was nearing 7:00 a.m. She had a sharecropper named Frank Young visiting her. He worked on the nearby Zama plantation. Amanda grabbed a bucket and told Willie and Frank to go back to the well near the barn and fill it with water. They got there and started the task. They could still hear the beating inside the barn. Willie and Frank tried to stay out of sight behind the pump.

A child's voice called out in pain, "Lord have mercy!"

"Get down, you Black bastard!" a deeper voice yelled.

The autopsy report would identify a broken skull, broken wrist bones, and a broken femur. An FBI investigator said it presented like a pistol-whipping.

"Mama, save me!" the child's voice cried again.

Willie Reed and Frank Young remained behind the well. J. W.

Milam came out to the pump. He wore a green nylon shirt and khaki pants and a U.S. Army .45 on a holster strapped to his hip. After taking a drink of cold water, he went back inside. Willie strained to hear. The screams had turned to whimpers and by the time the water bucket was full, the sounds stopped entirely. The sun was overhead and the farmhands were getting ready for church. Willie still needed to get changed. He and Frank took the water to the Bradley house. Willie went on to the store. The white men pulled a tractor out of the center of the barn and drove the green-and-white pickup truck in. They covered the back with a tarp.

Willie shopped and paid and turned back. When he passed the barn again on his way back home, the pickup truck was gone. Roughly three hours had passed since Willie first saw the truck arrive at Leslie Milam's farm. The morning was still. The blood on the floor of the barn was covered in cottonseed, soaking up the proof.

PATRICK AND I SPENT HOURS driving through the Delta. Long car rides are central to life here. When I was a child my parents thought nothing of a hundred-mile drive to eat dinner. People weren't from individual farms or towns so much as they were from the Delta. The drives inevitably became time travel. Respected elders always seemed to narrate: this was the old Buchanan place, and this is where I painted propane tanks one hot summer, and this is where Muddy Waters lived, and of course all the solemn nods to the sites of terrible violence. I know the exact spot on the highway where a high school classmate drunkenly ran over and killed a young Black woman; I also know that a local judge determined that his only punishment should be probation and a requirement that he graduate from college. Patrick had mapped out a specific route through space and time. We were saving the barn for last. Once he took a group from the Kellogg Foundation there and half the people refused to get out of the van.

Patrick directed me toward a river bend near Glendora. I shifted into four-wheel drive. We stopped at the latest historical marker his group had erected on the banks of the Tallahatchie River, reachable only by a farm road. It was the fourth sign they'd bought, fashioned from half-inch-thick AR500 steel, the same material used in military body armor, only twice as thick, covered with a replaceable polycarbonate plate. That's all a fancy way of saying bulletproof. They had to install a bulletproof sign to remember Emmett Till on the banks of the Tallahatchie River. The first sign, paid for by Morgan Freeman, was stolen and thrown in the river six months after being erected. The second sign got shot 317 times in eight years, so riddled with bullets that the Smithsonian has approached Weems about displaying it. The third sign made it thirty-five days before it allegedly got shot by three Ole Miss frat boys. The ETIC launched what it called the Emmett Till Memory Project. A tug-of-war emerged, each side acting in the shadows, with some people trying to preserve a memory and others trying, with guns, to erase it. A fourth sign went up, the bulletproof one, and two weeks later a group of white nationalists gathered on the site to film a recruitment video.

Next we went to the ruins of Bryant's Grocery, which is almost invisible behind the fungal ivy and vegetation growing over its collapsed husk. Weems wants to buy it but the current owners want four million dollars. They are the children and grandchildren of Ray Tribble, one of the jurors who freed Till's killers. The store remains the most visited Till site, in tension with the barn: decaying versus preserved, known versus invisible. The roof is gone and the walls are crumbling.

Emmett had come to Mississippi in 1955 to stay with his great-uncle Moses Wright and his cousin Simeon, who like everybody else called Emmett "Bobo." Simeon Wright didn't even know the name *Emmett* until the newspapers started using it. Simeon had stood outside the Money store and heard Bobo whistle at Carolyn Bryant. Emmett saw the look of horror and fear on Simeon's face, and he knew he'd made a mistake. He begged Simeon not to tell Moses what he'd done. He didn't want to get in trouble. For the rest of his life, Simeon would regret not saying anything. His silence didn't matter in the end; Moses and his wife, Elizabeth Wright, both heard the rumors about what had happened at the store.

The night Bobo died, he and Simeon shared a small bed. Simeon heard talking in his room and woke up to Moses standing over the bed next to half brothers Roy Bryant and J. W. Milam. Milam held his pistol in one hand and a flashlight in the other. Simeon heard the fear in his mother's voice as she begged the men not to take the boy. Elizabeth Wright offered what little money she had. Simeon huddled beneath the covers and pretended to sleep. He'd never forget how long it took Bobo to get his shoes on. Moses followed them outside. He heard a woman say they'd gotten the right kid. Simeon's mom ran to ask their white neighbor for help. The husband refused. Moses just stood outside staring toward the town of Money, long after the dusty trail disappeared. People prayed. Simeon's mom swore she'd never sleep in that house another night, and she didn't. She immediately moved to Chicago. Simeon and Moses Wright soon followed.

As an old man, Simeon came down to Mississippi over and over.

He'd drive from the spot where he'd lived in 1955 to the East Money Church of God in Christ and measure the exact distance: nine tenths of a mile. Then he'd go drive from where he lived to the railroad tracks in Money. Three miles exactly. Other folks on the road who saw the distinguished-looking Black man with a white mustache driving a Honda couldn't know they were watching a man measuring his past down to the tenth of a mile. Later in life Simeon Wright became a good golfer and kept his clubs in the trunk of his car. Next to them he kept his cotton-picking sack, just to remind himself how far he'd come and all he'd outrun. He saw the alpha and omega every time he reached for his sticks. It made him smile.

He and Weems got to be friendly. Once they stood together with a group of activists outside the store in Money, a place heavy with the lingering vapors of menace. Simeon didn't feel good there but he was willing to go if his presence helped Emmett's story be told. But his willingness to absorb pain for a larger good had limits. The next stop on that day's agenda was the barn. One of the people asked Simeon if he wanted to ride over with them.

"I'm not ready," he said.

SIMEON WRIGHT HATED ALL white people for a long time after his cousin's murder. The killing forced him into exile and curdled his beautiful childhood memories, like the smell of honeysuckle, which forever after made him remember the sleepless summer night when Emmett got marched out of the tiny bed they shared. He remembered how J. W. Milam's breath smelled. He remembered the sound of boots on the old wooden floor. But the older he got, the more he believed that hate only destroys the hater. "He finally got to a point that he said, 'I can't keep doing this forever,'" Weems told me. "He enjoyed teaching people about Emmett Till."

He got involved with white people he trusted, like Weems, and with white people he didn't trust, if it helped the cause. On one trip back to Mississippi, he agreed to meet with the Tribble family, who owned the store in Money. Years after serving on the jury, Tribble basically bought the whole town in the 1980s. There's something odd about buying in the Delta that late, especially for a family with such deep roots in the hill villages on the ridges around the small town of Charleston, looking down into the flat floodplain of rich black dirt. A *New York Times* reporter found him in 1995 and asked him about the jury verdict. Tribble explained that the corpse had chest hair and everyone knew Black people didn't grow chest hair until they were "about thirty" and so it could not have been Emmett Till. He believed that a vast conspiracy, cooked up by the NAACP, planted the body as a way to make Mississippi look bad and further a communist agenda hell-bent on tearing down freedom.

IN THE YEARS before Simeon's death, he would return many times to the spot where he heard his cousin whistle and all their lives broke into before and after.

"What was it like here with Simeon?" I asked Weems.

"You just don't talk," Weems says. "You just sit there. I mean, Simeon is whisked away, you know, he's twelve in 1955 and then the next day he's gone to Chicago. His cousin Wheeler is still alive."

That was a new name for me.

"Who's that?"

"The cousin who came down on the train with Emmett."

———

WHEELER PARKER JR. was Emmett's best friend, next-door neighbor, and cousin. They rode bikes and fished together. Before Mamie Till-Mobley died, she asked Wheeler to be one of the people who would keep her son's memory alive. Though Wheeler struggles sometimes with the attention, he does his best to keep his word. Not long ago he released an essential memoir, *A Few Days Full of Trouble*. He's a minister in Argo, Illinois, the pastor of the church Emmett's grandmother founded. Lots of people call themselves "the Till family," and cable news producers don't seem to have any mechanism for vetting, but Wheeler is the only person officially designated by Mamie's estate to speak for the family. He carries the ghosts of Simeon and Emmett with him. Weems told me Parker was coming south soon to work on plans to memorialize his friend.

"Where all is he going to go?" I asked.

"That's the question mark," Weems said. "He's never been to the barn."

There is a limit to how far Wheeler Parker is willing to follow Emmett into the darkness.

"River site, no problem being at the river site. Bryant's Grocery, no problem. The only site that I've seen him kind of be shaken was at the church in Chicago and he wouldn't come in. We all went into the main sanctuary and he wouldn't go in there. It took him like thirty minutes to enter."

Weems and I took Sunny Side Road across the Little Tallahatchie River away from what's left of Money. We talked about the abandoned and overgrown store. An activist once described the Delta to me as the picture of Dorian Gray: a place that wore its sins on its surface. We cut across back roads until we got on Highway

442 headed west to Schlater, pronounced "slaughter," the little town where Wheeler Parker was born before his family migrated north to Chicago. We passed a wheelchair and a rocking chair on the front porch of a house that looked abandoned. A corner store sold catfish and chicken and hot dogs. We kept on through town. A few miles later we stopped at the exact spot, the intersection of 442 and the Quiver River, where Wheeler Parker was born.

We turned north toward Drew. If we'd kept going on 442 for a few more miles we would have driven through the Eastland plantation, formerly the property of segregationist U.S. senator James O. Eastland, whose home sits 14.5 miles south of the barn. He took office in 1941, a proud white supremacist, and died in 1986. In 1984, my dad, a liberal Democratic fundraiser, needed to quickly collect a large amount of money for the fighter pilot and astronaut hero John Glenn, who was running for president. Someone said my dad needed to go kiss the Eastland ring, so he drove to Doddsville, down this same road, and he and the senator drank whiskey on the front porch. Eastland made a call. A steady stream of pickup trucks pulled into his driveway to drop off checks. When he and my dad finished their whiskey, Senator Glenn had his money. That's the kind of power "Big Jim" wielded in the Delta for half a century.

Weems and I left the main roads somewhere near Drew and navigated through turnrows and around the edges of fields. Not many farmers had cotton planted. That commodity chain has mostly moved on. For the most part we saw nothing but soybeans and corn. We were close to the barn. Long rolls of plastic poly pipe ran the length of landformed fields. Soybeans grew on the spot of the Patterson store. Corn grew on the site of Amanda Bradley's house. We'd been driving for a long time today and it didn't escape our attention that it was about the same length of time Emmett Till spent held hostage in the bed of a truck. He got kidnapped around 2:00 a.m. and Willie Reed didn't see him until after sunrise, four hours later.

After a little jog around a bean field, there it was.

"Here we are," Weems said softly. "Ground zero."

WILLIE REED FELT SCARED to tell the truth about what he'd seen, to challenge the dominant power structure, and he hoped silence might render that fear powerless. Then he opened a local newspaper to find a story about a missing child from Chicago. That was the first time Reed ever heard the name Emmett Till. A photograph of Till accompanied the story. Willie turned to his grandparents.

"That's him!"

He knew then that people would come looking for him. Rumors and whispers dominated life in the plantations. In the fields, on the gin yard, down at the country store. People talked. Reed just waited. Soon an armed J. W. Milam appeared in the field where he worked.

"Boy, did you see anything?" Milam asked.

"No, sir," Reed said.

"Boy, did you hear anything?"

"No, sir."

AFTER THE BODY WAS FOUND, Frank Young, who'd helped Willie Reed fill up the bucket at Leslie Milam's well, felt compelled to tell someone. Young, like Reed, knew that the story the lawyers and cops were repeating over in the Sumner courthouse and in the papers wasn't the whole truth. So he got himself to Mound Bayou and found the house of Dr. T.R.M. Howard, a civil rights leader and prominent Black businessman. Everyone knew Howard was leading the charge for justice. Something about the killing of this one particular child, in a place where white folks had been killing Black folks for centuries, had sent him into a rage.

Howard lived on hundreds of acres. Armed guards patrolled the grounds and checked any cars coming onto his property. Young found a war room and safe house inside the compound, a protected place for Black witnesses, activists, and journalists. This is where Michigan congressman Charles Diggs would stay during the trial, so he could represent his many Detroit constituents with Delta roots while also ensuring his safety at night. Howard slept with two pistols by his head and a Thompson submachine gun at his feet. His home bristled with weapons and men who looked willing to use them.

Young knocked on his door.

He told Dr. Howard the story. About Willie Reed and Amanda Bradley, and the green-and-white truck, and the barn. The screams and the silence. Howard called a white reporter he knew he could trust, Clark Porteous, from the *Memphis Press-Scimitar*.

Dr. Howard set up a meeting with the sheriffs of Sunflower and Leflore Counties and all the witnesses they'd found. The plan was to gather at 8:00 p.m. in the Drew office of a local attorney, Pascal Townsend. When the appointed hour arrived, none of the witnesses showed. The sheriffs went out and investigated. They found "some white men" had made the rounds of the plantations on Willie Reed's road, intimidating witnesses into silence.

Howard and the team started looking. Nobody planned on getting much sleep.

Meanwhile journalists looked for the Black men who'd been with Milam and Bryant during the murder. They'd vanished, too. Years later, a graduate student at Florida State would get law enforcement officials to admit that the men had been arrested under false names and kept away from the prosecutors in the Charleston jail.

While Howard was out searching plantations, a car pulled up to the law office. Inside was Frank Young, who'd come to repeat the story he'd told in Mound Bayou. The driver was his plantation owner, a widow named Ella Zama. Her husband, a child of Italian immigrants and a World War I veteran, had died two years before. Ella grew up in a social class that taught her how to write neatly in ballpoint pen with big, identical loops on her number threes. She and Frank Young waited hours for Howard to return before they gave up and disappeared into the night. After 1955, nobody connected to the case ever saw Frank Young again.

Leflore County sheriff George Smith led the search for the missing witnesses that night. A ruddy man, Sheriff Smith felt happiest hunting in the woods with a rifle on his shoulder. He, nearly alone among his tribe, tried to do the right thing about the murder. He arrested and charged Milam and Bryant almost immediately. The trial might have turned out differently had he run the case and not the cartoonishly racist Tallahatchie County sheriff Henry Clarence Strider. Smith knew right from wrong but didn't forcefully make his case; Strider also knew right from wrong but just didn't care. Sheriff Strider, as much a mob boss as a law enforcement official, ran his own plantation in Tallahatchie County. Locals joked that he got 100 percent of the crop-duster vote because he spelled out the letters of his name on seven sharecropper shacks lined up on the farm: S-T-R-I-D-E-R. Strider fought to claim jurisdiction over the case, which made him a hero to his constituents.

Smith, meanwhile, had caught hell when he said he'd join the NAACP activists and journalists who were trying to investigate.

He violated a code simply by trying to do his job. As the search mission began he'd told reporters, "These witnesses have a story to tell. We've got to find them if it takes all night."

Only twelve hours remained to get these men and women into the courtroom.

They needed to find Willie Reed.

THE JOURNALISTS WHO HELPED the local law enforcement officers search were a group of brave men, reporters who'd fought in wars and covered them, too, and who'd spend the next decade and a half risking their lives to cover the civil rights movement.

Black reporter Simeon Booker had been with *Jet* magazine only a year. Almost everything history books tell you about the killing of Emmett Till is known because Booker reported it. He got to the story first, sitting with Mamie Till in a South Side Chicago funeral home, taking notes about her tears and her resolve. When she looked down at her son's body and tried to find a part of him to recognize, Booker was there, recording her words. He wrote: "Her face wet with tears, she leaned over the body, just removed from a rubber bag in a Chicago funeral home, and cried out, 'Darling, you have not died in vain. Your life has been sacrificed for something.'"

There was Moses Newson, who is still alive and a legend in the journalism world. He was the civil rights correspondent for Memphis's *Tri-State Defender* and faced danger with the frequency of a second lieutenant in an infantry company. Clark Porteous, the white reporter trusted by the Black community, followed, too. Twenty-two years later he'd write the hometown paper's obituary for Elvis. The headline stretched across page A1: A LONELY LIFE

ENDS ON ELVIS PRESLEY BOULEVARD. Jim Featherston, of the *Jackson Daily News*, had won a Pulitzer Prize the year before. His colleague, W. C. Shoemaker, had survived the Korean War. Eight years later he'd be one of the last people to see Medgar Evers alive.

And there was James Hicks, editor of the *Amsterdam News* and later *The New York Voice*, whose accounts of these terrifying weeks in American history still resonate today. He was the first Black reporter to cover the war in Korea and the first Black American credentialed by the United Nations, and wherever the great national original sin reared its head in the culture, whether a school in Little Rock or a barn in the Mississippi Delta, Hicks was on the ground. His beat, if it can be described so reductively, was to find American heroes risking their lives to make the country live up to its ideals. The cops and reporters rode over the dark plantation roads surrounding the barn, traveling in a caravan, seventy miles an hour on the straightaways, racing the clock.

HEADLIGHTS FLASHED OFF BAYOUS and cypress trees. They had until morning. Everyone knew by now that witnesses put the murder in Sunflower County, not Tallahatchie County, which would give prosecutors a much greater chance of convicting Milam and Bryant.

Sheriff Strider was working to uphold the system. Sheriff Smith was working that long night to uphold the law.

The plan was to send Black reporters to plead with people to testify. Smith promised not to issue warrants or drag anyone from their home. He was going to let each man or woman decide. That felt like the empathetic thing to do. Smith understood what he was asking. A few hours remained before court reconvened. The Black reporters dressed in the simple clothes of the sharecroppers. The cars turned into Leslie Milam's place and found Amanda Bradley's home near the barn. The search party begged her for ten minutes to open her door and let them in. She refused and at first denied even knowing about the killing. The back-and-forth continued until a local Black pastor finally convinced her to open the door. Ultimately she agreed to testify, a decision she'd come to regret.

An hour later they found Willie Reed down the road.

They parked on Clint Shurden's place, in the shadow of Dougherty Bayou and Leslie Milam's barn, and knocked on the door of Add Reed, Willie's grandfather. They asked to come inside. Imagine Willie Reed in that moment. The radio stations had been filling the air with talk of the dead boy. The people he trusted most in the world told him not to say a word about what he'd seen. But Willie Reed thought about the cries he'd heard coming from the barn, thought about how impotent he'd felt hiding behind the well, weighed the cost of talking against the cost of his silence. If he'd have kept quiet, Emmett's final hours would have been forever expunged from the American story.

He agreed to tell the jury what he'd seen and heard.

JEFF ANDREWS OWNS the barn now.

His voice sounded real country on the phone. We set a time to meet at his house a few miles outside Drew, where he keeps his dental office. The road into Drew is lined with abandoned and rusted cotton gins. The potholes in town are six inches deep and twice as wide. In Drew, waiting on Andrews, I pulled up on a gray-haired country gentleman shoveling sand into a pothole in the middle of a city street. "It's hell on an old man," he said and then looked away.

I headed west out of town, past the spot where Clint Shurden's house once stood, and felt the road turn from blacktop to gravel beneath my tires. Behind me in the rearview hung a familiar cloud of brownish-red dust. A johnboat floated in the Dougherty Bayou, a fisherman pulling out crappie and bream and the newly introduced bass. The slow water, sliding around the gnarled open palms of the cypress tree knobs, looked delicate and peaceful. Jeff Andrews's manicured lawn swooped up toward a little hillock where his house stood. He had built it. Leslie Milam's old house was gone. It burned on Easter Sunday, 1994, not long after Andrews bought the place, according to land records.

The dentist was a few minutes late, so I looked around at his swimming pool with an outdoor fireplace and covered patio. A pergola of vines and flowers fought a losing battle against the sun. The air felt thick like sludge. A northern mockingbird sang in the cypress trees as the dentist's truck came into view. His tires kicked up a wake of dust when he turned off the Drew-Ruleville Road and headed across the bayou and up toward his house. He got out of the truck, still wearing his scrubs, and with a smile extended his hand.

Bird songs echoed across the flat Mississippi Delta countryside. Sounds here carry and distort how a person processes basic things like distance and time. The mockingbird, with no song of its own, threw out the calls of the wren and the chickadee. In between the cornfield and the house was a garden, with tin-wire tomato columns covered in vines waiting to flower and fruit. Andrews told me he rarely eats a store-bought tomato.

He's the fourth owner of the barn since Leslie Milam. I asked him what happened to the old house, the one that burned. He smiled. It cost a lot of money to haul boards and wires and pipes away, so when his contractors dug the foundation for his new home, he had them push all the wreckage into the hole and cover it. The ruins of the Milam house were literally beneath our feet.

The gravel crunched as he walked to the barn, which is long and narrow with sliding doors in the middle. Nobody knows when it was built exactly but its cypress-board walls were already weathered in the summer of 1955.

Andrews rolled up the firehouse-style garage door he'd installed.

Our eyes adjusted to the darkness.

His Christmas decorations leaned up against the left wall. Within reach lay a lawn mower and a Johnson 9.9-horsepower outboard motor. Gnarled Mississippi River driftwood was stacked in a corner. Dirt covered the spot where Emmett Till died. Jeff had ripped up the floorboards a few years back and hadn't yet installed anything else in their place. He pointed to the central wooden rafter beam with a notch worn in the center.

"That right there is where he was hung at," he said.

CLINT SHURDEN DROVE a terrified but determined Willie Reed to the Sumner courthouse and stayed there, to signal to folks that an attack on Reed would be an attack on Clint and his powerful family. He looked intimidating with a crew-cut receding hairline atop his rectangle-shaped, jowly head. It was a short drive to Sumner. Strider limited the number of Black citizens who could attend but people still flooded the town square. Vendors sold ham sandwiches and Cokes.

Judge Curtis Swango invited Reed into his chambers. Willie declined to sit. The judge asked what he'd seen and Reed told him about the truck and the beating in the barn, and how J. W. Milam walked to get a drink of water before going back to beat the child some more. As he talked, the two defendants propped their feet up on the judge's desk. When Willie finished, the judge approved him as a witness.

Mamie Till testified first. Her interrogators questioned her with casual cruelty. She fought back tears when a lawyer shoved a photograph of her tortured son in her face. The defense argued she couldn't recognize her own son and that the body found in the Tallahatchie River had been planted by the NAACP. That's the closest the true pathology of my home gets to the surface, when something insane feels easier to believe than a grieving mother's tears. The defense attorneys insinuated she'd hidden her son to cash in on an insurance policy, and that he was alive and well in Chicago or Detroit. She kept her composure and stepped down from the witness box.

Back at her seat she cooled herself with a black fan dotted with red roses.

Willie Reed went next. He felt afraid but seeing Congressman Diggs sitting in the audience calmed him. He looked at Mamie and knew he had to tell the truth. Only four years separated him and Emmett. He knew it could have been his body found in the Tallahatchie—a local man casually, and almost gleefully, told a national reporter, "The river's full of n——s"—and so he stood there and told the truth. The prosecutor asked him to identify the man he saw drinking water from the well. He did as he was asked.

Milam stared back at him and smiled.

WILLIE REED RODE HOME from court with Clint Shurden. The Shurdens had come to own most of the land around the barn by 1955. They'd come from Ireland before the Revolutionary War.

The family passed down the story of how they arrived in a cattle boat, which may or may not be true. The Shurdens had been mule traders in the old country. Three of Clint's great-uncles died in the Civil War but his grandfather survived. He came to Mississippi and couldn't read or write. Clint's father, George Shurden, was born fourteen months before Fort Sumter and died ten months before Pearl Harbor. Clint and his many siblings fed off the family garden: huge cabbages, butter beans, collards, string beans, bunch beans, tomatoes, turnips. His mother picked fruit from the peach and apple trees to make tarts. His dad raised hogs, cattle, and sheep.

Their father eventually moved from the Hills down into the Delta, chasing his fortune. That chase is what put his sons in Drew, Mississippi, in the summer of 1955. They started as sharecroppers and rose up through the post–World War I boom to escape the gravitational pull of one social class and enter another, briefly reaching even higher still. The Shurdens were in between rednecks like the Milams and the aristocratic Sturdivants, or the Dockerys, who lived just over the river from the barn.

They got close to the levers of power, real power, and learned about the ambivalence rooted in the true nature of that power: how it made people split in two, unable to do the right thing when the rewards they wanted were there for the taking. Clint's brother Otha became close with Senator Eastland. They went into the cattle business together along with oil titans D. A. Biglane and Bunker Hunt, a major funder of the John Birch Society whose brother created the Super Bowl and whose nephew owns the Kansas City Chiefs. On August 9, 1968, a Friday, the White House diary of President Johnson's day at his ranch in Texas includes a notation for 4:05 p.m., when LBJ went back to the main house to meet "Senator James Eastland, Mr. W. O. Shurden, Mr. D. A. Biglane."

The three men had been on a private jet to look at cattle in Mexico. They stopped for customs in San Antonio and Eastland figured he'd better make a courtesy call to the president.

"You're coming out here," Johnson told Eastland. "I'll have Lady Bird meet you at the Johnson City airport."

They got back on the plane and made the short hop. Lady Bird and the Secret Service drove them to the ranch. The president gave his guests a tour. Johnson showed his guests where he was born and then took them to a small cemetery. A tremor shook his voice.

"Gentlemen," he said, "right over there is where I'm going to be buried, and I don't think it will be very long."

Otha thought the president looked sad. He praised Johnson's tenure as president, told him about the great standard of living they enjoyed. Johnson perked up.

"And yet, Mr. President," Otha said, "there are some things we don't like."

Johnson smiled.

"Well, let me have it," he said. "My skin is thick."

Otha told him that the federal guidelines for integrating the public schools—this was fourteen years after *Brown v. Board* and the schools were *still* segregated—were unfair and that Mississippi should have the right to determine if white children and Black children shared classrooms. The president radioed the Secret Service to bring him some scotch. The men started drinking and went to Lady Bird's favorite place on the ranch, an oak tree on a bluff overlooking the Pedernales River flowing down below.

Johnson insisted on sending the men home on his plane, Air Force One, not the smaller jet that had brought them in. Otha went back to Drew.

JEFF ANDREWS AND I walked past the old well over to his swimming pool and sat down to talk. He wore scrubs. We heard the mockingbirds. They start early in the morning, right around sunrise. I wanted to know how he could swim and flip burgers and drink Bud Light so close to the site of such violence and death.

I kept looking back at the barn. He knew what I was doing.

"We don't think about it," he said.

Andrews understands the historical value of his barn, and the emotional power it holds for the Till family members he welcomes onto his land, and he winces a little bit when he sees people noticing his Christmas decorations. "I hate to have to show people this," he said one day, "cause I got so much shit in here."

There's buckshot mud in the distance, a sign of mediocre land, not the sandy, loamy black dirt the most expensive farms enjoy. Nobody wants to talk about it but the Delta soil requires more and more chemicals and fertilizers to hit yield numbers that make the effort worth it. The barn, though, looks like it might stand another hundred years. Architects who have examined it say it shouldn't still be upright. Something to do with how the interior struts are designed. It's a bit of a miracle that a big wind hasn't just knocked it down.

Sitting in the shade by his pool, Jeff pointed behind him.

"My parents' house is on the Drew-Merigold Road," he said.

His family is from this tiny patch of land and those roots mean something to him. A professor who studies Till once asked him if he'd be willing to sell the barn. Jeff just shrugged.

"I like my shed," he replied finally.

He told me they'd had a lot of rain.

"What did that do to your yields?" I asked later.

He sighed. "Probably about ten bushels to an acre less."

"What are you normally? Sixty-seven? Seventy?"

"Yeah, usually sixty-five, sixty-three, sixty-five, something like that."

His daily life is occupied with his current crop. He almost never looks into the past, an inherited habit. His father told him about the barn's history only after he'd signed the papers to buy it.

"I didn't even know," he said. "Really and truly. I didn't even know about the damn history of the place when I purchased it. . . . I didn't find out about that until afterwards. I know my dad knew I was gonna buy that but he never said anything about it. He was around, and hell, he was two miles down the road, so you know damn well he knew all about it. I think he even knew Roy Bryant and J. W. Milam."

He'd been on a call earlier in the day with preservationists talking about his barn. I started to ask him about the call and he interrupted me.

"They're all still blown away that this isn't a big deal to us. It's in the past. I mean, why would we talk about it on a daily basis? We're so stigmatized by what everybody else thinks Mississippi is, but it's like I told them today. I said, 'I promise you,' I said, 'I can take you into the elementary school—like the first grade through sixth grade and we can poll all them damn kids who Emmett Till is,' and I said, 'I bet you ninety-five percent of them won't even know who Emmett Till is.'"

There's a bitterness that lives close to the surface even now, a feeling of white victimhood that bleeds into nearly every political and social urge.

"It's everybody from up north and shit that keep, you know, I mean, they still think of us as *Mississippi Burning*," he said. "And that's what chaps my ass, you know, hell, I mean, you grew up in the Mississippi Delta, too."

His dad never told him about the history of the barn even though they drove past it thousands of times. Never. Not even once, in passing, after a long day in the cab of a pickup truck. This omertà, even between fathers and sons, perhaps *especially* between fathers and sons, is the way the white people in the Delta have forged their lives in the years after the civil rights era.

"It's in the past," Andrews said.

His yellow lab rolled in the hot grass near the cornfields. Her name is Dixie.

ONE DAY MY PHONE RANG and it was Stafford Shurden, the grandson of Reg, who bought the barn after Leslie Milam moved out in late 1955 six weeks after the trial. His great-uncles were Otha, who drank scotch with LBJ, and Clint, who drove Willie Reed to the courthouse. Stafford is the last of his kind, one of the only members of his farming family still around Drew. We met on a little side street just off the highway. He rolled down his window and smiled, a mop of blond hair on his head, with a youthful energy that hid the lines around his eyes. He was nearly fifty. Stafford owns the little café in town and is always trying to help Drew become a thriving place again, organizing duck gumbo contests, or Mardi Gras parades with lawnmowers, or crawfish boils. He served as a local judge but is now retired from the bench. He's lived his whole life in a ten-mile circle, except for college, and he never knew

Emmett Till was killed in his hometown, or that one of the key witnesses worked for his relatives. That knowledge never passed a single person's lips.

"Just as a race, I mean, let's just pretend it ain't never happened," he said and sighed. "And it's totally indefensible for sure. . . . Now I realize you have to talk about it."

His grandparents lived in the old farmhouse after Leslie Milam moved out, shunned by the same wealthy families who had agreed to help finance his ascent out of peckerwood status. The Shurdens lived there for maybe three years before his grandmother insisted they move out, even though they owned the land and the house was free. Something about it disturbed her. She never spoke about why.

"She always told me she hated it out there," Stafford said through his open truck window. "Everybody in town knew that old house. It was vacant when I was a kid. It was just in disrepair."

He told me his aunt was talking one day about the modern Ku Klux Klan, which never really had a hold in the Delta outside the community of Drew for reasons I never understood. In the rest of the Delta the paternal landowning class—Sturdivants, Dockerys— kept the Klan away from their plantations and their workers.

"I never met anyone that was in the Klan," he told her.

"You never met anyone you *knew* was in the Klan," she replied.

THERE'S A LONG-OUT-OF-PRINT history book about Drew that nearly every current and former resident keeps on their shelves. Otherwise it's just about impossible to find. I borrowed Stafford's copy and read about how this community and these farms were carved out of the wilderness that covered the Delta. The book includes the most detailed account of Nathan Bedford Forrest's nighttime run from Friars Point to Yazoo City, which took him through the wilderness between Drew and Dockery.

There's a good reason Forrest would have chosen that route. His brother lived near the Dougherty Bayou: the Forrest place was owned by the slave trader and Confederate officer Aaron Forrest. At that time, Aaron Forrest was one of the few white people who had ventured as far into the interior of the Delta as what is now Drew. The town wouldn't exist for another fifty years. The oldest people in the area still repeat the stories they heard from their grandparents about how hated Aaron Forrest was in the community. He never returned after the war but his old farm kept his name. The founder of the town, Andrew Jackson Daniel, lived on the Forrest place and worked as a sharecropper until he could afford land of his own. His daughter was Drew Ann Daniel. The town where Emmett Till died is named after a girl who was raised on a farm owned by a founding family of the Ku Klux Klan. The barn where Till died is within eyeshot of that very land. Nearly a century before J. W. Milam's pickup truck came rumbling down Dougherty Bayou, the cavalry of Nathan Bedford Forrest moved through the swamp from the other direction, and in some dimension where time doesn't exist, they still pass each other day after day.

The white history of the area, a sanitized version, exists in that Drew history book. The Black history exists only in memory, and a shrinking number of memories at that. A man named Carl Watson is one of its custodians. He's a pillar of the small community of Black landowners who live down from the barn on the Drew-Ruleville Road, and he agreed one afternoon to help me see the people and homes that have been lost to all but a few people like him. He's lived near the barn most of his life. His smoker is often rolling along at 250 degrees as his neighbors—family, really, as everyone here is related in some way—crowd around his picnic table and drink cold beer and wait for the food. If the grill temperature starts to go down, he's got a few chain saws lying around. He grew up on a plantation on the east side of the barn, almost directly across from Clint Shurden's home. We drove and he narrated life as it used to be. He pointed to a broken-down house, collapsing into the vines and the trees, almost in a fetal position.

"Detroit," he said.

Names unspoken for decades passed his lips. We skirted a pecan grove and then a stand of trees across the road. That's where his brother lived before he went north, one of the millions of Black citizens who left the South to find a better job, or to keep their family safe. He pointed to empty pieces of grass and listed the names of the families who had lived in houses that now existed only in his mind. The Williamses lived by the tree line. The Miller brothers' store was on the left. This past year a big corporation has been landforming, which requires huge tractors and graders and bulldozers to move around a field in a delicate dance, guided by GPS coordinates and satellites, trying to make the land better to irrigate and easier to farm. Watson can hear the machines moving dirt at night as he tries to sleep. It's strange to have the land around you change overnight. Normally it's the kind of tectonic movement that takes a thousand years. Now it happens in a few hours. Nature long ago lost a vote.

We passed the barn.

Watson didn't know Emmett Till had been killed there until his dad told him in the late 1980s. He was born four years after the killing, just down the road from the barn, and he doesn't know why his father never told him. Several generations grew up seeing the barn every day and were never told about it, perhaps owing to some well-intentioned parental desire to protect their children from what their ancestors experienced, a palpable silence laid over the land like a blanket being snapped and spread. White mothers and fathers in this part of Sunflower County didn't talk about it. Black mothers and fathers didn't either.

We kept driving, connecting dots, closing distance across the vast Delta landscape, and he pointed to where the New Hope church had stood. It collapsed in the 1990s. One living former member remained. Carl asked me to turn left on Radio Station Road. That's where he was born. We stopped at the spot. He could still see it and smell it. Two houses, boys in one, girls in the other, each three rooms with a coal stove in the middle. They also had a smokehouse and his dad made sage-laced country sausage that barely exists anymore. Then his father moved down the road toward Ruleville to take more of a manager's job with the Roy Clark plantation, where Willie Reed's girlfriend lived in 1955.

Watson's dad forbade his sons to drive tractors. He didn't want them even learning. They had three choices: a job away from the plantation, college, or the military. Carl joined the Marines. When he finished his service he came back here. His dad owned his house before him. They bought it from their friend Fannie Lou Hamer's Freedom Farm. She and her husband, Pap Hamer, became national political figures in the 1960s and '70s, advocating for voting rights and equality. Carl can see Pap Hamer coming down the road in his truck, stopping to pick up Carl and his brothers to ride in the back out to some plantation to chop cotton. All those people are gone. He told me he read a news story recently that said the modern tractors need people only to turn them around. The GPS does the actual farming. Soon, the story said, they won't need people at all to plant and harvest these crops. Almost all the tenant houses are gone. We passed two on the right side of the farm, still owned by the Clark family, both empty. When they finally come down, whether by a wrecking ball or by neglect, no visible signs of the sharecropping South will remain on the road.

"These are the last two," Carl said.

We made a final stop. His family church burned down not long ago and only soot and concrete steps are left. The cemetery remains. That's where his parents rest alongside their friends. The Jacksons. The Williamses, who lived by the long line of trees. His mother and father lie in the shade by the Dougherty Bayou, which flows into the Sunflower River out near Dockery Farms.

Isaac Watson. August 11, 1913 to January 9, 1999.
Clara Watson. May 11, 1912 to March 21, 2001.

ONE AFTERNOON Stafford Shurden took me through his family's land. A Taurus semiautomatic pistol rested casually on his console. His family footprint once stretched to the gates of Parchman, the infamous Gothic prison farm that serves as the Mississippi State Penitentiary, one of the worst and most feared prisons in the country. The front gate is twelve miles north of the barn.

At the end of the drive we stopped at his family's old farm office, which would have been buzzing with people back when the Shurdens ran this little corner of the world. Now it's empty. He found a key on a big ring and opened the door.

We stepped into the dark, silent room. The first thing Stafford did was go sit in his father's old desk chair made out of a green bucket seat from an old classic Thunderbird. He hoped the old man would be proud of him. A painting showed Black cotton pickers moving through a field with their long bags, with the Shurden Farms logo on the trailers parked around them. Stafford sighed.

"Tell me this ain't the most racist shit you've ever seen," he said.

There was a walk-in safe and a poster on the wall: *Every morning in Africa, a lion wakes up. It knows it must run faster than the slowest gazelle, or it will starve. It doesn't matter whether you're the lion or a gazelle—when the sun comes up, you'd better be running.*

There was an oil painting of a stern old woman.

"That's Grandma Shurden," Stafford told me. "She had eighteen kids."

A family crest, commissioned by Otha Shurden in 1969, has soybeans, cotton, and catfish on it. Grandma Shurden was Clint's mom, too. In a little side office was a huge map of their part of Sunflower County. It documented who owned every piece of land, divided into squares and rectangles and trapezoids, into little homesteads and big plantations. I looked down at the corner and saw the date: "Jan 1, 1956."

This was the first county land map made after the murder. I ran my finger along the sides of the map and found the barn: Township 22 North, Range 4 West, Section 2, West Half, measured from the Choctaw Meridian. Familiar names claimed plots all around the old Milam farm. Smaller pieces of land were marked only by initials. I found the Dougherty Bayou and all the nearby farms and then the barn. It was the only piece of dirt on the map without a name.

THOMAS JEFFERSON WROTE A LAW that would pass Congress as the Land Ordinance of 1785. His goal was simple. He wanted the empty open space of his new country to be broken into small blocks and sold to yeoman farmers—small, entirely independent (white) landowners—and so he took a system invented by a military engineer named Thomas Hutchins and codified it into law. Many ancient cultures were built around the idea of shared land. America was built around the idea of owning parceled land. That foundational urge was born in the moment when Jefferson put pen to page. Yeomen weren't plantation lords like Jefferson and they weren't poor white trash. To Jefferson their protection and elevation in American life was the hill upon which this new nation would live or die. The first draft of the bill broke the country into ten-mile-by-ten-mile squares called hundreds, while a second reduced them to seven-mile-by-seven-mile squares called townships. On May 3, 1785, William Grayson of Virginia made a motion to change the seven to a six and James Monroe seconded the motion. They would send surveyors out into every bit of new territory America amassed—starting with the land won from the English in the Revolutionary War—and divide it into thirty-six-square-mile blocks, which would be divided into thirty-six smaller squares named sections. Each section was 640 acres, or one square mile, and the sale of all this public land would pay down the war debt of the new nation, which hadn't yet been able to agree on a way to raise money through taxes. A permanent grid appeared overnight.

A central American conflict was baked into this first drawing of the new nation. Jefferson wanted the land to be settled by yeomen. But the price for the newly available land was simply too high for most farmers to pay. In the decades that followed, Alexander Hamilton's Federalist Party and Jefferson's Republican Party fought over this issue. From John Adams through Jefferson and into Madison and Monroe, the minimum purchase amount (and the price) rose and fell depending on whether those in power wanted to help capitalist landowners or small, independent farmers. The Land Law of 1800 reduced the minimum purchase to 320 acres, which was cut to 160, then again to 80, and finally, in 1832, to 40 acres. The base price was about a dollar an acre. This fight between capitalized investors and small farmers dominated the politics of the new nation and would play out brutally on the land surrounding Drew, Mississippi.

THE BARN SITS ON the southwest quarter of Section 2, Township 22 North, Range 4 West, measured from the Choctaw Meridian. That's its exact legal location on Jefferson's grid: a square mile per section, thirty-six sections per township, over and over again across the new nation. The thirty-six square miles of Township 22 North, Range 4 West, have borne witness to the birth of the blues at the nearby Dockery Plantation, to the struggle of Fannie Lou Hamer, to the machinations of a founding family of the Klan, and to the death of Emmett Till.

To get to Dockery, take a right out of Jeff Andrews's driveway, take another right on Ralph Ray Road toward the Bolivar County line, and then turn left on Dockery Road. Dockery Farms has been called the birthplace of the Delta blues by B. B. King and many others. It's not an accident then that this land fueled the first protest music. The blues came from the land around the barn. From Charley Patton, the Black grandson of a white man. Patton's music flowed from a place of rage about how he lived a small, threatened life because his grandmother was Black—"skin the color of rape," the poet Caroline Randall Williams wrote. He became the first blues star, the man who taught Son House, who taught Robert Johnson, who taught Muddy Waters, who hailed from the same Delta town as Sam Cooke and Nate Dogg, all these genres making the same protest music against the same forces as Patton—Delta blues or G-funk, Muddy and "I'm a full-grown man" or Sam's "A Change Is Gonna Come" or Ice Cube and "Fuck tha Police." Eazy-E's grandparents ran a grocery store sixteen blocks up Broadway in Greenville from the house where J. W. Milam lived when he died.

The Dockery family still owns their plantation. Now the granddaughters of the founder control the business. One of them, a distinguished elderly woman named Douglas Dockery Thomas, agreed to meet me in her New York apartment. Her building is on the Upper East Side, overlooking the Metropolitan Museum and Central Park. She's on the board at the Metropolitan Opera and is one of the central patrons of the Met. The doorman was expecting me. The elevator opened directly into her apartment, which covered an entire floor, easily more than four thousand square feet.

She led me into a formal parlor with a piano under tall ceilings and crown molding. I looked down at the museum and the yellow cabs on Fifth Avenue. Hers is some of the most expensive residential real estate in the world. The final vapors of the Gilded Age moved through the empty rooms in a world where history stopped in 1929, or maybe 1955. Nothing we talk about can be on the record, she says. The family remains very private. Her son, I've read, is an incredibly successful venture capitalist, the money behind Venmo and *BuzzFeed*, among others. We talked about Mississippi. Our families knew each other. On a side table was a picture of her with King Charles III when he was Prince of Wales. I noticed her sharp cheekbones and delicate wrists. She loves the opera but also loves the blues and has set up Dockery as a living museum to honor her parents, Joe Rice and Keith, and the music that came to life on the family farm. Her mother especially seemed to understand that the line all white southerners need to see or be shown wasn't between good and bad, but between cowardly and brave.

"If I had not been married to Joe," Keith said, "I might have been out on the streets marching with the protestors. But I was, and I didn't."

WILLIE REED STEPPED OUT OF his family home for the last time on a Friday night. He moved alone into the darkness. He had been told the plan and followed it carefully. Lots of people wanted him dead. He'd dared to accuse a white man of murder. In his arms he carried a coat and an extra pair of pants. Everything else he left behind. No account survives of the feelings in that dark house, the sorrow and fear, the words spoken and unspoken. It must have felt like a scene from a different time, a man forced into exile, facing a kind of ancient judgment surely not possible in 1955. The history books say he walked six miles in the dark. Nobody knows for sure which direction but when you look at the map, and understand who lived in the houses lining the roads, there's only one route he could have taken: down the Drew-Cleveland Road, now the Drew-Ruleville Road, skirting the edge of Dockery Farms.

I've driven that road at night, in a big, modern Chevrolet four-wheel-drive, with my armor of white skin, with a .40-caliber semi-automatic pistol in the glove box, and even then it's spooky. The darkness of rural Mississippi remains a physical thing, heavy and alive, a sonic experience, too, loud with bugs and birds. There is no safety outside the civilization of headlights. If someone wanted to kill you, there would be nobody to hear you scream. If someone approached, there would be no place to hide. This road was by far Reed's safest option, lined with poor Black families. He only had two other options to escape. The first, the Drew-Merigold Road, would have taken him through the only real community of small, poor, white farmers in the Delta. That was suicide. He could have run into the town of Drew. Also suicide. That left Ruleville, which is 6.6 miles from his house and still risky. One of the policemen in the city of Ruleville was J. W. Milam and Roy Bryant's brother. Reed likely passed his girlfriend Ella Mae Stubbs's home. He didn't have time to tell her goodbye.

A car waited in the dark at the end of the road. The driver took Reed north on Highway 61 through Cleveland and Merigold, finally reaching Mound Bayou and safety. Another car awaited him there. The man behind the steering wheel was Medgar Evers. The other passenger was Congressman Diggs. The three men drove north in Evers's Oldsmobile 88 with a big-block V-8, which he had bought specifically to outrun the white terrorists who'd follow and chase him through the backroads of the rural state. His speedometer glowed red whenever he got over sixty miles an hour, which he did as the three men roared toward Memphis Airport. When they arrived, Diggs and Reed went inside the terminal. They probably took the 10:00 a.m. Delta-C&S 686 from Memphis to Chicago, with a stop in Saint Louis, each leg exactly an hour and nine minutes. That's three hours with the layover to try to imagine what awaited them when the plane touched down. In Chicago, Diggs took Willie to Congressman William Dawson's office. Dawson had represented the South Side of Chicago since 1943. An uncle met him up there. Two strangers approached them.

"Willie?"

"Willie Reed?"

Both Reed and his uncle felt terror. He'd already been found. The fear eased when the men introduced themselves as Chicago police officers. They'd been assigned to make sure Reed was safe in his new home. Reed struggled to focus as his uncle took him to his mother's walk-up apartment at 2103 South Michigan, two blocks from what is now the Marriott Marquis, across the street from the Chess Records studio where the Rolling Stones would one day visit and find their hero Muddy Waters painting the walls of the lobby.

Reporters met Reed there in the first hours of his exile.

"Everybody is scared," he told them. "Why? What did we do?"

They asked him about the world he'd left behind.

"I feel kind of lonely for Ella Mae," he said.

The next morning charitable strangers offered to write blank checks to bring Ella Mae Stubbs to Chicago. Mississippi reporters went out to the Clark Plantation and found her father, Ernest Stubbs, and asked his opinion. He said his daughter barely knew Willie Reed and that his family was perfectly happy in Mississippi.

Willie Reed never saw Ella Mae Stubbs again.

A *Jackson Daily News* reporter, Bill Spell, flew up to Chicago in a state-owned airplane to "interview" him. The whole point was to let Willie know that Mississippi could reach him anytime it wanted. Spell would confess later in life that Senator Eastland's office was actively digging up dirt on the Till family and actually delivering prewritten hatchet jobs to the Jackson paper where he worked. The reporter, a member of the National Guard, got his commanding officer to approve a military flight to Chicago. Spell found Reed in Michael Reese Hospital, located in Bronzeville on the South Side, with what best can be described as a nervous breakdown. His room was in between the train station where Emmett's body would arrive and the little piece of sidewalk where Sonny Boy Williamson got murdered as he walked home from a gig. A month later, Reed swallowed his fear and returned to Mississippi to testify in Leflore

County as a grand jury debated indicting Milam and Bryant for kidnapping. He told his story and flew back to Chicago. The grand jury declined to bring charges, just as the jury in Sumner had acquitted Milam and Bryant, and with that the legal proceedings in the case of Emmett Till ended.

Reed changed his name to Willie Louis soon after. That had been his father's last name and he wanted to be anonymous again. Every day he went to work as a surgical technician in a South Side hospital, located between Michelle Obama's childhood home and the house of poet Gwendolyn Brooks. Mamie Till-Mobley, Simeon Wright, and Wheeler Parker all lost touch with him and thought he'd been killed. Willie Louis vanished into working-class Chicago. He would go many years before telling another person about what he'd heard that morning inside Leslie Milam's barn.

THE COURTHOUSE IN INDIANOLA, Mississippi, a few blocks from the juke joint where B. B. King played whenever he returned to his hometown, has a room full of old, heavy books. They sit on long tables and hold the history of every section of land in the county. I began with the present and looked to see who currently owned all the land in the township around the barn. One of the standard attacks a white conservative southerner uses against a white liberal southerner is to mock them for being full of guilt. Everyone will say that the past is the past, that they didn't own enslaved people or employ sharecroppers and they aren't responsible for the sins of their fathers and grandfathers. Nobody will admit to anything. But I noticed something as I penciled in current landowners onto a map. Most of the land around that part of Sunflower County was owned locally. There were two huge swaths of land, however, that were not. As I shaded in the map with locals and outsiders, a pattern emerged. At first I didn't believe it was real, so I checked and then checked again. The two big plots of land owned by out-of-state investors were both shaped like cones and both spread out from the barn, a literal blast radius of shame, so that a map with local owners in green and absentee owners shaded yellow looked exactly like an hourglass with Jeff Andrews's barn sitting in the middle.

One of those outside owners was a publicly traded company, which wasn't surprising. The global river of capital has always flowed through Township 22 North. Records show lenders from New York and England and the Netherlands dropping money all over this square of Sunflower County. Their purchases filled page after page in the courthouse. Go pull one of the books that track ownership. The section of land directly to the east of the barn, and the section of land directly to the west, were once owned by the Delta & Pine Land Company, a speculation outfit founded in 1886. Three and a half decades later, the company was bought by Fine Spinners and Doublers of Manchester, a huge textile-manufacturing conglomerate seeking to vertically integrate its supply chain by actually buying Mississippi Delta plantations instead of just lending them money. That company has changed names and hands over the years but still exists, with sprawling factories all over Asia that make lingerie, men's underwear, and baby clothes for Marks & Spencer and Victoria's Secret. The Manchester textile firm eventually divested itself of Delta & Pine, which remade itself as a chemical company. It was later owned by Monsanto and is now owned by Bayer—which itself was once owned by the chemical conglomerate in Germany that developed and produced the Nazis' Zyklon B gas. The parent company ran a slave-labor plant connected to Auschwitz and other concentration camps, and the director of the factory at Monowitz became board chair of Bayer after the war. All of which is to say that money's only ethic is to reproduce itself, and it keeps on moving, circling, finding the best margins. Once upon a time it found those best margins in the Mississippi Delta.

AS I SPENT MORE and more time wandering the square of Township 22 North, I marked the corners. The southwest one is a tall radio tower broadcasting gospel and Black sermons, six thousand watts of power, pushing the Word out over seven counties. The southern line of the township runs parallel to Highway 8, past the Dockery Farms gin and the turn to Robert Johnson's crossroads, which is only 2.8 miles from the grave of one of Emmett Till's killers, Roy Bryant, which is 7.1 miles from the barn. He's buried almost exactly on the township line, below an exposed, sunbaked patch of grass. Sometimes people vandalize the headstone.

The Marlow family cemetery is also on the township line. All three W. D. Marlows are buried there. W.D. III, "Dee," is the man who fired Fannie Lou Hamer for trying to register to vote. She and her husband, Pap, worked on his plantation for decades. She kept the daily farm records. Pap drove a tractor and made moonshine and ran a juke joint. The toilet in the Hamers' house broke and Marlow refused to fix it, sending them to an outhouse. One day she was cleaning Marlow's house and scrubbing the toilets. One of the Marlow kids, Maud, told her not to worry about one in particular.

"It's just old Honey's," she said.

Honey was the family dog. Hamer kept her rage inside until she returned home to Pap, where she exploded. *A dog!* Something clicked, a desire for a different life. The family wouldn't let her eat meals at their table, even alone, so she started using their spoons and not telling them. On the day she went to Indianola to register to vote, the plantation owner, Dee Marlow, came to their home in a rage. She had helped raise him. When he was off fighting in World War II, she had baked and mailed him the cookies she knew he liked. Now he was screaming at Pap.

"We ain't gonna have that now! It ain't gonna do nothing but stir up a lot of stuff. We ain't ready for it now!"

She got back from the courthouse.

Dee Marlow appeared again at their screen door.

"We are not gonna have this in Mississippi and you will have to withdraw."

He gave her until dawn to decide.

She slept on it and her resolve only steeled. She refused to withdraw. Dee Marlow, who'd looked forward to her homemade baking in a war zone, now threw her off the plantation where she'd lived for eighteen years. She went to a friend's house in Ruleville that night and her civil rights career began. Now she's gone, and Pap's gone, and the Marlows still own the land.

The southeast corner is by the dual water towers in Ruleville, Hamer's home after leaving the plantation. One tower is marked "Hot" and the other is marked "Cold." Ruleville is also where Roy Bryant lived out his days, running a little store and selling fruit on the side of the road. Sometimes Roy drove into Cleveland to eat at a local Chinese restaurant. My friend Don Joe's parents owned it. Don worked there with his brother Wally. None of the Joes knew about Roy's past. He'd come sit by himself and order fried shrimp. Then he'd talk to the Joe boys with his eyes closed, almost in a trance, and without warning, his eyes would snap open. It freaked them out. In 1995 the Jackson newspaper ran a story on the fortieth anniversary of the murder. Don opened the paper and started to read.

"That was the first I ever heard of Emmett Till," he told me. "I read that whole story and it nauseated me."

Then he saw a familiar face.

"Look at this! Look at this!" Don shouted.

His brother came over.

"Holy shit," Wally said.

The northeast corner is on the Drew-Merigold Road, which runs through the heart of what used to be the Sunflower Plantation, owned by New York timber barons and railroad executives. Sunflower often needed more labor than it could attract, so folks from neighboring plantations, like Fannie Lou Hamer, came out here to pick cotton for three dollars a day once their own crop was out of the fields. One day she walked her rows next to Mae Bertha Carter.

"You pick the cleanest row of anybody," Carter said.

"Everything I do, I try to do the best I can," Hamer replied.

The Carter family lived on the northwest corner of Township 22 North, Range 4 West. There's no sign to tell the story of how this family once did a very brave and dangerous thing here. It's marked only by a stand of trees in the middle of a field, bordered by a muddy, almost impassable road. Once this was called the Busy Line, a main dirt thoroughfare stretching from the Drew-Merigold Road to Highway 61. Families lived on both sides for several miles. A whole plantation world existed out here, land changing hands over the years. The Birch plantation. The Zumbro plantation. The sprawling Sunflower Plantation. Widow Parker's place with its big Indian mounds, where the owner, Belle Parker, would ride a horse to visit sharecroppers with her long white hair flowing out behind her like a medieval tapestry. Smith & Wiggins. The Pemble place, which is where Mae Bertha Carter and her husband, Matthew, lived when they decided to send their children to the all-white Drew High School and end segregation.

Thomas Pemble, the plantation boss, sent the manager, Ramsey Thornton, to their house to demand they withdraw their children from the Drew school. Mae Bertha raged at his approach. She also laughed. Pemble didn't even have the courage to do it himself.

Thornton honked his horn when he whipped up to their home.

Matthew looked at his wife and spoke softly.

"It's starting," he said.

He pulled himself up and went outside. By "it," he meant the certain intimidation he could see coming for his family. One night soon somebody would shoot up the Carters' house. The family would huddle on the floor for safety. The Carters' livestock, which they needed to survive, would be stolen as a threat. Soon Matthew Carter would be lying prone on their living room floor with a loaded shotgun, defending his family from terrorists. When the threats didn't work, the Pembles would do what landowners have long done: throw them off the plantation, sure they'd end up home-less and unable to live in the school district. A northern Quaker charity would buy a house in Drew for the Carters, foiling the plan. Those are just a few examples of what Matthew knew was starting when the plantation manager stepped out of his truck.

Thornton explained that the children would be so much better off at the Black school and offered to help the family withdraw them. Mae Bertha stood inside the screen door and listened. She dragged a chair outside to the porch. On it she sat a small record player, close enough to the door for the cord to reach to a plug in-side the house. In her hand she held a single record: June 11, 1963, President John F. Kennedy's speech in favor of a national Civil Rights Act. Medgar Evers was assassinated the night after Kennedy gave that speech, another straight line between politics and violence in Mississippi. Mae Bertha's son had bought the record up north and given it to her. That kind of thing would have been hard to find in the Delta. As the plantation manager got more and more angry that Matthew Carter wouldn't agree to withdraw his children from the school, Mae Bertha placed the needle on the outermost groove and turned up the volume. The real heroes of Township 22 North, any thorough history reveals, were determined mothers who refused to let the state limit their children. Mae Bertha stood in the doorway, arms crossed in determination, as the president's voice filtered out through the cotton fields surrounding them, east to the barn, south to the Walford Indian mounds, west toward Highway 61, north to the Drew-Merigold Road. Matthew and Thornton kept talking at the truck but Kennedy's speech couldn't be ignored. Finally Thornton said he'd go wait at the barn to give the couple time to talk.

"You go out there to the barn," Mae Bertha told her husband, "and you tell Mr. Thornton that I am a grown woman. I birthed those children and bore the pain. He cannot tell me what to do about my children."

Matthew went to the barn and told Thornton that his children would get the best education they could have, and if that meant Drew High School, then so be it. One of those children is Gloria Dickerson, who had a successful career as an executive and recently moved back home.

GLORIA DICKERSON'S NONPROFIT OFFICE is on the depressed Main Street in Drew, and one of her many programs is a mentorship school named the Emmett Till Academy. She grew up hearing the stories about the blood in the dirt. Her mother showed her the barn and told her the story of Emmett Till.

"Drew can't be transformed," Gloria says, "until we realize Emmett was killed right outside Drew. A lot of people in town don't know that."

She passes the barn every time she drives the short back way to Ruleville, looking up onto the hill and feeling a little of that terrible energy collect in her heart. There are quotes from Mamie Till-Mobley painted on the walls of her office, which are bright lime green, the color reflecting off the shiny linoleum floors. There are inspirational quotes posted around the building. Many are about never giving up. Her work here requires introducing painful history to young people who haven't been taught how to shoulder such a heavy burden. She gets it. The hope, for her, is to help the children entrusted to her care evolve past their own hardwired sense of limitation. To teach them about the past so they might understand how their world came to be, so their knowledge might render the past powerless.

"To remember and to do better," she says. "Remember and make it better."

After she and her siblings integrated the Drew school system, they found great careers with the education their parents suffered to give them. All of them except one moved away, including Gloria. Over the years Gloria accumulated money and titles, trying to honor her mom and dad's bravery. Her parents risked their lives for something as simple as a normal education. The Carter kids felt a responsibility to earn that sacrifice. "Then when I retired," Gloria says, "I'm like, 'What have I really done with my life?' And so I came back to Drew because it seemed like everything that I went through here in Drew was in vain."

Drew looks like it's been bombed. I've seen wrecked cities on magazine assignment in Bosnia, Iraq, and Ukraine. That's what it feels like to drive past insurance-fraud house-fire carcasses and boarded-up buildings and broken streets with deep holes that just wreck suspensions. Archie Manning's childhood home is falling down, the walls bowing out at the bottom, the floor rotted out, appliances dropped through to the ground. When Gloria came back she couldn't get over the ruin. She kept telling people that somebody needed to do something. That became her mantra. Somebody needed to do something.

"Why don't you do it?" a friend finally responded.

And just like that she had a nonprofit named We2gether Creating Change, and office space on Main Street, and a group of students coming to her mentorship program. She ran for Sunflower County supervisor and ended up in a showdown with Roy Bryant's cousin. Her opponent wasn't spiritually related to Emmett's murderers, nor politically or philosophically related. He was actually related.

She won, and he challenged her in court, and she won there, too.

She bought a house in Drew. Her siblings just couldn't understand. For Gloria, the home was a statement of intention: *I am here to stay.*

One of her missions in her hometown is to teach people that Emmett Till got killed in their community. The town had never, in any official or even unofficial way, acknowledged the lynching. She wanted her students to see the hidden history of their home, not to change how they felt about it, but to understand how it came to be.

The past year had brought new attention to the barn. When Dickerson first heard that Weems and others wanted to turn the barn into some kind of memorial, she smiled. An idea that radical was exactly what she had in mind.

"I don't know what the reaction would be," she says. "I think they'd go nuts. I think the whole county would go nuts. They tried to keep it a secret about Sunflower County anyway."

"For a long time," I say.

"'Why y'all bringing that up? You just need to let that alone.'" She laughs bitterly. "'Why are you bringing it up?' Because it needs to be brought up. It's still the same attitude. That's what I told my kids. A lot of people, when they focus on Emmett Till, they focus on the fact that he didn't get justice. I know that he didn't get justice. We want to know: Why did it happen? What attitudes brought this up? What was the intention of the people when they did this? That's what we need to talk more about. He didn't get justice. A lot of folks hadn't gotten justice. Why did it happen to him?"

Why bring it up? Why not, as Jeff Andrews said, leave the past in the past? Why did it happen? What about this land, this valuable dirt, created fertile conditions for violence? When were the fates of all these actors—Emmett Till, J. W. and Leslie Milam, Roy Bryant, Mae Bertha and Matthew Carter, Clint Shurden and his brothers, the Dockerys, the Forrests—written on some tablet atop some unseen mountain? What if those tablets could be discovered, deciphered, understood, shared? Isn't that what Gloria really wanted for her students? Not to show them the tablets, which are a mystery to her, too, but to deputize another generation to go out and continue looking for them? Why did it happen *to him?* Which is a way of asking, Why did a bright, hopeful child get murdered for whistling in 1955? What about the intersection of Emmett and the Mississippi Delta at that specific time led to his death? The attitudes and intentions are why we should bring it up, to interrogate the present to see what of the past remains. Because our present day potential for violence is alive and undiminished.

Gloria told me something about the infant mortality rate in the Delta. A lot of babies die here. The rate is higher than those of El Salvador, Mexico, and Iran. More than double that of China and the rest of the United States. Four times that of the European Union.

"We need to talk about how we got here," she said. "And I can say that with Emmett Till. We need to talk about what led up to that. Not that he didn't get justice. We all can say that. Anybody can say that. A lot of the white folks say that, oh, he didn't get justice."

We2gether's mentorship program is named after Emmett to honor Mamie, out of respect and in the hope that her students might look back far enough into the past to make sense of their current lives. To her, his death isn't merely a story about what a group of racist killers did, or what a brave mother did, or what a corrupt judicial system did or did not do. She wants everyone to go excavating. Dig down in the dirt.

"Why did it happen like this? And what's the real cause of this? It started a long, long time ago. It started building and building and building. You have to go all the way back to figure out how we got here. And I realized that you have to go back to slavery time really, when people weren't treated as human beings. That's where it started. And so, in my mind, people were oppressed so long. And when slavery ended, they were so far behind in terms of knowledge, in terms of power, in terms of wealth. They were still poor, living in poverty. They didn't have jobs. They didn't know how to read. All those things happened."

"And then every law passed made it harder to catch up?" I asked.

"Right. To make it harder to catch up. Not easier. We as a society put things in places that made that not get any easier. Black Wall Street? Burned down. All that Reconstruction, you know? We weren't allowed to go to school to learn how to read or how to speak. Or how to talk, or learn anything about politics and the way the system works."

"What year did you go to Drew High School?"

"In sixty-five."

"That's not that long ago."

"No, it wasn't that long ago. I graduated in seventy-one. That's not that long ago. Somebody on TV said we don't treat people differently because of the color of their skin. This man on TV said that, I'm like, 'Where'd you come from? You didn't come from the Mississippi Delta.' We've been treated like that and I can talk about it personally. That's another reason I came back. I still feel it in my heart. I feel so much in my heart that I need to help people because it is not easy. Moving from poverty to prosperity is not easy."

Gloria works with high school students who do not believe that a different life is possible. Students who've never left Sunflower County. Students who have never heard of Emmett Till, much less know he was killed a few miles from them. "They believe things will always be this way," she says. "I'll just stay home and take care of my kids and get the little money I get in the mail. The kids are not interested in being creative. They're not interested in being curious. Curiosity is not there."

Her future is here now.

"People ask, 'Why you want to live in the Delta?'" she said. "They even asked me when I was in Michigan, 'Why do you wanna go back to Mississippi?' I said, 'That's my home.' That's why I came back. Mama kept saying, 'Break the cycle.' We got to break the cycle."

I asked her if the house in Township 22 North where she grew up was still standing.

"It's gone," she said. "Everything on that road is torn down now."

WILLIE LOUIS WALKED DOWN his street on the South Side of Chicago. It was 2002. *Willie Reed* hadn't been his name in a long time. Along with his wife, Juliet, he lived in Englewood. They both worked at Jackson Park Hospital, he as a surgical technician, she as an intensive-care nurse. That's where they met. She liked him and just walked up to him one day and gave him a kiss. He was smitten. That was three decades ago. They lived with their collie named Hercules and liked to take cruises to the Caribbean.

He walked slowly because of bad circulation.

Two strangers stepped out of a car and approached him.

One of them was filmmaker Stanley Nelson.

"Mr. Reed? Mr. Reed?" Nelson called.

He stopped. "No, no, no, no, no," he said.

"Yes, yes, yes, yes," Nelson said.

Nobody in their neighborhood knew his secret. He never spoke about it. Even Juliet hadn't known until more than a decade after they met. If it weren't for his aunt Mae, she might have never known. One afternoon in the 1980s Mae called Juliet.

"Do you know who Willie is?" she said.

"All I know is he's Willie," Juliet said.

"He's the boy that testified at the Emmett Till trial," she said.

That was the first Juliet had ever heard about a man named Willie Reed and what he'd seen at Leslie Milam's barn. At least his nightmares made more sense. She'd always wondered why he cried out in his sleep. That same aunt is the one who told the filmmaker how and where to find the vanished witness to the Till murder. Willie was very angry with her but his southern manners won out. Willie said that he was indeed the witness. Later Nelson took him to Mamie Till-Mobley's house, where she welcomed him as a prodigal son. She'd always thought he'd been killed. Wheeler Parker and Simeon Wright were there, too, and they all embraced. They saw Willie as a hero.

That visit seemed to open something up in Willie. Not much of it was good. He was a quiet man who loved being a deacon in his church and enjoyed drinking a six-pack of cheap beer and watching a basketball game on television. He loved the Lakers. Now he started talking more about 1955. The nightmares increased. Other times he got quiet and seemed to disappear.

"Willie, what's wrong?" Juliet would say.

"I was just thinking about Emmett," he'd say.

A YEAR LATER an FBI agent knocked on the door. His name was Dale Killinger, a decorated former army Ranger and paratrooper. It was his job to reinvestigate the Emmett Till murder and see what new information might come to light. The Department of Justice wanted to reopen the case. That meant the United States of America needed Willie Reed to return to Mississippi for the first time in fifty years.

Killinger promised nothing would happen to him. Willie saw in his eyes he meant it and agreed. The FBI bought Willie and Juliet plane tickets and flew them back down south to Memphis. They crossed into Mississippi. Killinger and a local cop got them settled at the Sheraton casino in Tunica. Juliet refused to visit the barn.

"This is as far as I'm going," she told her husband.

She asked him, "Are you scared?"

He said he wasn't.

The next morning Killinger picked him up in a truck the FBI

had confiscated from a drug dealer. It was a black Chevrolet Z71 with black windows and twenty-inch rims. Willie looked out on newly planted cotton fields as they drove deeper into the old share-cropper Delta. The cotton looked the same. Little else did. Killinger would get chills years later thinking about the courage of this man. Willie talked about leaving Mississippi in 1955, and about his job sterilizing operating rooms at the hospital back up in Chicago.

Ninety minutes passed.

They turned on the Drew-Ruleville Road and parked. Willie Louis became Willie Reed again. He stood on the empty grass where he'd once lived. His grandfather's house was gone and so was the country store, and so was Ella Mae's house, and Ella Mae herself, and everyone he'd ever known in the first eighteen years of his life. The FBI agent wanted to know about life on the Shurden place and about Add Reed and Amanda Bradley. Reed remembered everything.

"You could just feel how powerful it was for him to be back there," Killinger would recall.

Reed moved slowly up the road. He walked across the bayou and past the dentist's manicured lawn and cypress trees, over to the well, which was still there, and finally to the barn.

"I could hear screaming," Reed said.

Reed's feet stood on the rough gravel and he suddenly seemed far away. The line between remembering a sound and hearing a sound blurred and vanished. He stayed with his memories until a voice pulled him back to the present.

Killinger asked which part of the barn.

"The right side," Reed said.

He couldn't believe the barn was still standing in the same spot he'd left it. How could everything be gone, changed, except this one terrible place? Killinger watched the old man closely. Reed wobbled, like he'd lost his balance, and threw his arms out to the sides to steady himself.

I GOT DOCUMENTS sent to me by the Bureau of Land Management, which is what the government now calls the office first created by the bill Thomas Jefferson wrote in 1785. The documents showed the original survey of Township 22 North, Range 4 West, and had a notation for the first land patent granted in the thirty-six-square-mile square. On September 1, 1848, forty acres in Section 8, roughly two and a half miles southwest of where the barn sits today, were transferred from the United States of America to John Clark. I had to read the name a few times and then do some research to make sure it was the same John Clark who founded my hometown, Clarksdale, and built a mansion next door to the house where I grew up: a big white house with twin gable dormers and six columns along the front of the porch. It's a bed-and-breakfast now but the Clark family still owned the house when I was a boy.

They'd let the trees and shrubs grow wild by then. It got noticeably darker when I slipped through the bushes into their yard. Not much light penetrated the canopy. A girl my age lived there but we didn't see her much. Once I remember going inside and when I close my eyes I see dark, empty rooms with tall, grand ceilings, more like an abandoned castle than a modern family residence. Cars pulled in and out of the circular drive all day and night. We never knew why but we suspected. The last time I saw the patriarch, Sean Clark, he was incoherent at a Van Morrison concert on the banks of the Mississippi River.

His great-grandfather, the first owner of land in Township 22

North, came to the United States from a manufacturing town in England. John Clark built a mansion and married the sister of a Confederate general–turned–governor and soon had a family of his own. He named his daughter Blanche. Blanche Clark married a dapper playboy lawyer named J. W. Cutrer and he built her an enormous mansion of her own, on the other side of her father's house, two doors down from me.

They called it Belvoir and threw wild, jewel-dripped parties in the huge front yard. The music of a full orchestra or a swing band would carry through the town. A young boy in the neighborhood used to sneak up and watch these parties. His name was Tennessee Williams and his grandfather was the rector at the nearby Episcopal church. When Williams became a playwright he mined his childhood for scenes and characters, the most famous of which was Blanche DuBois. She's really Blanche Clark Cutrer.

Lots of his characters are based on real people from Clarksdale. One of my mom's best friends is the son of the actual Baby Doll. That's what people called her. At her funeral, the priest said something like *We now commit our sister Baby Doll.* . . . It wasn't until college that I realized how central the theme of decay and the fading memory of wealth was in Williams's work. My whole early life was surrounded by a fable of lost grandeur. The mythic ascendency of that fable, I'd learn as a grown man, stole the oxygen from any other stories that might have been told, that needed to be told.

My family has owned our current farm for more than a century. One day I might run it. We have always called it a planting company—even in the 1950s, my family refused to refer to the farm as a plantation, recoiling from that word as deep investments and familial ties prevented us from recoiling from the land itself. Time is armor, too, namely the myth of comfort drawn from its passing. Nearly a decade ago local activist Jessie Jaynes-Diming led a group of Till family members out to the barn. It was the anniversary of the killing. They arrived with a police escort, less out of a fear of danger and more as a sign of respect. As they walked across the bayou a young white woman roared up on a four-wheeler. Jaynes-Diming explained who they were and what they were doing. The young woman sped away. As Emmett Till's family stood outside the barn where he died, the young woman and her friend started shooting, clay pigeons or Coke cans or something. They were out of eyeshot but nearby. There was so much gunfire that the sheriff's escorts came around to make sure there was no danger. "It just lets you know that 1955 may be gone," Jaynes-Diming says, "but the hearts of Milam and Bryant and all those individuals that were there that night, they're still lurking around in their children."

One day, long past the point when my investigation had turned into an obsession, I heard a rumor that J. W. Milam's gun wasn't thrown in a river, and it isn't displayed in a museum. Nobody melted it down. When I was first told that the murder weapon might be floating around the Delta, I didn't take it seriously. Then someone gave me a name to call. He was a crop duster pilot. When I got him on the phone he told me that, yes, he owned it jointly with his sister. He told me they also owned the holster, the one strapped to J. W. Milam's hip as Willie Reed watched him drink water. So many artifacts from 1955 have vanished but the gun remains. The siblings don't really know what to do with the pistol. Objects matter. The gun in the drawer will always carry traces of its malice. They're getting older. There is no way to match ballistics but the FBI believes it is the murder weapon. The man explained that their father had gotten it from Sheriff Strider, and upon their father's death it passed to them. The man told me the gun is locked away in a safety deposit box in Greenwood, Mississippi. It's black and cold, a model M1911-A1 .45-caliber semiautomatic made by Ithaca, serial number 2102279, government issue. It still fires.

NEAR THE EAST END of the Drew-Ruleville Road is the pecan grove where Clint Shurden lived, in a low-slung white house with a big front porch. In the middle of the pecan grove is where the Shurden plantation commissary offered groceries and supplies to its tenants. Clint died in 1969 on a Sunday fourteen years to the day after Emmett Till, Wheeler Parker, and Simeon Wright went to Bryant's Grocery. His son, Sidney, moved into the house.

Sidney was fourteen years old in the summer of 1955, the same age as Emmett Till. He loved the land and history and found all sorts of Civil War artifacts in the ground around his home, which supports the local story about Nathan Bedford Forrest. Sidney loved to go play the guitar in juke joints where the Black adults who worked for his dad drank after work. One of his dad's workers, James Totten, taught him how to play and they'd go work the clubs together. Sidney always knew on some level he'd been born into a collapsing empire and even understood intellectually that its collapse was proof that justice existed somewhere in the cosmos. "As Sidney said late in his life, 'I came to realize that we probably did things we shouldn't have done growing up,'" his widow, Lynn Shurden, told me in her cottage on a quiet, leafy street near Delta State University in Cleveland.

They got married in 1978 and he told her lots of stories about the murder and the trial and Willie Reed.

"There was a little country store," she told me, "and it was still there when we married. Just across the bayou. Willie heard it as he was going to that store. And came back and talked about it to Sidney's daddy, evidently."

Clint's relationship with the Reed family was strange, because he took advantage of them and protected them, looked down on them and respected them, had enough power to scare off some people who'd do them harm but was ultimately impotent against the same forces that helped create his plantation in the first place.

"I just know that Sidney said his father was so afraid that something was going to happen to Willie that he went every day," Lynn Shurden said, thinking about the trial.

In the years after, Sidney and his children became the "black sheep" of the Shurden clan, according to his son Jason Shurden. He never really knew if it was because his dad was the first in the family to go bankrupt in the declining farm economy, or if it was because Clint was so public in his support of Willie Reed.

"I've always wondered," Jason said, "if Dad wasn't treated the same because of what Clint did."

Sidney and Lynn loved spring out in the country. Lynn would open all the doors and a wonderful breeze would blow throughout the house. It pleased Sidney that he was the fourth generation to live in the place. His neighbors didn't know what to make of a man who moved so easily between the white and Black worlds.

"He was kind of a weird bird," Jeff Andrews told me once.

Sidney was proud of his family name but not blind. Maybe that's why he spent his entire life trying to correct a mistake in the historical record. In the first rush of news stories about the murder of Emmett Till, a reporter incorrectly said the killing happened on Clint Shurden's plantation, and the mistake was repeated in book after book on the killing. Sidney went to the big Memphis public library to dig through old newspapers and find the published correction. Armed with facts, for years Sidney Shurden wrote letters to book publishers asking them to correct reprinted editions. His widow even confronted authors who'd repeated the old mistake.

"He talked about it forever," Lynn says. "It was important to him that . . ."

She paused.

"Let's be honest . . . ," she says finally. "The Eastland and Shurden names have been tied together forever. Not always under the best circumstances. It was something he just wanted corrected. You know, it bothered him that his family name was tied to a horrendous, horrendous thing. And that it happened down the bayou. I mean, it's just right down the road."

Sidney's health slipped and they moved to the nearby town of Cleveland, walking distance from her church, but they kept the old Shurden family home. "He was damned and determined that nobody but family would ever live there because family were the only people who ever lived there," Lynn said. "And so when we decided to buy a little place over here, he said, 'We're not going to rent it out.'"

He died in 2010. Lynn kept the country place but fretted about its future. She didn't rent it. She couldn't sell it. To save money and protect it from fire—several houses had burned down in the area from old electrical wires giving out—she disconnected the power. Then one morning she received a call from their farm manager with bad news. She rushed out to the Drew-Ruleville Road and found the place burned off the face of the earth. The ground was still hot. There were no storms in the area. No electricity to short-circuit. Probably just some kids smoking dope. "Or Sidney sent a bolt down," Lynn Shurden says with a laugh. "That's what I choose to believe. It burned in October after he died in May."

———

I GOT TO THE ADDRESS in Englewood, on the South Side of Chicago, and knocked on the door.

"Mrs. Louis?" I called.

She unlocked a dead bolt and swung open the door.

"Come in!" she said with a huge smile.

A display tower held gold cats, a statue of the Virgin Mary with Jesus, and awards from work. Blankets covered the windows and my eyes took a minute to adjust. A cross hung over the door with a quote: *Home Is Where You Hang Your Head*. Next to the stereo stood a rack of 45s. Beams of light flowed through a break in the dining room curtains. She pointed toward a plush recliner in the front left corner of the living room, facing the television. It looked like it hadn't been used in a long time.

"Oh, if Willie was here," she said, "he'd be trying to find him a ball game."

Willie Louis died in 2013 and she feels his presence all over their house and especially when she goes up to Ohio to camp and fish. As he got older, Willie took every chance to slip off to the woods. He never stopped missing home, from the moment he climbed in that car with Medgar Evers to his last breath in the hospital. He liked to go down to a local club and let Muddy Waters and B. B. King take him back to the Delta.

"He liked the blues," she said.

When he got to pick the menu he chose mustard greens, turnip greens, hog maw, potato salad, and corn bread. I asked her what he called the land of his birth, whether he called it Mississippi or the Delta or what.

"He would just say 'down home,'" she said.

He kept to himself. His mother, who had left him as a child, didn't really take him in when he arrived on her doorstep in 1955. Juliet's family became his family, too, enough that he is buried in her hometown in Ohio. He knew her kin would check on his grave and keep it clean. She also had a funeral for him in Chicago. Wheeler Parker arrived and took his seat. Simeon Wright had a prior engagement in New York City. He got as far as the Chicago airport before something stopped him. Juliet looked back at the crowd just before the funeral began and saw him walk into the church.

She told me what happened when Dale Killinger dropped Willie back at the hotel after he visited the barn. They went down to the casino floor. He liked the Double Diamond machine. Willie and Juliet played in silence. She could sense his sadness.

"It brought back a whole lot of bad memories for him," she told me.

They went upstairs and went to sleep. The next morning they flew back to Chicago on American Airlines. Seats 4B and 4C. Neither talked that much.

"Well," he told his wife finally, "I'm hoping this is over with. I sure don't want to go through this anymore."

The nightmares never went away. Sometimes people wanted to talk about the murder and the trial and he'd oblige but he always felt bad afterward. A year after he went back to the barn, doctors had to amputate both his legs, and he spent the rest of his life in a red wheelchair. Word did get out in the neighborhood that a civil rights hero lived in their midst. Juliet bought a new stove and the delivery people just dropped it on the sidewalk. She didn't know what to do. Some neighborhood kids, standing on the corner, walked over and to her surprise offered to help. Once they got it in the house she offered to pay them.

"You don't have to pay us," one of them said. "We know your husband. We know what he did."

They never had children of their own but Willie raised Juliet's son. Willie loved Sollie and Sollie loved him. When Sollie grew up he fell in love and married a white woman.

"How did Willie feel about having a white family?" I asked.

Juliet laughed.

"Well, and how did I feel, too?" she said.

I laughed with her.

"At first I didn't really like it," she says. "But I had to. That was his life and he can live his life the way he wants."

She told me Willie knew his white daughter-in-law was his family, and he was hers, when he was dying in the hospital. She was faithfully by his side. Juliet was, too. Surrounded by loved ones, understanding the end was close, Willie heard a noise.

"What was that?" he asked.

His daughter-in-law didn't hear anything. Juliet said she didn't know what he was talking about.

"He said a white light came to him," she said. "I knew that he probably wasn't going to make it."

She went down to get food from a burger place across the street. When she got back she sat in the chair watching television, just keeping him company.

"Juliet," he said. "Come here."

She went to him.

"I don't feel good," he said.

His eyes rolled back and she called for a nurse.

"They come running in and he was gone," she told me softly. "I was right there with him. When he left me I was right at that bedside with him."

I WENT BACK TO the South Side on a Sunday afternoon to pick up Juliet Louis and go out to the suburbs for a day of remembrance. In Emmett Till's hometown of Argo, Illinois, Wheeler Parker's church was dedicating a marker to his cousin at his boyhood home, just down the street from the Argo Temple Church of God in Christ. I'd heard Parker preach there and felt the room come alive with his power and faith. People call Argo "Little Mississippi." "I'd like to see some Ole Miss students come to this neighborhood and try to shoot holes in that sign," local civic leader Dallis Anderson told me with a laugh.

Juliet and I caught up as we headed west. Patrick Weems and a young man from Cleveland, Mississippi, named Jay Rushing rode with us. Rushing wanted his picture with Juliet, nervous even to talk to her. Willie Reed's bravery still resonated in the Delta. Juliet told stories about Willie while we rode. She laughed and we all laughed, too.

We arrived in Argo just as church was letting out. Parker walked down the sidewalk in his flowing robes. He waved at me. We saw Annie Wright, Simeon Wright's widow. Her Simmy had been dead since 2017 and she carried on his work preserving the memory of his cousin Emmett. She kept Simeon's cotton sack and golf clubs now.

"Mrs. Wright," I said, "this is Juliet Louis. Her husband was Willie Reed."

Annie got a huge, warm smile on her face.

"I know Juliet," she said with deep love in her voice.

It felt beautiful to watch these two women together again, connected first by a killing in a barn, connected again by an act of remembering. Black southerners in exile, they listened as Wheeler

Parker stood beside the newly unveiled historical marker and began talking about 1955, and the beginning of Emmett Till's journey to Leslie Milam's barn. The sound of boots on the floor, and the bright shine of a flashlight, and the black of a pistol in the dark.

"Blacker than a thousand midnights," Parker said.

WHEELER PARKER DROVE ME around Argo and showed me the places where he and Emmett grew up. They were young and innocent. He told me more about the group of old men who went to elementary school with Till all those decades ago. They were planning a reunion on what would have been Emmett's eightieth birthday. Parker said the old guys spend a lot of time reminiscing about home. Even after all this time and suffering, he still felt connected to the land where he was born.

"Oh," he said, "Mississippi is talked about all the time."

He laughed.

"Behind the iron curtain," he said.

He's the last living eyewitness. Every time he talks about the murder he speaks for his uncle Simeon and for his friend Willie Reed, whom he sees as a hero of this terrible story, and for his grandfather Moses, and for Mamie, and Mamie's mother, and the entire community of people who felt the loss of Emmett every day of their lives. The murder happened to a nation, and a race of people, yes, but it also happened to an actual family that still exists and deals with the fresh pain of Emmett's death every day. Wheeler lives next door to one of his siblings and across the street from another. There are memories all over the streets of Argo. He finally stopped in front of the empty lot where the new marker now sits. The engine idled as he spoke. "Emmett Till's house was right here," he said as he pointed to the empty grass. "And 7524, our house, was right next door here."

He carries around many complicated feelings about the Mississippi Delta, about what it took from him, and about what it put in him that he can never let go. He is still called back. Like Gloria, he has questions about how it got to be the way it is today. He and his wife, Marvel, are pushing hard for a national monument in Chicago and Mississippi honoring their family, to make sure that once they die, and the others who knew Emmett die, too, his story will still be remembered. Because Wheeler survived. Because he and Emmett rode their bikes on this street. Because the gun still fires, because the barn is a barn, because time is thin and fragile, because the dirt Jeff Andrews and I were taught to love is very different from the dirt Wheeler Parker was taught to fear.

II

Destinies

G loria Dickerson sat behind the wheel of her sky-blue Lexus and steered us into the heart of Township 22 North. The violence in the barn doesn't make any sense, she tells me, unless you know the whole story of how a barn came to be out here in a former cypress swamp. We rode toward the overgrown turnrow where she grew up. Her people have lived in this square of land for generations. This is where they lived when she went to the white school in Drew. We drove past fields of soybeans and corn. The old store where her dad got credit to help them make it until harvest is someone's house now.

"That was the store owner there. Bob Pope, that was his name."

"What do you remember about Bob Pope?"

"I remember him telling Daddy he couldn't get any more groceries there because we were in the school," she said, not long before she spotted her old road, the Busy Line. Up ahead to the right a stand of anemic-looking trees grew. She pointed. That's where her father set up a defensive firing position with a shotgun when

Klansmen fired into their home, where her mother defiantly played the John F. Kennedy speech on her record player.

Her car rode low to the ground. We should have taken my truck. The tires started to spin and the back end slipped loose.

"Oh, slow down, girl," she whispered.

Thick diamonds of mud flew in the air. The back tires sank.

"I guess I'm stuck," she said. "Look at that mud."

MONTHS LATER I PULLED OVER by the Indian mounds a few thousand yards from the barn, not far from where Gloria and I got stuck. I knelt down. The dirt felt cool as it ran through my fingers. Nothing hits the nose quite like freshly tilled topsoil, carrying the scent of life and death. The ground around here smells rotten after a rain, gray buckshot petrichor, grabbing tires and axles and feet. I've lost shoes in this mud. Delta folks call it gumbo and it feels hungry, aggressive even, as if it actively wants to pull more living things down into its stinking maw. Mosquitoes search for stagnant flats of water. Runoff marches ruthlessly toward low ground. There's a story Patrick Weems told me about a poor new teacher over at the now-defunct Strider Academy, named after the sheriff who helped secure acquittals for Till's killers. Strider Academy sits at the edge of the Delta and the Hills in Tallahatchie County. The closest town is Charleston, home to three of the twelve jurors and the killers they set free. This teacher wanted to do a good job teaching history to her students and so for one class project, she asked her students to research the 1955 murder of Emmett Till. That was a mistake. "The teacher got cussed up one side and down the other for assigning that," Weems said. "Because the kids came home and said, 'Tell me about Emmett Till.' These are Strider Academy kids asking their parents about Emmett Till and no shit did they have a connection."

The connections I found in the land around the barn centered it for me in the American story. I first found Nathan Bedford Forrest in this same tight square where white supremacists murdered Emmett Till, but others quickly revealed themselves: I learned of ancient ruins, Indian mounds that would become known as the Walford site, buried nearby in the dirt. Archaeologists had been digging in Township 22 North since the start of World War II, removing artifacts to Jackson and Cambridge, Massachusetts. I found out about the New York timber-baron plantation, and the blues legends at Dockery Farms, and the mostly anonymous sharecroppers who made the world turn, including Gloria Dickerson's ancestors on both her mother's and father's sides. The connections created a map that led, always, to the barn, and then to the truth. The story of Till's death is the story of the rise and rot of a tribe of people, of which I am one.

The barn will not allow you to live free of the image of a tortured child. That, it turns out, is its curse but also its blessing. It will not let you go. Why was Emmett Till murdered? One cannot see the barn without being faced with that question. A question with many faces. Why was he killed in this place? Why the Delta, why Sunflower County, why Township 22 North, Range 4 West, why Section 2? The barn renders you mute at first. Seventy feet long and twenty feet high, it hunkers on a hill that rises slightly, a foot of added elevation every fifteen or so paces. A century of exposure weathered the cypress boards gray, and rust long ago patinaed the hinges and blacksmithed nails. The silence is immediately followed by an overwhelming impulse to speak, to shout, to say what happened here, and why, so that this knowledge inoculates us against its happening again. That urge requires a journey of understanding, requires action in pursuit of answers to these questions.

Emmett Till died in Section 2 because that's where Leslie Milam farmed, and Leslie Milam farmed there because for a very long time human beings have been trying to extract wealth from this square of land. The secret history of how the Mississippi Delta came to be defined by its rich land and poor people, by extreme structural value attached to dirt and a corresponding worthlessness attached to life, is the story of how a group of people all ended up in the same barn on the same night in 1955. The Milams and Bryants had been pushing westward for generations, cursed by greed and a kind of naive simpleness that would have made them almost sympathetic characters had their failure not curdled to unforgivable violence. They intersected with Till because the forces acting on him were in opposition to the ones acting on them. Where Milam and Bryant saw a setting sun Till saw a towering sky. Where they saw boundaries to protect he was just beginning to see boundaries to explore. They saw endings where he saw beginnings. Why was Emmett Till murdered? Why was he taken to Leslie Milam's barn? The answers live in the soil itself. In the land. In the grid square called Township 22 North, Range 4 West, measured from the Choctaw Meridian.

THE BARN IS ALMOST the exact geographic center of the Mississippi Delta, which was the last of the alluvial plain to be settled, still an uninhabitable wilderness long after most of the country had been populated and tamed. Drew wasn't founded until 1899. The barn sits in what until very recently was a vast, terrifying forest. When the loggers arrived in the 1880s and '90s some of these woodland floors hadn't seen sunshine in a thousand years. Geronimo was in chains and the Census Bureau had declared the frontier closed and the army massacred more than three hundred Lakota at Wounded Knee. The OK Corral shoot-out had already become legend but the west half of Township 22 North, Range 4 West, Section 2, remained a wilderness. Robert Ford had killed Jesse James before anyone grew a stalk of cotton in most of this part of Sunflower County. If the process of becoming America was about fulfilling the secular prophecy of Manifest Destiny, then there is a case to be made that the last bit of the continent settled was not the Wild West or the harsh upper plains but a pit of swamp and cypress trees where one day an unknown farmer would build a barn.

For thousands of years white oaks and willow oaks towered above the river and creek banks. The topsoil went deeper than two hundred feet, the river flooding year after year. Sycamore trees grew thick from the nutrients, records sizing some of them as wide around as shipping containers are long. Cypress groves spread complex cages of roots and secondary trunks. Cottonwood trees reached skyward with furrowed bark two full hand lengths deep. Oak, gum, hickory, ash, holly. An undergrowth of dogwoods and crab apples. Thick blue canebrakes choked off the open spaces. At night wolves howled and panthers screamed. Turkeys strutted in and out of the foliage. Herds of white-tailed deer rutted in the heavy undergrowth of vines and brambles. Huge birds dominated the canopies closest to the sky. Their songs were the first music of this place. Much later traders and log runners riding the rivers gasped in fear at the towering walls of hardwood trees rising on the banks. They couldn't see three feet into the dark woods but had to shout in their boats to be heard over the singing birds: Bachman's warblers and Carolina parakeets and the ivory-billed woodpecker—enormous, two feet across from wing to tip, valued as currency for its spiritual power and physical dimensions and beauty, called the Lord God Bird, as in, "Lord God, look at the size of that bird!" The woodpeckers lived in virgin timber runs of cottonwood and red gum, of hackberry, ash-leaf maple, and cypress. The kings of the forests were the songbirds.

IF THERE WAS A GREAT cosmic clock counting down to Emmett Till's murder in Leslie Milam's barn, that unspooling began when the first plow dug into the first row and broke open this ground to serve the appetites of human beings. *Break.* That's the agricultural lingo for cutting into the topsoil with sharp knives, unlocking the commercial potential of all that buried nitrogen. Those first native farmers built a town on what is now the Ralph Ray Road, connecting the Drew-Ruleville Road with Highway 61. Archaeologists have found measurable erosion beginning in the Delta five thousand years ago, the land's first human alteration.

Scientists still call the ruins of that town the Walford site, after the family who owned the land when Harvard's Peabody Museum arrived in 1940. The site consists of two remaining mound structures and a great deal of pottery and other evidence. So much about life at Walford mirrored how life would play out in the sharecropper South centuries later: a functional monocrop, with a caste system rising out of its cultivation, the land worked by slaves captured from rival tribes. Violence inflicted, violence absorbed, as critical to large-scale agriculture as photosynthesis.

A thousand years ago homes dotted the farmland around the main mounds and public squares. Defensive fortifications ringed the main square, the religious and cultural buildings, and the homes of the leaders. A wall, twelve to fifteen feet tall, formed a barrier on three sides with the fourth protected by the Sunflower River. The land, even today, moans with the faded echoes of war. Every forty yards, a bastion stuck out of the wall with elevated shooting platforms for warriors armed with bows and arrows, spaced to create interlocking fields of fire.

One reason the site attracts interest is because the military wall existed here before archaeologists believed such an invention was possible. Desperate, creative people built a wall that kept arrows out while allowing them to return fire. Their enemy has been lost to time. So have they. The city marked on maps as the Walford site was gone long before the Spanish explorer Hernando de Soto first arrived in the Mississippi Delta in 1541.

THE ARRIVAL OF THE SPANISH led to the mapping of this land, which pulled it out of the unknowable past and placed it squarely in a new modern world. I found the first map of what would become Township 22 in a museum in Seville, Spain. Alonso de Santa Cruz drew it in 1544 after interviewing the survivors of de Soto's failed campaign. I awoke early one morning and walked the old streets of Seville amid the noise of singing birds and the ringing of distant bells. Narrow cobblestone alleys and ornate recessed palace gates smelled of hidden gardens. I'd come to visit the General Archive of the Indies, which stores the paper trail for all that Spanish gold brought back in all those galleons, and for all that violence committed in the search for it. I stood outside and waited for the place to open. A familiar tree growing amid the hedges and palm trees caught my eye. The brown color of the sunburned leaves and the clenched fists of unopened bulbs looked familiar, but for a minute I couldn't place them. Then I saw a white flower, and another and another, and it hit me. There was a single magnolia tree growing in the front yard of the archive. Southern magnolias are the state flower and tree of Mississippi, even though the species is not native to the Delta, which is okay because almost nothing and no one is. I walked over to smell home.

The 9:00 a.m. bells finally rang all over the city and a man let me inside.

"Second floor," he said.

The archive staff showed me to a reading station, number 18, at a wood table in a high-ceilinged room. I requested the drawing known in research circles as the de Soto map. In the late fifteenth century Spain and Portugal were in a frenzied race to claim every unknown piece of the world. To bring order to the situation, in 1493, Pope Alexander VI issued the papal bull *Inter caetera*, which drew a line through the Atlantic Ocean 100 leagues west of the Azores and declared everything west of that line to be Spanish, leaving everything east to the Portuguese. A treaty a year later further formalized this. In 1504, an amendment increased the distance to 370 leagues, never mind that neither of the aggrieved parties, nor their churchly mediator, had ever actually seen the real estate they were greedily dividing between themselves. The papal bull claimed the future Mississippi Delta as the property of the king of Spain. In 1513, Spanish soldier Juan Ponce de León landed at a place he named La Florida. Cortés reached Mexico in 1519. Pizarro found the Incas. In 1538 a soldier named Hernando de Soto left Spain to travel to Ponce de León's La Florida and then push inward toward those undiscovered but already claimed possessions.

All this voyaging required oversight, and early on the Spanish government created Casa de la Contratación, the House of Trade, which was responsible for maintaining the Padrón Real—a secret, constantly updated map of the known world. Whenever a pilot on a galleon left Spain, he took with him a chart traced from the Padrón Real by a licensed mapmaker. While at sea, he marked any errors or new discoveries, which he swore an oath not to publish or reveal to any foreigner. When he returned to Spain he sat for interviews to share what he had learned. One of the men in charge of these interviews, and the subsequent adjustments to the map, was the sailor Amerigo Vespucci, whom America was named after.

I waited at reading spot number 18. Horse hooves clip-clopped on the cobblestones outside. Finally a man stood over me. He held a big white paper envelope.

The ink on Santa Cruz's map is now the color of copper, drawn in delicate pen strokes on heavy linen paper. The white space covering most of the bottom third of the page is the Gulf of Mexico, and Florida is labeled and recognizable on the far right. Santa Cruz drew little circles just south of what is now Miami. Moving up the west coast of Florida, he marked a large bay with islands, two rivers, then another bay. His role here was to create an organized system for stripping wealth from distant strangers. The map he drew, like every map of Mississippi drawn from then until now, served as the central article of justification. As the coastline turned west and flattened into the panhandle he drew a big cloud-shaped bay fed by a river. That's Mobile, Alabama. He drew many rivers that didn't exist. One river did: he drew a huge dog-head bay with a river running north to south into it that he named Río del Espíritu Santo. The local people called it the Mississippi.

THE HISTORY OF TOWNSHIP 22 is revealed through maps, which measure time as much as geography. I've got hundreds of them. One map sat on my desk for a year before I learned enough of the area's history to realize it had been trying to tell me something: the story of how Gloria Dickerson came to live on this square of land. The original, which is in the collection of Harvard's Peabody Museum, was completed by the Army Corps of Engineers in 1911. It lists a Township 22 landowner by the name of Bony Parker. That's a typo. His name was Bonny Parker and he worked his 160 acres, a quarter section, with his wife, Belle, a short woman with long white hair hanging down past her knees. One Friday in 1916, Mr. Parker sat on his horse as a ferry pulled him across the Sunflower River near his home. It was around Dockery. Just as the craft approached the shore his horse bolted. Bonny Parker broke his neck and lingered for a few days, then died. Belle Parker took over the place.

She hired a sharecropper named Willie Boyd to manage her hogs and mules. His salary was twenty-five dollars a month. Widow Belle, as she was known, also gave Boyd the house next to hers. Willie's girlfriend was Luvenia Slaughter, who sharecropped and worked as a maid for Belle. Luvenia was Gloria Dickerson's grandmother. She came to Township 22 North in 1908 with her parents and grew up on a plantation owned as an investment by midwestern railroad men. People from the North who met Luvenia got confused at her light skin and blue eyes. People from the South understood perfectly.

Luvenia spent much of her time with Widow Belle, who covered her pale skin in the summer, wearing gloves, long sleeves, and a hat to keep from getting burned. Belle especially liked Luvenia's daughter (and Gloria's mom) Mae Bertha, who'd churn butter in Belle's kitchen and talk about salvation.

"I got it now," Mae Bertha said. "I got the good religion."

"How you know you got it?"

"I can feel it burning in my heart. I can see a shooting star."

Belle Parker got old. She hung a bell on her porch and ran a rope back to her bedroom, where she could summon help. That bell rang out across the fields.

Three of the Black families who worked for Belle Parker were related, all of them having come from Georgia just after the turn of the century, chasing the cotton boom. A man named William Kelly brought his mother and sisters. One of his nephews was Matthew Carter, who drove Belle around in her beige-and-chocolate two-tone 1928 Model T Ford. Mae Bertha Slaughter and Matthew Carter fancied each other. They got married and started a family—Gloria and her siblings. The Carter children loved to sit and hear the stories from Matthew's grandmother, Lucy Scott, who'd been an enslaved woman in Georgia. She told them of huge eagles that'd swoop low over the fields and how the plantation owner would shoot them down from the sky and stack them up in wagons, fearful these big birds of prey would steal his slaves.

One of those great-granddaughters was Gloria Dickerson, my friend from Drew who got stuck with me out in Township 22 North. That day we'd both climbed out of the car, our feet immediately sinking in the gumbo mud, and assessed the situation. It looked escapable and a few engine revs and carefully timed switches between drive and reverse later, we climbed out of the hole and spun to safety. After we got ourselves unstuck we drove away from the mudhole to the empty ground where her family's church once stood. The only thing left are graves beneath beautiful oak trees flecked with beams of light.

"That's where Mama and Daddy are buried."

She thought for a moment.

"I wouldn't mind being buried out there."

———

THE FRENCH FOLLOWED THE SPANISH. In 1673, Louis Jolliet and Jacques Marquette piloted canoes down the Mississippi. Jolliet was a trader. Marquette was a priest. They made it to the Mississippi Delta, as far as what would one day be Prentiss. I grew up hearing about the legend of Prentiss, a cautionary tale about the fragility of our homeland. Once it was a thriving river town, until the river changed course and covered the place in dirt and mud, burying the churches and the courthouse and the homes and everything else. It stayed that way until 1954, the year before Emmett Till came south alive and returned home dead. Then the river turned again and land sloughed off into the water and revealed half of the old courthouse just hanging out in space. My mom's family drove over to see it. She was seven. Bootleg vendors sold Cokes and sandwiches. Water takes and gives what and when it wants. The reservoirs built to control all this water covered up entire communities, the streets and places of business and worship abandoned to the deep. People swear they can hear church bells ringing when the current moves right.

Jolliet and Marquette found natives with guns, axes, hoes, knives, and glass bottles, bought from Europeans encroaching from the East Coast. They turned back and took a different route home. They followed the Illinois River up through tributaries until they arrived at what would become the city of Chicago.

AFTER GETTING UNSTUCK and driving past the cemetery, Gloria and I drove to a car wash in Cleveland.

"Well, that was an adventure," she said.

We headed back toward Drew. On the left we passed the sign for North Sunflower Academy. Jeff Andrews, a proud alum, is currently the president of the school board. The mascot is the Rebels. It's one of the Delta's many segregation academies, which were private schools founded around the state after the federal government ordered all public classrooms to be integrated. Before it even opened its doors, the public school system gave its best books and supplies to the new academy. The books they didn't need, instead of going to the public school the Black students now attended, were thrown into the Sunflower River.

The sign said the school was established in 1966.

I turned to Gloria.

"What year did you guys get to Drew High School?"

"Sixty-five," she said.

THE FRENCH INFILTRATED the Choctaws' matrilineal society, traders meeting the daughters of chiefs and marrying them. The Europeans were conquering the Choctaw by becoming them and then pulling them into the world of credit and debt.

Greenwood LeFlore, the last chief of the Choctaw nation east of the Mississippi, was the son of a Frenchman named Louis LeFleur, who worked as a trader for Panton, Leslie & Company. No part of tribal life remained unaffected by the arrival of the market. Tribes reorganized their daily lives around this new economy. Some ran inns and saloons along the old walking trails. Others carried the mail. Some made salt. But the most common item sold to both the French and the English was deerskin. Between 1699 and 1715, English ships took at least 50,000 hides across the Atlantic annually. Some years that number topped 100,000. Soon the French in

Louisiana were exporting a similar number. Native families devoted all their energy to procuring and delivering the hides.

By 1721 the French and the Choctaw had agreed on set prices. Four deerskins bought a meter of woolen cloth or an axe. Two bought a blanket or a tomahawk. The deerskin trade peaked, historians believe, during the 1750s, when something like a million deer were killed per year, thinning the herds, putting pressure on both food gathering and the ways in which traditions were passed down. Soon hunters found themselves crossing the Mississippi into Arkansas and Louisiana looking for game.

The Natchez tribal leaders saw the future. They tried to fight back against the French and their Choctaw allies. A French commander demanded a Natchez village turn its home over to his men. The tribal leaders gathered. One respected leader rose to speak.

"Before the French came among us we were men," he said. A plan for war developed. On November 28, 1729, two hundred miles south of the barn, the Natchez attacked the French at Fort Rosalie, killing all the men and taking the women and children as slaves. They killed the military leaders and a priest. Two hundred twenty-nine French settlers died in all. The white males were scalped and beheaded. Reports said some slaves joined in on the side of the Natchez and attacked their owners. The Natchez fled in victory and for the next year the French and the Choctaw hunted them. Finally only four hundred free Natchez remained. On January 25, 1731, they surrendered, including the remaining chiefs. A few months later, those prisoners were sold into slavery to work in what is now Haiti. One of the slaves was a former chief. The Natchez vanished. Their name is now mostly known for being the name of the city that was the capital of the antebellum cotton world. Only a few records exist about what happened to these great warriors in slavery.

It seems most ended up working in sugarcane fields or slaughter-houses. There's no record of when or where the Natchez chief died. His last recorded sighting was on the docks of what is now Cap-Haïtien. A French bureaucrat who'd met the chief in Mississippi recognized him and walked over to reminisce about their days as enemies. The chief greeted his old foe with melancholy in his eyes and said he wanted to go home.

THE WORD *MISSISSIPPIAN* today carries many different mean-ings around the world, many of them born in the violence of 1955, but there was a time when the word had never been spoken. Then in the year 1719 one man made it code for extravagance, corruption, and foolish fiscal shenanigans. The man, named John Law, the son of a wealthy Scottish goldsmith, is the true founder of modern Mis-sissippi. His plan first turned this wilderness into a global invest-ment opportunity.

Law didn't do much, unless you count gambling, killing rivals in duels, drinking, eating, and escaping the odd death sentence when it behooved him to simply run. He loved to play tennis. Once he got into a feud with a gentleman named Edward Wilson, likely over a woman. He and Wilson were drinking and hurling insults at the Fountain Tavern in London, across the street from where the Savoy Hotel is today. They left the pub and then ran into each other again in Bloomsbury Square. The men drew their swords and Law killed Wilson, leaving him bleeding in the street. Law escaped to Paris and ran the faro game at a famous underground casino, talked loudly about money, was thrown out of the city, and washed up in Genoa and Venice and Turin. He played cards and chased prosti-tutes with the Duke of Orléans, the nephew of Louis XIV, the Sun

King. Smart, but not as smart as he imagined, Law studied the financial markets across Europe and made a mistake common to financial neophytes: he mistook the abundance of currency for an abundance of capital. Credit, he told anyone who'd listen, could unlock the world. He bounded forward like a puppy.

Law set up the first private bank in France. Then he sold shares in the Mississippi Company, each offering investors a piece of the river valley stretching from the gulf to the high bluffs where the city of Memphis would soon be founded. His new organization was a holding company for all the business being done on the new American frontier, home to a French monopoly centered around New Orleans. The company's value, adjusted to 2024 dollars, was greater than Apple and Microsoft combined. Ordinary people who got in early became rich. Law's driver retired. The instant millionaires became known in France as Mississippians. It was a slur, like calling someone reality-television famous, or new-money rich, or simply tacky, vulgar, and plain. One writer described them on the prowl in Paris: "the age of Roman corruption; furniture of gold and silver, dazzling jewels, precious odors, fountains of perfumed water, fruits from both continents, monstrous fish, marvelous automatons, half-naked courtesans."

Law's company founded the city of New Orleans. Two years later his bank had been merged with the national bank of France. Law suddenly oversaw the entire country's finances. Then the stock started to slide. The French economy stopped working. John Law fled under an assumed name while behind him burst what would come to be known as the Mississippi Bubble—the first of a series of famous corruption scandals in the foundational history of the state. Had Mississippi not spent the next three centuries turning its name into a code word for racial violence, the mere utterance of the state's name would signify the marriage of financial and political corruption, for a refusal to accept responsibility or pay bills or do business in an ethical way. Whenever some modern scandal hits the state, like the retired football star Brett Favre and former governor Phil Bryant allegedly conspiring to use welfare money to line private pockets or one of Emmett Till's killers being arrested twice for food stamp fraud in the years after 1955, there is a thread stretching back to the past all the way to John Law. He first put the Yazoo-Mississippi Valley into the global vocabulary as shorthand for speculation and theft. Law died in Venice broke and hounded by creditors. His grave is inside a church there.

THE CHICANERY EMBEDDED in the soil of Mississippi, and therefore Township 22 North, did not end with John Law. Rather it began. John Law's perverted morals would define civic and financial life in the state long after his name slipped from popular memory. Fresh from victory in the Revolutionary War, the new state of Georgia claimed ownership of the millions of acres stretching all the way west to the Mississippi River. Georgia politicians wanted this land sold so the state could benefit financially. By 1794 time was of the essence. The other states had already deeded to the federal government all their unsettled frontier.

Georgia had claimed all the land between the Atlantic and the Mississippi even though it could not control or defend this territory. Georgia politicians knew they needed to sell it now or perhaps lose the ability to sell it at all. Yazooists, the speculators and corrupt officials were called. They were named after the Yazoo-Mississippi Delta, which was part of the land that Georgia was feverishly trying to unload on the unsuspecting public. The corrupt politicians needed people to imagine these uninhabitable Mississippi swamps as an undiscovered paradise and so in a place whose name already meant wild speculation and market bubbles, the word *Yazoo* and its accompanying floodplain became the riskiest bet in that enormous rural casino. The Yazooists came like locusts. U.S. senator James Gunn led the investors from four different companies who wanted different parts of the territory. He offered fifty thousand acres to a member of the Georgia house in exchange for his support of the corrupt land deal. Bribes happened out in the open. One lawmaker sold his vote for $600 and then complained that others were getting $2,000. Another politician was offered "eight to ten" slaves. Eli Whitney, inventor of the cotton gin, was a Yazooist. More and more people arrived in Augusta, Georgia, to buy votes and land. An associate justice of the United States Supreme Court walked through the statehouse with $25,000 in cash buying votes.

The land beneath the barn ended up in the hands of James Gunn's Georgia Company, which got seventeen million acres for $250,000. Gunn and his fellow investors flipped their purchase almost immediately, selling most of it in the summer of 1795 to James Greenleaf, the land speculator who developed Washington, DC. Greenleaf flipped it, too, to a man who would become one of the most powerful investors in the country. Nathaniel Prime dominated the cotton trade on Wall Street and was the first president of the New York Stock Exchange. A decade after the Yazoo land deal, he ran one of the nation's first investment banks, which was named Prime & Ward. He later combined his firm with King & Gracie, whose founder lived in the big Manhattan mansion that is now the official home of the city's mayor. Among Prime's biggest clients was the London merchant bank Baring Brothers, which would make more off Mississippi cotton than perhaps any other entity in the world.

All these institutions engaged in the national pastime of land speculating, where the slips of paper traded around the financial capitals of the Eastern Seaboard had nothing to do with the actual wilderness those contracts represented. Deer walked carefully around sycamore trees while in every major city in the country, investors bought Yazoo land certificates for two and three times the original purchase price, sometimes as much as five times higher, betting that the collective political might of all these wealthy, old American families could convince Congress to honor their claims. Alexander Hamilton weighed in, adding confidence to the investment, assuring people that the new Constitution prevented the annulment of any land sales.

Then Georgia annulled the sales. The stench of corruption had risen too high. The citizens of the state started hunting their elected officials. A mob tried to seize the state senator from Hancock County and tie him to a tree for whipping. When he ran to South Carolina one of his constituents found him alone in a cabin and shot him dead. Gunn went into hiding. His wife killed herself. The state's other senator, James Jackson, resigned his seat and came home to try to overturn the law and reclaim the land for the yeomen of his home state. Jackson wrote beautiful, clear, angry essays under a pseudonym in the two big newspapers in the state, comparing the Yazooists to the worst decadence of Marie Antoinette, who'd been beheaded two years earlier. Jackson told voters he'd been offered half a million acres if he'd participate in the plot to sell the Yazoo land at far below market value. Nearly the entire assembly turned over in the next election and the very first law passed was to declare the entire Yazoo land deal void. A scripted and ritualized ceremony on the statehouse steps followed. It was February 15, 1796. The Georgia politicians exited the building. They carried all the records of the land sales. The bills, the notes, the receipts. The president of the senate gave them to the speaker of the house, who gave them to the clerk. A man took a magnifying glass from his pocket and started a fire. The pages kindled and burned.

THE COTTON GIN, invented in 1793, turned cotton into the most valuable commodity in the mechanizing world, a place atop the global financial food chain it would maintain until the 1930s. Without it there would have been no Mississippi, no Delta, no sharecropper family for Till to visit in the late summer of 1955. The gin was one of many new machines unleashed on the world at roughly the same time. It was a new age. This explosion of technology and capital shrank and connected the world, accelerating the spread of corruption and convenience in equal measure. When my mother was a girl, her father subscribed to *The Manchester Guardian*, historically the newspaper of the British cotton and textile industry, and it got mailed across the Atlantic Ocean once a week. He wanted to understand the link between their world of dirt and the world of machines across the ocean. The Mississippi Delta has long been deeply connected with Manchester and Liverpool. Slave narratives report the connection between the "Liverpool price" for cotton and the severity and frequency of violence. The small Mississippi town of Yazoo City, where part of my family lives, used to be named Manchester.

The industrial inventions around textile production killed home weaving, a thousand-year tradition that allowed the yeoman farmer to clothe his family and make a little extra. In just fifteen years an eight-spindle machine became a thousand-spindle machine, still run by one person. This was a century of unrelenting change. The first piano. The first mercury thermometer, invented by Daniel

Gabriel Fahrenheit. The fire extinguisher. The telegraph machine, threshing machines, and self-winding clocks. The parachute and guillotine. Doctors found a new mental health crisis: people driven insane by trying to keep pace with machines. Every living thing adapted or died. The peppered moth evolved in real time, changing its color to black to match the color of the polluted Manchester sky.

RECORDKEEPERS IN THE Georgia government, because of the ill-considered burning of records, didn't know who had purchased what. The land scripts had been sold and resold by savvy investors and powerful institutions that now found this paper worthless. A fight was brewing. The state of Georgia, after all its boasting and strutting, meekly signed over all its western lands to the federal government. The holders of the Yazoo land wanted to be made whole. The people of Georgia, supported by men like Thomas Jefferson, wanted the entire American frontier to be populated by small, landowning white farmers. Yeomen. The desire was ideological, to protect against the kind of class system that drove many early colonists away from Europe, but also practical: tough, resilient, armed men could protect the fragile borders of the new nation as well as or better than an actual army. On the other side were the connected, the old-moneyed, the powerful, the educated, the elites of New York and Boston and Philadelphia and Savannah and Charleston and New Orleans, and of course across the Atlantic, too. Benjamin Franklin's grandson worked for a London-based speculation outfit that wanted in on the action. Stuck in the middle, as always, were slaves and natives; the people who actually lived on the land had nothing to say about its future use. Only money spoke. The fight would last fourteen years and, as much as any moment in

American financial history, cemented the primacy of shareholder value as the nation's foundational principle.

The money won. In 1810 the Supreme Court ruled that the Yazoo land sale was binding.

THE LAND WHERE THE BARN now stands still slept. Sometimes when I walk or ride horses through the unfarmable river side of the levee, I feel like I've gone back in time to the days before people arrived in this bend of the Sunflower River. The backside of the levee, the batture now reserved for million-dollar hunting camps, is where the spirit of the old Delta lives. That land is the dominion of old planter families like mine, and the more modern folks who can afford the steep initiation fees and annual bills. Places like Burkes and Donaldson Point, the Merigold Hunting Club, which was run for decades by one of my uncles, and Concordia Rod & Gun, which was founded by another. The land behind the levee feels like virgin forest but of course it is not. An enormous amount of money was spent to turn back the clock and make this *feel* untouched. The money was well spent, because the world created with it does in fact give a window into that early Delta, before the arrival of things like money. Early one morning my uncle and I climbed up into saddles, the only first-light noise coming from the jangling spin of his spurs, and we wound through second- and third-growth cottonwood trees. A deer found persimmon trees and heard something snap in the woods. His head swiveled to look toward the noise, a big rack of antlers in the green canopy glow, free to eat the undergrowth and rut his horns against a tree. The whole forest knew he was ready to mate. His feet crackled on the leaves around the trunks. His neck blended into his shoulders, full rut, his antlers outside his ears. At sunrise the clouds above him glowed red and orange. Poison oak climbed the maple trees. The buck took deliberate steps. Then he was gone. My uncle and I pushed the horses toward a clearing and emerged onto a bluff rising high above the Mississippi River. A tugboat pushed a barge slowly past us toward New Orleans. We whipped the reins back toward the forest and before long ended up in another clearing. Huge industrial pipes and wheels ran through an erector set superstructure, all of it overgrown and abandoned. This was the old Bunge grain terminal, built to load soybeans onto ships bound for markets around the world. A new one got built just up the river and this was left to rust.

LESLIE MILAM'S ROAD TO THE barn stretches back to faded records in archives and old colonial courthouses up and down the Eastern Seaboard. Those records are incomplete, so his family tree prior to the American Revolution is ultimately an educated guess. The probable first member of the Milam family to cross the Atlantic was named John Mylan. He landed in Boston with his brother Humphrey. Most likely their ship docked in 1623, just three years after the *Mayflower* landed in Plymouth. Back home John and Humphrey Mylan had built barrels in a rural precinct west of London, near where Heathrow Airport is today. In America John got rich working as a cooper and speculating in land. His property abutted Boston Harbor. Soon he owned a mill and six enslaved people and a share in three ships named the *Zebulon*, the *John*, and the *Supply*. All three carried enslaved people on the Middle Passage: ships took raw goods from the Americas to England and took finished textile products from England to Africa, where they traded the goods for slaves to take back to the Americas. The family's fortunes would constrict with each succeeding generation, following a spiraling path of diminishment from their first steps in the New World until the bitter summer of 1955. John had a son named Joseph who had a son named John Maylem, a new spelling. He graduated from Harvard College in 1715 and had a son named John Milam, the third and final name change, who had a son named Samuel who had a son named Jordan, a soldier in the revolution who had a son named John, a veteran of the Battle of New Orleans, who had a son named Jefferson who had a son named Dave who had a son named Leslie who had sons named Leslie and J.W., who murdered a child in the family barn on the west half of section 2, in Township 22 North, Range 4 West, measured from the Choctaw Meridian.

THE CREATION OF THE GREAT American land grid required a fundamental change in what it meant to be an American. Land-hungry southerners eager to replicate the old wealth they saw in the original colonies needed to wait until George Washington died, which he did in 1799. Washington had believed the native tribes should remain independent nations within the United States but he could tell this was a losing battle. His correspondence is full of his fear that the nation he'd helped found would erase these tribes. "If the same causes continue," his friend Henry Knox wrote in a letter, "the same effects will happen and in a short period the idea of an Indian on this side of the Mississippi will only be found in the page of the historian."

While he was alive Washington used his prestige and power to protect native tribes from the land companies and politicians like Andrew Jackson. One of the first pieces of legislation Jackson passed after being elected president was the Indian Removal Act.

Only fifteen years earlier he'd fought side by side in New Orleans with the great Choctaw warrior chief Pushmataha, who earned a battlefield commission of colonel after leading his men on a successful lightning counterattack. Pushmataha, grandfather to the last great preremoval Choctaw chief, Greenwood LeFlore, thought he'd earned respect, but that respect would never come in his lifetime. In Jackson's speech arguing for the Removal Act, he described the new law as "benevolent" and said no man had the right to slow down the march of progress across the wide continent.

IN THE FALL OF 1805 Pushmataha had traveled north via boat to meet with Thomas Jefferson. That meeting shook the great Choctaw leader, who'd been forced to trade four million acres to settle a $46,000 debt to the Panton Company. The government had figured out how to clear the South of the people who had been living there so the new grid could be laid atop all that newly emptied land. Pushmataha came home and gathered his people. The sun set and the stars lit the sky. Sparks rose from the fire. Pushmataha began to tell a story about a bird whose song filled the trees with beauty. This forest music sounded like a beam of light shot through a cloud after a morning rain. The bird was small but strong and his song nurtured all the living things in the forests and the swamps. But it needed food and one day a creature arrived and promised abundance for a price.

"If you bring me the flowers of the field," the creature said, "I will feed you."

The bird traded and traded until all the flowers were gone. The creature let the bird continue to eat but warned of a coming reckoning.

"Finally the day came when the creature demanded payment," he said.

"In payment of your debt, I demand your song."

The stars twinkled in the night sky and the air turned cool.

"Please do not take my song," the tiny bird begged.

Nobody spoke.

"As with the tiny bird, the day has now come when payment is due. The white trader demands that what he is owed be repaid. But the Choctaw has no ability to repay. The deer are no more. The Choctaw has nothing of value to the white man—except land."

Pushmataha sighed.

"I speak tonight with anguish in my heart," Pushmataha said. "My voice trembles with the words that I bring from the White Chief in Washington. I come as the tiny bird whose song has been ripped from his throat."

THE LOBBYING CAMPAIGN TO legitimize the sale of Mississippi by the Georgia legislature launched a land rush. Decades before the country would print paper money, Yazoo securities flooded the frontier in denominations of $25, $75, $150, $300, $600, and $1,000. These could be redeemed for cash at the Treasury in Washington or for land at any federal land office in the Mississippi Territory. I've driven past the site of the government office on the edge of the Delta many times. A cluster of families lives there now, yards decorated with abandoned tractors.

These certificates granted not just land but government-backed access to global credit markets, promising the bearer the land at just 1.25 percent money down. Historians have written about how the Yazoo land securities "stitched" together slavery and capitalism.

The old indigo and tobacco lands of the Eastern Seaboard had been bled of nutrients and could never have supported the cotton revolution to come in the next five decades. Virginia politicians began seriously contemplating freeing enslaved people to get them off the plantation payrolls. Then the Yazoo lands opened at the moment the cotton gin was invented. These two events directly caused a doubling then tripling of the enslaved population of the United States. A system that had briefly looked like part of an old economic order suddenly became the foundation for the entire global economy. Had the Yazoo lands not been sold to speculators, who formed them into enormous plantations that were financed from London and New York—as opposed to the small forty-acre farms that would have likely populated the South had the Yazoo sale not been validated—there never would have been a King Cotton. A train of humanity stretched down the muddy and winding southeastern roads. Hundreds of thousands of enslaved people were "sold down the river" from the areas where rice, sugar, and tobacco couldn't promise the same kind of wealth. They came chained and manacled, on what historian Ira Berlin has called "the second middle passage."

A slave trader named Walker, his first name lost to history, shipped enslaved people from Saint Louis down through the Delta to New Orleans. During one trip a mother carried her nursing newborn. The baby cried most of the day. Walker demanded the mother make the infant stop. The sunburned shoulders and quickened tempers. Many of the enslaved got sick from mosquito-borne diseases, enough that plantation owners called the first few months in the Yazoo Delta "seasoning" as people acclimated to the swampy new hell of their lives.

That night Walker's chained caravan of human beings stopped

at an inn. The next morning, first thing, the baby began to cry again. Walker demanded the child. The women "tremblingly" complied, according to a witness. Walker held the baby by one arm and walked back into the inn and found the woman running it.

"Madam," he said, "I will make you a present of this little n——. It keeps making such a noise that I can't bear it."

"Thank you, sir," the woman replied.

The mother threw herself at the feet of the slaver and begged. Walker tried to kick her away but she gripped his legs tight. She pleaded and wept.

"Oh, my child," she wailed. "My child."

Walker pushed her back to resume the forced march, alone.

BETWEEN 1800 AND 1810 the population of the Mississippi Territory doubled and then doubled again. Soon this region would produce half the nation's cotton. The price per bale soared because a volcanic eruption in modern Indonesia left the global cotton crop short. Historians call 1816 the year without summer. The short crop collided with global capital markets eager to loan money; the Haitian Revolution had taken the lucrative French sugar and coffee plantations offline and left investors hungry for a new place to invest. Speculators ran wild around the southern United States. Mississippi became a state in December of 1817. Then the European economy and agricultural sector recovered from the volcano and at the same time England increased the amount of cotton imported from India. Cotton prices began to fall. In January of 1819 cotton fell 25 percent in a day and land values plummeted. The Panic of 1819, it would be called. The landowners lured west couldn't afford the debt on their new farms, and entire counties were reclaimed by the United States, which would own the land for many decades to come. The rush had lasted nine years and then the dirt shrugged off the invaders and returned to nature. None of these enslavers and speculators and land- and stockjobbers made it to the middle Delta where a barn now sits on the Drew-Ruleville Road.

The Panic of 1819 would build to another panic just eighteen years later, the bubble expanded by the same land speculation, the lesson unlearned. These two events led to Mississippi's global reputation as a place that did not honor its word. As late as the 1930s the nation of Monaco was trying to get the delinquent state to pay its debts. No part of America had a worse reputation for bad credit.

ROY BRYANT'S FATHER WAS NAMED Henry. Everyone called him Big Boy. His father was William, whose father was Henry, whose father was Josiah, whose father was Dr. Fortunatus Bryan. Doc Forts, as his plantation neighbors called him with affection. His father had fought in the Revolutionary War and formed a relationship with Thomas Jefferson. The future president taught him to survey land and served as a protector and benefactor. On April 30, 1805, Fortunatus Bryan married Elizabeth DuPont at her sister's plantation on the Congaree River in South Carolina. The bride came from the famous DuPont family.

The wedding venue sat white and tiered on a little rise just above Beaver Creek, with 180-degree views out over the river and several ridgelines. An enormous line of oak trees formed a canopy drive to the front door. One tree remains today. Vast gardens surrounded the Greek Revival mansion, with its tall white columns. All the bedrooms were upstairs overlooking a wide interior piazza. The sound of the wedding would have carried up and down the river between Columbia and Charleston.

They lived on a growing plantation until Doc Forts got sick and died. A bitter fight awaited his widow once her husband died. His estate was immediately valued at $9,450, or about $250,000 today. It included among other things three horses, two mules, twenty head of stock cattle, seven head of sheep, surgical tools for amputation, a ginhouse, a library, two wagons, four thousand pounds of picked cotton, forty acres of unpicked cotton, and twenty-five enslaved human beings, including Flora, Nancy, Charlotte, Charles, Jimmy, Phillis, Priscilla, Toby, Lindy, Elsey, Carolina, Jeff, Jacob, Stephen, Lucy, Molly, Amelia, and Mourning.

The will took years to probate and the money started disappearing almost immediately. One executor of the estate resigned and the other, an Irish attorney based in Beaufort, insisted that there wasn't nearly as much money as the widow Forts thought because Doc Forts had accumulated significant debts. All the money vanished. The plantation home burned in 1825.

The two Bryan boys migrated to the Lowcountry in their grief. Doc Forts's older son remained there and had four girls. The younger son, Josiah DuPont Bryan, the last without the *t*, moved to Alabama and died less than a week before his thirty-third birthday. His son, Henry, pushed to the edge of the Mississippi Delta, in the poor bluffs of Tallahatchie County. His grandmother had been a DuPont, a name that would come to symbolize the essential connection between military power and capitalism, and yet he lived in frontier squalor. The Milams were already there. For the next four generations these families pressed their noses against the glass of history's last cotton gold rush. The Hills rose steeply above the Delta, which only intensified the feeling of being on the outside looking in. They could see the wealth but could not touch it or make it for themselves.

They called the little town in Tallahatchie County where they lived New Hope.

FOLLOW THEM THROUGH TIME.

Henry Bryant, Doc Forts's grandson, died at age thirty-eight. Before he died, he'd lose a leg in the Civil War, according to family history passed down to modern ancestors. He wasn't alone in his maiming and disfigurement. After the war a fifth of Mississippi's budget would be spent on artificial limbs. Henry's widow stayed in New Hope and lived two doors down from the Milams. The families started a multigenerational pattern of intermarriage. Eula Morgan, the mother of three of Emmett Till's killers and the mother-in-law of an alleged fourth, married both a Milam *and* a Bryant. Through a web of backwoods intermarrying and inbreeding, Henry Bryan is the grandfather of both Eula's husbands, William Leslie "Eslie" Milam and Henry "Big Boy" Bryant. That means, bizarrely, that the murdering half brothers Roy Bryant and J. W. Milam had different fathers but the same great-grandfather.

The census takers a decade after the war found the Milams and Bryants, and most of their neighbors, unemployed for at least ten months the previous year. Around this time a third of the cotton crop simply didn't come up. None of their children attended school and many of the adults reported not being able to read or write. They grew up believing they deserved something that had been taken away. The central role of the next two hundred years of politicians would be telling this mass of Americans born into decline who to blame. In 1881 Ed Devaney, the oldest juror in the Emmett

Till trial, was born just up the road. All these people knew each other. This was an interconnected tribe of people. When the relative of one juror wanted a road built from New Hope to a nearby mill, a grandfather of the murderers was appointed to assist him.

There was a constellation of little villages, hemmed in together by narrow valleys, which functioned as a single place. The mere mention of these town names in polite planter society evoked the image of a medieval boondocks: New Hope, Paynes, Cascilla, and Leverett, clinging to existence on either side of the Charleston-to-Grenada Road, now Highway 35, the unofficial dividing line between the Hills and the Delta. The Milams and Bryants and Thomases were from New Hope; the Tribbles were from Paynes; the Striders were from Cascilla. The jurors' fathers grew up together. Their grandfathers cleared land together. When the local newspaper welcomed Roy Bryant into the world, the next sentence informed concerned friends that juror Ray Tribble's grandmother had the flu. In all, eight of the jurors, the lead defense attorney, and the sheriff who drove the acquittal—and the sitting U.S. congressman from the district during the trial—were not just from the same place but from the same clan. They shared the same codes and interests.

The Milam and Bryant men died violent deaths. Including J.W. and Roy, four straight generations either took a life or lost theirs in a gruesome way. Dave Milam, the grandfather of the killers, started a fight with another poor farmer. Milam and his seventeen-year-old son, Robert, accosted Joe Coleman and his two daughters. Robert attacked and wounded Coleman. The girls ran back to the house to get their dad's gun. Coleman escaped the beating and ran toward his house, where about halfway he met his returning daughters, who armed him. The scene turned even more wild when Dave Milam's wife showed up and started to attack Coleman with a cornstalk. Coleman waved his gun at the woman and Dave Milam approached with his own weapon. At this point Coleman shot and killed Dave Milam. He went to trial and was acquitted, the jury ruling that the killing of Dave Milam had been justified self-defense. Dave was forty-two when he died. His son Leslie, the father of Leslie and J.W., died at thirty-two. The Milam men hadn't seen fifty in generations. Dave's father, Jefferson Milam, also died at forty-two during the Civil War. He enlisted in the spring of '62 as a private and died of illness before the year was out. His oldest son died on the first day of Chickamauga. The boy was nineteen. The temperature dropped that night and some of the wounded froze to death out in the bloody field. Jefferson's father died at forty-seven. The Bryants didn't fare much better. One-legged Henry died at thirty-eight. His grandson, Roy's father, died at forty-eight. This was a violent, sullen place. A yellow fever epidemic almost erased the next town over. Life showed no signs of some magical improvement in their station or outlook. In the last decade of the century residents changed the name of their town from New Hope to Murphreesboro.

THE CHOCTAW HAD SETTLED another huge debt by selling more territory to the government in the 1820 Treaty of Doak's Stand, which handed over about half the Mississippi Delta but not the barn land. The great Pushmataha came north in 1824 to ask why the government had not yet made the payment promised by the treaty, just one in a series of unfulfilled promises made by the Monroe administration. By now he knew that even as he cut the best deal he could, his people were dealing from a place of increasing weakness and eventually would be killed or forced out of Mississippi. He'd spent three years exploring Oklahoma and Arkansas, finding the good and bad land, understanding the geography. He knew far more about the territory than the white men negotiating with him, including future president Andrew Jackson, who described the Choctaws' potential new home inaccurately and bristled when Pushmataha pointed out the error. Jackson, who insisted he knew everything but rarely did the work to learn, cursed and screamed at the chief, insisting he'd been called a liar. Pushmataha, as if dealing with a toddler, placated Jackson and rephrased his complaint by saying, "The paper is untrue."

The Choctaw took rooms at Tennison's Hotel at the corner of Fourteenth Street and Pennsylvania, two blocks from the White House. It's the Willard Hotel now. Pushmataha had a cough he couldn't shake. That didn't stop him from enjoying the city. He and his men did what soldiers do in the safety of peacetime. They drank, running up an enormous hotel bar tab, waiting on President Monroe to find time in his schedule. Pushmataha's cough got worse and worse. Doctors came to his bedside and diagnosed a severe case of croup. There was nothing more they could do. Jackson came to sit with the dying chief and told people he'd never met a braver man.

Pushmataha addressed his men.

"I am about to die but you will return to our country," he told them. "As you go along the paths, you will see the flowers and hear the birds sing but Pushmataha will see and hear them no more. When you reach home they will ask you, 'Where is Pushmataha?' And you will say to them, 'He is no more.' They will hear your words as they do the fall of the great oak in the stillness of the midnight woods."

The man spent his last hours in a Washington, DC, hotel room, far from the woods of his youth. His time had come and gone. The deer had all been killed. The hunting grounds kept getting sold to pay off debt. No more flowers remained to pay tribute. A terrible creature had finally come to take away his song. It was Thursday night. Pushmataha lay dying in his hotel.

He found his voice for one last request.

"When I am gone," he asked, "let the big guns be fired over me."

Two days later, thousands of Washingtonians lined the streets leading to the Congressional Cemetery overlooking the Anacostia River. Newspaper reports put the crowd between one and two thousand, lined up for at least half a mile along the approach to the burial ground. I walked the cemetery once on a chilly morning, with a bright, cold sun above the dormant cherry trees. It's a quiet place most days but not on the day of Pushmataha's funeral. The Marine Corps band marched in the procession along with Andrew Jackson, followed by carriages and mounted cavalry. The chief's last request was granted. The respect between warriors of different cultures was genuine. The secretary of war ordered the cannons at the Capitol to fire a volley every minute for twenty-one minutes. Minute guns at the cemetery fired, too. The band led the procession. An honor guard of seven soldiers fired a volley of rifle shots, then another, then another. When the drums and the cannons and the guns fell silent, the crowd departed from the grave of Pushmataha.

THE LAST CHOCTAW CHIEF east of the Mississippi, Greenwood LeFlore, was the grandson of Pushmataha. When Jackson signed the Indian Removal Act of 1830, which had passed by five votes in the House, only six years separated the military funeral of Leflore's heroic grandfather and the vote to make Pushmataha's descendants leave the only hunting grounds their people had known for centuries.

The bill's opponents predicted the bloody future in frightening detail on the floor of Congress. Massachusetts congressman Edward Everett said, "The evil, Sir, is enormous; the inevitable suffering incalculable. . . . Nations of dependent Indians, against their will, under color of law, are driven from their homes into the wilderness. You cannot explain it; you cannot reason it away. And we ourselves, Sir, when the interests and passions of the day are past, shall look back upon it, I fear, with self-reproach, and a regret as bitter as unavailing."

Chief LeFlore's mandate was to get the best possible terms. The American government sent John Eaton and John Coffee to negotiate. They gathered between the forks of Dancing Rabbit Creek. The government loaded in coffee, beef, and pork to feed the crowds. Someone opened a temporary liquor store. A casino sprouted and the Choctaw held dances and played games. Those who'd converted to Christianity prayed and sang hymns. For days the government and the tribe debated and argued and threatened and fought until the conference ended with no agreement. Most of the Choctaw packed up and started the journey back home.

Eaton waited two days and regathered the remaining chiefs.

He insulted them.

They were a burden, he said, nothing more than "Choctaw children."

He threatened them. The United States, he said with menace, was going to simply leave them at the mercy of the expanding cotton-rich state of Mississippi and give them no new land, no money, no concessions, no annual annuity. Just extinction.

"The Choctaws knew not what to do," one witness aid.

Their allies the French had long ago vanished across the sea.

They couldn't win a war against the Americans. They couldn't negotiate in good faith, knowing the Americans had broken treaties in the past and would again. But with no other good options, the Choctaw leaders reluctantly agreed.

The Treaty of Dancing Rabbit Creek demanded the Choctaw leave in three waves, during the falls of 1831, 1832, and 1833. Congress appropriated eighty thousand dollars to pay for the moves. Most of that money would be stolen from the federal government by corrupt contractors, which would lead to many people starving or freezing to death between Mississippi and Oklahoma.

The land the chiefs signed away that day included the land beneath the barn.

A BLACKSMITH NAMED WILLIAM FORREST crossed the state line into Mississippi in the months after the last Choctaw left. The Forrest family, busted and out of options in Tennessee, joined the same human wagon train that included the Milams and the Bryants. One of his oldest son's many biographers would later write that "the Forrests had been on the move for a good many years. They were a part of that vast restlessness which had spread over Europe after the breakdown of medieval life, and which, because it could not be contained entirely by the rigid discipline of nationalism, continued by overflowing into the Americas. Here, in the newly occupied continent of North America, the Europeans set about to appease their nostalgia for feudalism."

On the ground, in the 1830s, the Forrest family lived ten miles from any neighbor. There were no roads, only narrow horse paths. William Forrest died suddenly and his son Nathan Bedford Forrest took over as head of the family. He was fifteen. In three decades the family would have an outpost in Township 22 North.

THE GOVERNMENT WAITED thirty-eight days after the last Choctaw left before offering a contract to survey the land that would be Township 22 North, Range 4 West. Like Santa Cruz and his Seville cartographers before him, a man named Hugh Stewart claimed the job. The price of cotton was rising above ten cents a pound, a year away from hitting fifteen cents a pound. Stewart and his crew carried chains sixty-six feet in length, with one hundred 7.92-inch links, to measure off the distances. A mile was 80 chains. He found thick lines of cane, the land dotted with water oaks, gum trees, and ash. Dense thickets covered Section 2. Stewart hacked through or went around and 79.76 chains later he arrived at the corner of Sections 2, 3, 10, and 11. He described Section 2 as "third rate" land, a technical description that meant it was almost unfit for cultivation. Stands of cane and ropes of thick vines tangled the land. For days Stewart and his team made their way through Township 22 North, finding cypress brakes and hardwood trees rising into the sky. Finally he finished and sent the completed map to a government land office, where it joined thousands of similar maps commissioned at the same time. All of them stitched together transformed a wide expanse of swampy frontier into a product. The owner who likely built the barn, who also planted the first cotton in Section 2, wouldn't buy the land for sixty-nine more years. A post marked the quarter-section line, a block of forty acres primed to sell. An overcup oak marked the spot where Gloria Dickerson and her family would one day live.

DESTINIES

———

NATHAN BEDFORD FORREST carved out a wealthy life for himself as a slave trader and when war came in 1861, he felt compelled to defend his new life. The ad he placed in a Memphis paper to find soldiers to ride with him said: "Come on boys, if you want a heap of fun and to kill some Yankees."

Forrest won and lost many battles. He lost many other things, too. He lost his famous good looks, aging decades during the four years of war. He lost a world where he could own other people. His unit lost in combat in Yazoo City to a unit of Black Union soldiers. He lost his plantation, the land in weed and ruin, and his money, which he spent on weapons and food for his men and his horses. He lost a lot of his soldiers, who revered him. When he led them in prayer before battles, tears streamed down his face. He lost two of his five brothers.

In the winter of 1864, southwest of Tupelo on the exact spot where Hernando de Soto crossed the Natchez Trace, Colonel Jeffrey Forrest spurred his horse in pursuit of General William Sooy Smith's soldiers. A Union officer later said the sky glowed red with burning cotton. An enemy shot Jeffrey through the neck and he died where he fell. Someone told General Forrest. Fighting new battles for a war already decided, trailing behind the arc of history like his family had been doing for three generations, he rushed to the front line, in range of the enemy, and called out his baby brother's name again and again. The Confederate soldiers quit shooting. The Union soldiers began a disorganized retreat and the field of battle went quiet. Everyone watched the general cradling the dead body of his brother. Cotton sold in Liverpool that morning for more than $1.50 a pound. Smoke from hot, silent barrels curled over the flat field. Forrest kissed

Jeffrey's corpse, rode back to his lines, and called the bugler to sound another charge.

THE CLOSEST THE CIVIL WAR ever got to Township 22 North was when Nathan Bedford Forrest reportedly took his cavalry down the road his brother had built. The edges of the Delta brimmed with plantation labor camps but the interior remained mostly a wilderness untouched by the violence and destruction.

In the settled South, Confederate leaders made a mistake common to people at the bottom of a supply chain. Their local power made them believe they mattered to the people up that chain. Confederate leaders banned the export of cotton, which was the fragile country's only source of revenue. The South burned bales of cotton to keep them out of the global market. The South didn't have enough paper to print the banknotes tied to the price of cotton that it couldn't get to market in the first place. In England imports of American cotton fell from more than 600,000 bales in 1860 to 4,169 in 1863. The Confederate strategy was doomed to fail because it ignored the most important data point when predicting the future price of cotton: the carryover, which is the number of bales produced by global farmers not used by global manufacturers. Nearly every price collapse is rooted in individual farmers responding to falling profits by planting more, staving off their own personal destruction for a year but directly contributing to their own future collapse. The only question southerners should have asked at the onset of war was this: How much cotton found its way to the mills and factories of Europe in previous years that did not get made into textile goods? Everyone knew the answer. The crops of 1859 and 1860 had been enormous and pumped more cotton than needed into the supply chain. When the

Civil War began, England had more than a million bales sitting in warehouses, and in China and India warehouses held hundreds of millions of pounds of unsold goods. An entire network was water-logged with raw material and finished product. Nobody needed any cotton.

FORREST LIVED ONLY TWELVE more years after he surrendered. He looked like a ghost when he walked the streets of Memphis. The town boomed in the years after the war, flooding with new immigrants. He'd lost his war but not his impulse to kill, and without an enemy to confront on the field the object of his hatred became Reconstruction. A year after the war veterans formed a secret society to try to scare newly freed Blacks and any whites who supported the federal government. One of the leaders was Forrest's former artillery captain John Morton, who many years later asked to be buried in his Confederate uniform. Forrest went to Nashville to visit. "John, I hear this Ku Klux Klan is organized in Nashville, and I know you are in it," he said. "I want to join."

Forrest attended his first organizational meeting that night, in room 10 at the Maxwell House Hotel during the fall of 1866. A group of members had previously left Nashville and traveled to Virginia on a special mission, to convince Robert E. Lee to be the leader of the KKK. He declined, suggesting Forrest instead, and so the leadership of the Klan found themselves in room 10. They asked for nominees, knowing that Lee's suggestion would carry the day.

"The Wizard of the Saddle," a man called. "General Nathan Bedford Forrest."

His men set out into the night to win by terror a victory that they had failed to win in open combat. A Klan group who called themselves Heggie's Scouts and operated in the Delta claimed to have killed 116 Black people and thrown their bodies in the Tallahatchie, where Emmett Till's body would be found nine decades later. Armed citizens in Yazoo City lynched a Black elected official inside the county courthouse. There were mob killings in Friars Point in the Delta, and in Clinton farther south. In 1871 about sixty members of Forrest's insurgency in Monroe County, south of Tupelo, killed local Black political leader Jack Dupree. They invaded his home and dragged him out the front door with his wife and three young children helpless to stop them. The murderers stripped his clothes and went to work with knives and blades.

Niambi M. Carter, an author and professor, has described lynching as "a type of racialized, sexual violence that uniquely harms black men." They slit Dupree's throat then cut out his heart and intestines before finally throwing what was left of his corpse into a creek. Soon after, near Starkville, twenty members of Forrest's insurgency beat independent Black farmers who were renting and working land themselves. When a local Black farmer named Dick Malone tried to defend himself and his neighbors, he was shot and killed. A witness explained that the point was to scare Black people away from renting land and force them to be sharecroppers. That same year the Klan killed a Mississippi judge.

Vicksburg voters elected a Black sheriff in 1874 and white mobs killed at least fifty Black citizens in response. Federal prosecutors argued that this was state-sanctioned violence and a violation of the Enforcement Acts. When they won a guilty jury verdict, the judge stepped in and declared the Enforcement Acts unconstitutional and dismissed the indictments. The future of America was actively being contested, battles won and lost on both sides, until the legal system put its finger on the scales of justice and predetermined the victor. The Supreme Court agreed with the judge and said that any violence by the Klan, which had been run by men from the same Confederate cavalry unit, was the work of private citizens—the spiritual ancestors of Milam and Bryant, *private citizens*, deemed to be defending their homeland from a foreign invader. In Mississippi alone, the Justice Department was forced to drop 179 different prosecutions of terrorists.

Trying to vote during Reconstruction if you were Black risked bringing masked riders to your house. Trying to help other people vote could get you tortured and killed. Silently wanting freedom was fine but expressing it was fatal, the tick of a ballot, a moment of eye contact, a whistle, a newspaper printed on the South Side of Chicago. A political battle for the future of Mississippi was being fought with guns and knives. The Klan was a well-planned terrorist organization, run by former high-ranking military officers who understood the power of fear and secrecy, who strategically used violence against unarmed civilians to achieve a political goal. Jim Crow segregation was built on the people killed in the years immediately following the Civil War. Forrest's terrorists did to unarmed citizens what they did not have the strength to do to Grant and Sherman's soldiers. Inspiring fear, inflicting pain—these were his banner and sword. So the surest sign to the general's former men that he was dying was when, with only a few months to live, he told a fellow old soldier, "I have seen too much of the violence."

SHARECROPPING, WHICH WAS ABOUT TO replace enslavement as the cotton industry's dominant system of labor, didn't just happen. After the war European cotton experts heard that most newly freed people just wanted to own tiny subsistence farms, and industry pundits concluded that this would bring "evil consequences" to the entire commodity chain that powered the world's economy. Cotton requires enormous amounts of credit from financial institutions. Harvard history professor Sven Beckert wrote of the freed people's desire for the freedom that only owning land could bring:

> The reconstruction of the empire of cotton, at its core, required the diligent effort of cotton industrialists, merchants, landowners, and state bureaucrats to undermine such preferences, drawing, in the process, on the powers of newly consolidating nation-states, and sanctioning legal—and often illegal—coercion to make rural farmers into the cultivators and eventually consumers of commodities. . . . They sought—and eventually found—what French colonial officials aptly called "a new mode of exploitation."

The four years when the South was disconnected from the global financial market allowed the world to adapt and kept southern farmers from ever truly dominating again. In 1865 the first cotton future was traded in Liverpool and the USDA published its first information on national cotton prices, supply, and demand. A year later the first transatlantic cable was laid on the ocean floor and the possibilities of profits and commissions in a borderless commodity market exploded. Three years after that the New York Cotton Exchange opened, quickly followed by exchanges in New Orleans, Le Havre, Bremen, Osaka, Shanghai, São Paulo, Bombay, and Alexandria. Everyone around the world making money on cotton wanted it to be grown in large-tract plantations in Mississippi. The

South had no functioning banking system and without an enslaved population, no collateral.

In the early years after the war some plantation owners experimented with paying a salary or renting land to tenant farmers, but the short crops of 1866 and 1867 ended that. The planters who chose wages found themselves broke after the planting season. The Black farmers who rented found themselves in the same situation, without enough profit after paying rent to make it through the winter. Sharecropping became a mutually-agreed-upon compromise that would get the crops in and out of the ground and still keep the international credit markets pumping cash into the Delta. It also bound tighter white capital and Black labor. Meanwhile the land around the barn remained asleep.

THE VIOLENCE AND REPRESSION of Jim Crow segregation emerged from laws written by a Mississippi congressman named James Robert Binford, who owned land in Township 22 North, Range 4 West, a few miles from the barn. Mississippians, including Binford, laid the cornerstone for Jim Crow with the 1890 state constitution, which added laws to the corruption and violence that had, up until then, kept white supremacy in place. Future governor James Vardaman said, "Mississippi's constitutional convention of 1890 was held for no other purpose than to eliminate the n——— from politics." The constitution accomplished its goals with brutal efficiency, and ten years after it was ratified the number of registered Black voters had dropped from more than 130,000 to just around 1,300. The new constitution reframed Reconstruction as an act of northern aggression. Soon the state passed textbook laws that controlled what information the children of the state could learn. That fight continues today. A dozen generations of students, including me, learned that Reconstruction was a violent military occupation run by corrupt and vile men intent on enriching themselves at the expense of the broken South. The Black citizens in our textbooks were described as naive, inferior pawns being used by outsiders. No consideration whatsoever was given in class to the idea that Black Mississippians might have enjoyed their newfound agency after the war.

The aftermath of the constitution, which was never put to the public for a vote, birthed the codes and customs that filled in the gaps between the laws. Jim Crow needed grease to work. Blacks learned to step off sidewalks and never make eye contact, especially with a white woman. Most of the customs dealt with sex; there has rarely been a culture in the world that spent so much time thinking about sex, particularly between Black men and white women. Studies show a similar obsession in Japan after the defeat of World War II, the sexual monster being all American soldiers.

In the coming decades, a web of cleverly conceived and written legislation stripped away more and more rights from Black citizens, who'd come to numerically dominate the South because of the enslaved people who followed the western land rush started by the Yazoo scandal. This process required so much creativity that in the 1930s a Nazi law student came to study segregation at the University of Arkansas, looking for inspiration for Germany's own new race laws.

Poor white farmers pushed the state to stop counting Black citizens when determining representation, so that the wealthy Delta counties would be stripped of power. A 1900 amendment to the new constitution divided the state into three equal units to accomplish that goal by legal means. All three electoral districts got the same amount of power, unrelated to population, a gerrymandering that diluted the agency of the majority-Black Delta. The main dividing line was Highway 51, which ran along the border between the Delta and the Hills. Everything west of the road was part of the Delta, even the little Hill towns like Murphreesboro (formerly New Hope), Cascilla, Charleston, and Paynes. The Milams and Bryants and other people like them were caught on the wrong side of an arbitrary line and lost even more political status and power.

JAMES ROBERT BINFORD FADED from history and died in 1918 at his home in Duck Hill, the town his father settled. His obituary proudly mentioned his authorship of the "separate coach law" alongside his military service. He invented the law that made Moses Wright, Wheeler Parker, and Emmett Till move to the segregated Jim Crow car in Cairo, Illinois, always attached at the front so that the Black customers bore the brunt of the billowing engine smoke. He served on the Franchise Committee in the 1890 constitutional convention, which meant he oversaw the disenfranchisement of the state's entire Black population. He raised a real weasel of a son along the way: Lloyd Binford, the infamous censor of Memphis between 1927 and 1955. He banned Charlie Chaplin and any film that depicted a Black character who was not subservient. On his orders, movies that featured Lena Horne had her scenes cut from the reels. Studio heads ranted against his total control of every screen and stage in the city. Lawsuits tried and failed to strip him of his power. Finally his attempt in 1955 to ban a Sidney Poitier movie drew enough ire that he got pushed out. He was eighty-nine years old and nearly completely blind. The next year he died. His family's plantation was just seven miles from the farm where Wheeler

Parker would hide before he could be put on a train out of Mississippi and travel back to his mother. I've driven that old road, mapping the distance between seemingly unrelated places and events, feeling their proximity. Wheeler rode right past the Binford farm on his way to catch the Illinois Central north to safety.

EMMETT TILL'S ROAD TO THE barn traveled through a complex of antebellum plantations in Mississippi where four of his eight great-grandparents lived when the Civil War began. Their enslavers were the Taliaferro family, which had migrated west with the cotton frontier. The Taliaferros were old Virginia money. When John Brown got led to the gallows, for instance, a Taliaferro was one of the two men overseeing the hanging. The *T* in *Booker T. Washington* was for *Taliaferro*; Washington's father was an unknown white man from Virginia. Like a lot of Virginia families, the Taliaferros sent their descendants into South Carolina, then Georgia, then Alabama and Mississippi, where they set up shop just after the Indian clearing. Their Spring Hill, Somerset, and Lucky Hit plantations covered all or part of fifteen 640-acre sections of land in between modern Highway 61 and I-55. At least two of the enslaved people on the plantations, including one of Emmett Till's kin, joined the American army and fought as infantry soldiers against the South. When the war ended, Till's ancestors picked their own last names: John Smith, Laura Taliaferro, Smith Brown, and Lizzie Sinclair. These four people would spread roots all across America.

The white Taliaferro and Brown men had a multigenerational habit of raising unacknowledged Black families alongside their white ones. Smith Brown, one of Till's great-great grandparents, was the son of the plantation owner Hezekiah G. D. Brown. The woman genealogists believe to be Brown's mother was listed as Black in 1870 and mulatto in 1910. But she certainly looked white in the photographs that remain. Likewise Laura Taliaferro was a slave on Spring Hill and the granddaughter of the plantation owners. Lizzie Sinclair's father, Isaiah, was listed on the census as mulatto but in photographs also looks very white. Isaiah's father was also a white Taliaferro. Emmett's family tree was, until recently, more white than Black.

Smith Brown, son of a white Confederate veteran, became the grandfather of Emmett Till's grandmother, Alma, who cofounded the Argo Temple Church of God in Christ now pastored by Wheeler Parker. One of Smith Brown's daughters married George Seaberry, who in 1955 lived just down the road from Moses Wright in East Money. The attack on Emmett was an attack on an enormous web of interconnected people by another enormous web of interconnected people. The Seaberrys are buried in the cemetery in East Money where Sheriff Strider tried to have Emmett's body buried so his family, and the world, could never see.

Smith Brown died in 1951, just four years before his great-great-grandson was murdered in a barn 7.9 miles from his house. He'd come to the Delta to work on the farm owned by P. H. Brooks, an enlightened man from Virginia who treated his workers fairly and with kindness, a trait that wasn't popular with his neighbors. The Brooks place later became Fannie Lou Hamer's Freedom Farm. Both are gone now except for wrecked and ruined barns. After leaving the Brooks farm, Brown took up the ministry and people called him Preacher Brown. His home in Ruleville was on Weber Street, less than a block from the little cigarette, beer, and bologna store that Roy Bryant owned and operated in the last decades of his life.

Smith Brown looked exactly like his white Confederate father. Years after he died, his grandson had a little girl named Beverly.

She came out lighter than her parents and as she got older, she started asking questions.

"Why am I so light?" she wanted to know.

"My mother's father was the slave master's son," Smith Brown's grandson said.

Then he told her something else.

"Don't ever forget," he said, "that Emmett Till was your cousin."

ON AUGUST 6, 1867, a newly freed man named Oliver Carter went to precinct number 6 in Wilkes County, Georgia, to register to vote. That's the same county where my family lived before moving to Mississippi. Records don't exist to show who had been the owner of Mr. Carter, but a white man named John Carter was one of the larger slaveholders in the county and also registered to vote at the same place on the same day. The first presidential election Carter voted in was Ulysses S. Grant versus Horatio Seymour.

Oliver Carter's wife was named America. Together they stepped into a new world, immigrants in the land of their birth. Oliver worked as a farmer and couldn't read or write. No record of his death exists but his son, John, was born in 1882 in Wilkes County, too. John was the first member of his family to move to the Mississippi Delta, settling his family on a plantation near Money. That's where his son, Matthew, was born and lived until he moved into Township 22 North, Range 4 West, working for Widow Parker with her long, flowing white hair. His daughter was, of course, my friend Gloria Dickerson. Her grandfather was born enslaved and couldn't read or write and she and all her siblings graduated from college.

IN THE YEARS BETWEEN THE WAR and the birth of the modern cotton Delta, old and new empires overlapped, and only when the time lines are laid atop one another does a mournful sense of inevitability appear. A warrior leans with his bow through a loophole in a palisade wall and a cavalry company moves to the ping and rustle of tack. Gloria Dickerson's grandfather registered to vote and became dangerous. This land had a destiny all along.

In 1865 Greenwood LeFlore died. Will Dockery, destined to become the most important planter near the barn, was born.

In 1870 the Reconstruction governor of Mississippi wrote of the need for federal levees in the Delta, launching the greatest wealth-creation project in the state's history. He is called a scalawag in southern history books instead of being celebrated, because a truthful recitation of the facts would discredit the idea that Reconstruction was ruinous for the state. Within a few years, the river washed Prentiss away and buried it in mud, where it would remain until 1954.

In 1873, another global financial panic began in Vienna and soon made its way across the Atlantic. The crisis ripped away fortunes and plunged the nation into five years of depression. Railroad speculators drove the collapse. This crash is what ruined Nathan Bedford Forrest. The New York Stock Exchange suspended trading for the first time and remained closed for a week and a half.

In 1874 the Mississippi state legislature had sixty-four Black elected officials. A Black man, Thomas Cardozo, was chosen to be superintendent of education. The next time the state went to the polls, which would signal the practical end of Reconstruction, the election was won at gunpoint. The Klan patrolled the registration places and the voting precincts. Baring Brothers in London closely followed the campaigns via its New Orleans partners. The newly elected white representatives and their supporters had a name for this new era of Mississippi history: the Redemption.

In 1877 Reconstruction officially ended.

In 1878 there was not a single marked settlement on a map of Sunflower County.

In 1880 cotton prices began to fall. Only 16 percent of farmers were sharecroppers. Forty years later that number would be 76 percent. Charley Patton, the first famous bluesman and spiritual father of the genre, was born. In 1881 Billy the Kid died. Phoenix, Arizona, was incorporated. A band of Teton Lakota went on the last great buffalo hunt. The Louisville, New Orleans and Texas Railroad bought 774,000 acres in Mississippi. The same year the rivers in Sunflower County roared out of their banks, crashing through fragile levees, bringing destruction and ruin. Wyatt Earp killed Curly Bill. The American West was almost closed. But one place remained wild even as the West was being won. In the untamed Mississippi Delta, after ten years of political failure by the small population who feared change, the first railroad project was approved. The great forests of the North were running out of hardwood. Not every square mile had fallen yet. Around the land where the barn would eventually be built, wild hogs rooted in the swamp and wild turkeys gobbled and strutted through the brakes.

A LUMBERJACK FAMILY who'd come to start chopping that hardwood stood together in a clearing a dozen miles north of Township 22. They lived at the extreme edge of the settled Delta. Their names were Frank and Mary Hamilton and their first home in the Delta was on land my family now owns. Timber men had cleared a twenty-mile right-of-way and graded it into a long, flat dirt bridge ready for tracks. The Yazoo Delta Railroad—known in blues lyrics as the Yellow Dog—ran between Moorhead, where it crossed the east-to-west Southern Railroad, and Ruleville. Frank led crews who turned all that virgin hardwood to smoldering stumps. The lumber industry brought the railroad. The South replaced the great North as the country's main source of timber. Capital moved quickly into the market, a lot of it to Memphis, and in the forty years after 1880, the amount of southern lumber grew from 1.6 to 15.4 billion board feet. Little towns appeared all over the formerly empty rural Delta. Clarksdale was incorporated in 1882. Cleveland and Shaw and Indianola were formed in 1886. Drew became a town in 1899. A year later, Shelby, Duncan, and Lula. In 1899 Tutwiler and Ruleville were chartered. A year after that Sumner, the scene of the trial and acquittal, was incorporated. Webb, Mamie Till's hometown, was incorporated at the turn of the century, too. Glendora, where J. W. Milam lived in 1955, was created in 1910.

Frank and Mary's daughter, Leslie, walked with her mom and looked down the clearing toward Drew. Mary figured it wouldn't be long until the green-and-yellow locomotives began blasting past their little home, so she told Leslie all about trains, about freight trains and passenger trains, about how dangerous they could be. She tried to end on a more hopeful note.

"It brings everything we wear or eat," Mary told her, "and it will bring civilization to our country."

Mary heard someone scoff and turned to see Frank standing next to them. He looked at the empty track. Soon there would be no panthers or bears.

"We have got to face it," he said. "Fight damnation and adjust ourselves to civilization—a disease spreading all over our land."

PEOPLE STARTED ARRIVING AROUND the barn land, slowly at first. The initial pioneers were lumberjacks like Frank and Mary Hamilton. Settlers followed close on their heels. These people wanted to grow a little cotton for cash but to devote most of their land to lush fields of vegetables to feed their families. The global banking and manufacturing industries wanted them to exist in service of progress and the free market. Only thirty years had passed since the end of the Civil War. The few thousand people on the far side of the Sunflower River farmed patches of subpar land. A few men called themselves planters and those names remain recognizable to a modern citizen of the Delta. One was the grandfather of the founder of the Double Quick chain of Delta gas stations, where a man can buy a box of chicken and a pickle soaked in Kool-Aid.

This was the final moment when a different future for this land still existed. There was no barn yet on Section 2. Please forgive me this act of imagination but I've thought about this inflection point obsessively. The Mississippi Delta has never once been governed for the people. I use the word *governed* with the broadest intended interpretation. Mississippi was from 1800 until 1955 a colony of a global manufacturing cabal linking shipping firms (and former enslavers) in Liverpool, factory owners in Manchester, and bankers in London, New York, Le Havre, Geneva, New Orleans, Cairo, Charleston, and beyond. Nearly every conflict in the state's history—often framed by those business interests in cynical ways pitting Mississippians against one another—is rooted in the conflict between capital's desire to multiply and the human desire to live free. This moment was the last time that battle was truly contested in Township 22 North. Soon it would be a realm of heavily capitalized businessmen. The future was being written on the land.

A man from near Peoria joined Company B of the 11th Illinois Cavalry and died at Vicksburg. His children and grandchildren moved to the Sunflower River. They lost a daughter at seventeen, an infant at birth, a son at sixteen, a daughter at one, and a son at eight. All are buried on the riverbank. Dozens of former enslaved men created tight-knit families far from any institutions that might bother them. Illiterate Mississippians and country doctors and the odd blacksmith joined them. Immigrants from Italy, Germany, Canada, Ireland, England (plus England with Irish parents, which is code for Manchester factory class, and Ireland with a son born in New York, which is a family working its way south in search of opportunity), Switzerland, Prussia, and France. One Italian immigrant buried a wife on the banks of the river, and his son made cabinets in East Nashville, and his descendants married Memphis doctors and retired to Florida. If this land had somehow remained free of the financial arteries connecting it to the rest of the world, if the few yeoman farmers in the swamps had been left alone to exist in peace, then this story would end here.

ONLY SOMEONE FROM THE PATRICIAN lawyer-and-planter class of the Mississippi Delta could have found the land records now stacked in front of me on a conference room table. These volumes contain the otherwise invisible history of Township 22 North. The big leather record books across the street at the circuit clerk's office started only with the turn of the century. The first deals, which had been made by a desperate state government, had simply vanished.

It was late November when the son of a Delta lawyer, whose dad knew my dad, told me about a hidden set of complete records. The air outside hung gray and chilly when I opened the first book.

The whole story was there. In 1876, just before the end of Reconstruction, the state of Mississippi opened its wild forests to northern investors for $1.25 an acre. Each acre of land might yield hundreds of dollars' worth of hardwood. Vast fortunes were made. A railroad company in 1881 got government approval to buy 225,000 acres in Bolivar County, where my farm is located, at 6.25 cents an acre, which it then sold to individuals for $10 to $15 an acre. Between 1881 and 1883 alone more than a million acres moved from public to private hands. Many millions more changed hands in the years before and after. The paper felt thick as I flipped through the pages. Old books have their own smell. These went much further back than the official records across the street, and I saw land in the township moving much earlier than the real books described. But mostly it sat on the rolls of the taxman, repossessed and held by the government.

Until two new players emerged.

The first group, a collective of London- and Chicago-based investors, found each other through shared railroad and manufacturing interests. They bought the land and slogged through infighting and legal challenges that went all the way to the United States Supreme Court. The investors named their holding company Delta & Pine Land. In 1888 DPL took ownership of Township 22 North, Range 4 West.

The other group, called the Sunflower Land & Manufacturing Company, were a group of Memphis-based investors with deep personal ties to Nathan Bedford Forrest, who'd become a symbol of southern blue-collar strength in the years since his death. Many were his former staff officers. The enormous swaths of DPL land trickled through the local financial ecosystem and on November 28, 1891, the Sunflower Land & Manufacturing Company signed mortgage papers with a Memphis bank for the southern half of Township 22 North, Range 4 West, Section 2.

AFTER DELTA & PINE SOLD land to General Forrest's cronies, it kept selling until all of Township 22 North eventually passed into the hands of private investors, who then sold huge pieces of uncleared timber to the two plantations who'd rule this land for the next four decades.

Will Dockery bought a lot of it. The second large landowner was Taylor & Crate, an enormous Buffalo-based lumber corporation. It cut timber for the first four or five years, working through vast stands of oak, ash, cypress, and gum. As land got cleared, little ten- and twenty-acre farms got planted. Soon the owners opened a commissary and sank a 950-foot artesian well that pumped ice-cold water. They built a cotton gin and a plantation home, running electric lights. The Buffalo businessmen installed a shortwave radio to check the price of cotton, which hadn't changed much since the Civil War. At first the farmers just planted around the stumps, until a dynamite man came and blew them up for five dollars an acre. Soon more than 170 Black families lived and worked on the farm. They named the sprawling rectangle of land the Sunflower Plantation.

Will Dockery rode horses and mules through the mud, silver like shotgun pellets when it dried. He suffered through dysentery and rotting bowels. He raged against the "negras, nigs, lazy nigs, coons, coloreds, n——s" and against the "hayseeds, rascals, rednecks, heathens, scoundrels, white trash." It rained all the time. The mud ran ten feet deep when the water got high. All Will cared about was building an empire. He'd caught gonorrhea as a young man but that was about it as far as vices went. He didn't drink coffee and rarely drank alcohol and he did not smoke.

Dockery bought huge tracts of cheap swampland. Most of the acreage was uncleared forest, so his crews began the decade-long task of clearing it. He hung back and watched the Black music being played on his farm. It started with men playing fiddles to keep the crowd dancing. He liked to listen. Six years later the first Sears, Roebuck & Co. catalog would be published and those fiddles would be replaced by guitars. He lived surrounded by the Black men who did the hardest part of this work then relaxed by listening to music, fishing, and playing "craps à la negro," as he told his wife. His store burned in 1892 and his cotton crop failed but he kept fighting the wilderness. He blamed Black men for the fire and threatened to hunt them down and kill them. He feared for his safety and hired a night watchman to keep guard while he slept.

"The free n—— is a failure at every capacity," he wrote.

IN 1891 WILL DOCKERY and Taylor & Crate cleared, burned, and drained hardwood swamps on the north half of Township 22 North, working from modern-day Highway 8 toward what is now the Drew-Merigold Road. This was a year after the Census Bureau declared the American frontier officially closed. It didn't feel closed to Will Dockery. The price of cotton was seven cents a pound.

In 1891 Willie Reed's grandfather, Add Reed, was born.

In 1892 Moses Wright was born. The price of cotton was eight cents a pound.

In 1893 William Leslie Milam was born. His son would rent the barn in sixty years. Hunters noticed there were no more bears to kill. Will Dockery lost $4,200 on his cotton crop but kept clearing land. The price of cotton had fallen back to seven cents.

In 1894 the price of cotton fell to four cents a pound. The next year Eula Morgan was born. A year later the Supreme Court's *Plessy v. Ferguson* decision cleared the way for total Jim Crow segregation. Captain Ben Sturdivant died. His grandson and namesake would rent this piece of land to Leslie Milam. The captain's son and barn-renting grandson are buried in the same cemetery as my father.

THE FIRST PASSENGER railroad in Township 22 North arrived in 1894, a narrow-gauge track connecting Dockery to the lumber town of Boyle and then running west across the Delta to Rosedale. Locals called it the Peavine because it wiggled and curved through the woods (other historians believe the crews laying the track named it after the infuriating tangle of peavines slowing the work). The first railroads in the Delta came in the 1870s, and by 1880 there were only seventy miles. Then in 1882 robber baron industrialist Collis P. Huntington, Leland Stanford's partner, decided that their many interests would benefit from a railroad between New Orleans and Memphis, running through the Delta. Boyle was where the 456-mile New Orleans–Memphis line was finally completed with a golden spike in 1884.

The Peavine's route got cleared by the Dockery and Boyle families. Every morning before sunrise, at 4:00 a.m., the train started its day in Cleveland, traveling south two miles to Boyle, then on to the Dockery depot, which had a full-time ticket taker. Then the train ran the hour and five minutes to Rosedale on the river before doing the whole thing again, day after day, year after year. Will Dockery's men did enough work for the railroad company that his workers and cotton rode for free. The depot sat across from the commissary and gin, just inside the boundary of Township 22 North, in between Robert Johnson's crossroads and what is now Mississippi Highway 8. Johnson sang about this particular crossroads because, as a musician in the 1920s and '30s who played gigs on the commissary porch and in the juke joints across the Sunflower River, he often hitchhiked these roads when he wasn't riding the Peavine.

The Illinois Central bought the Yazoo and Mississippi Valley Railroad in 1892 and the New York–based railroad financiers now had their hooks in the Delta. Year to year the price of cotton went up and down, but the price of transporting all that cotton to a port remained stable, so the railroads stood to make enormous and constant sums of money if the land could be cleared of trees and turned into plantations. Between 1888 and 1892, local traffic jumped by 117.2 percent. The railroads unloaded their millions of acres, making a profit and creating customers at the same time. Between 1894 and 1897, the Illinois Central sold nearly all of its 579,000 acres for more than six dollars an acre. In 1896 the land went for as much as fifteen dollars an acre.

The railroad financed these transactions, making a profit that way, too. Much of the land did not end up with farmers, at least not yet. First it passed through the hands of timber firms, which stripped the hardwood and sold the stump-laced wastelands. Farmers then burned the stumps and girdled the remaining trees, allowing rot to kill them. These smoky apocalypse zones became known as deadenings. More and more track got laid down. Between 1880 and 1900 the total miles grew from seventy to seven hundred. Between 1900 and 1920, that number would grow to more than a thousand.

The Illinois Merchants Trust, which would become Continental

Bank, bought a plantation in Mississippi. The president of the Illinois Central Railroad, Stuyvesant Fish, bought a ten-thousand-acre Delta plantation, along with U.S. Speaker of the House Joe Cannon, and they invited President Theodore Roosevelt on several bear hunts. On one of those hunts, when Roosevelt refused to shoot a tied-up bear, the term *Teddy Bear* got introduced into the national lexicon. On another of those trips he stayed at the big house on the Sunflower Plantation. A gingko tree he gave to his hosts still stands in Township 22 North.

The Illinois Central would remake almost every aspect of daily life in both Mississippi and Chicago. The relationship between Chicago and the Delta was always a financial marriage. There would even be an 1895 reconciliation ceremony between the white businessmen in the North and the South. A statue went up in Chicago's Oak Woods Cemetery to honor the Confederate prisoners of war who died at a nearby camp. More than fifty thousand people attended. Sixty-one-year-old Mississippi Confederate general Stephen D. Lee spoke: "We accept your friendship. . . . We invite you again to invade us, not with your bayonets this time, but with your business. We want to hear in our land the voices of your industries."

THE RAILROAD CHANGED Will Dockery's life. The blues historians who have studied the matter the most generally put 1895 as the year Dockery Farms became a force, with eight thousand acres in cultivation in Township 22 North and at least that many in other places around the Delta. He started making money and became a local hub for train traffic. He built a commissary and a gin and tenant houses for the workers and their families and a Baptist church. When payment time came he gave his workers what they were owed, and word spread of a man who'd deal fair. The commissary at Dockery didn't charge interest and treated credit purchases the same as cash. Black workers from around the state arrived in Dockery, including a man named Bill Patton, who brought his son Charley with him. Patton's descendants would be among the last to leave the farm, and then only when they died of old age, long after sharecroppers had been replaced by machines. Fair dealing, of course, was relative. Thieves still got whipped. Justice got handled on the farm. Killings happened enough that the absence of them felt newsworthy enough to mention in letters.

Dockery grew confident.

"I am master of my own plantation," he wrote to his wife.

A community of thousands quickly arose around his property. Soon 250 families would call it home. Baptisms happened in the mule-and-horse trough. Dockery opened a doctor's office. In 1898 the tax rolls showed his holdings had exploded. Will Dockery owned 72,900 cleared acres and 215,971 uncleared acres in Sunflower County alone. His commissary accepted the paper money he printed and the coins he minted. Five clerks worked the counters and shelves. Twice-weekly steamboat runs on the Sunflower River to his dock kept the place equipped. The packet ships *Ruth*, *Livonia*, and *Lake Palmira* became regular visitors. He owned a business called Dockery & Donelson on South Front Street in Memphis that sold equipment and processed cotton so that he made a little profit from nearly every link in the commodity chain until the cotton left for Europe. Payday happened on Friday and Saturday and musicians would play for free on the commissary steps to advertise for the show in a juke joint that night. The Peavine whistle blew loud and long and could be heard for miles across the cotton fields.

———

THIS SHARECROPPER cotton empire was a product of northern and global capital and the willingness of Mississippi planters to act like socialists just long enough to protect and grow their farms. Without either of those urges, there wouldn't have been family for Emmett Till to go visit, and there wouldn't have been a barn where he would be killed. The flood of 1897 forced the state to spend real time and money on a solution to the constant flooding of the alluvial plain. Too many well-connected investors had too much money at stake to keep letting Mother Nature have the final say. The engineers investigated the data after the water receded and found that Arkansas's levees were newer and better than the ones in Mississippi, which increased the pressure on the east bank of the river. In February 1898, just months after the flood, a new state law authorized bonds to reclaim swampland with new taxes. By 1900 new drainage projects—done at a scale possible only by cooperative drainage districts—reclaimed land where people couldn't live through the summer, much less plant, tend, and harvest crops. Most individual farmers had been unable to afford to take on even the cheapest cutover lowlands. Without government intervention, the great plantation experiment of the early twentieth century, even with the railroad and timber capital, would have remained a dream. The cost to dig enough ditches to drain an acre of land was more than fifteen dollars. Now these drainage districts hired steam-powered floating dredges, rigged with dipper buckets that could cut through a thousand cubic yards of swampland a day. These ditches cost three thousand dollars a mile, which got passed along to the planters. Fights broke out over the allocation of the expense, but the vast swamps got drained. Deutsche Bank began investing heavily in irrigation.

I HAVE A MAP from around this time that shows every mile of railroad track laid in the Mississippi Delta. You can see all the routes, the lines connecting Dockery to Boyle, Clarksdale to Friars Point, Greenwood to Greenville. The whole grid is complete except for one small missing piece. One empty space of trackless land. The rails stop at Dockery from the south and at Lombardy from the north, while a separate line passes through Merigold to the west, and still another passes through Drew to the east. The lines literally just stop at Lombardy and Dockery. End of the road. The uncivilized square in between the broken tracks is Township 22 North, Range 4 West, which was the last bit of the Delta waiting to be connected to the railroad grid, the final bit of wilderness in the final bit of wilderness. There is a case to be made that the settling of the continent came to its conclusion in Township 22 North, Range 4 West. The physical closing of geography was accompanied by a wider closing of human possibility. All the land had been surveyed, mapped, owned, put into operation, harvested according to interconnected global markets. One of the last bits of land to be pulled into the American experiment was the piece of land where Emmett Till was tortured and killed.

IN 1901 MANY OF THE men on the board of Sunflower Land & Manufacturing laid the cornerstone for a new monument to Nathan Bedford Forrest in Memphis. The location they chose, a leafy park on Union Avenue, was just a block east of the home where the general's brother Jesse Forrest lived until his death in 1889. The home is gone but the spot is directly across the street from Sun Studio.

They wrote a check to the famous sculptor Charles Henry Niehaus for the design. Forrest had been dead for twenty-four years. All his siblings were dead. His former junior officers, nearing the nostalgia of retirement, ran the city. The term *Lost Cause* had first appeared in Mississippi newspapers just months after the end of the war and had become ubiquitous. By 1887 Confederate veterans were dying in clusters, more every day. That's the year the first effort to build a Nathan Bedford Forrest statue in Memphis began, formalized into an association in 1891. Down in Mississippi, politicians took away the Black right to vote but added payments to Confederate veterans and their widows. The pervasive idea of the Lost Cause reframed the Civil War to be about states' rights and not slavery. It turned the Confederate soldiers from traitors into American patriots defending the original ideals of the nation. This mythology took root as those old soldiers began dying in droves, another one every day, and their sons and daughters tried to sort out what their beloved parents had done in their lives and what they had done it for.

The city buzzed as the dedication ceremony approached. "The great leader of this secret clan rides once more," a local reporter wrote. An old man pulled out his old Confederate uniform and wore it to the park to sit vigil. Three times a day he stood at attention and saluted. He smiled at all the children playing in the park and on the statue.

"General Forrest loved children," he said.

Thousands lined the streets on dedication day. Mounted police escorted the parade. Forrest's son and grandson rode in the lead carriage. His surviving staff marched in uniform behind the family. The sight of so many old warriors moved the newspaper writer covering the event to write: "They are vanishing one by one. New men and new ideas and new interests are thrusting aside the broken fragments of the past. The shadows darken about the survivors of Forrest. A little later and these survivors will become shadows themselves."

Between fifteen thousand and twenty thousand people were on hand as Kathleen Bradley, the general's great-granddaughter, stepped onto the platform. She grabbed the cords that held the bunting that covered the general's face. As the little girl looked up, the crowd hushed. Then she let the cords slip and the wind carried away the veil as the crowd roared. An old veteran wept. The band played "Dixie."

A YEAR LATER the barn land finally became a cotton farm. On Tuesday, June 24, 1902, a local farmer named J. W. Riddell bought the southwest quarter of Section 2 from an Iowa-based timber company. He'd brought his family into a harsh square of land, risking everything for the chance of wealth and ownership. To finally— after generations of wandering—be lord of the manor, or at least *a* manor. Riddell, who went by James, had stepped into a difficult planting season. He wore short ties and straw hats and a kind smile that softened his face. That winter, near the end of March, his neighbor Will Dockery rode his horse through a flood. He found his corn wrecked and worried he might have to replant almost all of the crop. The next morning Dockery awoke to find the water had risen another foot. Riddell was the son of a Confederate veteran. The price of cotton when he bought Section 2 was seven cents a pound. A year later it rose three cents, then fell a cent and a half, then rose a cent and a half, then fell a cent, then rose a cent, then fell a cent. The future felt fragile but it also felt like a future. For the first time, John Hancock, Hartford, and Prudential agreed to offer life insurance policies in the Mississippi Delta. Across the bayou Will Dockery ginned nearly $35,000 worth of cotton that year and cut more than five hundred cords of wood, enough to heat a home for 115 years. The plantations around Riddell burned stumps and undergrowth every day. The air always looked hazy and smelled like smoke.

IN 1904 THE LOCAL NEWSPAPER in Charleston ran an item saying that Guy Thomas and Leslie Milam spent Sunday together. That was March 6. Leslie was the father of two of the men who murdered Emmett Till. Guy Thomas was a cousin of trial juror Travis Thomas. The daily lives of the killers and the men who freed them overlapped again and again. Their family trees did, too. Travis Thomas's sister married a Milam. Guy's daughter was Mary Milam. Leslie's brother was Travis's brother-in-law. In the coming fifty-one years, there would be many times when the families of the killers and the families of the jurors who would acquit them went to town together, built bridges together, attended weddings and funerals together, hunted deer and canned vegetables together. These are the people who would feel their culture under threat in 1955 and their response would exist inside, and not outside, their familiar rhythms of life. Nothing about the murder of Emmett Till was random. One tribe, related by blood and history, killed a child of another tribe.

IN 1904 A SHARECROPPER named Henry Sloan lived in Dockery. He played rhythmic dancing music on a guitar. Patient zero of the Delta blues. Mentor to Charley Patton, the first blues star, who mentored or influenced Son House, Robert Johnson, Muddy Waters, Howlin' Wolf, and Pops Staples. Sloan is a ghost. No recordings of him exist. There's one grainy photograph. Patton, whose family had moved to Dockery about four years before, was a young man then. Nobody knows for sure exactly when he was born. These early musicians blink out at daylight from the ether. Nobody can even agree on how to spell Patton's first name. Charley? Charlie? The man invented modern American music—fathering every rock-star trope in the process—and we aren't sure about his name. But the sound remains. The Delta blues emerged as evidence of the enduring violence that birthed it, a left-behind record of lives built and broken, buried and erased. Its rise happened at the historical moment this violence became inescapable.

Patton's grandfather was a white man from Vicksburg named Bill Patton, which was Charley's father's name, too. The white Bill Patton and his Black girlfriend lived together on the edge of the National Cemetery in Vicksburg, and in the terrible years of 1866 to 1868 they got paid by the U.S. Army to exhume and rebury the eighteen thousand Union soldiers who died in the assault on the southern port city. Blues scholar David Evans found a W. D. Patton who worked as an overseer on a plantation for an absentee northern landlord when the war broke out. Evidence suggests this is the correct man. W. D. Patton had a white and a Black family. He fathered a white Bill Jr. and a Black Bill Jr. He owned one enslaved woman, who Evans speculates was his mistress Rose, who was

Charley's grandmother. Vicksburg fell on July 4, 1863. Nine months later the Black Bill Patton Jr. was born. Seven years later, white W.D. was back with his white wife and white children.

Patton was white *and* Black. He was Mississippi—one part of himself at war with another part. Mississippi was killing itself and the blues was the soundtrack. His songs did something new and dangerous. He sang in aggressive first person and addressed present-day life. He talked about floods and lumber camps and the boll weevil. He sang critically about local white men, a dangerous game of chicken, and he name-checked Will Dockery in a lyric. The crowds went nuts for him. This was the first American protest music. Dissent like this could live only in the shadows, set to the rhythm of a guitar and dancing feet.

"Oh, I'm gonna leave Mississippi now," he sang, "before it be too late."

Music floated on the rivers and bayous. There was only one phonograph in Sunflower County then, owned by the Lombardy family upriver from Dockery. The tin horn amplified the sound, audible for a mile up and down the dark water. That was the only music in the air until the blues arrived. Then hundreds of share-croppers would fill juke joints and tenant houses with the furniture moved outside, music and gambling inside, the overflow of people spilling into the yard. On stage Patton stomped, and swiveled his hips, and played his guitar behind his back, and rode it like a mule, or like somebody else's wife. Men crowded the edge of the dance floor. Once Charley got his throat slit by a jealous man. He survived and changed nothing about his delivery. Dangerous noise was the point. Sometimes he strapped metal cleats to his shoes and when he stomped them on the cypress floors he did it with every ounce of strength in his legs. Every now and then he'd play the guitar with his feet. He beat on it when he wasn't strumming chords. *Aww when the sun goes down.* Sometimes Patton looked white. White men called him Black. Howlin' Wolf, who learned to play the guitar sitting at Patton's feet, thought he looked Mexican. Women thought he looked Choctaw. Once a friend asked if he had any Chinese blood.

"Hell, I don't know," Charley told him. "I'm here, that's all I know."

ON FEBRUARY 4, 1908, a hit national touring play named *The Clansman* opened its third run in Memphis. Carriages parked on Second Street, a half block from Nathan Bedford Forrest's old slave market. The lights on the marquee shined brightly enough that the theater kept a generating station in the basement because the city grid couldn't handle the wattage. The guest of honor was William Forrest, the aging son of the general. Flags were draped like bunting over his suite, including the actual Confederate battle flag his father's unit had carried into combat.

The air outside felt chilly as the crowd came inside to find their seats. It had rained that morning but now only clouds hung over the city. Up at the New York cotton futures market, prices fell all day. The city waited nervously for a report due in two days from the National Ginners Association that would give the markets some idea of the global supply and demand. Inside the theater the mood was festive, cozy, the Spanish-themed interior painted yellow, gold, and a bright imperial green.

The Clansman was a play written by Thomas Dixon, based on his book, which had sold more than a million copies. In seven years, the play would find its way to the big screen with its new name, *The*

Birth of a Nation, which gave a new life to the long-dormant Ku Klux Klan. The show ran only fifty-one nights on Broadway. Crowds and critics in northern cities hated it. But in the South it became a sensation. The crowds especially loved the part in the second act when Nathan Bedford Forrest, the Grand Wizard of the Klan, strode across the stage. That always brought cheers. In Baltimore, when a young Klansman tears down a proclamation about racial equality that has been nailed to his door, the crowd rose in an enormous cheer. Later, when the same Klansman gives an order to lynch a Black man and throw his dead body at the feet of a carpetbagger politician, the crowd stood and roared again. Dixon himself spoke after that show, his speech stopped after every sentence by applause.

"The play is not only a picture of the past, it is a prophecy," he told the crowd.

Cheers rang out.

"I have sons," he told them. "I am not afraid they will remember too much. My constant anxiety is they may forget too much."

In the Memphis theater, William Forrest settled into the right-hand stage box.

As a teenager he'd served as an aide to his father during the war. He suffered wounds at Fort Donelson and Shiloh. For years he'd refused to talk about combat, but like all aging men, he had recently started telling stories and seemed like he might never stop. He told about the time that a Union officer pointed a pistol at him during a battle and then William saw a flash approaching, his father on horseback with saber drawn and glinting, and he watched his dad decapitate the Union officer, then spur his horse back to the battle.

The plan that night at the theater was for William to go on stage and surprise the crowd. His son, Nathan Bedford Forrest II, sat with him, along with veterans in uniform. The play began, set during a Reconstruction stylized by Dixon as a hellscape of Black equality and the rape of white women. The plot builds toward an alleged rapist being lynched.

Forrest stared down at the stage. Something awoke inside him when the climactic moment arrived. An actor playing his father, dead for three decades now, stepped onto the Lyceum stage, looking up at the son of the man he portrayed. William Forrest looked back at him, suffered a massive stroke, and fell unconscious on the floor of his box. His family held his hand and called for medical help. A former staff officer of Forrest helped load the dying man into a carriage and took him back to his son's house on Adams Avenue, his father's old home, where William had lived as a boy. He hung on for three more days, surrounded by his son Nathan Bedford Forrest II, who'd later become the Grand Dragon of the Georgia Klan, and by three-year-old Nathan Bedford Forrest III, who would become the first American general killed in action by the Nazis. William Forrest died early in the morning, 6:15, and was buried at Elmwood in a military ceremony, his casket carried by his father's surviving men.

BY 1910 CHARLEY PATTON played on plantations and in towns, setting up shop in Ruleville at Mack's Café on Greasy Street, where drinkers ate fish sandwiches for ballast. It's where Pops Staples would hear Patton, and Willie Brown, and Howlin' Wolf. The music itself pulled from the sounds of the plantation. A palm-muted strum sounded like the cocking of a shotgun. Listen for the heavy, fast strums of a two-man saw team, a guitar like the crack of a rifle. Everything carried a backbeat of the locomotive. These were the days of steam exhales and sharp whistle blasts and phantom pains of escape when the train had long faded from view.

The Sunflower County population had jumped 80 percent in the decade after 1900. Most of the new arrivals were poor and Black. On the Dockery and Sunflower plantations a culture evolved. Schools and churches and stores opened. Huge gardens grew corn, beans, cabbage, greens, sweet potatoes, and tomatoes. Sharecroppers killed hogs in the winter to survive. Washed chitterlings hung on lines to dry. Hunters brought home squirrels and rabbits. Women canned beef and pork. A sharecropping life was a subsistence life. In 1880, before the clearing of the forests began in earnest, only 16 percent of Delta farmers were sharecroppers. In 1910 that number passed 50 percent and a decade later would be 74 percent. The only way out of sharecropping was access to credit, and the caste system meant Black people had virtually no access to credit.

IN 1911 THE MANCHESTER Fine Spinners and Doublers Association looked at the state of the cotton business and decided the time had come to vertically integrate its supply chain. It had endless credit. The manufacturing conglomerate combined some of the biggest mill owners in the world, like A&G Murray and McConnel & Co. Eventually it would control sixty factories and thirty thousand workers. One rainy afternoon on assignment in Manchester, I ducked into a hipster coffee shop that served pour-overs and free-trade beans. The coffee shop, a historical marker said, had once been a sprawling factory complex. I was in Ancoats, the first industrial working-class neighborhood, which once sat at the heart of the global cotton economy. The sign retold the history of this factory and said it had been owned by the Manchester Fine

Spinners and Doublers. I stopped to talk to the security guard manning the big glass entrance. His ancestors worked grim, dangerous jobs back when this was a factory.

"A lot of people died here," he said.

Then he held his hand out at about thigh level, his palm resting atop the imaginary head of some little boy or girl. Not all the workers were adults.

"Kids, too," he said.

The British company wanted a Mississippi Delta plantation to keep direct and secure access to raw cotton. Some of their executives ended up on a waterfowl hunting trip with a Michigan land speculator and a Rosedale planter. The Englishmen spent $4.5 million for 38,000 acres and began clearing and draining and bringing in sharecropper families. Farming in the Delta had always been a profit center for outsiders, who controlled the dirt but never had to endure living on it, or dying in it, or being buried under it. The arrival of the English industrialists was part of a long tradition.

There was only one hurdle to the sale. The dirt-farmer politicians had passed a law prohibiting any farms larger than ten thousand acres. But the law had a loophole, probably placed there intentionally, which grandfathered in companies chartered between 1886 and 1889. The law allowed Fine Spinners to search out an old, defunct company, still in existence and therefore grandfathered in, and take it out of mothballs. The company it used to get around the law was the Delta & Pine Land Company. It bought the name for its new plantation.

THE UNITED STATES ENTERED World War I on April 6, 1917, and the sudden demand for uniforms and gun cotton drove the price per bale to record highs. *The New York Times* reported daily on the boom. Cotton surged, then "soared," made "a wild leap," then kept going up, rising and rising and rising. In 1919 some cotton in the Mississippi Delta was selling for a dollar a pound, more than the current price in 2024. A loaf of bread went for 10 cents in 1919 and today Wonder Bread goes for $3.50 a loaf, while a modern cotton farmer gets less money per pound than his great-grandfather did a century ago. The crops of 1917, 1918, and 1919 made fortunes that still exist. If that price existed today—accounting for inflation—then a farmer with ten thousand acres in cultivation like the Sunflower Plantation or Will Dockery would gross more than $200 million a year.

"A riot of extravagance followed," one Mississippi history book said.

More drainage systems were built. Consolidated high schools in new brick buildings rose in every town. New gravel roads connected students in the rural areas with those schools. Cornerstones for big new churches were laid. Clarksdale got a new freight depot, where Emmett Till's body would be loaded onto a train back to his mother. Clarksdale High School got a brand-new building that year, and then another one a decade later. That campus is abandoned now but the local school board refused to sell the buildings to a vibrant charter school out of jealousy. They exist as a monument for a moment now forgotten, when the classified ads in the Memphis papers listed plantations for sale at skyrocketing land prices. Land valued at $50 an acre in 1915 went for $300 an acre. So a farmer who bought one thousand acres for $1.50 an acre and spent another $7 an acre to clear it spent $8,500 on property now worth $300,000. Huge fortunes accrued overnight—in both cash flow and capital value.

In 1917 J. W. Riddell bought stock in the Bank of Drew. Charley

Patton's father stopped renting at Dockery and bought his own farm. John Lee Hooker was born. Ford Motor Company introduced its Fordson tractor, the first mechanized farm vehicle that was light and affordable enough to be useful. The booming cotton prices resulted in a corresponding boom in the sale of tractors: the slow march to replace people with machines in the Delta had begun. Will Dockery, looking into the future, invested in the Southern Cotton Picker Company, which wanted machines to do the work of the men, women, and children pulling long white sacks. All the new roads threatened the old order of things. The Dockery ferry across the Sunflower River was abandoned. The state tried to close the Peavine railroad stop in Dockery but Will fought them off successfully. Muddy Waters moved to Stovall Plantation to live with his grandmother. Expectations in the Delta soared.

In between the harvest of the 1918 crop and the planting of the 1919 crop, at the height of the boom, J. W. Milam was born.

THIS PEAK OF WHITE WEALTH and economic power coincided with the first mass exodus of Black families from the Delta, and from all over the state, and the South. Factories in the North sent hiring agents down south during the war to encourage Black families to leave the cotton fields and come to the cities. The same cotton boom that financed luxury and expansion also bought the $11.60 tickets on the Illinois Central from the Delta to Chicago. More than 500,000 Black people had left by 1920. The families who left Township 22 North likely boarded the Peavine at Dockery headed toward the station at Boyle and the connection to the main line. The last thing they would have seen out the window of the train as it left, often obscured in the steam and smoke, was the True Light Cemetery, where Dockery sharecroppers were buried.

Black soldiers returned from the war changed. France, free from the South's caste system, had been a revelation. They'd seen another way of living and came back wanting the same freedom they'd fought to give the British and the French.

"We return from fighting," W.E.B. Du Bois said. "We return fighting."

The Klan returned, too. In 1918 the Ku Klux Press published a pamphlet called "The Practice of Klanishness." The enemies of the poor white men were made clear: planters and their "alien friends" like Catholics, Jews, and Black workers—along with big-business capitalism and Wall Street. At the same time, between 1918 and 1919, the NAACP's membership jumped from 9,200 to 62,200. These were the first breaths of the modern civil rights movement, and of the southern response to attempts at full Black citizenship.

The first returning Black veteran to die, Private Charles Lewis, was killed a month after the war ended. In Pickens, Mississippi, an unnamed Black veteran paid a Black woman to help him write a note to a white girl. Local leaders found him and hanged him on the outskirts of town. They hanged the woman who'd helped with the letter, too. Enough people died that President Wilson wrote an open letter to the country about extrajudicial justice. The NAACP reported that between 1889 and 1918 more than 2,500 Black Americans were lynched, surely a significant underestimate. It was a period of intense racial violence, an outbreak of pogroms in at least twenty-five cities around the nation. Those months earned the nickname Red Summer, for the fear of communists and the Black blood spilled in the streets. There had never been large numbers of

Black people in the urban North and Midwest. In Washington, DC, the mere rumor of an assault on a white woman brought out roving gangs of white servicemen and sailors. The DC Black community fought back, attacking random white people, a flicker of a race war until Wilson returned from his yacht trip on the Potomac to send in the army. Two hundred sharecroppers died in Elaine, Arkansas. Twenty-three people died in Chicago. There were two different mob attacks in Memphis. A lynching in Ellisville, Mississippi, was announced on the front page of the Jackson paper and all the factories within fifty miles closed so the workers could attend. As many as ten thousand people came. For the crime of having a white girlfriend John Hartfield was hung, shot too many times to count— kept alive by a local doctor to allow the torture to continue—and then finally burned. In Clarke County, Mississippi, a mob hung two brothers and two pregnant sisters from a bridge. The crowd who came to gawk and celebrate noted that they could still see the dying babies wriggling in their dead mother's bellies. Six human beings, two unborn, died on that bridge. The NAACP sent Mississippi governor Theodore Bilbo a telegram protesting the killing.

"Go to hell," he responded.

The Black exodus intensified. Violence was such a part of basic problem-solving in Mississippi that it bent almost every part of daily life to its rhythms and unspoken laws. Sometime between 1917 and 1919, according to oral histories taken about Drew by blues researchers, a white man named Arnold was murdered. This killing sparked an exodus of blues musicians afraid of indiscriminate lynch mobs. Men moved to other places in the Delta, sometimes just a few plantations away. They moved to Chicago and Gary, Indiana. Willie Brown left. Dick Bankston left. Charley Patton moved away, although he'd return to Dockery as a visitor off and on for most his life. Musicians Jack Hicks, Cap Holmes, Tommy Johnson, and Paul Baskett all fled in fear.

"During the 1920s many of the blues singers left the Drew area," the music historian David Evans wrote. "The local blues tradition in Drew in the 1930s and later was apparently much weaker than it had been in the 1920s and earlier. Very few new local musicians emerged, and most of the older ones eventually left or quit music."

IN FEBRUARY OF 1920 the cotton market collapsed. The newspapers clocked the local price falling from a dollar to fifteen or twenty cents a pound. Nobody saw it coming. The day the crash came, *The New York Times* ran a feature story about the brand-new wealth in cotton country. The reporter wrote a funny scene about almost being run over by fourteen Black drivers in fourteen new cars. That issue of the paper landed on doorsteps and a few hours later much of the wealth had vanished. The next week brought nothing but bad news. India reported a huge crop. Rumors spread about the stockpiles of raw cotton in England putting a halt to all imports. A statement out of Cairo warned all Egyptian farmers who rented land that an apocalypse was coming for them, and that held true for renters across world. Owning the land, and holding enough equity to borrow money, might buy a farmer an extra year or two.

The reasons for the collapse appear complex in the detangling but start with simple fear. High prices pushed cotton farmers to plant more cotton, and people who'd normally plant corn to plant cotton, and people who'd never even seen a plow or a mule to try and plant cotton, too. This happened in Sunflower County, and the

Delta, and all over the South, from Texas to South Carolina, and in India and Egypt and Brazil. The warehouses in Manchester filled with raw cotton. That meant abnormally high carryover. The Yazoo City newspaper figured that there was enough unspun cotton in the world to last for the next two years. The price kept falling. Membership in the Klan rose dramatically. Buried violence is a perennial bulb that is fertilized by fear and watered by insecurity. The dominant white culture instinctively turned to force in defense of resources. The specific problems might have changed over the centuries but the instinctive response did not.

October brought a *New York Times* headline that said COTTON DROPS AGAIN ON LIVERPOOL NEWS.

Larger fundamental problems pulled the price down, too. Scientists around the world looked for ways to replace cotton with synthetics. The price of 150-denier cotton filament yarn was $6 a pound in 1920. Two years later that price would be $2.80, and a little more than a decade later the price would be 55 cents. The cotton textile industry, which was the reason Sunflower County land held any value at all, was dying. In 1919 the American cotton crop set a record with a value of $2.1 billion. In 1920 the value fell to $940 million. Bad news kept coming. A year later a government research facility did a series of tests and released shocking and devastating news: the fertile soil of the Delta was losing its nutrients.

The short harvest of 1922 brought even more ruin. That was the last crop a lot of farmers made. On January 2, 1923, a Tuesday, the Wilson Banking Company took Section 2 from J. W. Riddell. Eleven days later, a few miles to the west, Gloria Dickerson's mother was born in a sharecropper's house. Her mother, Luvenia Slaughter, lived next door to her father-in-law, who had made enough money during the cotton boom to rent his own land and try to climb out of poverty. But the cotton bust destroyed all those plans and he ended up sharecropping again.

THE GREAT MISSISSIPPI Delta cotton boom lasted twenty years. The suffering and killing and decay that would follow for the next century were the price of three great years and a dozen good ones. These two decades also marked the peak of the Lost Cause mythology. Consider when all these Confederate statues went up around the state. Consider the history of cotton in the Delta. The land clearing finished around 1900. The price of cotton collapsed for good in 1923. And what happened in between?

Port Gibson and Aberdeen raised statues in 1900.

Macon in 1901.

Fayette in 1904.

Carrollton and Beulah and Okolona in 1905.

Tupelo and Ole Miss in 1906.

Brandon and Oxford and West Point in 1907.

Cleveland and Lexington and Raymond and Duck Hill in 1908.

Greenville and Winona in 1909.

Hattiesburg, twice, and Grenada in 1910.

Gulfport and Kosciusko and Quitman and Ripley and Brooksville and Heidelberg in 1911.

Columbus and Laurel and Meridian and Philadelphia and Vaiden in 1912.

Greenwood and Sumner in 1913.

Greenwood again in 1915.

Hazlehurst in 1917.

Louisville in 1921.

Many of these were placed, quite intentionally, on the lawns of local courthouses, sending a message about the law and whom it was designed to protect. Most of the monuments around the state were built during the brief but emotionally powerful cotton boom. Not a single courthouse statue in the state of Mississippi was erected after 1923. The Lost Cause was *always* about cotton and money.

GLORIA DICKERSON HAD A RELATIVE named Son Ham, and not long after the global textile collapse a mob of local white men lynched him. They made his family get the body and load it in a cotton sack. The killers tied Son Ham to the front of their Ford and drove through the little towns of Merigold and Shaw as a warning. Then they took him back to the Sunflower Plantation and buried him there. They would not tell the family where they put the body, just to be cruel. Jeff Slaughter, Gloria's great-grandfather, told this story over and over to his son Zeke. Zeke was one of the family members forced to deal with the body. He came home covered in his friend's blood and every time he drove his daughter, Mae Bertha, over the Sunflower River toward Township 22 North, he passed the same haunted field and told the same haunted story.

"Right in that field, a mob crew shot Son Ham down like a rabbit."

Zeke always used the same phrase. They killed Son Ham like a rabbit. Gloria's family, like so many Black families in the Delta, were as committed to the act of remembering as their white neighbors were committed to the act of forgetting.

"When they shot him, it blew the hat right off his head," Mae Bertha Carter said. "No one would even go pick up poor old Son Ham's hat. The people were too afraid. That hat, it just blew and blew across the fields."

———

ON FRIDAY, DECEMBER 14, 1923, a sharecropper outside Drew named Joe Pullum went to visit his plantation manager, Tom Sanders, to settle his annual accounts. Pullum carried a .38-caliber revolver. He'd learned to shoot fighting with the famous U.S. Army Buffalo Soldiers in the hills of Cuba during the Spanish-American War. When he returned home to farm, he lived with his family in a small tenant house east of town. The crop had been harvested and now came the tense settlement day. The only input a farmer controlled was the price of labor, a fundamental that remains true today, and for some men the temptation to cheat people with no legal recourse remained too great. Settlement day was an annual test of honesty and honor and most men failed. Pullum already suspected his boss would try to cheat him.

It had been another terrible year, the third in a row. Rain fell for nearly the entire cotton season and many farmers picked the worst crop they'd picked in decades, ten acres to make one bale in some places instead of three bales an acre. These plagues of sun and sky felt biblical. Banks wanted money or land from farmers. A third fewer bales got picked statewide and many farmers just abandoned the crop in the fields rather than pick at a loss. The jarring sign of untouched cotton in winter haunted the memories of farmers for a generation. It was the smallest crop in fifty years. That was a problem for management.

Pullum wanted his money.

Sanders said Pullum owed *him* fifty dollars.

They began to shout at each other. Nobody knows who drew his weapon first. Sanders and his manager, John Manning, stood on a back porch. Pullum stood on the ground below them and shot both men before fleeing east toward the Brooks plantation headquarters—the same land that in five decades would become Fannie Lou Hamer's Freedom Farm.

Sanders was dead. John Manning was wounded. Pullum ran to his house and loaded his shotgun with the only ammunition he had: lightweight bird shot. The posse went to Pullum's house. Pullum aimed at their heads because of the low-caliber bird shot. He shot R. L. Methvin in the face and killed him. He wounded another man, then slid into the Wild Bill Bayou and started trying to move north. His mother sharecropped on the next road to the north and, under threat, he tried to make it to her. A witness saw him cross Brooks Road to the west side of the bayou. The posse couldn't follow him through the thick swamps, still uncleared, and lost his trail at an abandoned tenant house. For two hours they searched, until someone found boot tracks leading down into a drainage ditch that fed back into the Wild Bill Bayou. They spread out along both sides of the swamp. Joe Pullum hid in the thick undergrowth, careful like those ancient deer about where he put his feet, and he listened as they approached. His military training kicked in.

The posse got closer and closer. Pullum waited.

Finally they were within pistol range. Just a few yards away. He shot Kenneth Blackwood in the face, Luther Hughes in the head, and Bob Stringfellow in the side and the arm. He shot Archie Manning, a local cotton gin employee and ancestor of the famous quarterback, in the face and the throat. The posse emptied eight or ten boxes of ammunition into the swamp but hit nothing. Pullum slipped silently away from his pursuers, moving through the bayou toward his mom's house on what is now Swoope Road.

The posse called for help. The sheriff from my hometown of Clarksdale, along with a half dozen prominent citizens, arrived with two Browning machine guns. Other men went into Drew and loaded ten fifty-five-gallon drums of gasoline onto a truck, which they drove as far as it could go into the muck. A wagon pulled by a team of four mules took it the rest of the way into the swamp. At 11:30 p.m., more than fourteen hours after the first shot was fired, the mob rolled the first barrel of gasoline into the swamp. They lit it on fire and ran down shooting wildly.

J. L. Doggett, from Clarksdale, saw something move in the darkness.

"There he is!" he shouted.

Pullum shot him immediately.

Doggett was a prominent lumberman. I knew his daughter when she was an old woman. She played bridge at the Clarksdale Country Club, in one of the rooms just off the snack bar, where kids would go to get chicken tenders and lemonade to charge to their parents' accounts.

"All my friends are dead and gone," she'd say.

Back at the Wild Bill Bayou the mob rolled a second barrel of gasoline into the water. The machine guns fired belts of withering rounds into the darkness. Pullum remained hidden and picked off his attackers whenever he got a clear shot. He had only a shotgun and a small pistol, so he had to get close to kill. The posse rolled a third barrel into the swamp and lit it on fire. This time the fire made Pullum move and the machine guns opened up and finally cut him down. Pullum had killed at least four people and wounded at least nine, although local oral accounts put that number higher.

The posse threw his dying body on a horse and they took him to a waiting car, which drove him to town. They left him to die on the cotton platform on Main Street. His shotgun got displayed in downtown Drew. Some older Black citizens tell how their parents and grandparents told them that parts of Pullum's body—multiple people mention his ear or ears—also got displayed for decades after that in local shop windows.

After the lynching Drew and other nearby towns enforced a strict curfew for Blacks. More lines got drawn on the Delta, unmarked on any map but understood by everyone as law. Boundaries governed more and more movements and spaces, and crossing one of those boundaries would be Emmett Till's fatal crime. When a local dance hall closed and the crowd didn't clear fast enough, the local sheriff shot and killed seven or eight people, including two of the musicians. The violence of Mississippi was detaching from its economic, social roots and was beginning to exist without cause or meaning, just a new fact of life.

The Franklin family left Sunflower County because of the killing. Their nine-year-old son, who would one day name his daughter Aretha, heard his parents talking about it. In nearby Webb, twenty-three miles from the barn and less from the spot where Pullum died, Mamie's father packed up his family and moved to Chicago.

Pullum's family disappeared. His great-grandson Thomas Pullum, who lives in Oakland, California, spends his free time trying to find out what happened to them, especially to Joe's two sons, who were never heard from again. Thomas came to Mississippi for the first time in 1967 and sat with his grandmother in the shadow of the Wild Bill Bayou. In a quiet moment he asked her to tell him about Joe. He saw a cloud of "pain and misery" pass over her face as tears welled in her eyes. But then something strange happened. Her eyes changed, a defiant sparkle emerging, and she smiled and settled back into the pillows on her bed and started to speak.

"I had heard of Mr. Joseph Pullum, your great-grandfather, all my life," she began and then told him the tale of a Black man who

had the courage to say no, to stand up for himself, and when it became clear he would not survive, a man who decided to send as
many of the enemy to hell as he could before they got him. Those
stories are all that's left, along with some newspaper clippings and a
smudged death certificate, signed by the same local doctor who
would later buy the house where Leslie Milam lived in 1955 and the
barn where Emmett Till was tortured to death.

THE NEXT YEAR Leslie "Eslie" Milam's house burned. It was
1924. He'd bought a little farm on credit, sitting right on the edge of
the Delta. Nobody in their family had made it out of the Hills before. The fire wiped him out. His friends and relatives up in the
Hills raised money to help; their tight community looked out for its
own. He and his wife, Eula, welcomed a boy the next year, named
Leslie after his father. Eslie was only thirty years old with a wife
and five children: Edward, Spencer, J.W., Daniel, and Leslie. He
took the best job he could get, digging gravel to make the new
roads laid across Tallahatchie County. One Thursday he and three
other men were working in a pit down in Leverett when the whole
thing caved in on them. Two men escaped serious injury. James
Bryant, Roy's uncle, died soon after arriving at the Grenada hospital. Eslie hung on for a few days with broken limbs and ribs but
pneumonia set in and he died, too, the third straight male in his
family tree to die young and violently. They buried him at the New
Hope Cemetery. He'd bought a little piece of land in the Delta to
try to get his family a new life but his widow couldn't make the payments. Two months after he died, the timber company he owed for
the land, Turner-Farber-Love, took it back. That would be the
family's last serious attempt at climbing up a financial and social

rung until his namesake son, Leslie Milam, tried to buy a Delta farm himself in 1953. The cotton collapse had moved all the pieces on the board: Mamie to Chicago for a new life, the barn land onto the open market, Moses Wright back into sharecropping, the Milam brothers off their land and toward the grocery-store economy of the Delta.

WILL DOCKERY SEEMED TO understand he'd outlived one time and slipped into another. His house on Dockery burned as the price of cotton collapsed, the fire taking all his keepsakes and photos. Little reminders of a life turned to ash. No boats cruised behind his gin blowing smoke and whistles. Fewer than forty steamboats now operated on the Mississippi River. Soon there would be none.

The population of Sunflower County peaked in 1930 and then started a long slide that remains ongoing. In the winter Will Dockery and Delta-born Senator LeRoy Percy would board the night train and head south to duck hunt in Louisiana. Will brought his son along for these hunts. They'd arrive in New Orleans, on the same train line that would take Emmett's body back home to his mother, and wait a few hours for the Boston Club to open. Cloistered, with an intimate bar and tall dining rooms with creole staples like turtle soup, the club served as a playground for the city's connected wealthy elite. Members were the ones who made the decision to blow the levees in 1927 to protect St. Charles Avenue at the expense of poor farms below the city. Joe Rice, Will Dockery's son, and Senator Percy played bridge and poker. Will Dockery would charter a private car, often a big Packard, and have the driver take him out to the battlefield where Pushmataha fought with

Andrew Jackson in 1815. He liked the ghosts. The day would finish with a meal at Antoine's and then another night train to Lake Charles for six days of duck hunting. The men bagged their limit every day and shipped fifty ducks to the University Club in Memphis and fifty ducks back to Dockery.

Once Will Dockery had written, "no time to think of anything but cotton and n———s," but now there was only time. He wanted to retire but didn't trust his son with the operation, so he soldiered on. Few people knew the soil better. Sometimes it was like he alone could see the locusts coming down in a black sheet, see the encroaching darkness, the killing of firstborn children, the water turning to blood. "We had the richest land on earth, naturally," he wrote, "but have abused it dreadfully and must change our methods for there is no more new land for us to take over."

In the twilight of Will's life he understood the cost of his fortune and who'd paid it. "We didn't exploit people, trick them out of their money because of their ignorance of mathematics and things like that," Joe Rice Dockery said many years later. "Some plantation owners did do that. But the system was wrong. Daddy knew that and I knew it. Everybody knew it."

THE STOCK MARKET COLLAPSE of 1929 pushed the price of cotton even lower. A few planters abandoned the tenant system and used tractors to plant the cotton and day pickers to harvest it. Abandoned shacks became a common roadside sight. That summer it didn't rain for one hundred straight days. Crops burned in the fields, and the rows that did get picked brought half the price they had a year before. The Delta's population shrank more and more each year. Meanwhile the little Delta towns like Cleveland and

Clarksdale, centers of power for people like the Milams and Bryants who were moving out of the Hills into the Delta, expanded. In *Deep Blues*, Robert Palmer wrote:

> They attracted more and more poor whites from the hills who brought to the Delta's paternalistic social structure an atmosphere of barely repressed violence, a burning need to acquire money and power, and an outspoken racism that neatly suited their purposes. They controlled most of the newer Delta towns economically and politically. The balance of power was shifting, and the planter class, never numerically strong, could only watch it shift. The Delta, already tense, coiled tighter and tighter.

IN 1929 PARAMOUNT RECORDS' first talent scout arrived at Dockery and tried to explain to the incredulous overseers that he was looking for a man named Charley Patton. Patton's fame messed with their most devoutly held beliefs about their place in the world, and his. A lot of plantation managers assumed the scout worked for a northern factory. Finally they gave him directions and the man traveled with his equipment fifteen miles right through the center of Township 22 North, Range 4 West. Patton leaned up against a tractor to tune his Stella guitar. When Patton finished tuning and got some whiskey in him, he kicked into gear and played.

Soon Charley Patton was standing in a northern studio and not long after that he was the most famous bluesman in the world. His records *sold*. He kept recording. In 1930 Charley Patton gathered his friends Willie Brown, Son House, and Louise Johnson. The group talked fellow musician Wheeler Ford into driving them to the recording studio in Grafton, Wisconsin, for another Paramount session. Patton sang of violent rural floods and the seductive call of Beale Street bars—dispatches from Dockery, really—songs about prison work gangs and dry summer crops burning in the field.

Willie Brown leaned into the microphone, the only time he'd ever record solo, and he sang about the long, dusty roads running through the completely drained swamps. The road he used most often was the one that runs past the barn.

> *Can't tell my future, and I can't tell my past*
> *Lord, it seems like every minute, sure gonna be my last*

Only five to eight copies of Willie Brown's "Future Blues" are believed to exist.

A DECADE HAD PASSED since the cotton market had collapsed. It was 1930. In DuPont's research facility, tucked into a bend of Brandywine Creek in Delaware, researchers invented synthetic rubber. The company had grown into an international juggernaut in the century since the Bryant family had been briefly connected to their rising star by marriage. The laboratory, named Purity Hall, buzzed with scientists hired away from the nation's top universities. In late April, not long after neoprene had been discovered, a scientist named Julian Hill worked with a new machine called a molecular still and formed polyester with previously unseen strength and elasticity. He'd made the first synthetic fiber. The Mississippi Delta didn't know it yet, but it was about to lose its importance to the bankers and manufacturers who had bent its culture to their ROI needs. In January 1931 Roy Bryant was born in Tallahatchie County.

That same month the financial structure of the Delta collapsed outright. Banks had no money to lend. Farmers planted some food crops for the first time in memory so people didn't starve. The cotton grew well, finally, but the price fell to five cents a pound, which didn't even cover the cost. It was the largest cotton crop ever grown in the United States, as falling prices forced farmers into a doom loop. All the banks in Indianola failed. The Illinois Central began to shut down lines.

The next year the economy of the Delta got worse. Cotton prices stayed low. Almost forty thousand farms went into foreclosure. Across the state 115 banks had failed in just two years. The Federal Farm Board asked farmers to plow up every third row of cotton. Nearly all growers refused. On one day in 1932, a quarter of all the land in the state was sold for delinquent tax bills. Historian John Otto wrote: "In many ways, 1932 was the darkest year since agricultural prices collapsed in 1920. For 12 years, bottomland planters, farmers, and tenants endured poor prices, droughts, floods, and boll weevils. They kept hoping that prices would eventually improve, so they could relive the prosperity of the World War I era. But in 1932, their hopes were finally dashed."

That fall Franklin Roosevelt ran for president and talked about controlling commodity prices by limiting the amount planted. He won the election easily. On the day of his inauguration in March, which was the rock bottom of the Delta cotton famine, farmers made plans to plant another enormous cotton crop, despite a carry-over of 12.5 million bales. The researchers at the DuPont laboratory kept working on synthetics. The five years it took for those scientists to advance from that first fiber to the first nylon were the last five years Eula Morgan and her boys lived in the Hills. They'd made it to the Delta, finally, at the exact moment King Cotton died.

She ran a store in Leflore County near Swan Lake. In the store one night Milam and Bryant's brother-in-law Melvin Campbell got angry at some Black customer's perceived act of disrespect and pistol-whipped him. The impact of the gunmetal split the man's skull and also released the hammer and fired off a round with a terrifying boom. Melvin's wife, who was Roy's sister Mary Louise, got blood splatter on her shirt. The sound of the pistol brought a family member rushing into the room. She surveyed the scene, convinced that Melvin had shot his wife, until she saw them both laughing hysterically as the Black man bled on the floor.

THE DEPRESSION KILLED Paramount Records. Some of the masters got sold as scrap metal, precious evidence lost. The rest just got abandoned in the Grafton, Wisconsin, chair factory where they'd been recorded and pressed. The staff gathered for the Christmas party and management fired them all. A group of them went up to the roof, standing in the freezing cold with the sound of the Milwaukee River rushing past down below. They'd brought up huge stacks of pressed 78 records and the masters that hadn't been sold as scrap. In a fury they began throwing them into the water. Some smashed on the rocks and others landed with a tiny splash. The workers read off the names from the records before flinging them into the night.

"Willie Brown."

"Skip James."

"Charley Patton."

Charley Patton kept playing his music around the Delta. He loved to sit on a porch and entertain children, taking his famous guitar and playing a singsong version of the alphabet and encouraging them to sing along. He liked to teach the children to buck dance and to move their hips like the crowds did in the clubs. Patton hadn't lived in Dockery for a long time but he found himself drawn there again and again, to see family, to chase women, to play a few songs on a porch, to satisfy the urge of a wandering man to go home. Around the same time the angry Paramount employees threw the masters into the freezing Milwaukee River, Patton went over to Dockery, likely to visit his sister, who still lived on the farm. Herman Jett, Will Dockery's close friend and manager, saw Patton hanging around and told him he could never come back. At least twice Charley had stolen other men's wives from the plantation and Jett didn't want any unrest among his workers. Patton left and never returned.

ON MAY 12, 1933, the federal government took control of the U.S. cotton industry, control it retains nearly a century later. The Agricultural Adjustment Act worked to limit production and refinance mortgages for farmers barely hanging on to their land. The plan worked. Farm income in 1935 was more than 50 percent higher than farm income in 1932. The Supreme Court overturned the law in 1936, on the grounds that agriculture should be controlled by the states, even if the states had done nothing to try to arrest the thirteen-year free fall. The Roosevelt administration rewrote the bill to account for the high court's reversal and it passed again. The Agricultural Adjustment Act of 1938 copied all the main provisions of the previous bill and added two new ones. First, it provided for crop insurance. Second, it instituted parity payments, which added a subsidy to the per-pound price of cotton to offset the permanent drop in the crop's value and global importance.

Everyone recognized that the next revolution would happen in science labs and petroleum wells, not in fields or factories, but many felt the families who had powered the old revolution should have their economic fall softened somehow. The government worked out the math to allow farmers to regain a standard of living erased by the collapse of the commodity market. Subsidies were given to make sure that falling crop prices and rising chemical and mechanical prices wouldn't impact the farmers' purchasing power. They picked a golden age of cotton—but before the boom triggered by the war—as the baseline: August 1909 to July 1914.

The experts came up with a plan that ultimately worked so well it still exists in an evolved form today. But nobody considered the accidental by-product, one more shortsighted decision in a place where the future didn't extend much past the next rain or drought. The caste system known as Jim Crow—invented by a landowner in Township 22 North, Range 4 West—grew hand in hand with the economics that required it. Then the forces of the market crushed those economics and would have cleared all the people out of the Delta, the natural end of a failed experiment, and likely taken the brutal caste system away with it. The long thirteen years should have led to the land going back to nature. If the free market had been allowed to work, there would have been nobody for Emmett Till to visit in 1955.

"Time will tell," a skeptical Sunflower County newspaper commented.

Look with me nearly one hundred years into the future and see the Delta today, which seems to all outside observers to be a place trapped in the past. That idea is the subject of countless books and films, none of which mention a principal reason the whole place feels stuck in some distant yesterday. The policy of the government statutorily locked the Delta between August 1909 and July 1914. If it feels like the distant past here, that's because it is.

CHARLEY PATTON WENT TO the doctor with shortness of breath. It was 1934. He had a recording trip to New York scheduled for three days later. The doctor told him not to go. He and his romantic and musical partner, Bertha Lee, ignored the advice, boarding a Southern Railway train for the long ride north. His Stella had been beat up too badly for a recording session and Patton carried a black-top Gibson. They arrived in a winter storm at Grand Central Station and went up to Harlem, where they stayed at the Hotel Theresa across the street from the Apollo Theater. They recorded twenty-nine songs in three days, sleeping all morning and going to work in the afternoon. He sounded great but the engineers noticed him breathing heavily between songs and struggling to hit the high notes, which had always come so easily and had let him cut through the noise of a loud country juke. The temperature fell below freezing at night. Finally they went back home. The label released five 78s and they didn't sell at all. His kind of blues was sliding into the past with the mule. Back around Dockery gasoline-powered tractors broke the land from the Sunflower River to Lombardy Road and already the maps showed abandoned tenant houses dotting the land.

In April of '34 Charley performed at a dance for local white people. The effort landed him in bed for three weeks. A doctor diagnosed bronchitis. He struggled to talk. Bertha Lee and Charley's families loaded him into a car to drive him to a hospital. The spring rains had left the roads crisscrossed in deep, unpassable ruts. The car got stuck and they carried a dying Charley back to his bed. There'd be no more hospitals or doctors. He started preaching from the book of Revelations. A few clouds smudged the tall, blue sky. The temperature rose into the eighties during the day and dropped below fifty at night. Family rushed to his side. He smiled and seemed content as he talked wistfully about the old blues.

Charley Patton died surrounded by his family and the violent power structure he sang against barely noticed at all. Not a single word was printed to mark his passing in the same newspapers that devoted a hundred column inches to the marriage of a plain-faced rich girl to the closeted gay son of a planter. But the news hit the sharecropper bars and tenant houses like the death of Elvis, with the same undertone of a lost world slipping forever from view. He had given voice to the voiceless and provided the soundtrack for decades of Saturday nights. His was the kind of death that made everyone stop and consider the passage of time. Patton's house filled with the men who'd traveled the circuit with him, names famous now to obscure record collectors. They sang over his body all night, finishing at daybreak with "I'll Meet You in the Sweet Bye and Bye."

IN 1936 THE BUFFALO timber concern Taylor & Crate found a willing buyer for its enormous Sunflower Plantation: the United States of America. Township 22 North, Range 4 West, would never be the same. A new kind of private-public hybrid agricultural market bloomed in the ruins of the crash. The rising racial violence of the coming two decades was on the surface a product of flailing against increased federal intervention in the moral affairs of the South, but its subtext was the shame tied to the impotence of being a ward of the state. That began in Township 22 North, Range 4 West, with the breaking apart of the Sunflower Plantation.

The Roosevelt White House had formed an organization called the Farm Security Administration, which among other things purchased plantations from industrialist types who didn't want them anymore, which allowed the wealthy capitalists to reinvest that money in more modern parts of the struggling economy, especially petroleum and steel, and allowed the government to try to help small-time farmers finally achieve Thomas Jefferson's yeoman dream, which the free market would never allow.

The FSA wanted to remove the Black families who'd been living on Sunflower for generations, removal having long ago become the default solution for any problem, and replace them with mostly white farmers from other states. Each family picked for the helping hand would get forty acres and a newly built house for $5,500 to $6,500. Each homestead came with a smokehouse and a shed. The government financed loans and set payment between $250 and $325 a year at 3 percent interest for forty years. These were sweetheart loans, designed to allow poor white families to build capital and wealth. That kind of helping hand could have changed the lives of the Black families who'd worked on the Sunflower Plantation. The land came with communal barns and mules and equipment and wells. It turns out that during the Roosevelt administration the United States did give folks forty acres and a mule. The government put up fences and gave the houses a fresh coat of paint along with electricity and running water. The barn area also had chicken and hog houses, a cotton gin, and an orchard.

At the plantation's peak before 1920 around 170 Black families lived in the tenant shacks on both sides of the Drew-Merigold Road. That number was down to around 115 and falling by 1936. Those families wanted to stay in the only home many could remember. They petitioned the government and were denied. They went to their white neighbors for help. Only one of them spoke up on their behalf.

J. W. Riddell, who'd been pushed out of the cotton business by the collapse of the global cotton order, sat down and wrote a letter to Mississippi senator Pat Harrison. He lived in the same house where Leslie Milam would live in 1955.

In his letter he said he did not understand why the government would enact a program to help small farmers and then remove small farmers who'd worked this exact land for decades and replace them with people who'd never even seen it before. These Black share-croppers had made Taylor & Crate incredible profits and now had a right to this dirt, in his opinion. They'd built a school. They'd buried generations of dead in the cemetery there on the riverbank.

"They have made good citizens," Riddell wrote.

The Roosevelt administration forced the Black farmers to move anyway. Riddell's letter failed to sway anyone with power. The unused tenant houses got torn down by the FSA and the lumber left over was burned. The new hand-selected white farmers started to move into the area. One of them was Earl Andrews, whose grandson, Jeff, now owns the barn.

ON OCTOBER 16, 1940, a young roughneck found his way to the local draft office in a little Louisiana swamp town on the banks of the Mississippi River. A clerk handed over a two-sided yellow card for him to fill out. The young man started with his name: John W. Milam. J.W. He'd migrated south to find work with a construction company out of Ruston, Louisiana, which was sending crews to Oklahoma to build a dam in the flats west of Tulsa. Until he needed to report, he lived in Morganza, which sat just two bends in the river south of the brutal state prison farm Angola. J.W. filled in the vital details, height and weight, skinnier than he'd be when he became notorious but still a barrel of a man. He went through all the lines one by one in childish, loopy handwriting. Then he got to the place where the army asked for a contact back home who would always know how to reach him. This space was reserved for a person who mattered a lot in the soldier's life. Milam wrote down James Tribble, whose nephew, Ray, would be a juror in the Till trial. Ray Tribble would vote to acquit his close family friend and would later buy the store where Emmett Till whistled. Less than half a year after Milam filled out his card, he got drafted.

FIVE MONTHS LATER, on a Wednesday, Alma Gaines took her pregnant daughter, Mamie, down Route 66 from their little town of Argo to Chicago's Cook County Hospital, a journey of about twelve miles. It was time for Mamie's baby to be born. She was nineteen years old, naive and scared. Nobody had prepared her for the next few days. The father, Louis Till, stayed at work, at the Corn Products plant in Argo that made Karo syrup and Argo starch, the product that gave the town its name.

The nurses put Mamie in a room with another lady in labor, who screamed and cursed as Alma came in and out. Thursday passed. Mamie thought the dark space—"like a government office," she'd write—didn't match the joy she felt about finally meeting her baby. Alma came in and asked if her water had broken. Mamie told her she thought so and had told a nurse but nobody had come to help. Alma marched to a nurse's station. The chastened staff whisked Mamie to a delivery room and as the doctor examined her, his voice changed. She'd never forget the doctor's anxiety. The baby was being born backward, a breech, and the next minutes were crucial. The doctor slipped on a mask and asked her to count backward from one hundred.

"Ninety-nine," she said.

That's the last thing she remembered until she woke up. Doctors worked on her now, nurses, too. She kept asking to see her baby. Later, they told her. Now, she insisted, and insisted again, until the nurses came in and handed her a tiny human.

It was July 25, 1941.

"Oooh, no," Mamie said.

There'd been a mistake. This baby looked white, with blond hair and blue eyes, but the nurses explained that a lot of Black babies came out like that. His tiny body was bruised and swollen. The doctors had used forceps and left scars on his forehead and nose. During the birth, the umbilical cord wrapped around his neck, right knee, and left wrist. He'd nearly been suffocated but had survived. Mamie lay in the white metal tube bed. Another nurse came in and asked for a name. She thought of her favorite uncle.

"Emmett," she said.

THE PEAVINE SHUT DOWN on August 1, 1942, the tracks ripped up, the spikes yanked out. The government's Metals Reserve Company needed the 4,150 tons of steel. The old railroad steel would find a new home in 230 different tanks, 17,000 bombs, 8,500 pieces of artillery, and several destroyers. Joe Rice Dockery, just six years into his reign over the family empire, started thinking about a world beyond cotton. Soon he'd popularize rice as a big crop in the Delta. As he tried to escape the monocrop yoke, he diversified into oil exploration, too, and then cattle. Dockery was changing from a plantation, an agricultural estate where the workers lived, to a farm, which is just a place people came to work. More and more the machines replaced people. Joe Rice often made the short walk to his landing strip, where his pilot flew him in one of his planes around the Southeast, maybe down to the Mississippi Gulf coast harbor where he kept his bronze-hulled yacht, the *Azara*, one of the last old schooners left afloat, or maybe a ride over to the white sands of Destin, where he could fish for wahoo and tarpon in the Gulf. Dockery belonged to him now. He and his wife, Keith, built a seventy-five-foot-long swimming pool. They collected art. A Degas painting of the New Orleans Cotton Exchange hung in Joe's office. The family played tennis with Shelby Foote and bridge with Walker Percy, talked positivity with Norman Vincent Peale at the Metropolitan Club in New York, and lunched at the Vanderbilt home at 640 Fifth Avenue. Joe Rice drove a red Lincoln and a Mercedes roadster. He donated the first Bully mascot bulldog to Mississippi State. Keith's rose garden mirrored the size of their private tennis court.

IN DECEMBER OF 1942 the Ithaca Gun Company switched its upstate New York assembly line from sporting shotguns to a government contract to mass-produce Colt .45 semiautomatic pistols, the sidearm of American officers. The plant drew power from the waterfalls on the adjacent Fall Creek. It sat up on a rise, still known as Gun Hill, on the south bank of the fast-moving water, a mile and change from Cornell University's Barton Hall, which was simply called Drill Hall during the year Joe Rice Dockery spent there as a student, before his father accused him of partying more than studying and demanded he return to the farm. Ithaca would make more than 335,000 of these weapons during the war. The fifth delivery to the military contained 59,300 guns, including the one bearing serial number 2102279, a black metal pistol with sharp angles and a magazine holding seven rounds. That same month, Township 22 North, Range 4 West, Section 2, long controlled by failing banks and bankruptcy trustees, finally found a new owner. A doctor from Drew, A. C. Kimbriel, bought the land.

IN 1943 Luvenia Slaughter, Gloria Dickerson's grandmother, left Township 22 North and moved to Ohio. She settled in Toledo, eventually buying a 1,600-square-foot house on Tecumseh Street. Family members would, over the years, try to convince her to move back south but she always refused. Never again, she swore. That year pulled a lot of Mississippians to cities up north. Muddy Waters left the Delta for Chicago in 1943. Son House moved to Rochester, where he worked as a porter for the New York Central Railroad and faded from view. His neighbors didn't know he'd ever been a bluesman, much less a recorded and celebrated one.

About the same time, an entrepreneur named Fowler McCormick, president of International Harvester, made an announcement. McCormick had long been at the forefront of mechanical farming and, as a close friend of Will Dockery, he stayed at Dockery Farms several times and conducted a lot of tractor and early cotton picker tests there. In 1944 at the Hopson Plantation just outside Clarksdale, McCormick's tractors and pickers planted, tended, and harvested the first cotton crop in history made completely with machines. One of the men test-driving those new machines was Pinetop Perkins, before he left the Delta and joined Muddy Waters's band.

An acre of cotton that had taken seventy-four hours to pick by hand now took just six hours. The sharecropper South was finished, even as the remaining sharecroppers, men like Moses Wright, hung on to the only way of life they'd ever known. A train from Cleveland took Luvenia away from her home, with two trunks and several small suitcases a neighbor helped load at the station. Gloria's grandmother saw the future clearly. She took six of her seven children with her to Ohio. Her oldest daughter, Mae Bertha, stayed behind with her husband, Matthew Carter, working on the Parker place even three years after Widow Parker died. The widow's sister ran the farm from afar and left the Carter family tremendous autonomy. The Carters lived in the widow's house near the barn.

IN APRIL 1944 a human being made the last confirmed sighting of an ivory-billed woodpecker. The fight to save them had failed. The last large hardwood patch in the Lower Mississippi Valley was eighty thousand acres in Louisiana called the Singer Tract, named after the sewing machine company that owned it. There were four nests in John's Bayou and a confirmed roost tree in Mack's Bayou. The company leased the land to the state as a hunting refuge but sold the timber rights to a big lumber firm out of Chicago. When the war began, Chicago Mill and Lumber, formerly Paepcke-Leicht Lumber, signed a contract with the military to deliver wood. It began cutting immediately. The National Audubon Society went to work to save the woodpecker habitat, lining up state and national support, even getting the War Department to agree to accept less wood in exchange for saving the bird. The company cut it all anyway. The company executive who answered all these pleas responded by saying, "We are just money grubbers, we are not concerned, as are you folks, with ethical considerations."

So many animals had vanished from these river hardwood

swamps. The red wolf, the cougar, the Carolina parakeet, and now the saws had come for the Lord God bird itself, the ivory-billed woodpecker. The wood got turned into military packing crates and plywood gasoline tanks for fighter planes. The Audubon Society sent a researcher back into the vanishing forest to see if any birds remained. He found one. The researcher told a colleague, who was also an artist, that if he ever wanted to draw an ivorybill from a living bird, the time was now. Don Eckelberry, just twenty-three, went south to the swamps. He searched and followed and looked for specific nests and trees. Walking through a swamp while looking up is a learned skill. One evening around dusk, as barred owls sang in anticipation of a nighttime kill, Eckelberry and his traveling companions heard a double knock. They silently waited. Thirteen minutes later the bird swooped through the clearing, flying above the broken tree corpses left by the lumbermen. Eckelberry notated the details in his journal. He stared at the last known ivory-billed woodpecker and would never forget its face.

"Hysterical pale eyes," he wrote.

J. W. MILAM SERVED IN the 75th Infantry Division, 289th Infantry Regiment, 2nd Battalion, Company E. They landed in Europe three days before the Germans launched the desperate offensive that came to be known as the Battle of the Bulge. Easy Company of the 289th Infantry, which included a future murderer named John Milam, briefly served in the tip of the American spear, the forwardmost unit engaged in combat with the German army.

Milam's company attacked on Christmas morning. German artillery shells exploded in the treetops as his unit captured and secured a ruined forest. They dug in and waited for morning. The last hours of Christmas night, 1944, seemed to last forever. Milam could see burning buildings and tracer fire. That night it snowed twelve inches. Hidden by the weather, the 22nd Panzer Division slipped through a hole in the line. The Americans had to regroup and repair their positions. Slowly, the Americans pushed the Germans back. Milam's unit, Company E, moved on the town of Bech and, despite heavy casualties, controlled it after six hours of hard combat. Company E cleared ridgelines and forests—ordered by their commanding general to push "to the limits of physical capacity"—and on January 19, after helping to win one of the decisive battles of the war, the unit got relieved. They moved by truck to a nearby town, where local women served them hot coffee and doughnuts. Ten days later they got pulled back into another fight, this time over the Colmar Pocket on the border between France and Germany. Milam arrived at the assembly area at three in the morning and four hours later his unit successfully attacked. Company E suffered hundreds of casualties. One of them was J. W. Milam. Shrapnel tore through his shoulder and thigh and the doctors at the field hospital left the wound open to guard against infection.

He moved from facility to facility until he rested in clean white sheets far from the front. When Milam got out of the hospital, he made moves to improve his station back home in Mississippi—to become an officer like all those Delta planters. Like my grandfathers, my uncles, and my father. So as the war ended, he attended and graduated from Officer Candidate School in a chateau in France. He was not, as some books and stories have reported, given a battlefield commission. But he did get commissioned a second lieutenant after his wounds healed. An officer and a gentleman. He got a single gold bar to pin on his collar and an Ithaca .45-caliber automatic pistol to wear on his hip.

———

WHEN EMMETT TILL TURNED six in the summer of 1947, he went south to visit his cousin Simeon and his great-uncle Moses Wright. His grandmother Alma took him. They rode on the Illinois Central with Alma's sister, Elizabeth, who was married to Moses. Folks in Chicago called the City of New Orleans line the Chicken Bone Express. Nervous families in the North would carefully pack shoeboxes with fried chicken and chocolate cake since Black people couldn't use the dining car, the packed meal an act of love and also something for worried hands to do. The ride took all day, with a stop in Cairo, Illinois, for the Black passengers to move to the segregated cars. The train clicked through Memphis and over the state line. Moses picked them up in Winona and drove across Highway 51, the Hills on one side and the flat Delta on the other, headed into the interior of the Delta and the gravel road to his home. Its original name was Darr's Ferry or Dark Ferry or Darfield, depending on whom you ask or which history you read, but the folks who lived on it in the 1940s called it Dark Fear. Because of the lynchings that had happened out there, Simeon Wright speculated in his book, or maybe just because night fell atop the cotton field houses like the end of the world.

Moses Wright, the child of slaves, was a sharecropper at John Ware's place outside Schlater where Highway 442 met the Quiver River. This job was a step back for Moses. For a decade during the last great cotton boom he had owned his own land. Then cotton prices fell and the stock market crashed and he lost it. If the markets had held steady, he never would have been in Money, and neither would his nephew Emmett Till. After the economy collapsed, Wright started renting land from local planter Grover Frederick.

This was the arrangement Moses liked best, because he did not want white men to be able to boss around his children. But the price of cotton kept falling and eventually he landed back on the lowest rung of the cotton chain: sharecropping. That's how he got to the Ware plantation, where he received an annual furnish and use of equipment in exchange for half his crop. Even if the landowner was scrupulously fair, there was barely a living to be made. Wright lived back in the woods off the main road between Schlater and Dodds-ville and the rest of his family lived in small houses between him and the road.

At the close of World War II, Ware sold that patch of land to a thief of a man named McShane. That year's crop was short, a finan-cial hole made deeper by McShane's shady accounting and his treat-ment of people. Moses told his new boss that he wouldn't be talked to with such disrespect and McShane told him to leave. Moses packed up his family and moved due east across the Delta to work for his old landlord Grover Frederick. Frederick treated people fairly. "He was German," Simeon Wright once explained. "He wasn't a bully. We never heard him say a racial word to any of us." Simeon always admired how his father navigated the white people living in their midst. He obeyed the codes, stepping off the side-walk when a white person approached, knowing his *sirs* and *ma'ams*, looking down at his feet when a white woman approached. But he was deeply suspicious and once he'd found an honest man, he hitched his wagon to him.

The Wrights moved into a spacious six-room, low-slung house with an enormous porch running thirty feet along the entire front. The family made money every year and kept a checking account in town at the Bank of Commerce. The year after Emmett's first visit, Wright would make two thousand dollars off his twenty-five acres of cotton. He kept two shotguns in the house. People on the farm called him Preacher. He pastored a church a half mile or so from his house called the East Money Church of God in Christ. Like his biblical namesake, Wright knew he would never take his family all the way to the promised land, but he could look at the life he'd built with some satisfaction. He'd taken them a long way indeed, set them up with a work ethic and a faith that could help them complete the journey he'd started. People admired him. He could pick two hundred pounds of cotton a day. Moses loved the country life. His wife, Elizabeth, talked from time to time about moving to Chicago. Moses refused, and when pressed, he'd state his intention to die in the state of Mississippi. This was his home. He kept ten hogs and three dogs. Chickens clucked around in the dirt. Emmett didn't understand these animals were destined for a table and he treated them like pets. He went down to the country store and bought peanuts and then came home and fed them to the birds. His uncle asked what in the world he was doing. Emmett explained that the chickens were hungry.

The rural way of life felt like another planet to Emmett Till. He stood in complete awe as milk came out of a cow. Back home he got his milk from the deliveryman, who doted on the young boy and sometimes snuck him a little container of chocolate milk for helping with his neighborhood run. Moses made his own country sausage and hung it in the smokehouse. The family loved cold buttermilk. Emmett tried it and thought it tasted sour. His aunt told his mom later that he didn't drink any milk down in Mississippi. Moses always kept a fresh bucket on the side porch.

Moses liked brains and eggs for breakfast. Everything got cooked on a wood-burning stove. He whistled in the house in the morning, pulling suspenders over his shoulders and putting on a wide-brimmed straw hat to keep the sun out of his eyes. His voice boomed through the house.

"Let's go back," he'd shout. "Let's go back. The work ain't hard and the man ain't mean."

When it rained and the fingers of water stretching across the Delta started to swell, the little lake across the road from the house flooded and the water ran clear beneath the house, which sat on little concrete stumps. It looked then like they were alone on the ocean.

A nearly identical house down the road a little toward town was home to the plantation manager. One day Emmett borrowed a hammer from him. When the man came back and asked for his hammer, Emmett looked up and said, "Just a minute. I'm not finished yet."

Everyone panicked.

His grandmother rushed in. She returned the hammer and quietly led the child away.

IN 1951 ROY BRYANT JOINED the army and went to Fort Jackson in the 13th Infantry Regiment, Company D. Everybody hated him, white and Black. A soldier in his unit used to imagine Roy's face on the paper targets during shooting drills. Bryant eventually got demoted from private first class to private and then went AWOL. By February of 1951, Bryant was home, and he and Carolyn Holloway were dating. Eula Morgan and four of her children lived in the heart of the Delta by now, in between two abandoned houses on Heathman Frazier Road, right on the same plantation where Charley Patton died. The Bryant home sat east of the cemetery where Patton's body was buried and forty miles south of the barn. Melvin

Campbell ran a store and lived between two Chinese families on River Road outside Minter City. The Little Tallahatchie ran right outside his door, winding in big cursive loops from Glendora down to Money. Leslie Milam farmed someone else's land, either renting or sharecropping, and lived with his wife on the Money Road, just seven minutes from the little store his half brother Roy would take over in two years.

Low wages and a closed labor system enforced with violence had been chasing off workers for thirty years now. In 1948, with a record crop, there weren't enough Black people in the Delta to pick it all. Cotton farmers estimated the 1951 crop was the largest ever, which meant that about fifteen thousand Mexican workers were needed in addition to all available Black hands. In Topeka, Kansas, that year, the NAACP filed a lawsuit on behalf of a railroad welder named Oliver Brown, who wanted to enroll his daughter, Linda, in an all-white school.

ON DECEMBER 22, 1952, plantation magnate Ben Sturdivant bought Section 2 in Township 22 North. Sturdivant didn't intend to farm the land, just make a little profit serving as a bank. He found a buyer who wanted to leave the lower-class grocery-store life and aspire to something better. The same day Ben bought the land he flipped it on credit to Leslie Milam and his brother J.W., who a few months later was written out of the legal documents, leaving Leslie solely responsible for the farm and all the buildings, including a deep well, a gas tank and pump, and a barn. Leslie and his wife, Frances, moved into the white house overlooking the bayou and the road, with a gallery bay window in the front for wide views. The first cotton crop Leslie planted was in 1953. As he harvested that first crop, prices fell lower than the year before, which were down from the year before that, which were down from the year before that.

His mother and siblings ran their loose network of stores that catered to the poorest Black sharecroppers. A fire burned down J.W.'s store in Glendora, along with much of the block, and the nearest firefighters refused to come help him. Two years later, six months before the murder, J.W.'s rebuilt store burned down again. To make ends meet the brothers operated trucks and mechanical cotton pickers to rent for custom jobs, as well as a healthy moonshine and bootlegging operation. Everyone knew a Bryant or Milam grocery always doubled as a liquor store. J.W. had pled guilty to bootlegging offenses five times. Other white people called them "white trash" and "peckerwoods" and tried to steer clear. "It was the 'N Word' all the time," Carolyn Bryant would say years later in an interview. "I've got this 'N' working over here doing this. . . . I'm gonna have to go get my money from that 'N' over there because he's not paying."

Everyone knew about these brothers' relentless, depraved malice. Just a few years before, they'd been arrested for assault and battery after kidnapping a man they suspected of robbing one of their stores over in Quitman County. Eula's oldest sons, Ed and Bud Milam, chased two white suspects down on the highway. One escaped but they caught the second and dragged him to the sheriff. Before turning him over, the suspect alleged to law officers, the brothers beat him. A year later, a Black man named A. C. Love worked for J.W. on a contract to build a movie theater in Mamie's hometown of Webb. According to Love's brother, Milam shot and killed A.C. after an argument over money. J.W. then found a third brother to threaten.

"I'll kill any n—— who argues with me about money."

That brother, Benjamin Love, also said that Milam later chased down his parents and siblings, who'd left a local plantation and moved across the river to Arkansas. Milam allegedly gathered a posse and armed himself with a shotgun. The mob kidnapped the family and brought them back to the Delta. Two Love family members said they saw Milam take their parents and two other siblings out into the woods. They heard screams coming from the trees, then watched Milam walk out alone. They asked where their family had gone.

"On a vacation," Milam told them.

The four Loves were never seen again.

Roy Bryant bought a dump truck and started a business. On the side he managed trucks for J.W. and Leslie. Part of that job required training new drivers; he gave lessons on his own truck. One student driver crashed the truck, and though both men escaped, it burst into flames and cooked down into a smoldering shell. Roy and Carolyn filed an insurance claim. The insurance company had declared bankruptcy just before the wreck and so they never received a dime. That sent the young family into a spiral. They never had enough money. His dream of building a company died with the fire. Near the end of that year, as Leslie harvested his first crop, Roy Bryant bought a store in Money without first telling his wife. They rented the building but owned all the contents. Roy and his brothers wanted to spruce up the living quarters and they painted the floors of the apartment red. The dining room abutted the back wall of the store and their bedroom was across the way. In the wall by the dining table was a little hole so the family could eat while still watching out for customers. The meat counter was on the wall opposite the table, and up front big glass cases held candy and other treats. Carolyn and Roy set out a checkerboard outside with bottle caps for pieces. Their customers called the couple Mr. and Mrs. Roy.

IN 1953 THE OLD DOCKERY COMMISSARY, one of the great venues in blues history, burned on a hot August afternoon. They blamed old wiring or rats. Nobody had used it since the war ended. All the new machines had ended the world of commissaries. Delta & Pine started its transition from working plantation to a seed and chemical research facility, which would lead to its purchase by Monsanto and then Bayer. The acres of cotton planted in the eastern United States dropped from 43 million to 17 million. The price hovered around twenty cents a pound. Worlds end with a whimper. Joe Rice Dockery sold his seat on the New York Cotton Exchange. He sold his Grumman seaplane to Miller Brewing. In just a few years the Department of Agriculture would drop sharecropping from its list of existing farm jobs.

IN 1953 MOSES AND ELIZABETH Wright of East Money, Mississippi, bought their first-ever refrigerator. That's five years after he made two thousand dollars in a single harvest and bought his first washing machine. Yet many parts of his life still felt ancient: his homemade sausage and the daily ritual of homemade biscuits, his rhythm of rising with the sun and quitting with its setting, a life ruled by the cycles of seeds and water and sun and big orange harvest moons. The government had finally run electricity to most plantations. Life had never been worse for a Mississippi Delta cotton planter and had never been better—if only in a material sense—for the few Black sharecroppers who'd resisted the call of Chicago.

On Dark Fear Road, across from the rising waters of Lake Never-Fail, Moses Wright and his sons lived with a foot in two worlds. Many of their days followed routines set by their enslaved ancestors, but more and more, new ideas arrived, messages sent from the future. Moses Wright listened to the radio and followed the presidential elections, even though he couldn't vote. He preferred Stevenson over Eisenhower. Emmett Till's uncle could pull cold milk from his fridge and enjoy it while the clothes washed themselves.

AS 1954 DAWNED IN THE Delta and across the South, the authorities worked, as they long had, to keep *The Chicago Defender* out of people's hands. The national powerhouse African American newspaper offered proof of a different kind of life. Railroad porters would throw bundles of it into the darkness from a moving train, trying to get news through an iron curtain. The folks in Township 22 North knew they could get a copy at the Black shoe store in Drew. One day in the summer of 1954, Mae Bertha Carter—Gloria Dickerson's mom—went to her regular church and heard a word she'd never heard before. A friend sidled up to Mae Bertha with news from the outside world that sounded like science fiction.

"The Supreme Court handed down something on the desegregation of public schools."

"You're gonna have to break that down for me. What's desegregation?"

"It's integration."

"What's integration?"

"Well, what they're saying, they're talking about Black and white children will all be going to school together."

Mae Bertha Carter sat with that news. She'd seen her kids go into the fields while white kids went to learn. *Brown v. Board* would ignite the latest wave of violence in Mississippi, rooted in the same old fear. Keeping the Carter kids uneducated was required to keep them compliant.

"Well, I'll be glad because when that day comes our children won't be starting school in November and stopping all the time to pick cotton. I know they will start in September and go nine months like the white children."

WHITE MISSISSIPPI REACTED TO the Supreme Court ruling like an endangered species facing extinction. Almost immediately a Sunflower County plantation manager named Robert "Tut" Patterson formed an organization named the Citizens' Council to help fight to keep segregation alive. Patterson, who worked the same farm where Eula Morgan ran her store in 1950 and where Charley Patton died and was buried, gave fiery speeches about protecting his daughters from race genocide and nearly certain rape. He played a recording alleged to be of a Howard professor claiming the real goal of *Brown v. Board* was "integration in the white bedroom," and even though the tape was quickly proved to be fake, the attorney general of Georgia followed Patterson's lead and mailed out transcripts on government letterhead. Rarely has a man talked about sex in public as much as Patterson. He was obsessed.

"If we white southerners submit," he said in 1954, "the malignant powers of mongrelization, communism, and atheism will surely destroy this Nation from within. Racial intermarriage has already begun in the North and unless stopped will spread to the South."

He spoke to the persecution complex so embedded in the southern identity. The newspapers celebrated him and his quickly growing organization. The Jackson paper quoted a Yazoo County planter who summed up the plan for keeping Black people out of the state's white schools. "We won't gin their cotton, we won't allow them credit and we won't rent them houses."

Patterson made his views clear to a New Jersey reporter.

"Sir, this is not the United States. This is Sunflower County, Mississippi."

UP IN CHICAGO, it was the Christmas season for three generations of an extended family of Mississippi Delta exiles. As 1955 approached, they had many reasons to give thanks. It had been thirty years since Mamie Till's father moved his family from their home in Webb to Chicago. They left friends and family behind, to be sure, but also all the traditions and rhythms that turn days into a life. Now they filled an entire two-story townhouse on South St. Lawrence Avenue on the South Side with blood relations.

In this holiday glow they picked out a Christmas tree. A big one, with wide green needles. Mamie wanted something nicer than the ones they'd had in the past, so her boyfriend, Gene, and her son, Emmett, went to pick it out. They chose a spruce, six or seven feet tall. Mamie covered it with decorations. On Christmas she spread out all the presents and took a step back and let gratitude wash over her. She thought about how far they'd come, and how her son was on the cusp of becoming a man. They opened gifts. She had bought Emmett a black suit. Gene got him a wide-brimmed fedora and a tie to go with the suit. Mamie got him shoes to match, too. Emmett bought her a scarf and a Whitman's Sampler box of chocolates.

The neighbors converged for a feast. It was Alma's production; the house was alive with the smells of Mississippi. She fixed turkey and dressing with gravy and yeast rolls. Magnolia made her greens with potlikker and cooked potatoes and sweet potato pies. Mamie baked a cake. Steam rose off the perfectly browned turkey, sitting at the center of the table, but nobody could eat until Alma blessed the meal. She felt the spirit that night, thanking God for delivering them out of their old lives and into their new ones, for the family around them who'd not let the chaos of exodus break their bonds. Gene kept nudging Mamie, who tried to hold in her laughter. There was an old family story about her grandfather, who'd sat at a table like this one back in Mississippi and listened to a preacher go on and on with the blessing. When the long-winded pastor finally said, "Amen," her grandfather cracked, "I was wiping my mouth."

Alma started praying for the upcoming year, 1955, asking for protection and grace, going on and on herself. Finally she finished.

"Amen," she said.

There was a pause, then Gene spoke. "I was just about ready to start wiping my mouth."

Everyone laughed, even Alma.

The spirit of joy hovered around the table as they ate. They loved Aunt Magnolia's greens. She cooked them down with pork, adding garlic and the southern trinity: onions, bell peppers, and celery. Then she added hot peppers, lots of them, so people would be crying from the heat and yet unable to stop asking for more. Everyone told stories and sighed with happiness, reaching for potatoes or turkey, the room alive with a chorus of *please pass me that*. Emmett Till sat with his family, still a boy to them, his cherubic face glowing in the soft electric light.

III

1955

On January 1, 1955, Mamie and Emmett ate the traditional greens and black-eyed peas to welcome in the new year. The greens represented money and the peas good luck. Mamie looked around at the glowing tree, and the home she and Emmett had made together—they laid the linoleum floor themselves—and felt they belonged on the cover of *The Saturday Evening Post*. She mentioned to a colleague how much she wanted to take this moment in her hands, hold it, preserve it. Emmett played with his young cousin Ollie, just seven, who lived in the garden apartment. "Well, from the eyes of a seven-year-old, it was a joyful time. Everybody got along well," Ollie remembers. "Emmett was a prankster, so somebody was always laughing. He was like our guardian angel."

There were always pots and pans on the stove. Emmett's mother and grandmother were great cooks. "I remember the yeast rolls and the famous turkey dinners," Ollie says. "And it was not just for Thanksgiving or Christmas; you could have that at any time. They made delicious rolls. I always remember those."

She can smell that house still.

"I'm not a pot roast person but Emmett's mother could make the best roast in the world with all the garlic. And to this day I'm still trying to perfect it."

On that same New Year's Day, Leslie Milam stepped out into a dry and chilly morning, forty-six degrees at daybreak, in a Township 22 North gripped by drought. His brother J. W. Milam woke up that morning in Glendora almost certainly hungover, in his little rental next to the turbine roar of a cotton gin. Roy Bryant woke up with his wife, Carolyn, in the back room of their store in Money. He could also hear a gin's engine turning. The sound of someone else's money. Moses Wright woke up nearby. Without a crop in the ground, he could settle into country rhythms, like hunting birds and game and putting up slaughtered hogs in the smokehouse.

Mamie's friend turned out to be a photographer who could take a family portrait. He came to the house on South St. Lawrence and captured the tree and the gifts. Emmett got dressed up in his new suit, with his crisp white shirt and sophisticated tie, complete with his fashionable tie pin. He posed for one photo alone with their Philco television set and another with his mother, the only proper photograph they'd ever take together. He smiled, a little shy with peach fuzz on his lip, and she just beamed. Emmett looked directly into the camera and Mamie looked at someone in the distance. She adored these pictures. The camera clicked in that beautiful light at the end of day, and the images captured the season's joy, the innocence, the love. The photographer took one of Emmett by himself, eyes young and hopeful, trying not to smile but his face giving him away. He wore his fedora, the brim cocked just like Gene showed him. The camera caught him trying on a version of himself along with that grown-up hat. These photographs are famous now. They are the ones Mamie would give to the newspapers when Emmett went missing.

1955

IT'S 2021, IN THE SUMMER, and I'm sitting in a hotel on Cotton Row in Cleveland, Mississippi, sixteen miles west of the barn. Wheeler and Marvel Parker have called a group of people together to brainstorm with an architecture firm that specializes in social justice monuments. I saw Marvel in the lobby. She told me she'd recently gotten a look at Carolyn Bryant's unpublished memoir and that Carolyn not only didn't apologize, she stuck to her story. The death of George Floyd a year earlier had launched an American reckoning and the name *Emmett Till* had suddenly come back into the news. Wheeler was writing a book with friend and Northwestern journalism professor Chris Benson about his experience over the last seven decades and Marvel had been typing out the work he'd done longhand. There were things on those pages she'd never known. A lot about how guilty he felt to have survived. Marvel worried all this remembering was coming at a cost. "It's hard on Wheeler," she said quietly. "It hurts him so bad. He said he thinks about Emmett every day."

Outside the clouds hung low, a strange shade of gray that put fear in the hearts of old-time farmers. A crop-killer rain had been falling for a few days. Last night another storm pummeled the Delta. A levee broke in two places between Charleston and the New Hope Cemetery. Twenty inches fell in a few hours. The Sunflower River at Indianola rose several feet in a day. The big rectangle of land between my farm and the barn took the brunt of the damage. The water that did manage to drain found the Bogue Phalia, a stream whose name comes from the Choctaw for "long creek," and the Sunflower River, which flowed in between Jeff Andrews's place and Dockery. Dougherty Bayou flooded its banks and started to climb up the hill toward the barn. The Army Corps of Engineers opened the gates at the south end of the Sunflower Basin, near Steele Bayou, to speed up the drainage. Fifty square miles of farms sounded general quarters like some old warship. Water closed Highway 49 between Drew and Parchman.

The Parkers had a driving tour planned for the architects and decided to try and proceed. A big bus sat parked outside to drive us from site to site. We climbed aboard. Wheeler sat in the front on the left side, beneath blue accent lights, and I sat a few rows behind him. Eventually we turned onto the Drew-Ruleville Road toward Jeff's house. Wheeler had never visited the barn. The bus driver made the big, sweeping curve and we could see the flood had washed out Dougherty Bayou and left the road to the barn submerged. It felt like a mercy. Most everyone got off the bus and stood alone or in small, silent groups staring at the gray barn atop the little hill. Wheeler Parker stared out the opposite window at the green soybean fields. He never left his seat.

EARLY JANUARY 1955 brought more freezing weather to Chicago. For the first time Mamie decided to let Emmett go alone into downtown Chicago to pay off all her Christmas bills. She gave strict instructions. Emmett repeated them back. Her fear did battle with her understanding that she must, at some point, send him into the world. He'd been asking for more responsibility. They argued about it, her standard and reflexive *no* coming into conflict with his adolescent desire to expand his world, to cross boundaries. She'd been giving up control inch by inch. Already he cooked most of the meals. The star of his repertoire was pork chops with corn, which came out yellow and black from all the pepper he put in them.

Mamie choked it down until finally she broke and asked him to ease up on the spice. When he boiled potatoes he always added too much salt, but his mother was appreciative. He talked about the future, how he wanted to be a motorcycle cop. They seemed like superheroes to him.

"I can pay those bills for you," Emmett kept telling her. She wanted to trust him. He'd earned some trust. But this was different. Mamie didn't have a checking account, so he'd be carrying cash. Cash she'd worked hard to earn and couldn't replace. For a while now he'd navigated the train system alone to visit family and friends in Argo. But a little bedroom village, where he knew and was likely related to every other person he saw, couldn't prepare him for downtown Chicago. She made him repeat the directions again.

"Go up to Sixty-Third Street," he told her.

She nodded. That got him a block and a half from home. Emmett had two places to catch the elevated train near their home, five blocks west to the South Park Station, five blocks east to Cottage Grove. Either stop would take him north into the Loop.

"Get off at Adams, walk over to the Fair Store . . . ," he said, going through all the turns and stores until finally she knew she needed to take a chance and trust him. Let him take baby steps toward adulthood. He took the El north on the number 4 Cottage Grove line, climbing aboard the green-and-cream-painted car through the back entrance, past the conductor, clicking and shaking north in his wooden seat. The bills stayed tucked in his pocket.

He went past Washington Park, through the famous Bronzeville neighborhood. Around Forty-First Street the line jogged to the left for its run into the canyons of downtown. As the train turned, a few blocks to the west stood Roberts Temple, where his own funeral would be. His El line ran just past the Twelfth Street Station, where his body would arrive in nine months. Wheeler always talks about how the actual person he knew and loved has been erased over the decades and replaced with a symbol. Bobo loved pranks. He liked to tell jokes, too, forcing people to wait for the punch line even when he stuttered. On some level he had to know he was overweight, and maybe his humor helped combat whatever angst his thirteen-year-old mind cooked up in the mirror.

Emmett passed Grant Park. He got off the loop at the Adams Street stop, a block from the end of Route 66. From there he hit the Fair Store on the corner of Adams and Dearborn. Across the street at Sears he handed over the money and the bill, which a clerk stamped "paid." That store smelled of roasted peanuts. Emmett needed to sprint beneath the Van Buren Street train tracks to avoid the pigeons dive-bombing pedestrians. He turned right and walked to Wieboldt's and then Carson's. Then he repeated his journey in reverse and laid the receipts and the change on his mother's nightstand. She got home and saw what he'd done. Then she read the note he'd left. Aunt Magnolia had given him permission to go visit a friend nearby. She smiled.

"I'll be home before dark," he wrote. "Don't worry."

IN THE LATE AFTERNOON of March 9, 1955, in the chamber of the House of Commons along the banks of the River Thames in London, the Industrial Revolution ended. It was a cold, clear day, wind blowing hard off the water. Members of Parliament came into the first-floor chamber with hacking coughs and sore throats. They were coming to hear Sir Harold Wilson make a plea for the government to save the Liverpool and Manchester cotton textile trade. He rose from his green bench beneath the towering ceilings and burled-wood walls.

"I beg to move," he began, "that this house notes with concern the serious situation which is developing in the cotton industry, and regrets the failure of Her Majesty's Government to take effective action to remedy the position."

A year earlier the government had shut down the Raw Cotton Commission, which had set the price for the textile industry during the war and kept the economy alive during the fragile years afterward. The rest of the world benefited from this artificial price protection and now it was gone.

The nation's cotton stocks were lower than they'd been even during the Battle of the Atlantic when German U-boats launched torpedoes into convoys of ships laden with bales from America, when German bombers firebombed the warehouses of Manchester and the burning cotton threw towers of flames into the sky. Exports of textile goods were at their lowest ebb since 1940.

England's former colonies were becoming nations and had learned their lessons well. Developing countries around the shrinking globe were setting up manufacturing hubs. Imports of Indian cloth had jumped from 16 million yards in 1953 to 133 million yards in 1954. In January of 1955 alone, 33 million yards of fabric had been imported into the country. From India, Pakistan, Hong Kong, and Egypt, cheaper clothes came into the country along with cheaper raw cloth, which forced clothing manufacturers who previously had made their own cloth to shut down their plants to try to compete.

"The fact is, and it is not too much of a flight in oratory to say it, that the cotton textile industry in Lancashire is bleeding to death," one minister said.

"Lancashire feels mutinous," he continued.

Wilson took aim directly at Prime Minister Winston Churchill.

"The Prime Minister may or may not have been elected to preside over the dissolution of the British Empire," he said, "but the Right Honorable Gentleman certainly may regard himself as having been elected to preside over the dissolution of our export cotton trade."

Colleagues began rising and sharing stories from their own districts. One mill had closed. Three more were on short time, with others considering the move. Factories all over the Northwest were cutting hours. In the spinning industry alone, there were 661 factories that had gone to short time. A year before that number had been 69. One colleague suggested that Manchester and Liverpool should form their own country and leave London's politicians behind.

Wilson's voice rose into the galleries. "This is not just an economic problem," he said, "it is a social problem as well. If this industry is destroyed, it will not merely be the destruction of a segment of our economic system; it will be the destruction of a community, a community which in the past has served this country, not only industrially but in many other ways, and can do so again in the future. It is wrong to look at Lancashire simply as a nursery of fast bowlers and wet weather."

The men listening could feel the world changing. The next day the Anti-Aircraft Command, which had run the searchlights and guns that bristled on the coasts and in city squares during the war, would quietly shut down. Wilson, who'd scrapped his way to an elite education with scholarships and grants, spoke for a corner of his country being left behind by those changes.

"It has produced some very great statesmen in industry and, indeed, in this House. It is utterly wrong, like some of the sneering financial journals of the City, to suggest that Lancashire goes all protectionist every time a problem arises and wants Government aid. Lancashire's record in this matter over many years is remarkable. In the American Civil War when many people were calling for the removal of the blockade on the trade with the Southern States, and when no one would have gained more from the removal of that blockade than Lancashire, it was Lancashire who held firm because of its belief in the rightness of the cause of the Northern States."

A colleague leaped up to speak.

"It was the Lancashire working classes!" he roared.

Wilson called for a specific remedy. The government should establish a buying agency for cotton yarn and goods, which could keep the industry alive. The Tory leadership called for a vote on Wilson's motion. Winston Churchill, sick with a cold, entered the chamber to vote no. He sat with Anthony Eden, his deputy, and read some documents before returning to Downing Street. The votes were counted: 288 no, 256 yes. The motion failed.

Cheap textiles, made with petroleum-based synthetics, were the future. Oil had replaced cotton as the most valuable commodity in the world and the politicians who voted no that night understood it. So did those voting yes, on a certain level, but sometimes people claw and fight to keep their past alive. The intermodal shipping container would be invented the next year and render longshoremen and warehouses redundant. The port city of Liverpool crumbled as fast as Manchester. Then Parliament passed the Cotton Industry Act of 1959, which paid to scrap machinery. A year later a popular television program, *Coronation Street*, premiered and recreated the nostalgic old Manchester that the decline of cotton destroyed. It remains on the air.

Two weeks later, at 4:30 p.m., as planned, the Cotton Board went to meet with Winston Churchill on Downing Street. Cotton leader Sir Raymond Streat, wearing a scowl and a fedora, led the most important cotton men in the country. They gathered in the Cabinet Room, long and narrow with four Corinthian pillars. Papers were passed around the table where Eisenhower had once spread war maps. Streat sat across the table from Churchill, who slumped in his chair, looking every bit his eighty years with heavy shoulders and his elbows on the arms of the chair. Streat noticed the old man fiddling from time to time with his hearing aid. Aides passed around a cigar box and glasses of whiskey and soda. Churchill took a drink of his and urged his guests to do the same. As Streat talked, a beam of sunlight came through the window, blinding Churchill until a thick curtain was closed to block out the light. When Streat was finished he introduced the manufacturing leaders who'd accompanied him. The Manchester industrialist representing the entire textile industry, William Winterbottom, stood up and spoke forcefully and directly, asking for an honest assessment of the condemned. It was a fair question. Capitalists needed to know if the time had come to find new homes for their capital.

"Tell us the cotton industry is expendable," he said.

Finally Churchill, after sipping his drink, rose to speak. He was kind but firm. His eyes remained piercing blue even if a little glassy now. He punctuated his sentences with thrusts of his big cigar, making eye contact with Streat. They laughed, perhaps a little wistfully, as he remembered political trips to Manchester and Liverpool when all the businessmen railed in favor of free trade. By the time Winston Churchill was out of office ten days later, the companies that owned the British factories had already turned their attention and capital away from the Mississippi Delta, whose sun was setting with the British Empire that had powered its rise. A curtain closed on centuries. Economic darkness was coming.

Streat led the cotton delegation out of 10 Downing. He was followed by Winterbottom, who was the chairman of the Manchester Fine Spinners and Doublers, which owned Delta & Pine, the same company that first started buying land around the little hill where Leslie Milam's barn now stood.

IN THE FIRST MONTHS of 1955 the politicians of Mississippi started passing laws designed to prevent the *Brown v. Board* decision from actually resulting in desegregation. While Winston Churchill and his advisers made hard economic decisions at 10 Downing, his Mississippi peers doubled down on social policy. On February 22, 1955, the legislature passed a resolution requiring "universal conformity to the doctrine of segregation." That wasn't the only business the hardworking public servants did that day. Another resolution offered support for National Hillbilly Music Day.

Less than a month later the legislature made it a crime for a white person to attend the same school as a Black person. A whole list of voter-registration requirements got approved. A written examination demanded new voters interpret a section of the state constitution. The state told circuit clerks they didn't have to keep records of this interpretation, so nobody could check to see if the tests were run fairly. Two weeks later the impoverished state spent $88 million to try to improve Black schools enough to make them actually be separate but equal—trying to obey a law only after it had been replaced by a new law it hated even more. That was $88 million the state did not have, but fiscal responsibility was never part of Mississippi's political DNA. That was the end of the legislative session. April Fools' Day. Rarely has a more cowardly collection of humans been put in the exact right place at the exact right time to do maximum damage. Even at the last minute, Mississippi held the power to pull back from the brink. Instead its leaders pressed for more speed on a suicidal glory charge.

Two more weeks passed and in Washington, with the cherry blossoms blooming pink, the Supreme Court began hearing arguments on the fight by some schools to delay the desegregation demanded by *Brown v. Board*. For four days the justices heard arguments. Mississippi attorney general J. P. Coleman flew up to sit in the audience. He held court with reporters and said confidently that Mississippi wouldn't be ruled by whatever decision the court might make. His voice boomed in the halls during breaks. U.S. congressman John Bell Williams, who'd later become Mississippi's governor, watched from the gallery, too.

"A kangaroo court," he called it.

Attorney Thurgood Marshall, later to become a justice himself, used his closing argument to ask the court to implement the law immediately. A justice asked him what to do about the achievement gap. Marshall said that shouldn't be a problem.

"Put the dumb Negro children with the dumb white children," he said, "and the smart Negro children with the smart white children."

The justices retired to make their decision, which most people expected would come before summer. Coleman flew home to Mississippi and on May 5, just two weeks after the Supreme Court hearings, announced his candidacy for governor.

Five people in all joined in the Democratic gubernatorial primary, which was the de facto general election in the one-party state. Coleman, former governor Fielding Wright, Ross Barnett, Paul Johnson Jr., and Mary Cain were the combatants. All five announced immediately they were for segregation and made the case for why they specifically would be the best person to keep Black kids out of white schools. That's what the entire election would be about.

"A hot summer away from the finish line," Sam Johnson wrote from the Jackson Associated Press bureau.

The talk in the cafés and in the newspapers was all about the Supreme Court. The wagons were circled. The state of Mississippi in the first months of 1955 was a wheel that turned faster and faster as politicians chased votes. One politician would say that what the state needed was "a few killings."

The president of the Mississippi Bar Association, John Satterfield, recommended "the gun and the torch" to keep schools white.

The editor of the *Jackson Daily News*, Frederick Sullens, said, "There will be bloodshed."

TWO DAYS AFTER THE FIVE candidates for governor announced their campaigns, on May 7, 1955, a preacher in Belzoni, Reverend George W. Lee, stared down a white man who'd come to threaten his life. The man demanded Lee tear up his poll tax receipt, the document that allowed him to vote.

Lee told him he'd rather die.

Lee had spent the spring registering Black citizens to vote. His print shop in Belzoni, a Delta town between Yazoo City and Indianola, turned out flyers and posters. In April of 1955 a crowd of seven thousand showed up in Mound Bayou to hear him speak. He had a deep baritone.

"Pray not for your mom and pop," he roared. "They've gone to heaven. No, pray you can make it through this hell."

The threats intensified as April turned to May. The local Citizens' Council made plans to "guard" the polls on Election Day. A lot of the local rhetoric focused on Lee. One man came to his store and said they believed killing him would scare the rest of the Black people in town enough to stop trying to vote.

The night of May 7 Lee drove around town almost like he'd resigned himself to his martyr's destiny. Between eleven fifteen and eleven thirty, he stopped outside the Ben Franklin store downtown and chatted with a friend. He talked about the visit early in the day and said he felt his situation had become dire. White people were angry, he told his friend. Nobody in town was more angry than Joe Watson, a member of the local Citizens' Council. A witness told the FBI that he'd overheard Watson say he was going to kill Reverend Lee if he could get somebody to drive the car.

That witness was the Belzoni chief of police, who didn't lift a finger.

Reverend Lee told his friend goodbye and got back behind the wheel to drive through downtown Belzoni. A green-and-yellow Mercury convertible followed him. The car ran with just its parking lights on. It belonged to Peck Ray, a handyman. The FBI believes Ray was driving and his friend Joe Watson rode in the passenger seat and that Watson held a sawed-off double-barreled 20-gauge shotgun loaded with number 3 buckshot. Deer rounds, enough metal to tear a man apart. Lee drove north on Church Street, toward the high school, and as he got to the intersection of Lowery Street, the tailing Mercury sped up. It was 11:45 p.m. Witnesses saw a muzzle flash and heard the shot. The Mercury pulled even with Lee's car and a second shot rang out. Lee lost control of his car and rammed into a sharecropper's home on Church Street so hard it was knocked three feet off its concrete blocks. A broken piece of wood flew through the windshield. The Mercury sped away and skidded around the corner onto Third Street toward the cotton fields east of town.

A Black taxi driver stopped and rushed to Lee's car. The windshield was shattered. Blood covered the steering wheel, the right side of the car, the interiors of the right front and rear windows, the upholstery above the right front door. The shotgun blasts had mutilated Lee's jaw and ripped open his face. The taxi driver rushed him to the hospital, where he was declared dead. It was the first lynching in Mississippi since 1951.

The Jackson paper ran a story with the headline NEGRO LEADER DIES IN ODD ACCIDENT. Some witnesses heard gunshots, the reporter said, but others heard a tire blowing out. The sheriff said the lead found in the dead man's skull was from his fillings, knocked out of his teeth by the force of the crash.

Two days later an anonymous citizen called the NAACP's Birmingham office and said he'd been involved with the coroner's inquest and the jurors were planning to "white wash" the case and call it a car accident. Congressman Diggs got the FBI involved and agents came down to Belzoni to a hostile reception.

The FBI proved Lee had been shot with number 3 buckshot. The sheriff changed his tune and suggested that Reverend Lee had been cheating on his wife and been killed by a jealous husband.

"A ladies' man," he told reporters.

Shortly after the shooting, the FBI found, Ray painted his car a different color. They quickly identified Ray and Watson as the suspects and interviewed them. Watson spoke to the FBI with a loaded .38 revolver tucked beneath his shirt.

"Vague and evasive" is how the agents described him.

Medgar Evers, in the first real campaign of his career, worked to get the governor to investigate. The governor refused. Police didn't arrest anyone. A local prosecutor declined to even bring the murder to a grand jury; the same man later successfully defended Byron De La Beckwith in the murder of Medgar Evers. George Lee's two alleged killers would live into the 1970s. The FBI returned the shotgun to Watson.

The front page of the Jackson *Clarion-Ledger* from May 10, 1955, didn't mention the lynching three days earlier. Instead there was a story about the dying Liverpool cotton markets, and one about J. P. Coleman leading a political procession from Jackson to Ackerman. A podium had been set up for him on the local high school football field. At the fevered crescendo of his forty-five-minute speech he railed against the Supreme Court violating the rights of Mississippi. "When you go to the polls on August 2," he said from the football field, "your ballot will most certainly determine the education of your children and the maintenance of segregation for the next four years, possibly for the next 50 years."

At George Lee's funeral, his friend T.R.M. Howard from Mound Bayou spoke. The church was packed. Rosebud Lee, his widow, made a brave decision. She left his casket lid open.

MY DAD USED TO TALK TO ME about his grandfather Ellis Wright's role with the Jackson Citizens' Council in 1955. Ellis and his son, John, had founded it and served as its leaders. My dad thought the difference between him and his relatives proved that Mississippi could change. There couldn't be two more different men, him and his grandfather. Ellis had led the effort against integration and my father cochaired the Coahoma County Democratic Party with civil rights icon Aaron Henry. On the same page of the Greenville newspaper in the tense 1950s, Ellis demanded that Millsaps College declare whether its faculty was for segregation, while in a column to the right, Aaron Henry wrote, "We are determined that the American right to vote will no longer be denied the Negro in our state."

When Ellis's son, my dad's uncle John, took over the Citizens' Council in the 1960s, he responded in a newspaper interview to a new biracial committee with Henry on the executive committee. He said he felt confident white people "will know how to deal with this threat to our community." Two decades later his nephew was working on a biracial committee with Henry. I can only imagine that John Wright felt that my father, too, was a threat. He never once called him to apologize or explain the comments he'd made about my dad's friend. As the descendant of liberals and conservatives, of owners of enslaved people and civil rights crusaders, I usually find it slimy to judge them from the moral safety of the future. It's trendy for southern writers to find a strawman ancestor in their past to malign. I find that generally disgusting. But the actions of a few of my family during this terrible year, when faced with an easy cowardly choice and a hard brave one, left a terrible stain on our name. On my name.

Ellis pushed for the state not to build a veterans' hospital because federal law required it to be integrated. He'd rather veterans of World War II and Korea just not be treated. Over and over he engaged in fights he'd lose both in the moment and in the years to come. Hodding Carter, the Pulitzer Prize–winning editor of the Greenville paper, mocked my great-grandfather in print: "The undertaker who is president of the Jackson Citizens' Council apparently is prepared to embalm and bury the remains of academic freedom in Mississippi. Neither Pope Pius XII, the rabbis of Judaism nor most of the ministers of the established Protestant denominations could pass through this Jackson thought embalmer's muster."

I sat on his knee when I was a boy. He gave me more money than the other great-grandchildren because I alone carried his name. Walter Wright Thompson, Junior. I remember his farm and the lake. Reading a celebratory profile of him in the Jackson paper written in 1955, I came across a new biographical detail. He was born in Missouri. Blame it on my mom's Delta planter roots but I felt a spike of anger. Not only was he not from the Delta but this guy wasn't even from Mississippi and he felt the moral authority to speak for the state? Moses Wright was born here. Ellis Wright was not.

We all shape an inheritance. We can be my great-grandfather, who tore apart the Jackson Methodist church over segregation, or we can be Reverend Dan Whitsett, who preached the gospel of love and tolerance. Whitsett called out the Citizens' Council as immoral and endured the wrath of Ellis. But the Bible is clear. Ellis either didn't believe it or thought he knew better. Either way his sins were hubris and hate. Ellis Wright was right about many things in his life. His business dealings were conducted, by every account, with a rigid morality. He led local civic organizations and charitable boards. But search his name now and none of those things come up. Once on his journey he faced a life-defining decision, without the benefit of knowing it had arrived, and he failed spectacularly. Whitsett, also born in the South, had the same available information as Ellis. He made a different choice.

The Citizens' Council always claimed to be nonviolent but again and again the lie was put to that. Here's one example. In April of 1955, Ellis Wright called Whitsett a communist. Then the KKK burned a cross in the preacher's yard in Alabama, four feet high and two feet wide, and an anonymous caller threatened that night to kill his wife and children. Wright loved to write statements for the newspaper. His smugness roars off the page even all these decades later. But he issued no statement denouncing the threats on Reverend Whitsett in 1955, just as he didn't say a single word about Emmett Till.

BY THE BEGINNING OF SUMMER in 1955, a long, multifront battle between the Earl Warren Supreme Court and the Eisenhower administration came to a head over the issue of southern integration. The *Brown II* case demanded a resolution. In the previous few years Warren had been urging his fellow justices to chip away at segregation: banning segregated beaches in Baltimore, banning segregated golf courses in Atlanta. He understood, though, that schools were more fraught. The unspoken issue at the core of the debate, he knew, was always sexual. It had always been about white girls sitting in desks next to Black boys. The southern farming class lived in mortal fear of Black men doing to them what the planters and overseers had done to Black women for two hundred years. The accusation, as it often is in Mississippi, was the confession. The Supreme Court promised a decision before it recessed in June and so every Monday morning, the capital and the southern states held their breath. None of them knew that the decision had actually already been made, on May 17, although the announcement wouldn't come for two more weeks.

Senator Eastland began attacking the justices on the floor of the Senate. It's like he knew already. He called them communists and demanded a congressional investigation. Four days after that speech, the ruling came down.

"All deliberate speed," the justices said.

The South must integrate its schools. No time line was set, which the governor of Mississippi, Hugh White, saw as a reprieve. Eastland, however, understood perfectly the forces unleashed by the ruling. He ranted and raved in the Senate and in the press. Down in Money, Mississippi, a relative of future governor (and President Obama's secretary of the navy) Ray Mabus hung a black wreath on her door. Six days after the decision the Mississippi NAACP got all the local branches to start petitioning school boards. Segregation was dying. Black parents were asking that their children be given the same education offered to white children. A week later all five candidates for governor appeared at an event sponsored by the Madison County Citizens' Council and all were asked about keeping Black kids out of white schools.

A newspaper reporter summed up the rhetoric: "On segregation, all candidates agree. They support it. Each argues that he can do a better job of keeping it."

All five candidates tried to prove they were more racist than their opponents, a sprint to the bottom, all promising to take any measure to stop the most dangerous and immediate threat to the Mississippi way of life, which apparently was a Black child who wanted to learn math. All of Hannibal's elephants and Genghis Khan's hordes lacked the world-destroying power of a bunch of first graders learning the alphabet and how to stay in line during the walk from recess to lunch.

ON JULY 1, 1955, Emmett Till was on the edge between one kind of life and another. His mother's boyfriend, Gene, had recently asked Emmett what he thought about Gene and Mamie getting married and being a real family.

Emmett considered the idea.

"We're not ready," he told Gene.

Every boy has that special summer, when childish things start to slip away and the first little steps toward adulthood begin. For Emmett Till that was the summer of 1955. Earlier that year he and his mother went together to the Plymouth dealership to pick out the first new car Mamie would buy on her own. It was red, with a white top and white interior, a beautiful-looking machine. The salesman drew up the paperwork and then Mamie told him that her son would cosign with her. Confused, the man said she didn't need a cosigner.

"My son and I are buying this car together," she insisted.

Then he got it. A lesson about responsibility and finances, and a formal declaration that Mamie and Emmett were united against the world. The salesman allowed Emmett to sign and Mamie told him she might need help one day on a payment. Emmett nodded earnestly and they drove together back to South St. Lawrence Avenue.

One Sunday in Argo he'd gotten on the streetcar headed back into the city when he saw his cousin Thelma waiting on her own ride. Like most of the family, Thelma went to services at the Argo Temple, which Emmett's grandmother, Alma, had cofounded. She and Emmett waved at each other. Thelma's friend Bennie Goodwin Jr. rode in the car with Emmett. He lived in the city, too, the son of the Argo Temple's preacher, now a student at the Moody Bible Institute. He and Emmett sat with each other. Bennie, compelled for reasons he never understood, asked if Emmett wanted to pray with him.

Emmett said yes.

Goodwin started to pray, and Emmett joined in. Bennie later told Thelma that he'd seen Emmett accept Jesus into his life.

On July 25, 1955, Emmett Till turned fourteen.

Mamie threw him a birthday party. He'd recently expressed interest in girls. Once he even took the train to Argo, picked up a date, took her to a movie in the city, and escorted her back to the suburbs. He and his mother talked about values and what kind of young woman he might marry one day.

At the birthday party the kids all hung out in a room away from the grown-ups. They started playing spin the bottle and Emmett leaped up and ran around the circle to try to make sure it stopped on him. Everyone laughed and the noise filtered up to the grown-ups, who just smiled to themselves. Mamie asked Gene if he'd sit down with Emmett for the talk. Nobody ever had it with her. She got pregnant with Emmett on her wedding night. Gene said he'd do it when the time felt right.

The temperature dropped that night, down into the sixties, with a little breeze coming in off the lake. It was raining in Mississippi. Mamie wanted to take Emmett on a road trip in their new car before school started. It was all set. Uncle Moses Wright was coming to visit in a few days and after he went back to Mississippi, they could head out on the open road. She promised she'd even let Emmett drive a little.

SIXTY-SIX YEARS LATER, on the weekend when Emmett would have turned eighty, his family held a reunion in Argo. They invited a group of people from Mississippi to come up and graciously included me. I pulled up to the community center Wheeler and Marvel founded at the end of Seventy-Sixth Street, where the town fades into a train embankment. Wheeler Parker looked down at the rails.

"Emmett played on these tracks," he said.

The center carries Emmett's name. Marvel and Wheeler had raised the money and gotten this building constructed and when they felt the communal love after it opened, it made them want to do more to preserve Emmett's memory. They held community and church events and the grounds often buzzed with the sound of playing children and laughing elders. Both imagined what it might feel like to take this small-town spirit and spread it around the world. We all walked inside the small room to see a picture of Emmett as a boy, wearing suspenders, with his big smile and soft eyes. A friend once described Till as the type of guy who would pull the fire alarm. He loved to laugh.

Another photo showed Moses Wright pointing in the courtroom. Another showed the faces of every white juror who let his killers go. They've never forgotten these men's names in Argo. A painting of the store in Money hung on the wall, too. Marvel, dazzling in turquoise, floated through the room as the consummate host, welcoming guests, overseeing the local folks who'd cooked food for the event. Pans of jerk chicken and fried fish, platters of ribs and barbecue spaghetti, filled the room with down home smells. Wheeler introduced me to his uncle Robert, an army veteran who wore his camo hat with his last name, *Wright*, on the back. All around were people, like Robert or one of his nephews, who actually knew all the human beings who were forever changed by Emmett's death.

"Was Moses your grandfather?" I asked a relative as we ate.

"Grandfather, yeah."

"What was he like?"

"A quiet man, and gentle, too. He was a preacher. In his later years he wasn't preaching but still was a very religious guy. And fifty-five, after the incident, he moved here. When Moses came here after the incident, he was afraid to stay there."

People fixed plates and laughed and told stories. Tomorrow's graveside prayer service would bring back a lot of pain but tonight the family broke bread and gave thanks. I sat back and watched in awe at the power of love to triumph over darkness. They lived their rebuttal to hate. Nearly every living person who actually knew Emmett Till was in the room. Marvel and Wheeler asked people to introduce themselves.

"My name is Walter Henry. I am a retired FBI agent."

"My name is Fatima Curry. I'm a documentarian for ABC News."

An elderly man named Joe Williams, who'd come all the way from Los Angeles, said he hadn't been back to Chicago in thirty years. He smiled and pointed to the famous photograph of Emmett on his bicycle. There are two other kids on bikes. One was Wheeler. The other was Joe.

"I'm often asked, 'Well, how old were you?'"

He looked over at Wheeler, who grinned back at him.

"Well, I was old enough to hang with the big boys," Williams said.

The whole room laughed.

"I'm Geralyn Johnson. I was mentored by Mamie for many years."

"Hello, everyone," a man said when he stood up. "I am affectionately known to the community as Uncle Bobby. I'm the uncle of Oscar Grant. How many of you have seen the movie *Fruitvale Station*?"

The crowd murmured yes.

"Oscar was my nephew. His mother, Wanda, was my baby sister."

One woman sang at Emmett's funeral. Another was the great-granddaughter of the founder of Roberts Temple, where the funeral was held. The woman who ran the AIDS Quilt project stood and said hello. Moses Wright's grandson introduced himself. A neighbor went next.

"My name is Bertha Jackson," a woman said. "The Parkers and I lived in the same building. The building was for two families, but four families lived there. So we were close every day. Emmett lived next door for twelve years, and he was such a prankster."

Wheeler stood and pointed toward the table close to the back wall.

"This is my uncle Robert," he said.

Robert, still wearing his army hat, stood up and waved.

"He was in the house with us when they took him," Wheeler said.

Robert looked down. The coming *but* hung in the air as Wheeler waited to drop the punch line.

"But . . ."

Wheeler grinned.

". . . he didn't wake up," he said.

Then a frail old woman stood up to address everyone. It was Moses Wright's daughter Thelma, who'd waved at Emmett as they waited on a ride back in 1955. She spoke in a soft voice.

"I wasn't there when he was taken," she almost whispered, "but I was there the night he was born."

AT TEN THIRTY ON a warm morning in July 1955, Memphis celebrated the birthday of Confederate general and Klan wizard Nathan Bedford Forrest. He would have been 134 years old. The

Tennessee National Guard stood at attention in uniform. Soldiers laid a wreath on his grave. It was a state holiday. All government offices closed. Ladies gathered at the Gayoso Hotel for a United Daughters of the Confederacy luncheon hosted by Mary Bradley, the general's granddaughter. "Appomattox marked the birth of soul and stature of this land," the luncheon speaker, a local newspaper reporter, told the crowd. There had been a resurgence in Confederate imagery and nostalgia. This collective act of memory, seen by historians as the second great wave of Lost Cause mythology, rose in defense of a stronghold under assault.

The Mississippi history book I studied in junior high school in the 1990s had its roots in the anxieties of 1955. I read it again recently at my mom's kitchen table in Clarksdale. A large photograph of Milam, Bryant, and Sheriff Strider dominated the page where reference to the murder was found. A single paragraph covered the entirety of the killing and the trial. It talked about the election that summer and how the governor "proved to be a moderating force during a very difficult time. Just after the election, Emmett Till, a young black man from Chicago, allegedly made a pass at a white woman in a rural store. Two men kidnapped him, beat him, killed him and threw his body in the Tallahatchie River. The coverage of the trial and acquittal of his accused murderers, who later admitted their guilt in an article in a national magazine, painted a poor picture of Mississippi and its white citizens."

A man, the history book said. *Made a pass.*

One hundred and seventeen words about the murder of a child that sparked the civil rights movement. Or, if you are a white student in a Mississippi Delta school, a case most newsworthy for how it made white people in the Delta look to the rest of the world. I pushed the chair back sharply from the table and read the passage again. I understood in that moment why a memorial for Emmett Till in the Delta wasn't just about justice or truth. Memorials in my homeland had always been about forgetting. Nathan Bedford Forrest in Memphis, the Confederate dead on countless Mississippi courthouse lawns. But this memorial would be about remembering. A first step in combining two tribes—the Tills and the Andrewses, the Moses Wrights and the Ellis Wrights—into one. The Delta needed to change to survive. The Delta hated, perhaps most of all, change. A monument would force a new conversation. Because right now a man made a pass that sure did make white people look bad, and feel bad, too. Mamie sent a healthy boy south and got a mauled corpse in return, but never forget that her loss "painted a poor picture of Mississippi and its white citizens."

THE LAST STOP ON EMMETT'S eightieth birthday was the Burr Oak Cemetery. Mother and son rest there together. Nearly every person buried in this ground came north during the migration. The founder of the Roberts Temple is buried here, and Willie Dixon from Vicksburg and Otis Spann from Belzoni and the lead singer of the Chi-Lites and a Black Purple Heart recipient from Vietnam. Plus generations of mothers and fathers, brothers and sisters. Emmett's death rattled every single family who thought they'd escaped the South. Mahalia Jackson bought his headstone.

Congressman Bobby Rush stepped forward to say a few words. He talked about how his father pulled him aside and showed him the photograph of Emmett in his casket. "Look, I want you to see this," his father said.

Standing in the cemetery, Rush looked down and searched for the composure to continue. The mourners wiped away tears. A replica of the marker naming a stretch of Chicago's Dan Ryan Expressway after Emmett stood watch over his flat grave marker. "Emmett Till Memorial Bridge," it read. That felt right. Rush, his once-powerful voice raspy and halting, spoke without notes.

"I've never forgotten," he said. "We can never forget the power of a mama's love for having the courage to open that casket and show the world what hatred looked like."

IN JULY OF 1955 the NAACP first entered the tightly insulated square of Township 22 North, Range 4 West, measured from the Choctaw Meridian. It was a Sunday afternoon out near the Walford Indian mounds. A beat-up old bus parked at the tenant house of Gloria Dickerson's parents, Mae Bertha and Matthew Carter. A preacher named Anderson got out and came to the door. Everyone knew him. He sharecropped at the nearby Zumbro plantation, owned then and now by my relatives, and he quietly ran membership and recruitment for Cleveland's NAACP chapter. It was a dangerous job. The Carters had never heard of the organization. Anderson told them he wanted to add their names to his list.

"Advancement for colored people?" Mae Bertha exclaimed. "I want to join!"

She and Matthew found six dollars, enough for a membership for each of them and for their four oldest children, and joined the group. Quietly she and Matthew began attending secret meetings every Wednesday night at the New Kingdom Baptist Church in Cleveland. Amzie Moore, who organized Anderson's recruitment missions into the plantations, ran the local operation out of his service station. He'd fought in the Pacific in World War II. He got sick in 1945 and ended up in a field hospital in Burma. On

December 13, 1945, he boarded a ship and sailed through the Bay of Bengal into the Gulf of Aden and the Red Sea. He looked out from the decks of the ship and saw Mount Sinai and felt its majesty. They stopped for a spell in Egypt. Being in Africa inspired him. They sailed through the Strait of Gibraltar, in the shadow of the rock, and finally landed in Camden, New Jersey. He took a night train back to Mississippi, after three years abroad, and the only place he could eat with white people was the Holiday Inn. Nothing had changed. That's where his second act began. He joined with Dr. Howard and Medgar Evers to pull the sharecroppers out of serfdom into something approaching the modern world. All that was just getting started in 1955. That's why Anderson went to the Carters' home and signed them up.

Black informers in Township 22 North snitched to the white power structure but Mae Bertha found a solution. She knew one man to be a traitor, so she just brought his wife along on an NAACP bus trip to Jackson so he had to stay quiet lest he implicate his own family. These were tense days but by the end of 1955 more than four thousand Black Mississippians had joined. Those discovered to be members got their names printed in the local papers, which quickly led to firings, evictions, and a loss of credit.

Poor people like the Carters took enormous risks to join. They wanted to show their children not to be afraid. That's the lesson Gloria took away from her parents. In the six weeks before Till came south to Mississippi, a schoolteacher named Dola Walters was fired from her job in Indianola for trying to use a white restroom. More than one hundred Black people signed an NAACP petition for integration in Vicksburg. Black citizens in Clarksdale circulated a petition demanding integration. Twenty-six Black people signed a similar petition in Natchez and nine days later Natchez started its branch of the Citizens' Council. In Clarksdale 303 Black people signed and immediately afterward my hometown opened its Citizens' Council branch. These petitions and the responses were all Mississippi talked about in July 1955 and into August.

Fifty-three Black people signed in Yazoo City. They were all concerned parents who followed local politics. That year Yazoo County spent $245 per white student and $3 per Black student, and in the next decade it would start a segregated private school, named after the English city that birthed the Mississippi Delta. Manchester Academy opened in 1969, the year before most of the state finally integrated, and until he died, my uncle Will was the football team doctor. Three of my cousins graduated from there. The roots of that school began with the petition signed by fifty-three Black people. It sent panic through the town's establishment and demanded a response. The Yazoo Citizens' Council bought a full-page ad to list their names and addresses. So many got fired, threatened, and cut off from credit or supply chains that soon only two signatures remained on the list. The Citizens' Council's newspaper list, which started the campaign against the parents who signed, was published on August 18, 1955. Two days later, Moses Wright was scheduled to leave Chicago to head back to Money, Mississippi, where he and his family needed to start the cotton-picking season. Wheeler Parker was going with him to visit his cousin Simeon and get his fix for the country way of life they'd left behind. His best friend, Emmett, wanted desperately to come along.

MOSES WRIGHT HAD BEEN STAYING at his daughter Willie Mae Jones's house. Before she moved to Chicago she'd lived out in the country next to Wheeler Parker at the intersection of Highway 442 and the Quiver River. A thin membrane existed between Chicago and Mississippi; the cheap train ticket made moving between the two worlds easy. Wright rode the El and explored the enormous city. He told his family about his life back home, about fishing in the streams and lakes, about how boys could run free in the woods around his house. Wheeler had already secured permission to travel back with him to Money for a last bit of summer vacation before school began again. Emmett kept begging his mother to let him go. She told him no. Mamie was against it. So was her mother.

Emmett stayed after her and finally Mamie decided to go and talk to Moses. When she arrived at Willie Mae's house she recognized her mother's car parked outside, which made her laugh. They both were thinking the same thing. Everyone inside the house laughed, too, "two hens coming to fuss over this one little chick," as she put it. Willie Mae made her famous fried chicken and Mamie got to sit with Moses. She called him Papa Mose. He promised her that the boys would not go to town alone. She gave in. Emmett could go to Mississippi.

She started teaching him the rules. It was, she realized, the very first conversation she'd ever had with him about race. She told him a Black man couldn't even be caught looking at a picture of a white woman.

"Mama," he said, "I know how to act. You taught me how to act."

She kept going over the rules. Don't start any conversations with a white person. Say "Yes, sir," "No, sir," "Yes, ma'am," "No, ma'am." *Put a handle on your answers.* If a white woman walks toward you, step off the sidewalk and lower your head. Do not under any circumstances look her in the eye.

"If you have to humble yourself," she told him, "then just do it. Get on your knees if you have to."

"Oh, Mama," he said. "It can't be that bad."

"Bo," she told him. "It's worse than that."

FOURTEEN YEARS EARLIER, in 1941, Muddy Waters was on his Mississippi porch playing his country blues for men from the Library of Congress. He would get a friend to write letters to one of the men for the next year, asking what became of those recordings. He wanted a life far away from Stovall Plantation, where his house sat at the foot of the same fields he plowed, and he knew his music, which he had learned from Son House, might be a way out. Son House, who'd been taught by Charley Patton, was two years from disappearing into the industrial North, where he'd leave his old life behind. Waters followed his mentor north but he had no intention of disappearing. He could hear a new sound. A train took him from Clarksdale to Memphis, where he boarded the Chicago Nine train north. Sixteen hours after he left home, he arrived. He spent his first night in Chicago with friends from Colonel Stovall's plantation, in the segregated part of town called Bronzeville.

From his very first night there at 3652 Calumet Avenue, Waters was surrounded in his new city home by Mississippi spirits. A half block down East Thirty-Seventh Street and a half block north was the mansion where journalist Ida B. Wells lived after she got famous. She was born in Holly Springs. If Muddy walked five blocks the other way down Thirty-Seventh Street and took a left on Indiana, he'd soon come upon the house where novelist Richard Wright lived when the FBI put him under surveillance. He was born in Roxie, Mississippi.

When Waters got to Chicago, the electric guitar was still being developed. John Deere released its first mechanical picking

machine the same year that Fender released the first Telecaster. Leo
Fender's company was founded the same year Muddy Waters left
the Delta, and after he arrived in Chicago, where a man made
$1,919 a year compared with $439 in Clarksdale, a musician handed
him one of these new machines. Muddy plugged it in and changed
the world.

A decade later, in 1952, Howlin' Wolf got to Chicago, leaving
behind Drew, Mississippi, where he'd worked and played in the
shadow of Leslie Milam's barn. He spent his first nights in Chicago
staying at Waters's house on South Lake Park Drive in Bronzeville.
Waters got him a gig at Pepper's, where the man with his rolling
cart would turn up around midnight and hawk pig ear sandwiches
on Forty-Third and Vincennes. The South Side was Clarksdale
with airports and pro sports. One block to the west and decades
later Muddy Waters would invite the Rolling Stones onstage with
him at another now-vanished South Side juke called the Checkerboard Lounge. He called for Keith by name. A young Richards had
once bonded with a young Mick Jagger on a London train platform
because both clutched Muddy Waters records in their hands.

How do you describe the totality of Bronzeville? This is the
world that Emmett Till saw every day. Imagine a neighborhood in
today's America where Barack Obama, Jay-Z, Skip Gates, Oprah
Winfrey, and LeBron James lived alongside dockworkers and hog
butchers and street hustlers, where Ernie Henderson sold so many
fried chicken sandwiches he bought a Rolls-Royce. If you wanted
to find a Black friend in Chicago, the saying went, just stand at the
corner of South Parkway and East Forty-Seventh Street and wait.
Long-ago-vanished pleasures: Sonny Boy Williamson and Little
Walter shooting pool in the dim light of an Indiana Street bunker
named Turner's Blue Lounge. The red sign is still there. Nat King

Cole visiting a young lady on Forty-Seventh Street by the OK Drug Store while the neighborhood kids peeked around corners and spied. Mixed drinks at the Palm Tavern, a fancy dinner out at Morris Eat Shop, chicken at Charlie and Ella Mae's, rib eye steaks at Cadillac Bob's, and Army and Lou's for that stewed or smothered taste of their youth. Hot tamales from vendor carts and Italian meals sold to go by ladies who spoke in their mother tongue.

Muddy Waters playing at the Zanzibar, at Pepper's and at Theresa's and at Smitty's Corner and the 708. In 1943 when it was called sharecroppers' music by the urban sophisticates who preferred jazz, in 1953 when it was the most dangerous music being made in America, in 1961 when the new militants saw it once more as sharecroppers' music. Smitty's Corner shared a block with the office of *The Chicago Defender*, the powerful Black newspaper whose editorials and news coverage lit the path of the Great Migration. Three blocks east to the Dreamland Café where Louis Armstrong and King Oliver made the music we now call jazz. It got torn down and the Stateway Gardens housing project went up on the spot. It was torn down in 2007.

From the end of the nineteenth century, politicians abandoned the neighborhood to the Irish and Italian mobs. Al Capone sold a lot of liquor in Bronzeville. Enemies culled their ranks. Nancy Green got run down by a car. You probably don't recognize her name. You know the brand of syrup that bore her actual face: Aunt Jemima. South Parkway and East Forty-Seventh is where she died. Private First Class Robert E. Robertson, Vietnam vet, 4th Infantry Division, died in 1966. He lived at South St. Lawrence and Forty-Second and is buried in the same cemetery as Emmett Till. There's a long history of soldiering in this part of Chicago. Milton Olive started working in Lexington, Mississippi, during the Freedom

Summer to register voters, and his grandmother got so scared for his life that she shipped him back up north to the South Side, where he joined the army to fight a different kind of enemy. That seemed safer; his family didn't fear the Vietcong nearly as much as white Mississippians. Milton learned how to jump out of airplanes and then, in a jungle clearing on a Friday, dove onto a grenade to save the lives of his friends, including his racist lieutenant. A year later President Johnson presented Olive's parents the Congressional Medal of Honor, the eighth ever given to a Black man. His dog tags are now on display at the intersection of East Thirty-Fifth and South Giles.

Joe Louis lived in Bronzeville. His mother owned two rooming houses over by the lake near the HillTop Lounge run by a corrupt cop named Two-Gun Pete. When Louis fought, you could walk through the streets at night and hear the tinny radio sounds coming out of every window, the tenements of sharecroppers new to the city and the swanky flats and mansions where men like Nat King Cole and Louis Armstrong lived. Armstrong would walk on nights like that in khaki pants and an undershirt, carrying a horn case through an alley, with a wake of children following behind him. On those Joe Louis fight nights, you could hear something else besides the radio call. The men and women of Bronzeville, southern sharecroppers in exile, refugees who'd found asylum in this new world, would be loudly urging Louis on.

IT'S BEEN NEARLY SEVENTY YEARS since the City of New Orleans left Chicago with Moses, Emmett, and Wheeler aboard. Wheeler found himself in the Memphis station not long ago. It's a fancy hotel now but it still serves as the station. Wheeler, Marvel, and Chris Benson were all there for a meeting with the FBI. Investigators wanted to know what the Till family would consider justice after all this time. It was late at night. A furious noise of metal and steam arose outside.

"Wow," Benson said. "This really is still a train station."

Parker laughed.

"That's what I've been telling you," he said.

"No, really," Benson said, pointing out the window. "And there's a train."

Wheeler turned to look.

"Wait," Chris said, "that's the City of New Orleans."

It took them all a moment to understand. This was the same train that had carried Wheeler and Emmett down to Mississippi together and carried Wheeler back to Chicago alone. He'd never forgotten seeing Mamie for the first time and feeling like he'd done something wrong. The light of the train called him and he rose from the table and walked to the windows. The train seemed to be exhaling, steam coming from big metal lungs like breath on a cold morning. He felt it carry him south into the Delta, back across time to 1955.

He remembered getting to Chicago's Central Station on Twelfth Street on the day they left. Emmett was going to meet them at Sixty-Third and Woodlawn on the South Side. Mamie handed him the usual meal for a train trip south: a shoebox packed lovingly with fried chicken and cake, the same she'd carried when she was a girl, all her love and anxiety visible in the carefully packaged meal. Emmett liked the dark meat. Wheeler remembers the train whistle blowing as Mamie was buying Emmett's ticket. The observation car glowed in the early-morning light. The conductor called all the passengers aboard. Emmett ran to make it.

Mamie called for him to stop and give her a kiss.

"Aw, Mama," he said.

But he turned and kissed her goodbye. He slipped his wrist-watch off his arm.

"Here," he told her, "take this."

Mamie held the watch and saw the train roll south as Emmett found Moses and Wheeler and took his seat. Emmett ran all around the train. His uncle told him over and over to sit down. They arrived in Winona Saturday afternoon. Emmett wore a hat, khaki pants, and a cotton shirt. He had a silver ring with his father's initials engraved on it. Maurice Wright, Moses's son, was waiting for them at the station in the family's 1946 Ford. They drove into the Delta on Highway 7, past the empty ground where a land office had opened in 1820 to bring the grid to this wild piece of earth. Maurice turned onto Dark Fear Road, at the cotton gin, the tires kicking up a cloud of dust on the gravel, filling the sky. And now, somehow, Emmett is a martyr and Wheeler is an old man and a bright light cuts through the night, and the steam hisses and coughs.

SENATOR EASTLAND AND segregationist Mississippi judge Tom Brady had both spoken in Senatobia a week before Emmett, Moses, and Wheeler arrived in Mississippi. More than two thousand people had gathered. Brady told them that God supported their desire for segregation. Standing in the glow of the high school football stadium lights, he spoke about the glory of their coming combat against these evil forces. "It is an unending battle," he said. "We are in the mouth of a cannon."

A cool breeze blew across the crowd. The stadium sat near Highway 51, a dividing line between the Delta and the Hills.

Senatobia was one of those towns that grew on the edge of the white gold rush. Hernando, Como, Sardis, Batesville, Oakland, Grenada, Duck Hill, Winona. Judge Brady talked about the death of Egyptian civilization at the hands of mongrelization. He talked about Karl Marx. He said the NAACP was the most powerful organization in the country. His words found their target. *An unending battle. The mouth of a cannon.*

Then Senator Eastland took the stage and shook his fist.

"We are going to have to stand together and present a united front," he said, "or we are going to be destroyed."

The stakes had been set. War loomed.

"They cannot force us to drink the black hemlock," he said to cheers.

That same day, 240 miles south of Senatobia, a World War I veteran named Lamar Smith had been encouraging Black people to vote in the upcoming runoff election. He stood in front of the Brookhaven courthouse with a box of absentee ballots, a tool that allowed voters to avoid the customary intimidation and violence at the polls. White politicians and bureaucrats worked hard to create a false narrative that absentee votes somehow wouldn't count; the intimidation was a key part of the disenfranchisement plan.

One witness said later that he heard Smith's last words: "No white man is big enough to run me out of Brookhaven!"

Someone shot Smith on the courthouse lawn at 10:00 a.m. in front of at least thirty white witnesses, including the sheriff, who let one of the alleged killers, Noah Smith, escape despite being covered in blood. A grand jury declined to indict any of the accused: Noah Smith, Mack Smith, or Charles Falvey. Nobody would testify. There was no law anymore.

Mississippi wound tighter and tighter. Almost no one noticed how wild the rhetoric had gotten until much later when historians started to try to understand this strange last stand. Mamie certainly didn't realize the atmosphere of frenzied hatred that awaited her son. She let him go like every parent lets their child go, finally, into the world alone.

Mamie listened until the sound of the train died away. A friend took her home. As she tried to make it into her house she just "crumbled," as she'd say later. Her friend helped her up the stairs and into bed.

Her friend Ollie Williams remembers how sick Mamie got right away. "Really, truly, you could tell how she was deteriorating from the time he left for Mississippi. It's like she knew something was wrong, because she became ill. I recall she didn't have any energy. She was lethargic. She was just pretty much bedridden. And I always say we have a connection with our children and sometimes you know something, you just can't pinpoint it. So it was as if she knew something was gravely wrong."

Emmett's train moved south, a trip Mamie knew well. His watch ticked. She knew that by two he'd be in Cairo, Illinois, moving to the Jim Crow car up front by the engine. She thought about standing on the platform kissing him goodbye and how a voice inside her was shouting not to let him go. Later she'd write: "What if I had paused at that point for just a moment longer and let the other side of me win, and let Emmett lose? How long would his disappointment have lasted? A moment, maybe? I would have a lifetime to consider all that, one moment at a time."

MAURICE WRIGHT, who'd met Emmett, Wheeler, and Moses at the station, parked the car in the front yard of Moses Wright's house.

Simeon Wright, Moses's son and Maurice's brother, ran outside to meet them. The first thing he noticed was that Bobo had grown chubby. The second thing he noticed was that his cousin, in khaki pants and a cotton polo shirt, did not look prepared for the cotton fields surrounding the house. Third he noticed Emmett's ring, an heirloom from his late father, silver with *LT* on it for *Louis Till*. Simeon really loved that ring and Emmett let him wear it for a few days. All the boys ran out to play. They fell into a timeless dreamscape. Country and blues music played from a Philco radio. Bobo wanted them to hear the hot new song out of Chicago and sang a few warbly bars of Bo Diddley. He showed off a Frankenstein comic book he'd brought from home.

They swam in the lake, going deep to touch the bottom, coming up with a handful of mud as proof. The water got colder the deeper they swam and the cool water felt good against the summer burn. Simeon showed him how to fish without tackle, putting bait in a glass jar and leaving it floating on the surface. The fish would go after the bait and be unable to reverse back to safety. The trick, Emmett learned, was to catch the jar once the fish got lodged inside. Back home they'd all listen to radio programs like *The Lone Ranger* and *Gunsmoke*. In the relative cool of late afternoon, they'd get the neighborhood kids and Maurice would drive the 1946 Ford sedan the three miles into Money to visit the stores. The Wright boys taught the Chicago boys how to buy bubble gum and candy from Bryant's Grocery, and everyone watched Maurice play checkers with soda bottle caps out on the front porch. A few days pass like lifetimes at a hot country crossroads. On Sunday they went to buy fireworks in Money and the local boys got terrified when Bobo set them off in town. Never do that again, they warned him. The white folks didn't like all that noise. Simeon and Emmett shared a bed and when the lights went out, Emmett told him about life in Chicago and the beautiful days of swimming and picnics at Lincoln Park.

On Monday morning, hot before sunrise, everyone including Emmett got up to go hit the fields. It was the first day of harvest and that energy of hope and competition filled the air. Emmett could feel it. He and Wheeler and Simeon got pulled from sleep by Moses's whistling and they ate grits, eggs, and bacon for breakfast. Moses had fed the hogs, watered the chickens, and milked the cow while they got themselves together.

"Let's go, boys," he told them.

They all knew what he was about to say next.

"The work ain't hard and the man ain't mean."

The crew left the house, biscuits in their pockets for later, dragging empty nine-foot sacks out to the field. They had twenty-five acres to pick. Two dollars for every hundred pounds. Wheeler and Emmett had begged to join them. The kids looked down at Emmett's feet and laughed. He was wearing penny loafers. It didn't take long for the novelty to wear off. Before 11:00 a.m., sweat poured down Emmett's face. Bobo moved slower and slower with each row and finished with just twenty-five pounds. That night he told Elizabeth Wright that he couldn't stand the heat.

After work they hung with kids from other plantations, from the O'Neal place out toward the East Money Church of God in Christ, and from the Carter place south of Money. A tractor driver from the Carter place tried to pick a fight and all the boys backed down and later Emmett scolded them for not defending their turf like he'd been taught to do in Chicago. Simeon, even at that age, saw his own meekness reflected in his cousin's boldness. Somehow he understood that he'd been trained to be quiet, and to hide himself, to be invisible. That shame would stick with him for a long time, and when he wrote about it six decades later in his memoir the hurt felt fresh.

The next day, Tuesday, Moses let Emmett stay home and help Elizabeth. Emmett, used to helping his mom, knew how to work the family's new Maytag washing machine. He picked vegetables from the garden with his aunt to help make supper. When his cousins got out of the field they all sat down for a meal.

It was Election Day and Moses followed the state and national elections. His favorite politician was Adlai Stevenson. "It never dawned on me that he couldn't vote," Simeon Wright would say. Moses hoped that the end of this virulent campaign might bring a little calm back to their world, which had been boiling for months. Afterward the kids raided a watermelon patch and each took one to the riverbank to eat. They busted them on the ground to get easier access to the sweeter part at the center. The juice ran down their faces. The next morning everyone but Emmett went back to the cotton fields. That evening, when the sun started to sink in the sky and the temperature dropped just enough to make folks feel human again, five or six of them piled into the 1946 Ford, a three-speed with first gear burned out. The plan was to go back to the little half-block downtown in Money. Less than twenty-four hours earlier, the closely contested governor's race had been won by J. P. Coleman, the guy my white textbook would call "a moderating force." Maurice got behind the wheel and followed the river into town, taking a left toward Bryant's, where the Yalobusha ran into the Little Tallahatchie. Simeon sat in the back seat next to Emmett and watched the sun slip from the sky just as they arrived in Money.

THAT SUMMER AND FALL *The Chicago Defender* ran letters from Black children all over the South who wanted pen pals. Hundreds of kids wrote in. One of them was Doris Jean Mosely. She was Emmett's age and lived on a rural road out from Vaughan, Mississippi, a little roadside dot on the edge of the Delta. She attended eighth grade at East Yazoo High. Her favorite things were dancing and baseball. Doris married Morey Moore. Her husband loved Christmas; people called him the Gingerbread Man. Every December he put out an elaborate light display, growing more elaborate with each passing year, until people from neighboring counties would ride out into the country to see it, directions spread by word of mouth until the paper finally printed them. His gravel road was two miles on the left from the antique store, if you were coming from Yazoo City. He died of lung cancer in November 1995 and that Christmas, his sons turned his lights on in tribute, and the cars came from all around to look at the glow of thirty thousand tiny bulbs. Morey Moore died two miles from where he was born. Doris still lives in their house. She's in her eighties.

THE KIDS GOT OUT of the car and walked up to the front porch of Bryant's Grocery: Emmett Till, Wheeler Parker, Maurice Wright, Simeon Wright, Ruthie Mae Crawford, and Roosevelt Crawford. All of them except Wheeler are dead now. Ruthie died just a few years ago. Wheeler told me the news. We both understood his unspoken meaning: *And then there was one.*

They knew they weren't supposed to be in Money. Moses had

promised Mamie, and Maurice, who didn't have a driver's license, had promised Moses. They were only supposed to go to the little country store out in East Money on the plantation. Never into Money itself. But now they were here, a little after 7:30 p.m. The sun was gone by the time they reached the porch, where other sharecropper kids played checkers.

In the coming weeks, when the details of a random teenage afternoon suddenly became national news, T.R.M. Howard would tell the story he'd heard. Outside the store with these new older boys Emmett bragged about how he went to school with white girls, and maybe even dated one, which is the kind of thing an insecure fourteen-year-old boy would say. He couldn't stand the heat enough to pick cotton, or wear the right clothes, and he looked pudgy and talked with a stutter, but he had something none of these country boys had, and he knew it and they knew it. He had Chicago. The other teenagers, Howard said, taunted him to go prove it and talk to that white woman in the store.

Wheeler and Simeon stood around the edge of the checkers game. Neither of them heard Emmett say anything about white girls or heard any of the other kids dare Emmett to go inside. Each would tell the story of these ninety seconds over and over for the rest of their lives, the frequency eclipsed only by the times they'd each silently replay it in their minds.

Their cousin Curtis Jones, whose mother hosted Moses Wright during his trip to Chicago, got interviewed about what happened on the porch during the famous *Eyes on the Prize* documentary that reintroduced the Till story to the country. He was the eyewitness on whose memory the story rested. Wheeler and Simeon, middle-aged men, watched the special on television. They heard the question and saw Curtis's face just before he answered. Both of them had the same reaction:

"He's about to start lying!"

They knew he was lying because Curtis hadn't been at the store with them. He didn't get into town until the next Saturday. Curtis told the story about dating white girls and even added a detail about Emmett showing off a photograph of his female white school friend. Simeon and Wheeler insisted, in hundreds of retellings each, that this never happened. T.R.M. Howard was also repeating a rumor that has been turned into fact by time and retelling.

Wheeler turned and walked into the store to get some soda.

The screen door creaked on the hinges, slow to open, fast to shut, with a couple of rebound slaps. People in the store could hear the conversation on the porch and people on the porch could hear the conversation in the store. A few seconds later, less than a minute, Emmett followed Wheeler inside. They shopped together for snacks.

Wheeler left the store and went back outside. He ate an ice cream cone. The only two people inside were Carolyn Bryant and Emmett Till.

Less than one minute passed. Maurice got worried and sent Simeon into the store.

Twelve days later the Memphis paper reported that a local man, Albert Johnson, who lived in Wheeler's hometown of Schlater, had intervened in the store and led Emmett out by the shoulder. Moses Wright said once that Johnson had been with the boys at the store. None of the other witnesses mentioned him.

A few minutes later Emmett and Simeon came out together. Just the two of them.

Wheeler looked up and clocked their exit.

"In America," Wheeler said at a podium one night a few years ago in Chicago, "we really embellish everything. . . . And so let's get back to the store."

He told the crowd that he knew how to talk to white people and not make them angry. The sirs and ma'ams, the meek eyes, the bent posture.

"It's something that he hadn't experienced," Wheeler said.

The moderator, Chris Benson, spoke.

"You can't have a crash course in hatred when you've only known love, right?"

"Exactly," Wheeler said.

"You don't think he had enough of that kind of awareness because he didn't live that reality?"

"He knew nothing about it," Wheeler said. "He had no way of knowing. No way of knowing. If you told him, he'd say, 'This makes no sense.'"

Ruthie Mae Crawford watched Emmett inside the store the whole time, she said later. She said she watched Emmett pay for his candy, never saying or doing anything else, and she saw him make a mistake. He put the money in Carolyn's hand, not on the counter. Their skin touched. That was forbidden and made Ruth worry.

Simeon Wright insisted more than fifty years later that Ruthie wasn't there at the store.

Simeon said he saw Emmett do nothing inappropriate. Big glass cases doubled as counters and the shopkeeper would get something either from the display or from the shelves behind her. The width of the countertop was too great for people to, say, hug.

Fifty years later Wheeler Parker sat on a panel at a college. Five scholars opined about Emmett Till. All had a take on what had happened, and why, and Wheeler just nodded along, impressed with the lofty ideas and beautiful language, the concise, powerful storytelling. Then came his turn to talk.

"I don't think I know this guy you guys are talking about," he said.

The energy in the room changed.

"It was beautiful but it wasn't accurate."

Wheeler looked out at the room. All these people taking the story and using it, often for good, but using it all the same. Changing details, fudging details, moving things around, making Emmett look better, or Carolyn look better, exaggerations, justifications, white lies, mistakes.

At the door Emmett told Carolyn Bryant, "Goodbye." He did not say "ma'am," according to Sheriff Smith and Maurice Wright. In the days before, Moses said, Emmett had delighted in not adopting that little soul-crushing bit of deference. Carolyn Bryant came rushing out of the store just after him, mad, headed to her sister-in-law's car parked alongside the store to get her gun. Every eyewitness agrees on what happened next.

Wheeler's more than eighty years old now, under stage lights as he tells his story yet again, answering questions again posed by Chris Benson, his most trusted moderator. "It's always painful for me to say I was not interviewed until thirty years later," Wheeler tells him, "and I was an eyewitness at the store. It's just mind-boggling."

Emmett whistled at Carolyn.

The rest happened fast.

"Boy, you know better than that," Maurice said.

Emmett didn't understand what was going on. Carolyn rushed to the car. Some witnesses said she'd already left to get her gun when he whistled. Others believe his whistle is what prompted her to want the gun in the first place. Everyone heard the whistle. All the boys looked at each other in fear and panic and then they ran, too. Emmett followed them. He limped a little from his bout of polio at age six. He wasn't laughing anymore. The kids dogpiled into the car and in his panic, Maurice dropped a lit cigarette on the floor. He frantically felt around for it as the other boys yelled at him to . . . *drive!*

"Let's go!" Till stuttered. "Let's go!"

THE BRYANTS WOULDN'T OWN the store in two months. All the sharecroppers in the area refused to shop there after the murder and the couple sold it to a local family, who in 1959 turned around and sold it again. The new owners, Bud Young and his wife, moved down from Paynes in the Hills, one of the tiny communities in the small circle of Tallahatchie County that produced the Milams and Bryants. They renamed the store after themselves. They operated it as the town of Money faded back into the dirt from which it was formed. They finally closed the doors in the early 1980s. By 1985 the place was abandoned. The Till juror Ray Tribble and his family bought the store (and much of the rest of the town over the next three decades) and just let it rot. The verdant grip of nature doesn't take long to strangle a place in Mississippi. The producers of *Eyes on the Prize* saw the decaying store as the center of a "haunted landscape." The porch fell in on itself in the early 1990s and a decade later the floors had rotted and collapsed. Hurricane Katrina ripped off the roof and wrecked part of an exterior wall. A few years later the Tribbles floated the idea of dismantling the store and selling each brick to Black people. Then the family, according to investigative journalist Jerry Mitchell, offered to sell it to Leflore County for $40 million. The family then lowered the ask to $4 million. Leflore countered with $50,000. Negotiations stopped at that point. The building continued to rot.

Mary Annette Morgan, a Tribble, helped lead a successful effort, culminating in 2014, to preserve the Ben Roy gas station next to the collapsing store. She said the restoration, which cost the state of Mississippi more than $200,000, would allow a visitors' center for the civil rights tourists who came to find the old Bryant's Grocery. They'd show the segregated bathrooms as the only nod toward the Delta's strict caste system. A source with the Mississippi Department of Archives and History (MDAH) told author Dave Tell that the state knew the gas station didn't really have any historical value but took a gamble that this act of engagement would bring the Tribble family to the table for the grocery. So the money got approved and spent.

In fact, the "renovated" gas station does not mark the segregated bathrooms. It revels in the fictional nostalgia of a racially harmonious Delta. The finished building, which has never been unlocked on any of the dozens of trips I've made to Money, does not mention Emmett Till or what happened at the shell of a grocery store next door. According to people who've been inside, the store is full of midcentury artifacts from rural life. When the family filled out the grant application, they stressed how the project would reflect "an era in the history of Mississippi," and in a way it does. It reflects the fictional history taught to folks like Mary Annette, and Jeff Andrews, and me. The application described the jukebox that once played the latest hits on the porch where white and Black people came together to share the communion of music. The "step back in time to the summer of 1955" the family promised on the application was a trip into a parallel universe of erasure. If you drive to

Money right now, there is a perfectly restored gas station designed to show how everybody got along back then, standing next to the collapsed wreck of a store where a fourteen-year-old boy whistled at a white woman and got tortured to death by a decorated combat veteran for it. Both are owned by the same family. As Dave Tell wrote, "While Bryant's Grocery stands as an indictment of the Delta, Ben Roy's is an apology for it. Thus we have nostalgia and ruins 67 feet apart from each other."

The old doors to the store are in a museum. Some people think the Tribble family has all sorts of artifacts, like the cases and the cash register, sitting in dusty storage. I've thought a lot about the family's motivations. Their decision to let the building rot has created its own kind of monument, more powerful than anything an architect could design. Ray Tribble was a juror who made a decision and would have faded into the background of this story. The actions of his family since his death have tied his decision to their decisions and made the store a metaphor for the way Mississippi has tried to stop time. A German student not long ago suggested to Weems her idea to interpret the store. Instead of buying it and fixing it up, just let it rot. Then build a statue across the street of Moses Wright standing in the witness box and pointing with his long finger at the wreck of a store, as if to say: *See.*

See the store in winter when it looks like a tomb from some recently rediscovered civilization. See it in summer when the poetic vines and trees grow from this bloody dirt so that it looks like a vaguely store-shaped tree. You might drive this way a hundred times without noticing the flashes of brick and splintered wood, without knowing a building stood here. This store had a Coca-Cola sign out front, and a big wooden porch, where a boy once whistled and then fled in a speeding car with his cousin Maurice behind the wheel. Emmett begged his cousins not to tell his uncle what had happened. He didn't want to get sent home.

As the days passed, the boys forgot about their fear. They would go to the fields to pick and go out to play once the work ended at sunset. Payday came. Simeon made fifteen dollars. Wheeler made eight. Emmett made four. They got busy with the usual Saturday search for rides into Greenwood. They wanted to go hang out on Johnson Street. These late-summer evenings in cotton railroad towns carried with them the warm glow of late boyhood. Emmett had never been to a juke joint street on a country Saturday night. Simeon and his friend John Crawford rode together to see a western at either the Dixie Theatre or the Walthall Theatre. Maurice, Emmett, Wheeler, and Roosevelt Crawford were not interested in a western. They wanted to meet girls. They went up and down the street, looking into the juke joints and seeing the shadows of dancers through the smoke. Johnson Street hummed with noise and smells. Vendors sold hot tamales and fried fish, ice cream cones and foot-long hot dogs.

Emmett and Wheeler walked the few blocks south across the railroad tracks to McLaurin Street, a wild strip of bars, pool halls, and underground casinos. They had no business in this part of town. On this Saturday night Emmett and his cousins found the nerve to walk into the Blue Light Tavern. Then they all piled back into the car and went to a house party on the Four-Fifths Plantation. Folks gambled and danced and drank moonshine corn whiskey. Simeon Wright and Wheeler Parker sat around one day in Chicago and talked about those last few hours of innocence.

"Four-Fifths," Wheeler said.

"Juke joint," Simeon said.

"It's still there," Wheeler said.

"It's dangerous over there," Simeon said. "Man, you guys . . ."

"We got some white lightning on Four-Fifths Plantation. Got home twelve thirty Saturday night."

The drive back to Moses's house from the party took them down a pitch-black gravel road. They turned right on Sunny Side Road and then made a quick left on Money Road by Bryant's Grocery, which was closed for the night. From the railroad tracks it was three miles home. Maurice ran over a dog in the 1946 Ford. Emmett begged Maurice to stop and let him check on the animal but Maurice refused. They kept driving. Emmett began to cry. He loved dogs. Nobody else said a word.

JOHNSON STREET IS ABANDONED NOW, boarded up, and early one morning as a dog wandered around in traffic, I sat next to Wheeler Parker, who was driving his navy-blue Mercedes-Benz sedan.

"This is the last place Emmett Till and I went," he said as his eyes searched the abandoned storefronts and his memories conjured them whole again. "Right here on Johnson Street."

He can still see it all like it was during Emmett's final few hours alive.

"This was it," he said.

His wife, Marvel, sat in the back of the car with their friend Therese Anderson. Therese and her husband, Dallis, are the Parkers' faithful friends and traveling companions and, more than anyone else, make sure Wheeler can move around the country to share his story. On this day, Therese wanted to go out into the country and visit her father's grave for the first time since his funeral. So we all met at a hotel downtown and headed out of town. Our first or second turn took us back into the last night of Emmett's life. Mississippi is full of trapdoors for Wheeler. Once he walked into the old drugstore in Sumner in the Delta and it felt so much like 1955 he immediately turned to leave. These moments sneak up on him. Like Johnson Street. Sometimes it's like he's narrating a movie only he can see.

He turned on Highway 49 East, which cut south into the fields. We passed an abandoned cotton gin on the left and then the big cotton warehouses.

"Time for another crop almost," Wheeler said.

Marvel asked what was growing on both sides of the road.

"Soybeans," he answered quickly.

Marvel beamed.

"He can tell everything," she said.

"At one time I could," he said.

They both still love Mississippi. They strongly, strongly dislike— Wheeler will not say hate—what happened here, but the pull of home only gets stronger with time. *Nostalgia* comes from the Greek words for homecoming and pain. Marvel always fills their trunk with hickory wood to use in their smoker back home. She loves local watermelon and loves it when I bring her hot tamales from Clarksdale or sweet corn from our farm in Shelby. She loves magnolia leaves. Three or four times they tried to plant magnolia trees in Argo but they never took.

Wheeler has lived many lives since walking Johnson Street with Emmett and Maurice. He joined the army and got stationed in Nuremburg. He went to stand in the public spaces where Hitler gave his speeches and he understood. His family continues to suffer the aftershocks of 1955. Some part of Maurice died that night. He drifted away from the family. Twenty years after the murder a family member accused Maurice in a Black history journal of telling Roy Bryant out of jealousy what Emmett had said to Carolyn. Simeon and Wheeler said over and over that was absurd, that there really wasn't a way for that to have happened: all the boys were together all the time that week. Wheeler felt like the unfounded accusation somehow sped up the shame spiral and pulled Maurice down. Once Simeon went out to California and found him living on the streets. Maurice didn't want to come home. He died on the streets of San Francisco the day after Christmas in 1991. He was taken to the morgue and in his pocket the coroner found his only possession: a piece of paper with a phone number for Simeon Wright, Argo, Illinois. The medical examiners called. A heartbroken Simeon flew out to San Francisco. He went to the morgue where a stranger pulled out a long metal tray. Simeon looked down and nodded and then brought his brother home.

We crossed the Holmes County line. Rows of corn joined the soybeans. A recent rain had left standing water in the soybean fields, drowning the crops just at harvest.

"You see how flat it is?" Wheeler said as he drove. "Get you a cotton row and go as far as the eye can see."

Wheeler's dad was 55 percent white. Wheeler is 24 percent. His dad was closer in blood to the men who took Emmett than to Emmett. That's flat-earth logic. Wheeler quoted Langston Hughes as he drove. Flat earth. None of this strange place makes sense until you understand how the land came to be so empty, and drained, and full of ghosts. He remembers what the sun felt like, what the sack felt like pulling from behind. He remembers his cousin being ripped from bed in the middle of the night.

"Nobody kills like America," Wheeler said as he drove. "We're raised on violence."

I GOT A PADDED MAILER at my house and tore it open to find a thumb drive. On it was Carolyn Bryant's embargoed and unpublished memoir. An anonymous source had mailed it to me. Carolyn was in hospice care by then, dying with family in Louisiana while protesters searched for her in Raleigh, North Carolina, and Bowling Green, Kentucky, two places she'd recently lived. These were her words from the grave, since she'd wanted this book to be published only after she died.

I flipped immediately to the part about the evening of the whistle.

She worked that day in the store, she said, watching their little boys, angry at Roy for slipping off to get a load of shrimp down on the coast. Delta men have, for generations, slipped off to party on the beach under the guise of bringing a load of seafood back north. When I was a boy, the Clarksdale airport buzzed with single-engine airplanes headed down to the coast to get croaker sacks of oysters.

So she spent her day beneath the rack of cigarette packs at the front counter, next to the cold drink cooler and the ice cream freezer. The store opened at 6:00 a.m., for the farmers, and closed at 10:00 p.m., for workers who'd been out in the hot sun all day. Gamblers came in during the day to sit at the slot machine in the back. She worked the counter until the sun went down. It wasn't light out, she wrote, but it wasn't really dark, either, when she first noticed the kids congregating outside. Emmett came inside and went straight to the candy counter. She went over to help him and got the candy he ordered. When she held out her hand for the money, she said he grabbed her hand and said, "Don't be afraid of me, I've been with white girls before."

She said his grip was strong.

"How about a date, baby," she said he said.

She said she felt fear for herself and for her children. She said she ran to get Roy's pistol as he grinned. Now she was in the open space. She said he grabbed her hips and said, "What's the matter, baby, can't you take it?"

She said she struggled free from his grasp.

"You needn't be afraid of me," she claimed he said. "I've fucked white women before."

She said she screamed.

She said she was shaking all over as she tried to jerk free. Just at that moment another "young man," she wrote, pulled Emmett off her and they left the store. She realized the pistol was in the car parked outside, so she said she ran out to get it. That's when he whistled, and as she rushed to get the gun, she wrote, the boys got into a tan luxury car and sped away.

THAT'S ALL A LIE. There are about a dozen different ways to prove it. Because Emmett stuttered too badly to say any of that, and because if she'd screamed, there were a lot of people within earshot, and because they didn't drive a luxury car, and because the screens allowed every word spoken inside to be heard on the porch, and because, perhaps most of all, her story kept changing. Her own sister-in-law didn't believe her and thought she invented the story to make Roy jealous enough that he'd never leave on one of these shrimp expeditions again. The story she wrote in her book is the one she told on the witness stand. That's not how she told the story until the defense lawyers got involved in shaping her testimony.

Two and a half weeks before she went on the stand she'd sat with her husband's attorneys in Sumner and told a different version, without the hip grabbing and without him talking about sex. She said she told Roy herself on Friday morning. The attorneys took notes, which ended up being discovered in an Ohio State archive a half century later, along with lots of other paperwork that revealed that most of what the public learned about the case, at trial, and in the famous *Look* magazine story that followed, had been invented by the lawyers to protect their clients first, and then to protect segregation itself generally, and to make sure Leslie Milam and his barn got written out of the history, since he remained vulnerable to prosecution. She sat in the Breland & Whitten law office in between the railroad tracks and the Sumner courthouse and described the events. That law office stands today with its long-dead founders' names still painted on the window.

She kept silent for decades.

"She could clear up a lot of stuff," Wheeler said once.

"If she'd just come clean," Till author Devery Anderson replied.

"It would have been over," Simeon said.

Once Wheeler signed up for an Ole Miss literary tour of the Delta. They all rode together through Greenwood as a guide narrated, not knowing Wheeler's history. He was just another anonymous literature lover who wanted to learn. They passed a simple house with three NO TRESPASSING signs in the yard. Wheeler pressed against the window in shock when the guide said casually that Carolyn Bryant lived there. He just stared at the house as they passed. He wanted so badly to knock and ask why she had lied. But Carolyn said nothing to anyone, not even to family, until she got old and started to watch friends and family die around her.

Through her daughter-in-law, Marsha, she got in touch with a writer and Duke professor named Tim Tyson. Carolyn gave Tyson her manuscript, which he appears to have edited, according to correspondence and marked-up pages. Tyson wrote in his book *The Blood of Emmett Till* that she recanted her testimony to him during an interview, which happened before he'd set up his recorder. He didn't tell anyone for nearly a decade until his book came out. His claim led the FBI to reinvestigate the case, again, and to think seriously for the first time about prosecuting Carolyn Bryant. Once the FBI got involved, though, Tyson's claims started to fall apart. A source said the FBI even considered prosecuting him for perjury before just letting it go. The FBI told Wheeler Parker that the Bureau did not believe Tyson, who has maintained that his account of the interaction was accurate. Wheeler called Tyson dishonest and has written about the pain that flicker of hope and vindication had caused him all these years later.

Carolyn's book should be taken with skepticism, but here's how she described what happened when Roy returned home on Friday. He walked into the store that afternoon, she wrote. They ate supper and put the kids to sleep. The next morning they ate breakfast. Roy snapped at a Black child in the store who didn't say "Yes, sir."

She worried he knew.

That night they smoked cigarettes at the kitchen table.

Then he asked how everything "really" went while he was out of town.

"Fine," she said. He knew she was lying. She could tell. The only person she'd told was Juanita Milam.

"I think you have something you need to tell me," Roy said.

"I don't."

"Oh, yes you do. I want to hear it now."

She kept quiet while Roy began telling *her* what had happened. As he narrated, he began screaming and the main thing he raged about was finding out from someone else. Little men always worry first about their pride. Scared men worry about how other men judge them. It's universal. Finally they fell asleep, until a loud banging in the middle of the night awoke them both.

Carolyn said she heard it first and flipped on the light.

She shook her husband awake and Roy pulled on his pants and yelled at the door. J.W. answered him and Roy went outside to talk. She said she couldn't hear the conversation. Roy came back inside with a "tone" and grabbed his pistol. She denied going with them, and denied identifying Till later, even though Moses Wright testified that he heard a woman's voice in the darkness and saw a Black man. Many believe that Black man was Johnny Washington, who hung around the Bryant store.

Johnny Washington left Money for good not long after the incident. Run out of town by the Black citizens is how Wheeler Parker and Simeon Wright described it. Moses Wright believed Washington told Milam and Bryant where Emmett was staying and accompanied them when they stepped outside that night. Nobody could ever prove it. Washington died in exile and the only reason people knew was because his wife received a life insurance check. They never divorced, according to Simeon Wright. Dale Killinger, the FBI agent, went to interview Washington's widow in her home in the Baptist Town neighborhood of Greenwood, not far from where Emmett, Wheeler, and Maurice had gone clubbing on that last boyhood Saturday night. She dodged his questions and he sensed she knew more than she was letting on. Finally he asked directly.

"Where was he that night?"

She turned away from him in shame and faced the wall.

J.W. AND ROY BOTH WORRIED about how their neighbors would judge them if they didn't do something, Carolyn Bryant wrote, if they didn't act like all the politicians urged them to act. The only thing that separated men like Milam and Bryant in their minds from the very bottom of society was their skin color and that was a fragile protection. Wealthy white people looked right through them so long as they didn't need a tractor repaired. It ate at them. If word spread of the insult they'd be judged harshly. The status quo depended on the dirty work being done out of sight.

There was also another terrible creation of the caste system working on Milam and Bryant, mixing with their tempers and their own rage about the station of their lives. Black folks so internalized Jim Crow that they came to expect violence from white men like Milam, and to judge them cowards if they weren't capable of administering it. Florida State grad student Hugh Whitaker wrote in 1963 that Roy felt compelled to do something because Black people in Money "had begun to talk because he didn't 'deal with the Chicago boy.'"

CAROLYN BRYANT WOULD FEEL FOLLOWED, hounded, for the rest of her life. She wrote that she, too, was a victim. And she insisted in her memoir that she had been justified. What kind of person carries a lie to the grave? That's what I kept wondering with each page of the memoir. Killinger spent time with FBI profilers before interviewing her and they all agreed that his chances of breaking her were slim because when a lie gets told that many times for that many years, the person telling the lie believes it. The story becomes memory, the memory becomes truth. That same emotional process protects modern white Mississippi. There is a story we were taught, me and Jeff Andrews and Mary Annette Morgan, handed down like tablets by every person of authority in our lives. We believe in the goodness of the people we love. We believe our ancestors must have shared our values because of the blood we share, and the land we share. We believe so that we might get up in the morning and walk into the light. But we know. Somewhere inside we know. Even Roy Bryant knew he'd done something unforgivable. Four years after 1955, their daughter Carolann was born. She wouldn't talk and Roy and Carolyn got worried. Carolyn took her to a doctor, who did an examination and broke the news. Their little girl was completely deaf. Carolyn took this news home and waited on Roy to finish work. He got home and poured himself a cup of coffee. Back then he still looked like the Roy Bryant from the news photos and not the broken shell of a human he'd become in his bleak final years. She told him the news.

He pushed his coffee away and tears started rolling down his face.

"The Lord is punishing her for what I did," he said.

Over and over he said that, the words coming out in repeated jumbles.

"I'm being punished and she's being punished for what I did."

He was sobbing now.

"It's my fault."

"It's my fault."

"It's my fault."

"It's my fault."

MOSES WRIGHT LIVED three miles down the road on the right. It was around 2:00 a.m. J. W. Milam drove. Roy rode with him. Two or three Black field hands rode in the back; though the eyewitness accounts don't agree, the two men most commonly identified as unwilling accomplices are Too Tight Collins and Henry Lee Loggins. Milam and Bryant parked the two-tone Chevy truck in Wright's yard. J.W. carried a five-cell flashlight in his left hand and his Ithaca .45 in his right.

Roy got to the front door and called Moses's nickname.

"Preacher!"

"Who is it?"

"This is Mr. Bryant."

"Yes, sir," Wright said and opened the door.

"I want that boy who did the talking down at Money," Bryant said.

He and J.W. stepped inside. A third man, who Moses thought was Black, stayed outside trying to cover his face. "He always said there was another person there," Simeon Wright would say. "He thought it was a Black man. He acted like a Black man."

The white men wanted lights but Moses told them the lights didn't work. By that time Elizabeth was awake. J.W. told her to shut up and get back in bed. Said he wanted to hear the springs creak. Roy wouldn't say another word. This was Milam's show now. The two brothers moved through the house. The first room they entered was where Wheeler slept. He didn't hear them come in.

"The one thing about when death is imminent," Wheeler Parker would say, "is you think about all the bad things you ever done, I don't know why. I think the Lord is trying to get you to get your life together. I started pleading with God and bargaining and begging. At sixteen you're not trying to die. I'm begging for life and shaking like a leaf on a tree and it's darker than a thousand midnights. You couldn't see the hand in front of your face and you've got the talking. Then all of a sudden, they're coming my way."

They shined the flashlight in Wheeler's face. He saw the light and the gun.

THIS IS A STORY WHEELER PARKER would tell hundreds of times, each one at a tiny cost to him, but he got to where he could do it on autopilot. Almost breezy, the result of years of calluses forming. But as the talk of monuments and memorials heated up in 2021, he got asked to record an oral history. He knew he was near the end of his life and that this version of the story would live on after him. The rolling tape held his dream of people never forgetting.

"I closed my eyes. They went to the next room and they found Emmett in the third room. They took Emmett. . . . He had no idea who he was dealing with or where he was at and, uh . . ."

Parker's voice cracked and he started to fight off tears.

"I'm reliving this too much," he said. "I'm reliving it too deep."

A friend sitting nearby had never heard him break down before, not in a decade of watching him tell the story. They sat in the church where Wheeler preached in Argo. He struggled to gain his composure and asked the film crew to forgive him.

MOSES SAID WHEELER wasn't the right boy. One room over and in the bed with Emmett, Simeon heard voices. The men went through the next room, where Curtis slept, and into Simeon's room, where Simeon and Emmett shared a bed. Simeon looked up into the bright circle of the flashlight. He rubbed his eyes and shielded them and Milam demanded he go back to sleep.

Emmett didn't wake up immediately.

Moses shook him.

J.W. demanded Emmett get dressed. That's when Simeon realized they were taking him. He felt terror. Elizabeth came into the room and begged them to leave the boy. Simeon heard the fear in her voice. She wept and pleaded. Years later Simeon would describe her as half talking to them and half praying to God. A room or two over, Curtis slept through it all. A tough man, he would later serve as a Chicago cop.

"I always thought if Curtis had woken up," Wheeler Parker would say, "there probably would have been some shooting. He wanted to stay there and wait for them to come back. He was ready to do war."

"He wasn't afraid," Simeon said.

Moses kept a 12-gauge and a .410 shotgun in a closet but never made a move to get them. There's no way he could have gotten a shot off against the armed intruders.

Milam spoke in the dark.

"Are you the n—— who did the smart talk up at Money?"

"Yeah," Emmett said.

"Don't you 'yeah' me, n——. I'll blow your head off. You say, 'Yes, sir.'" Emmett dressed sitting on the side of the bed. It was dark except for the swinging flashlight beams. Moses told them to just take him outside and whip him. Elizabeth begged and cried as they took Emmett away. She offered the intruders money. Then Moses tried to find out where they were taking him.

"Nowhere if he's not the right one," Milam said.

Milam looked hard at Wright.

"How old are you?"

"Sixty-four."

"Well, if you know any of us here tonight, then you will never live to get to be sixty-five."

Then they left.

Elizabeth Wright ran next door and begged to use their white neighbors' phone. The Chamblees. My mom taught one of their relatives. The wife wanted to help but her husband said no. Wheeler and Simeon stayed frozen in the darkness, terrified to move or speak. Robert and Maurice and Curtis still slept soundly. Wheeler put on his shoes and decided if the men returned, he was running out back into the woods to hide.

"It was horrible," he said. "It seemed like day would never come."

WHEELER WAS STILL EMOTIONAL as the camera kept rolling on the oral history project. He alone carries this memory now, the whole family standing on his shoulders. That responsibility weighs heavy on him. He composed himself.

"They left with him and that was the last time I saw him alive," he said.

He's replayed that night over and over.

Once he told me he thinks about it every day.

"See, I wouldn't have gone," he said. "I probably would've gotten killed because I knew where I was at and I knew what I was dealing with. He had no idea. They said they were going to bring him back, but . . . that didn't happen."

NOTHING ABOUT THIS HOME invasion was unique. White people could go into Black homes with impunity and often did. It's why Marvel's dad left Mississippi in 1938. The only thing different about Emmett Till's death was that the world bore witness.

The house stood in a little bunch of trees, with a road out front and cotton fields in back. It's gone now. A tornado destroyed it in February of 1971. It was a strange storm. The winter temperature spiked. Daffodils bloomed early along the bayou. Skies darkened to black in late afternoon. Then the temperature plummeted to the thirties and a strong wind blew across the fields. The tornado crossed the Yazoo River south of the juke joint where Robert Johnson played his last show, which a different tornado had erased twenty-nine years earlier, headed almost directly over his grave and passed across the Money Road straight toward Moses Wright's house. The funnel cloud destroyed the home and then lifted it off the ground and away into the air, wiping the scene of this kidnapping from the face of the earth, leaving behind the metal barns just to the east and the other home just to the west.

Outside the house in East Money the last moments of the kidnapping played out. Milam's truck was about twenty-five feet from the front door. Moses didn't see the third man, who'd been hiding his face. One of the kidnappers asked someone in the dark if this was the "right one," and a voice said yes. Moses said it was a woman's voice. He believed until his dying day that the voice in the truck was Carolyn Bryant's voice. Milam supposedly told an interviewer named Bonnie Blue that Carolyn had been in the truck and got dropped off in Money immediately afterward. The men put Emmett in the back bed of the truck and drove with the headlights off back toward Money. Carolyn wrote in her memoir that she had not been at the house but instead J.W. and Roy had brought Emmett to the store for her to identify.

Dale Killinger believes that at the store in Money Emmett jumped out of the truck and tried to escape. One of the Black accomplices brought him back. One account, by writer Bonnie Blue, said Emmett begged for his mother and said he wanted to go home. J. W. Milam's Black employee and alleged forced accomplice, Too Tight Collins, yelled at him and made him stay put, riding through the Delta by the light of a full moon. The next four hours were known only to the people in that pickup truck, and all of them are dead now.

Moses Wright stood silent outside his home for a long time, staring west toward town.

THEY TOOK HIM to the barn.

August 28, 1955, sunrise. Township 22 North, Range 4 West, Section 2.

Within sight of Willie Reed, who became Willie Louis, who stood on this same land as an old man.

In the shadow of the mounds at Walford.

Destruction was coming.

The end of the boy. And of the world the murderers killed to protect.

Emmett Till cried for his mama in the last hour.

And she somehow heard him.

The killers smelled of whiskey and sweat.

Grown men. Soldiers once.

They laughed about what they'd done to his body.

7.5 bird shot fired from a .45 automatic.

The crepe-soled shoes he put on in the hurried dark of a strange room were never found.

WHO WAS AT THE BARN?

Emmett Till was there.

J. W. Milam was there.

Roy Bryant was there.

Leslie Milam was there.

Carolyn Bryant told her family that her brother-in-law Melvin Campbell was there and she claimed he actually pulled the trigger.

Too Tight Collins was there.

Henry Lee Loggins was there.

J. W. Milam told an acquaintance that a man named Hugh Clark was there.

After the murder Carolyn let it slip that an associate of Roy and J.W. named Elmer Kimbell was there.

I went to the New Orleans home of the secretive but influential Till researcher Plater Robinson, who has thirty years of interviews he's never released, including many with now-dead primary sources.

"But Kimbell had a boy, didn't he?" he asked me.

"Did you talk to him?"

"No, but I think that he was there that night."

"You think he brought his son?"

"I do," he said.

Filmmaker Keith Beauchamp claimed that as many as fourteen people were there. Willie Reed said he saw seven people with Emmett in the truck. Three in the back. Four in the front. Any one of them could have stopped the murder.

Just as the barn is a place that stores Black trauma, it is also a vault for white secrets. Whenever I found myself there, I would wonder what knowledge was held by these cypress walls, made from boards sawed, sanded, and planed from the trees cut down to make room for the cotton fields. I've been to the barn maybe a hundred times now. Once I went out there before sunrise on the anniversary of the murder: August 28, 2021. A year later there'd be the first-ever public acknowledgment that the barn existed. But now, in the hot mosquito darkness, ETIC museum director Ben Saulsberry and I looked at each other and then at the far west side of the barn.

"A child was murdered here," he said. "On the other hand, how many other places have we walked around in the Delta where . . ."

"You start playing around with Mississippi, like how far away from right here is far enough?"

"Yeah."

"Were your parents or grandparents alive in fifty-five?"

"My mother was five years old when the Emmett Till tragedy took place," he told me.

"Have you ever asked her about it?"

"Oh, yeah."

"What'd she say?"

"I remember her saying she was really young and she really couldn't grasp all of that. But she could absolutely remember how nervous and scared she was for her brothers coming home at night.

And she said she could pinpoint this tragedy to that anxiety. She wasn't able to settle until all four of her brothers came home."

IN THE HOURS AFTER the kidnapping, Moses Wright got a friend to drive him to the Bryants' store in Money. They parked and walked to the door on the side. Wright knocked. Sundays moved slowly in these little railroad depot towns. Nobody came to answer but Moses got this strange feeling like somebody was there. He knocked again and waited.

"They're not here," Moses said finally.

They both knew then. Moses started to drive through the country to look under bridges and on the banks of rivers and bayous. He wasn't looking for a living boy. Curtis Jones went to landowner Grover Frederick's home to make a long-distance call. Jones rang his mother, Willie Mae, who knew she was about to have the hardest conversation of her life. She needed to tell Mamie that Bobo was missing.

"I don't know how to tell you this," she began.

All she could say at first was his name.

"Bo."

Mamie's blood rushed to her head.

"Bo what?" she asked.

Willie Mae told her and burst into tears. She sobbed so hard Mamie couldn't ask questions because she couldn't understand the answers. Time for Mamie stopped and would never start back again. *Missing in Mississippi? Oh, my God. Oh, dear Lord, no. Please, no.* Mamie didn't know what to do, so she called her mama. Alma begged Mamie to get to her as quick as she could. They'd face this together as a family. Gene readied the car. Mamie picked up

Emmett's watch and put it on her wrist. After a mile she yelled at Gene for driving too slow and made him trade places. Alma wasn't hysterical like everyone else. She was just silent. Willie Mae came with more information. Emmett had whistled at a white woman.

Mamie contacted the newspapers.

The reporters arrived and Mamie told them her son was missing in Money, Mississippi. She looked at her silent mother and realized Alma had already given up. White men in the middle of the night meant death. Mamie hung on to her hope. She'd been so young when she and her family left Mississippi. News spread through the far-flung community of Black Mississippi expats in urban centers around the industrial Midwest. Newspapers reported on the missing child. A friend of the family, Rayfield Mooty, who'd gotten to know Bobo around town, ran the local steelworkers' union. He came to the house and found Mamie with tears and mucus running down her face as she heaved and struggled to speak.

This annoyed Moody, who didn't yet know the news.

"Just blow your nose and stop crying," he said.

"They took Emmett," she said.

"Emmett? Who's Emmett?"

"My son!" she said. "Emmett Till."

It occurred to her then that most people didn't know his full name.

"Mr. Mooty," she said, "that's Bobo."

She said his face "lost all expression" and he did not say a word in reply. Mooty simply swiveled and practically fled from the room. He was gone a long time. Maybe ten minutes. Then he returned, tears visible just barely beneath the surface. The Chicago steelworkers went to war for Bobo. Mooty got on the phone and mobilized serious people with serious power. Before long they'd activated the Chicago political machine and brought pressure to bear. The governor of Illinois called the governor of Mississippi.

Back in the Delta, Crosby Smith, Emmett Till's great-uncle, took all the information his sister, Elizabeth Wright, gave him and went to tell Leflore County sheriff George Smith.

The sheriff heard the story and turned to his deputy.

"Don't you reckon that's Bryant and Milam?" he asked. "They done something like that in Glendora once."

Up in Chicago the entire community packed into the Argo Church of God in Christ to have a prayer vigil. Word had reached Argo that morning in time for the preacher to tell the congregation from the pulpit. Mamie and her mother rallied support.

Moses drove his wife to her brother's house in Sumner early that morning. She'd leave the state for good in a few days. Her brother Crosby rode back to Money with Moses. They took up positions on the front porch of Moses's place in East Money and waited for a car to bring Emmett back. The younger boys watched them in silence. The men waited for hours, staring at the road and praying a car would come kicking up dust down the road.

"Not even a dog walked past that house," Crosby said later.

A crowd slowly gathered at Moses Wright's place in East Money, people flocking from the little plantations along Dark Fear Road. The mood was despondent. Simeon Wright wrote: "August 28, 1955 had been the longest day of my life. It was the first day there was no laughter in our house."

Simeon and Robert were hidden with a neighbor named Clint Lewis. They owned a homestead way back deep in the country. A group of families held down this part of Leflore County, just down from the Hills, where Greenwood LeFlore himself had lived and was buried. The Wrights, the Seaberrys, the Purnells, the Tidwells, the Loves, the Lewises. These were old Delta names, linked to white and Black families—all tied to common ancestors at some point.

Moses Wright stayed behind to guard the house alone. Two days later, on Tuesday, Simeon and Robert saw their dad's bravery and decided they felt safer with him than with the neighbors. They wanted to be brave, too.

Up in Chicago, a subtle but real fault line broke open in the family. The night of the kidnapping, Moses Wright's house had been full of people. Kids of various ages slept beneath his roof. Emmett Till was the only one not related by blood to Moses. Moses would carry that guilt with him forever, and no matter how many times Mamie said she didn't blame anyone, the feeling lingered inside the family that Wright wouldn't have let those men take one of his own. Of course he'd had a gun trained on him the whole time and would have been dead before he got halfway to his own weapon. But the guilt remained.

The murder destroyed the close-knit East Money community. The families who'd been there since Reconstruction and the cotton boom left. They sent their teenage boys away first. The murder sped up the last wave of the Great Migration from the Delta. Even Grover Frederick, who'd lived in East Money since 1897, left four years after the murder.

"Mechanization hadn't hit them yet in fifty-five," Simeon Wright said. "After the Emmett Till trial a lot of the teenagers left. A lot of families left the South. They were forced in the area we lived in to buy cotton pickers."

The search continued, everyone in Chicago and Mississippi hoping for a happy ending. For a brief moment, those prayers and hopes looked like they were coming true. Mamie walked into her mother's house to hear incredible news. The Chicago Police Department had called Alma's three times to tell them Emmett had been released, found, and put on a train home. A miracle! One she needed to hear for herself. So she called the police and got transferred around until someone broke the news. There had been no official call to Alma's and no discovery in Mississippi. It was a cruel hoax. She didn't know it then but her son's dead body was already beneath the brown, slow water of the Tallahatchie River.

WITH NO SIGN OF EMMETT, Willie Mae Jones made a second phone call to Wheeler's mom and dad. She told them to get their son home immediately. The Parkers realized they had family nearby. The plan was to get Wheeler on the first train headed north to Chicago. An uncle, William Parker, lived on his farm a few miles outside the little town of Duck Hill. He owned his own land, which made his place a citadel. The Winona station was just a few miles away. They all got in the Ford, with Maurice driving, and took Wheeler to William's house. I've made that drive with Wheeler's cousin and William's daughter, Joy Parker.

"Do you remember him showing up at your house?"

"Oh, yes," Joy said. "Of course I do."

We drove together eight miles down Highway 404 out from Duck Hill. Joy said she likes the Hills more than the Delta. It feels safer up there than down in the cauldron below.

Wheeler's dad begged his brother, "Get my son safe to me," and William Parker took that as a request from God himself.

"I'm going to do it," he said.

"He did it," Joy said to me.

Wheeler arrived in Duck Hill late in the afternoon. William

Parker immediately drove him to Winona, in his 1954 green-and-white Chevrolet Bel Air, to catch the train. They arrived too late and had to return. A very long night awaited them all. Joy remembers the tension. Everyone listened for the sound of a car rolling slowly over the gravel road to the house. There was no reason for anyone to happen upon them. Headlights meant trouble. Joy went and slipped into bed between her parents. She could hear Wheeler pacing the house all night long, moving back and forth to the windows so he could peer out into the darkness. She heard his footsteps reach the door of her parents' bedroom.

Wheeler came inside.

"Uncle William," he asked, "is it time for me to go?"

"Oh, no, boy. No, boy. Go on back in there and go to bed."

Wheeler walked away and paced some more.

He came back and asked again.

"Uncle William," he asked, "is it time for me to go?"

"Oh, no, boy."

He paced some more and returned.

"Uncle William," he asked, "is it time for me to go?"

"Oh, no, boy."

Joy won't ever forget how scared he sounded when he spoke. "I told Daddy later, I said, 'Daddy, we should've been up praying and hugging Wheeler,'" she said. "Dad, being that old, he didn't understand the fear."

They lived on a hill. They had three porches, a dining room, a kitchen, and three bedrooms. The first room inside the door belonged to her parents. That's where they burned firewood to heat the house. For a while their grandfather moved in with them. He was William and Wheeler Sr.'s dad. Mittie Parker. He'd been born in 1878 a few miles over in Lodi, south of Alva in the backwoods, the son of an enslaved man. A family of white Parkers lived in Alva, which is probably where they got their name. Judge Samuel Parker started buying land from the federal government in 1840, moving into the space left behind by the Choctaw removal. Township 20 North, Range 7 East. The white Parkers came from Alabama, and their parents had been born in North Carolina, a standard genealogy for a Mississippian. A lot of the Black Parkers had very light skin. Mittie died in 1954, a year and a few months before the long night when Wheeler came briefly into their lives.

William Parker built a bubble around his family.

"He was a man," Joy said. "And his home was his glory, okay?"

All four of his daughters went to college, paid for out of William Parker's cotton patch. Joy got a master's degree from Michigan State. Her sister, Gladiola, rose through the corporate ranks to run a New York City hospital.

"They named a wing of the hospital in Queens, New York, after her," she said.

Joy loves to brag on her sister.

"Coming from the cotton field of Duck Hill, Mississippi."

Joy and I rode down Highway 404, the mother road of the white and Black Parkers of Lodi and Alva, until we arrived at a tangle of vegetation. The plants have retaken the wreck of her old house, which is only visible if you look hard.

"This is what Wheeler had to come through at night," she said.

That night William Parker kept his pistol and his single-shot rifle with him. Joy heard her father finally take Wheeler away in the dark, putting him on a train north and arriving back in Duck Hill just as the sun began to rise. Wheeler got on the train alone in Winona in the middle of the night. He rode along the ridge separating the Hills from the Delta in darkness and arrived in Memphis to change trains. He unwittingly tried to use a white restroom in the Memphis station, which sat across the street from the Lorraine Motel on the Black side of town. Some Black soldiers stopped him from going inside. He continued north, leaving the Jim Crow car behind in Cairo, Checkpoint Charlie in the "iron curtain," arriving finally in Chicago. Someone in his family met him at the station. They took him straight to Mamie's home on South St. Lawrence Street. Inside he found the family sitting vigil. Down in Mississippi the authorities were still searching for Emmett. Wheeler locked eyes with Mamie. She looked at him with compassion.

"Go hug your mother," she said. He did.

WHEELER FINALLY WENT BACK to Mississippi with Marvel in 1968. They went to Teoc to see her family, driving down Highway 7 past a cotton gin in a little unincorporated map dot called Whaley. A gravel road ran into the highway there by the gin. That was Dark Fear Road, which led to Moses Wright's house and the store in Money, just a few miles away. Wheeler never mentioned a word about what happened in 1955.

Teoc was home to the McCain Plantation, which is where Marvel McCain Parker grew up before she and her family moved to Chicago. It's forty-eight miles southeast of the barn. Marvel didn't grow up working on a white man's plantation; her dad owned and farmed his own small square of land. Her people had been on this land, as enslaved people and then sharecroppers and finally owners, since before the Civil War. Most of what you can see down below from the bluff belonged to a plantation owner named William

Alexander McCain, whose white descendants still own the large plantation that dominated the flat land below the Teoc bluffs.

He had a white son and a Black son, splitting the family into two. The white son, named John Sidney McCain, had a son who became an admiral, who had a son who became an admiral, who had a son who became a Vietnam war hero and a senator. John McCain is the same rung on the family tree as Marvel's father. In Teoc there are the white McCains and the Black McCains, all of whom share a common ancestor, which of course makes them one family. The mental and emotional gymnastics it takes to obscure that fact is roughly the amount of exertion that makes the modern state of Mississippi possible. During Senator McCain's run for president he claimed he never knew his family owned slaves, which is absurd.

Marvel McCain Parker, whose contemporary on the family tree is Meghan McCain, is a firecracker of a woman, with a smile that can light a room and a scowl that can clear one. She does not tolerate any insult to her family. She's also understandably skeptical of white people and wears that skepticism in terse emails and her unwillingness to let a smile and a bit of charm work as unearned social grease. Have you ever looked at somebody, really looked into their eyes, and realized they were a warrior? It made me think about those three generations of navy heroes on the white side, and the war and civil rights heroes on the Black side, and wonder if there is something wired into the McCain genetic code that passes along bravery. Wheeler makes jokes all the time about her controlling him, which makes both of them laugh, because very few people can control Wheeler and because Marvel is absolutely one of them. We drove through the Delta one day, him behind the wheel of their beautiful blue Mercedes sedan, and her leaned up into the space between the driver and passenger seats.

"You have to slow down!" she said. "You're driving too fast!"

Just then the dashboard and console lights started flashing.

Marvel grinned.

"Even the car knows!" she said triumphantly.

Everyone laughed. She's got a contagious laugh. The hard outer shell, a layer of callus built up over a lifetime, hides an emotional core that reveals itself from time to time. Once we stood next to each other looking at photographs and came across a famous one of Mamie Till-Mobley waiting at Twelfth Street Station in Chicago to collect her son's body.

"Mamie," she said, then made a sound laced with pain and understanding.

After Marvel brought Wheeler back to Mississippi thirteen years after the murder, he grew more comfortable with the idea of returning. Now he comes all the time. They've even discussed retiring back to Mississippi, he misses home so much. On every trip until William Parker died in 2008 at the incredible age of 105, Wheeler made Marvel drive them to visit him out in Duck Hill. To be honest, she got a little annoyed because Duck Hill is in the middle of nowhere. He never told her he did it out of respect for the enormous risks his uncle took that night. There are different kinds of secrets. Some are kept out of shame. Others are kept out of love. Not long before William died, he let a secret slip. A few nights after he put his nephew on that train headed north, white terrorists came out to the place looking for Wheeler, who'd already arrived back in his mother's arms.

IN THE DAYS AFTER the kidnapping, the Wright family of East Money, Mississippi, all went back into the fields to keep picking

Moses's twenty-five acres. The horror of that gets glossed over. For two full, hot, long days, Moses and Simeon and the rest of the Wrights had walked up and down the rows carrying nine-foot sacks. The repetition of picking cotton turns a man into a machine and leaves his mind free to wander. It's a hard way to spend a day. Simeon and his sisters Thelma and Hallie didn't eat. Hallie lost ten pounds in ten days. The Wrights picked cotton all day Monday and Tuesday, and Wednesday morning got up to do it again. At noon Simeon saw a sheriff's deputy park his car and walk across the field to whisper something to Moses, who walked alone out of the field.

Moses left home with another sheriff's deputy, who drove him toward Glendora. A local seventeen-year-old kid named Robert Hodges had been fishing early that morning at Pecan Point, down the river a bit from Graball Landing. He'd gone out to check his trotlines, which kept hooks in the water overnight. Stuff gets hung up in them all the time. He saw something snagged on one and he motored over to check. Legs. Human legs.

He rushed home to tell his father, who called his landlord, B. L. Mims, who relayed the information to the police. The Talla-hatchie County sheriff's office dispatched people to the scene. A deputy got there first, Garland Melton, and he went with Mims and towed the body back to shore. A gin fan was tied to his neck with barbed wire. Sheriff Strider arrived eventually. The corpse smelled so bad he couldn't get close. The left eyeball was about to fall out of its socket. His face looked chopped up with an axe. It was Em-mett Till.

Moses Wright identified the body. He returned to East Money to tell everyone the news. Then he went to sit alone on the front porch swing. His sons had never seen him like this before. Some part of

Moses Wright never returned from the riverside. He didn't make words so much as sounds. He sat on his porch, moaning.

SEVEN DECADES LATER the Parkers rode an elevator down to the lobby of a hotel in Washington's Navy Yard. Today they were headed to a ceremony at the Smithsonian Museum of American History. Patrick Weems had brought up the historical marker from the River Site, the one shot 317 times. Cars dropped us all off at the museum, where we gathered around a small stage. Dwight Eisenhower created this museum two years after J. W. Milam and Roy Bryant stepped into Moses Wright's home. I found a seat next to Annie Wright, Simeon's widow, who kept talking about the number of holes in the sign. The head of the Smithsonian, Lonnie Bunch, spoke to the crowd from a video screen. He couldn't make the event but, as a longtime friend of Mamie, wanted to welcome everyone.

"She wondered who would carry that burden when she was gone," he said.

Marvel nodded from the front row. She knew what he meant. Mamie had asked Wheeler to never let people forget, a charge he's taken as seriously as a human being can take something.

Wheeler Parker spoke to the crowd. The only sound was his voice.

"Sixty-six years ago last Saturday," he began, "I was sixteen years old."

The South is built, he said, on never talking about the things right in front of your face. But the sign speaks. It cannot be ignored and here in this place of national honor, it cannot be forgotten.

Long ago he decided that remembering is best done by speaking, and that by speaking, he remembers.

"And his mother asked me, personally, to carry on his legacy," he said.

This trip to Washington had made Wheeler feel that he'd really accomplished something, that he'd done right by his friend. It also made him want more time to really push this mission now that he'd seen so much success.

"I'm eighty-two years old," he said.

A NEWSPAPER IN CHICAGO heard that the body had been found. They didn't know if anybody had called Mamie, so they dialed her number. She answered. They asked if she'd received any news. When she said no, they politely thanked her and then called her best friend, Ollie Williams, who was at work at Inland Steel. Ollie waited as long as she could and then drove over.

She broke the news.

He'd been found dead. He'd been beaten and his body tied to a cotton gin fan.

Mamie felt herself split in two. She took calm, careful notes and then repeated them to her mother, Alma, and to her aunt Marie. Marie started screaming.

"Take her out of here!" Mamie barked.

She went into a defensive crouch, determined to offer her son a measure of protection in death that she'd been unable to provide in life. His last words, the witnesses reported, had been crying out for her. She sent a telegram to President Eisenhower and demanded he use the powerful tools of the federal government to bring justice to the men who had lynched her son. "Awaiting a direct reply from you," her message ended. She got no response.

Down in Mississippi, the bigoted Sheriff Strider wanted the body buried immediately. Two men even dug the hole in the little graveyard outside the East Money Church of God in Christ. I've walked that cemetery more than once trying to see if there's a sunken rectangle where a grave was dug and not filled. A hearse brought Emmett and parked along the gravel road. It's clear the Mississippi officials who'd seen the body understood what the torture represented. Curtis Jones slipped off to find a phone to call his mother, who called Mamie. Mamie wanted her son home. She called her cousin in the Delta, Crosby Smith, who promised he'd bring her son home to her if he had to pack a pickup truck with ice and drive it himself. Crosby got a Leflore County sheriff's deputy, one of the heroes of these awful few days, and they rushed to East Money. They walked to the group of men preparing to bury Emmett. The deputy told everybody that whatever Crosby Smith said was the law. Smith demanded the body be sent to Chicago.

Eventually the white state and local officials agreed to put the body on a train under one condition. The casket would be sealed with official state of Mississippi tape and was never to be opened. They, too, knew what would happen if people ever saw this particular corpse. The embalmer, Woodrow Jackson, did careful work. He cut tiny slits in the body and submerged it in formaldehyde for thirty-six hours. They took the remains north on Highway 49 to the Clarksdale train depot. They loaded the redwood box carrying the best casket available in Tutwiler, Mississippi, onto the Illinois Central and the train pulled out of the station.

Crosby Smith, Elizabeth Wright, and Curtis Jones all took the same train north. They rode through the little town of Lyon, the home of Son House, and past the Bobo-Mosely cotton gin. The tracks paralleled Highway 61 headed north. The train rode through the night and arrived in Chicago at 9:00 a.m., the same schedule the City of New Orleans keeps today.

Mamie waited at Twelfth Street Station.

She collapsed when she saw the box.

"I know I was on your mind when you died," she cried.

They went to the Rayner funeral home. Mr. Rayner refused to open the casket at first. He'd promised the state of Mississippi. But a grieving mother cannot be denied. Mamie went into the room and stood over the body.

She recognized his nose and his forehead.

The remaining eye was the right color.

That was one side. She wanted to see the other. Rayner asked her to go home for an hour and let them dress the body. She complied and when she returned, she saw the evidence of her son's final hours. A photographer from *Jet* magazine, David Jackson, took pictures of Emmett's face. Rayner asked Mamie, gently, if she wanted his team to do some work on the body. Make it more presentable.

"No," Mamie said. "Let the world see what I've seen."

Rayner placed Emmett in a shiny casket. Three pictures of him from that Christmas photo shoot were pinned to the soft lining of the lid. More than fifty thousand people would walk past that casket at the funeral at Roberts Temple. Mamie was changing. Soon she'd emerge from this pain as a focused, relentless woman. She went out on the road and told her story to anyone who would listen. She spoke to huge crowds. Former sharecroppers and their descendants, just two generations removed from enslavement, listened in

Detroit, and in Harlem, in Omaha, Nebraska—everywhere the diaspora had settled outside the South. The month after the funeral she'd visit thirty-three cities in nineteen states. At every stop she told the crowds her sadness had been replaced by anger. Nothing in her past had trained her for this new role but her friends and family watched, a little stunned, as she completed her transformation from a young mother into a powerful leader. This road she traveled for the rest of her life began in Roberts Temple when she invited the South Side of Chicago—the true capital of the Black Mississippi Delta—to come see what J.W., Leslie, Roy, and Melvin had done to her son. Inside the sanctuary on September 6, 1955, Wheeler Parker kept telling himself that it was not his friend and cousin in that box and that they'd see each other again one day. Mamie came to the front of the church to see her son and she leaned over his body. She'd asked the world to see. But when she got to the front of the church, she closed her eyes. A glass cover protected the body. She leaned over the casket and wept.

THE WASHINGTON MONUMENT rose over Wheeler Parker's shoulder as we walked toward the front door of the Smithsonian's National Museum of African American History and Culture. We walked down the long descending ramps toward the Emmett Till exhibit. The museum had been opened especially for Wheeler and his guests. Wheeler peeked past Patrick Weems to get a better look at an old plantation slave cabin. A guard tower from the Angola State Prison in Louisiana rose above the other exhibits. Where could a story with this much pain, tempered by a chain of individual acts of courage, be leading? Finally we arrived at Emmett Till's original casket. The Smithsonian had rescued it after the FBI's reinvestigation of the murder prompted the 2004 exhumation of Till's body, followed by his reburial in a new casket three days later.

The family went into the room alone.

Annie Wright saw video of her late husband and started to cry. She wiped her eyes. They saw Papa Mose and heard Mamie's voice. The casket was shiny and narrow. Marvel sat in a wheelchair close to the video screen, her feet rocking slowly back and forth, the soles of her shoes slowly grinding. From behind she seemed to be caving in on herself. Wheeler was silent. He walked out first. Annie Wright followed behind him, turning to take one last look at the casket.

Wheeler leaned up against the wall.

He didn't speak so much as he made noises, noises like the ones he'd heard Moses Wright make on his porch after he'd identified the body. A television played speeches nearby—Obama, Martin Luther King, James Baldwin—so Wheeler's pain had a strange, mournful soundtrack.

"What does the Negro want?"

"Mmmmmm."

"He wants what every other American wants."

"Mmmmmmm."

Finally he spoke. I stood next to him. Strong memories of walking through cotton fields flooded back, he told me later.

"You know, Saturday was the sixtieth anniversary of the abduction," he said. "The thing I relive most is the kidnapping."

We walked up the ramps out of the museum. He passed the slave cabin and talked about being six years old out in the fields picking cotton. Something about that theft of his youth seemed particularly cruel to him. A worry settled over Wheeler, a sense of time rushing away. He seemed lit from the inside with a sense of purpose and power.

The museum staff lined up by the door.

"Our children don't know this," Wheeler said.

THE POLICE ARRESTED J. W. Milam and Roy Bryant for the kidnapping and murder of Emmett Till. For a few news cycles the story got presented, even locally, as a pretty clear case of good versus evil, until the partisan political machine recast it as a battle between the NAACP and Mississippi white people. On cue an old beauty pageant picture of Carolyn Bryant suddenly appeared in newspapers around the country. Scholars have long wondered who leaked that photo, whether it was the local attorneys or the sophisticated media operations of Senator Eastland or Senator John Stennis. The real defendant, it was becoming clear, was the state of Mississippi itself. After the photo's release the language used to describe her started adding the word *pretty* before *wife*. The ability to protect white women was suddenly on trial, too.

The Milams and Bryants huddled together. They kept moving Carolyn around and refused to let even her mother or siblings know where they had her stashed. Leflore County had issued a warrant for her arrest. They moved between the different stores the family owned around the Delta. They went to Eula's store, then to Melvin and Mary Louise's in Minter City, then to Bud Milam's store and back again.

Bud Milam came to Carolyn one night and told her they were driving out into the country to Leslie's house for dinner. She gathered her two boys and headed down the Drew-Ruleville Road.

They took a left across the bayou just past Add and Willie Reed's house. They passed the barn and parked and went inside the house.

Then J.W. and Roy walked in. They'd been let out of jail for the evening to see their families. *Sauntered* is the word Carolyn would use in her memoir. Rage shot through her as she watched them act like nothing was wrong. Roy Jr. ran to his father and Lamar toddled over. They all hugged and Roy threw them in the air and caught them, then they all rolled around on the floor as they screamed with laughter. Someone in the barn could have heard the joyous reunion. Carolyn seethed and wouldn't go hug her husband. A hurt look settled over his face. They all gathered around the table and ate supper like they weren't on the eve of a murder trial. Someone came to Leslie's front door around 2:00 a.m. It was time for the prisoners to return to jail. The ride back to their cell took them toward Drew. They turned on Highway 49. There were cotton fields on both sides of the road, some picked, some unpicked. Leslie got to work in the morning on his own crop, the last one he'd ever make.

NINETEEN YEARS LATER Leslie Milam lay in his pajamas on the couch in the front room of his house on Colonial Drive. He had less than twenty-four hours to live. His street dead-ended into cotton fields. He was forty-six years old and riddled with cancer. Just three years earlier he'd been arrested for meth possession with intent to distribute.

His wife, Frances, called their preacher, Macklyn Hubbell, and asked him to come to the house.

"Leslie needs to talk to you," she said.

Almost fifty years later, Hubbell, now in his nineties, welcomed me onto his back deck in Cleveland, Mississippi. He told me about her request. Hubbell has been retired for a long time now. He has that beatific preacher's face reserved for actual men of God, unravaged by sin. He continued his story about 1974.

He drove over to the Milam house and walked up to the door. Frances let him inside. Light flooded the room. Leslie Milam was stretched out on the couch.

"I remember exactly," Hubbell told me. "I remember approaching the couch where he was lying."

Leslie wanted to tell him something. The preacher pulled up a straight-backed chair.

Milam looked him right in the eyes.

"It was a confession between Leslie and me," Hubbell told me. "And I didn't share it with anybody until Leslie was gone and Frances was gone. Because they are gone, I can tell you what Leslie said."

It had been nineteen years since Emmett Till died. The burden of the barn followed Leslie and Frances Milam. After all the legal proceedings ended, Leslie Milam's financial overlord, the powerful Delta planter Ben Sturdivant, threw him off the land outside Drew and sold the land to Stafford Shurden's granddad. A savvy businessman, Ben surely sensed that one day people would start digging into records and ask some questions. One summer morning his grandson Walker Sturdivant escorted me into his office on their sprawling farm. We passed framed newspaper clippings of his father, a high-profile progressive Democrat. All around were the telltale signs of old Delta money: a chair from the Woodberry Forest School, a Union Planters Bank espresso cup, photographs from ski vacations. Not long ago he went down to the courthouse himself to pull up the old rental agreements and land records so he'd have his facts straight. It's all there in those red leatherbound books we both read.

"Immediately after it happened," he said, "that's when he exited from his relationship. Dad always said J. W. Milam and Roy Bryant both had been ostracized in the white community after what they had done. The people just decided, even though there were a lot of pretty staunch racists, at least the code said you don't do that to children."

During the trial people put up mason jars in stores around the Delta to raise money for the killers, but once they were acquitted and confessed in a national magazine, people understood that these men were living mirrors. Anyone who looked too long at a member of the Milam or Bryant family saw the worst of themselves reflected back. Leslie Milam ended up unable to farm because he couldn't get a workforce. He sold used cars. He dealt drugs. The night in August 1955 was never mentioned.

Dale Killinger discovered these bonds of silence still intact decades later when he reopened the case and started knocking on doors. Killinger found Frances Milam's total obliviousness perhaps the most infuriating. She pled ignorance and blamed her ignorance on her young age in 1955. He knew she was lying. Once when Killinger and I spoke on the phone, he described for me the violence that happened so close to the room where Frances slept and the kitchen where she'd surely gone for breakfast or coffee by the time the beating began. The next time we talked, he told me his wife had been in the next room during that graphic conversation and when he hung up with me, through her rage and tears, she asked him why they'd done it.

"Don't you understand?" he told her. "They were *entertained* by this."

"What do you mean?" she cried.

"They could've killed and tortured him anywhere they wanted to," he told her. "They chose to take him to a barn where they could control the environment and do what they wanted. In my mind, they were entertaining themselves."

He told me he's imagined the sounds of that night over and over.

"Frances Milam was home," he said. "She was in the house. You think she heard what was going on?"

Killinger laughed bitterly and answered his own question. He's seen some terrible people in his career at war and fighting drug cartels and corrupt politicians. Frances was up there with the worst of them.

"Hell, yeah, she did," he said. "It's 1955 and you don't have air-conditioning. So she admitted that they brought him to the farm in the middle of the night. That's in the FBI report. So she was there and they were beating him and eventually somebody shot him in that barn in the head. You hear everything in Mississippi! You know? The windows are open. You have window screening, that's all you have. You hear a car coming a mile away. You hear somebody getting beat in your barn! You hear a gunshot! . . . Think about why they chose to go to that barn. They chose it because Leslie Milam controlled that space. And they could go in there and do what they wanted, how they wanted. And why would you do that? You could have taken him off in the woods and killed him if you wanted to. Right? Dump the body anywhere. They went out of their way."

By the time Leslie Milam lay dying, nobody talked about the Till murder anymore. Melvin Campbell had recently died but all the other killers were alive. Nobody really knew for sure how many had participated, nor who they were, except of course for the murderers themselves. And none of them said a word. Until Leslie confessed to Hubbell.

"I remember that he said he was involved in the killing of Emmett Till," Hubbell said. "He wanted to tell me because he perceived me to be a man of God. He was releasing himself of guilt. He was belching out guilt."

Hubbell said a prayer with Milam and then walked back to his car. Leslie Milam stayed on that couch. He didn't live to see the sun rise again.

THE TRIAL BEGAN ON September 19, 1955. During the long selection of jurors, the four little Milam and Bryant boys shot water pistols in the courtroom and ran around with their shirts off. "Every time a stranger looked at J.W. and wanted to hate him," Murray Kempton of the *New York Post* wrote from the trial, "there was always a little boy in the line of vision." The jury, once selected, was sequestered at the nearby Delta Inn, where a cross was burned in the yard the morning of opening arguments.

It's well established that this trial was corrupted from the beginning by the familial ties stretching from the Hills down to the courthouse in Sumner. The killers and most of the jurors, the defense attorneys and the sheriff and the local congressman, were all from the same tiny corner of Tallahatchie hill country. Murphreesboro had nearly vanished by then.

In 1955 the only surviving center of Milam and Bryant's world was the New Hope Presbyterian Church, which got heated by a potbelly stove. Worshippers brought their own wood with them to Sunday-evening service. The preacher wore a heavy coat and a hat and his breath came out in big clouds during the winter. The preacher at the New Hope Presbyterian Church in September of 1955 was an idealistic young man named Maynard Fountain, who'd brought his young family to Charleston and conducted services at the big church in town and then out in New Hope, too.

"I called it No Hope," his son, Dr. William Maynard Fountain III, told me. "In the church there was not a deacon or an elder who could read or write his own name. . . . That may be a little bit of an exaggeration but that's what my father said. When they would take up the offering, they had two clans in the church. They would put the money out on a table that had been picked up and they had to have one representative from each of the clans counting the money."

Fountain III remembers the trial. He remembers his mom, a trusting, naive lady, talking to a member of the church named Mr. Brown after a Wednesday-night prayer meeting.

"I am so glad they caught those terrible men," she said.

Mr. Brown had throat cancer and could talk only by putting a vibrating machine up to a hole in his throat. He got right in Mrs. Fountain's face.

"Don't you ever say anything like that in this town again," Mr. Brown said.

Fountain tried to address these issues with the Bible as his guide. One Wednesday, he asked the kids to stay at home because he was going to talk about racial relations in the Delta and didn't want them to hear the angry responses. When he finished his sermon, he asked for questions. A woman stood up after a long silence.

"We love our n——s," she said.

The room stayed quiet.

Congressman Whitten, a member of the church, stood up.

"I think we've discussed this issue quite enough," he said. "I move we adjourn."

Then the whole congregation stood up and left.

Fountain's son told me that 1955 in Charleston stole something from his father. Some belief in the innate goodness of people. "He went there as a white, well-educated man," he said. "He left there at age thirty-four feeling like he was defeated in life, like he had failed at what he needed to do. My father passed away almost five years ago. I tried to pick his brain for the last few years about different things relating to this very topic. He would not talk about them. He'd either get up and walk out of the room or grunt."

MOSES WRIGHT TOOK THE STAND on the third day of the trial. He was sixty-four years old and had lived in Mississippi his whole life. The defense lawyers hurled aggressive and intentionally confusing questions at him, which he parried with confidence. He wore a white shirt, suspenders, and a tie. It was boiling inside the courtroom, nearly one hundred degrees. Kempton would describe the grilling about to commence as "the hardest half hour of the hardest life possible for a human being in these United States."

Wright got asked to identify J. W. Milam, who stared back at him with a lit cigarette in his hand. Wright reached out his arm and pointed clearly and defiantly with his index finger.

"There he is," he said.

Wright didn't say "thar he," as some of the people in the room claimed. He was a professional preacher. He enunciated quite clearly. *There. He. Is.* Wright could feel the energy in the room change when he pointed. He told family members he could feel the blood of all the white people boiling. Nobody made a sound. He could hear the sound of the ceiling fans cutting through the air. A single shutter click sounded like a gun going off. That's the famous photograph.

The last defense attorney to question him was Sidney Carlton, who mocked and badgered him but never really developed a successful line of attack. Carlton was getting owned by an old man with a seventh-grade education, and reading through the transcript feels like watching the last scene of an action movie. Moses Wright, whose life had been controlled by the caste system for decades, broke free. He stopped addressing Carlton as "sir." His courage irked at least one of the jurors, who muttered, "Sambo, Sambo, Sambo."

Sidney Carlton died at aged fifty.

Moses Wright lived until eighty-six.

That evening, in September 1955, Moses Wright stood alone on the courthouse lawn. A United Packinghouse Workers union rep, in town to support Mamie, approached him.

"Where did you get the courage to testify in the face of probable death?" he asked.

"There are some things worse than death," Wright replied.

MOSES WRIGHT SPENT three more days in Mississippi after he left the courtroom. He wanted to stay but the death threats grew too scary to ignore. Everyone in East Money, he told *The Chicago Defender*, was "scared to death," and he just couldn't risk his life anymore. He loved his home but men came out in the night looking for him and he slept in his car down at the church where Emmett had almost been buried. He couldn't even finish picking his crop. All that cotton he just left to rot in the fields. On the day he left forever he stood in his front yard and kept looking at his three dogs. He couldn't take them. He'd already sold his furniture and his chickens.

His favorite dog was named Dallas. As Wright looked at him, he started to cry.

"I hate to leave this dog," he said. "He's the best dog in seven states."

Wright patted the dog on the head and wiped away a tear. It was time. A neighbor led Dallas away. The dog looked back and whimpered. Wright and his sons got into the 1946 Ford and drove to the Winona train station. He parked his car in the lot there and left it. His brother said he'd try to sell it and some of the corn from the family garden. They rode north with what they could carry and started a new life. For a few months he got taken on a speaking tour by the NAACP.

"After the speaking tour," his son Simeon said, "I don't remember too many people seeking him out."

He got jobs he could do alone. For twenty-two years he went in at 2:00 a.m., the same time the kidnappers knocked on his door, and cleaned up a local playhouse. There's a restaurant there in Argo called El Famous where he bused tables. His sons never heard a word about Emmett Till's death.

"He didn't talk," Simeon Wright said. "Not even to me."

Moses Wright never drove a car again. He never fished or hunted again. When Simeon joined the army, Moses moved into a housing project on Sixty-Third Place. After many years he and Alma, Mamie's mom, finally cleared the air. She'd held a grudge against him for not doing more but she came to realize there was nothing anyone could have done once J. W. Milam stepped onto Moses's porch. His wife, Elizabeth, died and he started going blind. Moses cooked cornbread from a box. Once he fell and lay on the floor for a day until someone found him. His family put him in a nursing home right off Route 66. His greatest joy came from his garden. That was the only time he touched his old life. The railroad gave him a little patch near the tracks and he and some other old men tended their plants like they'd once tended crops down south. Wright put a wheel on a plow to replace the mules he used to drive. He and the other old men planted tomatoes and cucumbers and butter beans and greens.

He died in 1977. They buried him in the same cemetery as Emmett.

ONE OF THOSE OLD MEN who tended the Argo garden with Moses Wright was an exiled former sharecropper from Louisiana. Frances Hampton worked at the Argo Starch company with many of Emmett's family and neighbors. The family called him Big Daddy and his wife, Iberia, got called Big Mama. Their son, Fred Hampton, grew up in Argo down the street from Wheeler Parker and turned seven two days after Emmett Till died. Thirteen years later he rose to prominence in the Black Panther Party and a year after that the Chicago Police Department killed him while he slept. Emmett Till's uncle gardened with Fred Hampton's father, silently moving up and down the rows of vegetables, both of them a long, long way from home. One afternoon I met Fred Hampton Jr. at the house where his grandparents moved when they left Argo, the house where his father grew up.

"Do you like sitting here?" I asked him. "Do you feel his presence?"

"Oh, yes," he said. "That's my charge-up."

Hampton told me he was leaving soon for Louisiana. He goes

now to see his father's grave, which also has been a magnet for vandalism.

"His tombstone, it's shot up annually," he said. "By law enforcement. And they're up front about it."

Apparently it's a tradition for cops to go out into rural Louisiana to shoot slugs at the ghost of a man killed in his bed by the Chicago Police Department.

"And it is up in the backwoods," he said, "so they come up in there and do it."

"Where's your daddy buried?" I asked.

"Haynesville, Louisiana. Right near Shreveport. And they shoot his tombstone up annually. And a lot of people say, 'Well, why don't you just get another tombstone?' And I said, nah. You know, like Emmett Till. So people can see."

I asked about Till's uncle Moses Wright. He smiled and pointed at Connie, his cousin, who'd just parked and walked up to the house. She grew up in Argo, he explained, and knew Emmett and his family.

"This is perfect timing," Fred Jr. said.

"I knew Mr. Moses," Connie said. "I just loved him. They lived in the next block from me. He was a little bitty guy. He didn't bother nobody."

"Did Moses ever talk about anything that had happened?"

"Never," she said.

Argo suffered tremendously from the murder of Emmett. His death felt like their death, because they knew him, and all his family, and because they *were* him and his family, expats from mostly the same place who came at the same time for the same reasons. His death was also the death of a way of looking at the future, the death of imagination and hope.

"I was just going through this stuff last night with a friend of mine," Connie said, "and I was telling him, 'That was the first time I saw my father cry, when Bobo got killed. When they came back from that funeral.'"

"Yeah," Fred said.

"I ain't never in my life seen my daddy cry."

"How old were you in 1955, if you don't mind me asking?" I asked.

"Five," Connie said.

"And you remember it?"

"Yes," she said. "Yeah, five years old. I remember. And I'll never forget the look on my father's face when he came back from that boy's funeral."

NO TRANSCRIPT OF THE closing arguments still exists. They've all been destroyed, lost, or hidden. (The FBI found the witness testimony only after a source tipped them off to a copy in private hands on the Mississippi Gulf coast.) That's obviously not an accident. That file was the most famous one in the entire courthouse and the biggest case any of the lawyers involved ever tried. Newspaper coverage mentioned a dramatic ratcheting up of racial rhetoric but quoted only a few passages from John Whitten's final plea to the jury. All the defense lawyers had been building toward this speech. The whole subtext of the trial had been about *Brown v. Board* and the sudden existential challenge to segregation. A way of life was being defended, not just two disposable rednecks. There's a reason people refer to Emmett Till's death as the spark of the modern civil rights movement. Everyone involved in the trial understood the stakes and yet nobody has a clue exactly what the defense lawyers said to an all-white, all-male jury in the steaming court-room. Their words, necessary in the moment but despicable to decent people even then, have been erased.

Reporters over the years have unearthed bits and pieces.

Devery Anderson quoted J. W. Kellum, who said a guilty plea would make their "forebears absolutely roll over in their graves."

Whitten had the last word in the whole trial. We know some of what he said. A court artist drew him with a hawkish nose, wearing glasses and a schoolmarm demeanor. He talked to the jury about how the case had brought so much negative attention and newspaper coverage to the South, rooting a not-guilty vote in the pervasive southern thin skin about any criticism. Residents of Sumner had been shouting at reporters on the street.

"You're making a mountain out of a molehill!" a man shouted. "The NAACP is really making you work!"

Whitten knew his audience when he invoked the "rabble rousers" who had come south to mess with their way of life. That's the gospel he preached to this jury. And then Whitten got to the real point. The beating heart of the whole trial. All the ridiculous questions they'd been asking were just a dog whistle for the real issue at hand. "I'm sure every last Anglo-Saxon one of you has the courage to free these men in the face of that pressure," he said. John Whitten's whole legal career has been reduced to that one word. *Anglo-Saxon.*

THE DELTA IS FULL OF dead and dying grandfatherly and horrible old men. John Whitten's son certainly learned his lessons well. John Whitten III became the county prosecutor and worked out of the same office in the same building as his dad. I never met him, although I drove past his house in Sumner to see all the military vehicles he stockpiled for the "race war," as he called it, which included a surplus British armored personnel carrier. Here's the only story you need to know about John Whitten III. Let's go back to the summer of 2020, when the quarantine forced me back to the house where I grew up, an old Cape Dutch showplace my father bought with the proceeds of his successful law practice. Sitting upstairs, I reached out to the son of another Clarksdale attorney. We'd both worked filing in our dads' offices growing up. Yet our lives had been very different, my Clarksdale full of sepia-toned contentment and his full of fear, because I was white and he was Black. Cornelius Pittman wrote back immediately and agreed to tell me the story of the day in 2009 when a mob of white men tried to lynch his brother in a cotton field outside Sumner, Mississippi. We met under the shade of a magnolia tree in the front yard of the Cutrer Mansion, the huge estate where Blanche Clark—Tennessee Williams's most famous muse and daughter of the founder of Clarksdale, John Clark, the first land patent owner in Township 22 North, Range 4 West—had moved when she got married. I brought lawn chairs.

Cornelius and I caught up for a while. We'd gone to different schools growing up; Clarksdale, like nearly everywhere in the Delta, remains functionally segregated. Pittman explained the rules for growing up Black in our hometown. He said he gets nervous when he sees a pickup truck. I looked over at the parking lot. I drive a black pickup truck.

I asked him to explain to me what it was like to be born Black in the Mississippi Delta, and he paused for a long time.

"It's hard," he said. "Real fucking hard."

Twenty-two more seconds of silence passed. I felt terrible for asking. His lip quivered and then he started to cry, big tears rolling down his cheeks, until finally he got out a few words. "Your life is in danger every day, all day," he said. "You're constantly paranoid. You ride by me too many times, I have to take a picture of your tag or something."

He stopped talking and twisted and retwisted a piece of paper in his hand until he felt composed enough to tell the story. His brother Will, who struggles with addiction, broke into a house in Sumner. He stole some stuff and ran off into the woods. Local men formed a posse led by John Whitten III, the son of Milam and Bryant's lead attorney. He led an actual posse in 2009. A maintenance worker from a nearby town put on a police shirt and pretended to be a cop. Lots of dudes stood around pickup trucks. Some were drinking beer. Nearly everyone was armed. Shotguns. Pistols. Assault rifles. One of the military vehicles had a .50-caliber machine gun. A local pilot went to the strip and got one of those bright-yellow crop dusters up in the sky. You know, air support.

During all this insanity Cornelius got a call. He needed to get out to Sumner. People were hunting his brother. A cop he knew told him they had Will pinned down in a field. He drove the twenty minutes from his dad's office in Clarksdale to Sumner and pulled up to a huge crowd. "It was about fifteen trucks like the truck there, F-150s, nothing but white faces," he says. "Everybody standing 'round with bottles and beer cans. Everybody out here got guns, drinking beers. This is going to be a lynching and a hanging."

Cornelius and Will used to play in these woods growing up. He knew his brother could navigate the fields and forests. Armed men searched the rows. Nobody could find him. The mob started talking about setting the cotton field on fire. "You don't get that feeling like I can call somebody and do something," he says. "Everybody around here has guns. I know these guys are not police officers. So I don't get the feeling that I'm safe."

The men taunted him. Pointed guns at him and made him pop his trunk. They joked about how they were going to kill his brother and about how annoying it would be to clean blood and guts off the tank treads. He says John Whitten III—the man who owned the military vehicles and *was the county prosecutor*—told him, "If we can't get him, one of his family members will do just as fine."

One of the posse members' wives offered Cornelius mosquito spray while her husband hunted his brother. Will Pittman finally snuck out of the field and through the woods and turned himself in. The mob converged on the jail and the man pretending to be a cop tried to sneak in carrying his weapon before Will's attorney father pushed him back outside.

There wasn't a story in the local paper. Just another day in the Delta. But people around town talked. They knew the players. They knew the name John Whitten III and they knew who his father was. They knew the crop duster pilot who flew air support, who had his own connection to the killing of Emmett Till. He and his family now owned the murder weapon. The Ithaca .45, serial number 2102279. His wife is the woman who offered Cornelius mosquito spray.

ON SEPTEMBER 23, 1955, the jury adjourned at 2:35 p.m.

A friend of my dad's was in the courtroom and he said he could hear them in there laughing. They'd joke later they needed to make it look better for the northern press, who had a pool going about how long the jury would pretend to deliberate. Mamie Till even got in on the action. She guessed forty-nine minutes. As the jury deliberated, she was gone. She'd asked Congressman Diggs to take her back to Mound Bayou.

"I would like for us to leave now," she said.

"What, and miss the verdict?" he said.

"This is one you will want to miss," she said.

Milam and Bryant stayed in their chairs, except when they went up to chat with the judge and drink cold water from his pitcher. Soon they emerged with a unanimous decision. Sixty-seven minutes. Black photographer Ernest Withers, who snuck the iconic photograph of Moses Wright, won the pool.

J. A. Shaw Jr., the foreman, handed over the verdict.

"Not guilty," the clerk read.

"Oh, no!" a Black spectator exclaimed.

J. W. Milam and Roy Bryant lit victory cigars. The photographers crowded around and asked the men to kiss their wives. Defense attorney Sidney Carlton came to shake hands with Milam. The other lawyers kept their distance. Milam made a joke about needing to buy a wig since his bald head made it so easy for Moses Wright to identify him.

The defense had painted a picture of a vast plot by people all over America, including right at home, involving such communist stooges as Moses Wright whose mission was to damage and discredit the good name of Mississippi and its humane and Christian system of segregation. The jurors bought that story because they'd long ago given up logic and common sense. A cult is built on believing the absurd if the absurd justifies the cult.

Shaw said the body pulled from the Tallahatchie River was not Emmett Till.

He mocked Mamie.

"If she had tried a little harder she might have got out a tear," he said.

Jim Pennington said that Willie Reed was an NAACP plant.

Ray Tribble agreed.

They all agreed on the following set of facts, as laid out by the defense: Emmett Till had been hidden by the NAACP in the North, in either Chicago or Detroit, and Willie Reed and Moses Wright had been coached by professional, probably communist agitators, and Mamie Till had played along with the plot in exchange for a life insurance payout for her not-dead son, and she'd flown down and lied about recognizing her son, lied about her tears and emotion, and all of this had been arranged by shadowy powers who wanted to overthrow the southern way of life as a precursor to an attack on the United States itself. The body pulled from the Tallahatchie River had been donated to the cause by a helpful mortician. These people had access to bodies, the defense attorneys had said. They would stop at nothing to attack Mississippi.

TWENTY-FIVE YEARS LATER a two-pack-a-day alcoholic walked into his doctor's office down in Jackson after he'd been pissing blood and tissue. He filled out the forms: John W. Milam, 615 Purcell Street, Greenville, Mississippi. His lower back hurt and the pain radiated down to his hips. It was the spring of 1980 and the farming economy was about to collapse. Milam was just sixty-one years old, flat broke with a ninth-grade education, and hadn't been to his job running heavy machinery since October of the previous year. The year before he'd made seven thousand dollars but all that dried up when he got sick. He didn't own a single thing in the world. He had zero dollars in the bank. His next Social Security check, for $296, was scheduled to arrive soon. He had a fever and elevated blood pressure. He couldn't stop coughing and felt a dull, aching pain on the left side of his chest. That day at the doctor they stuck him with a bunch of needles and ran scans and found cancer in his lungs that had spread to his bladder. He stayed in the hospital for a month and went home. Then he went back, this time for thirty-eight more days, and he received twenty-five doses of radiation. Sometimes pieces of tissue got stuck in his penis and made him feel on fire. His pants smelled like urine because he dribbled all the time. He only felt good lying down, just a dying old man who lived on the Black side of town. His home was a former Black church.

He'd been forgotten by then, pushed to the fringes by a society that didn't like what his existence said about it. A year after his acquittal, in 1956, J. W. Milam found himself living near the barn on a farm between Ruleville and Cleveland. Nobody in Tallahatchie County would rent him land to farm. His brother-in-law finally helped him rent a couple hundred acres near the barn and John Whitten helped him get a small crop loan from the Bank of Webb to get a cotton crop in the ground. He lived in a tenant house with no running water, probably a home left behind by the Black sharecroppers fleeing men like him.

"I had a lot of friends a year ago," he said then.

The Sunflower County sheriff refused his application to carry a gun. Two years later he lived in a different tenant house. The *New York Post* gleefully published a witness's account of seeing him standing in a bread line. Once he stole a whiskey still and drove it in his truck right through the middle of Charleston. One of the jurors complained, "To think of all we did for him and he goes and does something like that."

He moved to Texas near Roy Bryant for a few years, where he made the most money he'd ever make in a year, twelve thousand dollars in 1965, but he soon returned to Greenville. He kept getting in trouble. A conviction for writing a bad check. Another for using a stolen credit card. Ten days in jail in 1972 for assault and battery. Devery Anderson interviewed a next-door neighbor and found that Milam was the only white person in his neighborhood. J.W. spent a lot of time alone on the porch with his mean attack dog. In the last months of his life, he started having long conversations with the writer Bonnie Blue, who said he confessed the details of the murder to her step-by-step, although many of the details in her reports remain uncorroborated by any of the other reporting done on the murder.

According to her, J.W. said that at the store Emmett tried to run and that it was Too Tight Collins who caught him. She said Melvin Campbell was there, and that Roy Bryant punched Emmett in the stomach and hit him in the head with his pistol. She said Leslie Milam was up and already working in the barn when J.W.'s truck pulled up that morning. She said that tears rolled down Emmett's face as he fought through his stutter to say, "I want my mama!"

By the fall of 1980 Milam weighed 187 pounds. He'd weighed 235 during the trial when he smoked his victory cigars and collected all the photographs the newspaper photographers had taken of him. Milam kept going down to Jackson. The doctors didn't like his vitals. He needed repeated blood transfusions. The forms made him recall his life before he'd killed a boy named Emmett Till. He faithfully wrote down the dates he'd been shot in France, and how he ended up in a general hospital in England. By November he walked into the doctor's office pale, depressed, and angry, with liquor on his breath. The doctor confronted him and he admitted only to taking a drink before leaving the Delta.

"Pain in both my hips and the bones of my legs," he told the doctor.

His pulse kept slowing down. The doctors told him not to drink. He cut back from two packs of cigarettes a day to one. Five days later he returned. The pain had gotten worse. He wanted to see a bone doctor. That's what he told the staff.

"A bone doctor," he begged.

His legs didn't bear weight. The doctors whacked him in the knee with a reflex hammer. Nothing. They pricked him with a needle. Nothing. Milam went home but on December 27, 1980, he checked back into the VA hospital in Jackson, the facility my great-grandfather tried to block because the government wanted to treat Black veterans there. Three days later Milam died.

IN NOVEMBER OF 1955, J. W. Milam and Roy Bryant faced a second charge in Leflore County: kidnapping. This one was an easy case to make. They'd confessed to the sheriff already. Moses Wright risked his life coming back south to testify. The grand jury refused to even return an indictment. There would be no trial for kidnapping, even though both men told the Leflore County sheriff that they had kidnapped Emmett. Simeon Wright said this news felt like "salt in a raw, open wound," and it taught the family to try to bury their feelings somewhere deep and safe. There would be no justice in Mississippi. There would be no memory. There would be only silence and erasure. On November 9, 1955, both men were released. Fourteen days later, Ben Sturdivant kicked Leslie and Frances Milam out of their home and sold the barn, the house, and the land to Reg Shurden, Stafford Shurden's grandfather, and when the next local land map came out, every piece of ground in the area had a name on it, except the one beneath the barn.

IV

Tomorrow

In Montgomery, Alabama, Rosa Parks got the 1955 issue of *Jet* with Beverly Weathersby on the cover and she wept when she turned to page 8. Two and a half months later she went to the Dexter Avenue Baptist Church for a political event. T.R.M. Howard, who organized Willie Reed's secret exit from Mississippi, spoke about the killings of Lamar Smith and George W. Lee. Then in disturbing detail he described the death of Emmett Till and the exoneration of his killers. The story haunted her. Four days later she finished her shift at the department store where she worked as a seamstress. Her shoulder hurt. She stopped at Lee's drugstore on an errand and then waited at Court Square for a bus back home. Her husband was cooking dinner that night. The city's Christmas decorations lit up the gloaming. A two-tone green-and-yellow city bus stopped and she paid her ten cents and took a seat. The bus was mostly empty but slowly it filled. At the next stop all twelve white seats were taken as well as all the twenty-two seats available to everyone. If the bus was full and a white person wanted a seat, a Black person had to stand.

A white man stood by the driver. He never asked for the seat. The bus driver, James Fred Blake, got pleasure from hassling Black riders. He'd given Parks trouble before.

"Let me have those front seats," he called.

Four Black people sat in the four middle seats closest to the driver.

None of them moved.

"You all better make it light on yourselves and let me have those seats."

Three of the people stood.

Parks stayed seated.

The driver got up and came back to stand over her. Arrest and a potential beating awaited if she refused his order. She thought about her grandfather, the son of a white plantation owner, and how he always kept a shotgun within reach to shoot back if some night riders came to do violence to his family.

She said later she thought in that moment about Emmett Till.

ON OCTOBER 28, 1955, an Alabama-born writer named Bill Huie sat down in the Breland & Whitten law office by the Sumner courthouse. J. W. Milam, Roy Bryant, Carolyn Bryant, and John Whitten joined him. Huie carried with him a large amount of cash advanced by *Look* magazine. The murderers in front of him needed as much of it as they could get. Just nine days earlier the Bryants put their store on the market. Black customers had boycotted them. J. W. Milam was equally a pariah. Eventually he'd be living in a shack without running water.

Huie took notes but made no recording, per a carefully lawyered agreement ironed out over a series of meetings. The killers would split 20 percent of Huie's net and their lawyers would split 10 percent. They talked for hours and when all that talk ended, the men shared a bottle of bourbon. This meeting would birth the famous *Look* magazine story that's now known as the confession.

The language Huie used in print mirrored language the lawyers had used in writing before. The defense team, whose real client was a system, crafted a very specific version of events. In the story Huie wrote, the killers never went to the barn and never entered Township 22 North or Sunflower County, which meant that Leslie Milam could not be tried for the murder. In Huie's original pitch letters to the magazine, after initially meeting with Whitten and Breland, he spoke consistently of four murderers, which made sense: J.W., Roy, Leslie, Melvin Campbell. After October 28, the story would be told with only J.W. and Roy, and without even a nod toward Leslie Milam and his barn. Leslie's brothers protected him even as they confessed for money.

The lawyers didn't just stage-manage the action reported in the story. They also supplied the motive. The quotes from J. W. Milam about fighting for the rights and pride of white men came straight from his lawyer, Breland, a Princeton grad who'd been practicing law in Sumner since 1915. In the negotiations for the interviews, Breland had spoken freely with Huie, using some of the language that would come from J.W.'s mouth when the story appeared. In those conversations Breland made it clear that he and his friends hoped this story would be a weapon against the local Blacks. *Let them read the true nature of depravity and violence. Drive some out and control the rest.* The lawyers in town, educated men all, genuinely believed that the Supreme Court, any day now, would reverse itself on *Brown v. Board*—"just like prohibition," Breland told Huie. He and Whitten wanted to "put the North and the NAACP and the n——s on notice."

It was a "good propaganda move," they told him.

Buried in the notes Huie kept was a description of the book he hoped to write on the back of this story. His work would study a "community approved murder" and he planned on naming it *The Case History of an Approved Murder*. That idea didn't embarrass Breland and Whitten. Quite the opposite. Breland said men like him needed to push dumb, poor white folks to fear and then let the violence grow on its own.

"We've got to have our Milams to fight our wars and keep the n——s in line."

The defense attorneys wanted to "turn the rednecks against the n——s and let the chips fall."

Breland wanted everyone who read *Look* magazine to plainly understand.

"We don't need the n——s no more," he told Huie. "And there ain't gonna be no integration. There ain't gonna be no n——s voting. And the sooner everybody in this country realizes it the better. If any more pressure is put on us, the Tallahatchie River won't hold all the n——s that'll be thrown into it."

Huie carefully orchestrated this moment of revelation. He'd been open for business from the beginning. The first partner he pitched for financial backing was the NAACP, but when that didn't work, he went to Milam, Bryant, and their lawyers. In them he found eager co-conspirators. In his correspondence he reveals himself as insufferable. I recognized immediately what I was seeing: a southerner putting on the myth for a northern friend. It's a favorite move for generations of Mississippians. Under the guise of saying his writing won't be cursed with affection, he describes this allegedly simple prose as "straight sex, hate, moonshine likker and violence."

The magazine editor insisted that one of his staffers check these men out in person. That sent Huie into a tizzy and in a series of numbered memos he laid out all sorts of advice for the selection of this comrade. Huie said "if your man is the liberal type" then a warning should be made, and in case the editor didn't know exactly what warning, Huie spelled that out, too, declaring, "I am capable of drinking out of the mug with Milam and letting him drink first."

In another letter he got even more wound up.

"He should at least be an Anglo who can drink bourbon straight out of the bottle without making a face," he wrote, "and who can ENJOY maybe a meal and an hour's 'good fellowship' with me and Bryant and Milam and Breland."

In correspondence about the magazine contract, Huie called himself "hot" in Hollywood and said his last book had sold more copies than any other book published in 1954. He writes these letters like he's wearing a smoking jacket with a pawnshop war medal dangling from the lapel, waving a signed first edition of *For Whom the Bell Tolls* and pronouncing the *B* instead of the *V* in *Havana*. Bill's byline was William Bradford Huie. Got him? Good. The pages drip with ego. Wheeler told me once that Huie's widow approached him after an event and actually scolded him for not giving her husband more credit.

But even with all his hubris, Huie did understand Mississippi in a way that Milam and Bryant, born and raised, never could. He knew the killers were inconvenient obstacles in the defense of a way of life and that once the late unpleasantness had been wrapped up and the northern reporters tucked back into their big-city cafés, then these two rednecks could be excommunicated for bringing all this heat down on Mississippi in the first place. "Three months from now," he said in his pitch for the story, "the folks who put up the money for his defense won't speak to him on the street."

The Huie account of the murder became the official record.

The barn disappeared from history. Emmett Till had been killed, but according to the state of Mississippi and *Look* magazine, there was no place where that killing occurred.

Almost nobody questioned the utter impossibility of the route laid out by Huie until recently when a student at Rhodes College in Memphis did her thesis on a debunking of the Huie time line and map. Till scholars immediately celebrated her work. This story was personal to her. She grew up in Sumner and her name was Ellen Whitten. John Whitten was her grandfather.

THE BARN SHOOK OFF its infamy and became, almost immediately, a barn again.

Clint Shurden's brother Reg moved into the farmhouse left behind when the Sturdivants ran Leslie Milam off the land. Reg Shurden didn't stay out there long. They never spoke of the murder. "When my grandmother was still living, I didn't realize that's where Emmett Till had been killed," Stafford Shurden had told me.

The Shurdens sold it in 1961 to a family from Missouri. The Buchanans moved to Drew and brought their two children with them. A lot of folks in town today still call Jeff's property the Buchanan place. Their son, Bob, was a junior in high school and fit right in. Bob rode horses around the place. He shot muskrats and snakes down in the bayou. His parents built him a little bedroom over the family garage. Just enough room for a closet, a bed, and a small bathroom. "I could almost get up the steps without my mother hearing me," he said with a laugh.

The land didn't produce good cotton yields, so they made do with soybeans, getting what living they could out of the stingy mud. "That piece of ground didn't have the reputation for being the most productive," Buchanan told me once.

He doesn't know if his father knew the history of the land when he bought it. They never discussed it. Bob remembers exactly when he found out what had happened in their barn. A shed, he called it, just like Jeff. There was an old post in there. One day they were inside working when one of the grown-ups pointed to the post and told him the story.

"That's where they tied up Emmett Till," the man told him.

Buchanan says he didn't think about it much after that. His memories of his childhood on the farm are warm. He played baseball with an eighth-grade shortstop named Archie Manning, who could rocket the ball around the infield. Archie became nationally famous as Ole Miss's quarterback at the end of the decade. Suddenly everyone had heard of this tiny, dusty town. To reporters who loved the country-boy-made-good story, Drew, Mississippi, existed in their copy as a perfect central-casting small southern town. Not a single story on Manning mentioned the famous murder. Archie's father, Buddy, ran the local Case tractor dealership out on Highway 49. People were losing their farms. Buddy Manning struggled with foreclosing on his neighbors. In the summer before Archie became nationally famous, Buddy killed himself with a shotgun. Archie found the body, and the mess, and cleaned up the scene so his mother and sister would never see. He almost never speaks about the suicide, even to his own children. Archie and Bob both describe their childhoods as idyllic.

"Mayberry," Archie described it to me.

"Mayberry," he told the Memphis *Commercial Appeal*.

"Mayberry," he told the New Orleans *Times-Picayune*.

"Mayberry," he told the Indianola *Enterprise-Tocsin*.

There are stories that cover other stories, alluvial sediment layers. Archie never knew Emmett Till had been tortured and killed 3.1 miles west of his childhood home.

ON JUNE 23, 1964, an elderly Black man sat on his steps in the late afternoon in Rochester. He had worked as a porter at the nearby train station. A red Volkswagen with three white college blues aficionados rolled slowly up Greig Street looking at the addresses. Nick Perls, Phil Spiro, and Dick Waterman wanted to find number 61. The three men lived on the East Coast and were part of a small group of people searching for time travelers from the vanished, erased Delta. They loved the blues and wanted to find "lost" bluesmen. The energy propelling them on this quest emanated from Dockery Farms. They were some of the first people outside the Delta to know the word *Dockery*. They talked about forgotten names like Charley Patton and Son House. These artists had just vanished, no death records, no newspaper obituaries, but their recordings remained.

The three men had driven two straight days to Rochester from Mississippi. They'd been down there chasing a rumor that Son House had been spotted in Memphis. He'd become popular again. A new release included liner notes that described to young folk fans the reception they should expect if they went to the Delta in search of this music: "Northwest Mississippi is one of the most vicious areas of human intolerance and brutality on the face of the earth. A stranger in a town like Avalon or Port Gibson is followed as he goes down the street. If a car is left outside a store a sheriff is leaning against it waiting to ask questions when the driver had come back outside."

Less than a decade had passed since the murder, but a world had died. All that violence to protect a way of life, and in the end, it just crumbled to dust. Emmett Till's murder had, in many ways, been the tipping point.

Wheeler Parker did a tour of duty in Nuremburg in 1964. The Liverpool Cotton Association ceased to exist. Joe Rice Dockery got named king of Memphis's Cotton Carnival and down at Joe's plantation blues researchers came to interview people who remembered Charley Patton. The songs they found on old Paramount records told them that the fight for equality on the nightly news had been going on for generations. All the fans looking for new music and new artists were academics in the folkways tradition. They always saw the music not as a Saturday-night dance beat but as evidence. These old musicians were rediscovered prophets, not entertainers. Then came the Freedom Summer and the search for Son House.

Waterman and his friends drove along plantation roads and found angry locals. They visited an old bluesman in a hospital bed who put them on the trail that finally revealed, after a series of meetings and phone calls, Son House to be residing in Rochester. These encounters bounced them between sons in the South and an ex-wife's new mother-in-law's son somewhere in the Northeast, who might connect them to a completely different man in Detroit, who'd point them back south again. The Black Delta existed as an idea more than a place by then. The man in Detroit gave them an address. They sent a telegram but got no reply. Eventually they connected with a man in Rochester who said he knew Son House. That friend, named James Knox, drove over to Son House's place and called the three young men. Knox handed the phone to House, who told the men that he was, in fact, the old bluesman. He'd stopped playing in public when he moved north in 1943, but whenever his old friend Willie Brown would come visit, they'd bust out the guitars and head back down south, if only in their fading memories. When Brown died a few years later, Son House stopped playing altogether. When the three young fans pulled up to his stoop, he had no idea anyone knew his name or his music, or that it had become popular. It stunned and delighted the old man.

That phone call happened on June 21, 1964, the same day three civil rights workers went missing in Philadelphia, Mississippi. James Chaney, Michael Schwerner, and Andrew Goodman had been working to register voters in an area with a powerful Ku Klux Klan presence. Their supervisors feared the worst but hadn't yet accepted a world where the three young men under their protection would become martyrs, the mere mention of their names an emotional and political trigger for a whole generation. Meanwhile the three young blues aficionados, one of whom had gone to high school in Manhattan with Goodman, arrived on Greig Street in Rochester two days later, June 23, 1964. They could have been the missing civil rights workers, and the missing civil rights workers could have been them. These two worlds, fighting for justice and searching for evidence of that justice through an old musical tradition, were one world. The same day the music fans arrived on Son House's street the burned car of the civil rights workers was found in Mississippi. They had been killed.

Son House sat on his stoop and waited. He didn't own a guitar and had forgotten how to play. Alcoholism had left him with the shakes.

His new friends would have to coach him back to his long-vanished skills. In the coming months Alan Wilson, a blues nut from the band Canned Heat, got the honor of teaching "Son House how to play like Son House" again. He did this work well. House would soon be playing Carnegie Hall. He didn't mention returning to Mississippi.

"He never had an interest in coming back," Waterman told me.

Waterman would become a famous rock-and-roll photographer, taking iconic images of Bob Dylan, Joan Baez, and the Rolling Stones. He and Son House would spend hundreds of hours together talking about the Delta and the land. "Son was very, very proud of being an exceptional tractor driver," he said. "He was just really good. Whenever Massey Ferguson or John Deere had a new model of tractor, they would bring the prototype and Son would be the driver who put this thing through its paces."

A year after Waterman drove down Greig Street in Rochester, Gloria Dickerson would leave her home in Township 22 North and with her siblings integrate the Drew public schools. A year after that North Sunflower Academy opened, the school where Jeff Andrews would learn his Mississippi history and later, as an adult, serve as basketball coach and president of the school board. As Waterman and his friends looked for Son House, to the south, Senator Eastland told President Johnson the civil rights workers weren't actually missing and that it was all a "publicity stunt" designed to make the good white people of Mississippi look bad. Eastland hung up. Exactly six minutes later Johnson got a call from the FBI telling him the burned wreck of a station wagon had been found thirty feet off the highway through the Bogue Chitto Swamp. Up in Rochester, New York, the hot summer air cooled down after sunset and House saw the red Volkswagen park and Perls, Spiro, and Waterman get out.

"Can you tell us which apartment Son House lives in?" one of them said.

Son House stood up and extended his hand.

"This is him," he said.

ALL OVER TOWNSHIP 22 NORTH, Range 4 West, and the entire Delta, the old families walked with stoicism toward an unseen cliff. The richest girls still went to the same boarding schools. The boys still went to Woodberry Forest in northern Virginia, Robert E. Lee country, where they relaxed after class on a Donald Ross–designed golf course on campus. Planter boys rushed Phi Delta Theta at Ole Miss. Delta daughters went Phi Mu or Chi Omega. Redneck boys with high and tights sweated out nights riding the circuit with the windows rolled up so all the rich girls would think they had air-conditioning.

The Dockery train station burned to the ground in 1965. The cotton gin shut down around the same time. Joe Rice just locked the door and when somebody got around to opening it decades later, the entire gin machinery sat dusty but intact. The general store burned in 1976. The Dockery post office closed in 1980. Two years later, Joe Rice Dockery died at a hospital in Memphis. His ashes were spread over Dockery.

The old families still farmed the land around them. Steve Shurden stepped in to rent the land from Mrs. Buchanan, who was Bob's mother. He put in two wells so the land could support rice and cotton. He remembers the year because his wife wanted to build a new house and instead he bought a John Deere 8440 four-wheel drive. He needed it to handle the Buchanan place.

He knew about the barn, he told me one day eating lunch at

Stafford Shurden's restaurant on Main Street in Drew. "We didn't think about it," Steve said. "I mean, it wasn't anything to talk about."

"As a kid I didn't know who Emmett Till was," Stafford said.

Out at Dockery after her husband's death Keith Dockery looked back at the world they'd inherited. She was a thoughtful, kind person. Great friends with my aunt Nan. The wild inequality of a working plantation had not escaped her notice. Her words on this subject linger for me because they identify the mistake my people have made over and over. Responsibility for the status quo falls on the heads of every single person living benefiting from the status quo. But the overriding urge and inherited moral imperative is to protect the land.

"What we've done and what we've left undone comes out pretty strong," she wrote. "It's embarrassing. Life just went on. And I recognize to my own sorrow that Molière was right: 'It is not what we do, but also what we do not do, for which we are accountable.'"

The thing "not done" was protecting a child, and then compounding that failure by not telling his story. Fewer and fewer people talked about the barn, even the people closest to it—perhaps *especially* the people closest to it—and slowly it vanished from memory, like so much else surrounding the actual facts of the Till murder. The erasing over the years has been blunt and brutally effective. The only copy of the trial transcript disappeared. Till's ring disappeared from evidence, too. The gun is in a safe, or at least it was until the crop duster pilot's sister started deteriorating from dementia and accusing everyone around her, including her brother, of trying to steal everything from her, including that heirloom gun. A lawyer in Sumner found the gin fan used to sink the body in the 1970s and took it home as a trophy but after a few creepy days went and threw it in the landfill.

In 1971, on the night of her high school graduation, a young Black woman named Joetha Collier walked through Drew's small downtown with her friends. An old-fashioned promenade with summer in the air. Three white young men, blackout drunk, rode past her in a truck. One of the boys lived near the barn. The other two came from one of the founding families of Drew, who'd been on a long generational slide into the tacky confines of peckerwoodville. One of them leaned out the window with a pistol and pulled the trigger. The bullet struck and killed Joetha. One of the boys served a little time and all three now live seemingly normal lives. One of the killers is still in the community. Once he called his local elected official, Gloria Dickerson, to ask her to come out to his house to listen to him complain about something going on with public services provided by Sunflower County. Of course she knew who he was and what he'd done. But this was her job. She shook her head and went to see what the murderer wanted.

Hugh Clark and Melvin Campbell, both alleged to have been in the barn, died of heart failure six days apart in 1972. A year later all of Milam and Bryant's military histories burned along with sixteen to eighteen million other records in a devastating fire in a Saint Louis archive facility. Eula Morgan died the year after that. So did the matriarch of the Shurden family. Sometime in the 1980s, an old farm worker named Willie Nesby said he saw J. W. Milam's old truck collecting rust on either the Sturdivant place or the Flautt place out in Glendora. Delta & Pine got sold to a company named Southwide, which would later sell it to Prudential, starting a run on Delta farmland by big investment houses that continues today. Muddy Waters won his first Grammy. Moses Wright died. And out on Section 2, Mrs. Buchanan finally moved to town, closer to her family and doctors, and abandoned her house.

———

ROY BRYANT RAN A LITTLE store on Highway 49 in Ruleville by then. It was near the intersection with Highway 8 and two turns and a few miles from the barn. The sign out front said BRYANT'S GROCERY. He'd moved there quietly in 1973 and as the years passed, he got old and fat and his eyes dimmed from years spent as a welder. Carolyn had divorced him in 1975. She got full custody of their children. He remarried a woman from Ruleville with big poofy hair. You know what they say: the bigger the hair, the smaller the town (and the closer to God). Polite people in town didn't like it when she spoke to them in public, lest someone think they were friends.

"You could buy beer and chicken," Ruleville native Mary Perry told me. "It was one of those stores where you could get anything. Old men hung out and drank beer. Probably craps games. That's big in the Delta."

Bryant walked his wooden floors and chain-smoked. A store cat liked to sleep on grocery sacks. He served plate lunches to hungry workers. If anyone asked about Till, Roy would answer, "Yeah, I killed a n——."

Perry shopped in the store all the time.

"He could be so polite and nice," she said, "but then he could turn and be so mean. It was shocking because you never knew. You never wanted to rile him. We didn't want to mess with him. He was very weird. He couldn't see well. We were scared to death of him."

Every few years, usually on some anniversary or after another character in the saga had died, reporters would come find him. Just laying eyes on him and getting yelled at was the point, in a way. "He hated it when they'd come," Perry told me. "You could tell. He'd get real uneasy. I think it made him nervous, to be honest.

He'd turned old and blind and he turned afraid because he didn't know who was coming at him."

The one big beer cooler held Budweiser tall boys. Gamblers liked to hang around the counter. Roy sold cigarettes and cans of dip.

"I hated it when he looked at me directly in the eyes," Perry said.

I WAS BORN IN 1976 and went to a high school called Lee Academy.

Now people who want to defend it insist that it was not named after General Robert E. Lee but after the middle name of a local planter who donated the land. But the school newspaper was named the *Traveller*. That was Robert E. Lee's horse. We got off school not for Martin Luther King Jr.'s birthday but for Robert E. Lee's birthday. Of course it's named for Robert E. Lee. These academies virtually all sprang to life at the same time: between the end of first semester 1969 and the start of second semester 1970. In between those dates, a federal judge demanded that Mississippi—sixteen years after *Brown v. Board*—finally integrate its schools. The moment had arrived. The ruling came on October 29, 1969. That date marks the real end of the formal Jim Crow caste system. The Delta schools went on Christmas break, and in that month the white power structure sprang into furious action. When my hometown of Clarksdale reopened its public schools on February 2, 1970, 574 of the 585 white students were missing.

Financed by powerful planters, such as the Pillows in Greenwood and the Shurdens in Drew and the Andersons in Clarksdale, the white ruling class formed a parallel school system in the Delta, a constellation of segregation academies like Lee Academy, Bayou Academy, and North Sunflower Academy. Frank Bryant, Roy and Carolyn's son, graduated from North Sunflower in 1975. He played football for the Rebels.

These new schools revolved around twin goals: to keep white and Black kids from becoming friends and making babies and to teach those white kids a newly invented gospel of the Delta, that there were good whites and bad whites, many more of the former than the latter. That was the creation myth of a new land stripped of everything that had happened since those first prehistoric native monocrop hunters moved south into the violent but nutrient-rich forest swamps. Generations of white Delta children have now been taught this myth from birth, including Jeff Andrews and me.

The academies are dying now. The population is down, so enrollment is down. Some big farmers now live in Oxford and commute the hour to their land every day. It's like it was before scientists figured out how to prevent malaria: landowners hiding their families in the Hills while dipping down into an alien place to make money.

Out on Highway 32, across from the ruins of the sheriff's old plantation, Strider Academy sits abandoned. Lee Academy was dying when I went there and is now on life support. There's only one way for it to survive. North Sunflower has Black students and while I reported this book, they took down the Confederate flag from its football press box. Jeff Andrews approved the removal. The Lee Academy cheerleading squad now has Black members. Greenville Christian, once thought of as the most redneck of the academies, is now the most diverse. Turns out, the only way for a segregation academy to survive is to integrate.

———

REG SHURDEN WALKED INTO 1980 confident enough to schedule a weeklong golf trip to a resort in Brownsville, Texas. The year
before, he'd farmed 4,099 acres, which he planted mostly in cotton
and beans. By early March he followed closely the futures for the
year, watching the price of cotton tick down a little more every day.
December cotton looked weak. The middle of the month brought a
deluge, more than a foot of rain, swelling Dougherty Bayou and
flooding all the land south of Drew. Reg hung out in his shop and
waited. Finally on May 3 he started planting cotton. His crew finished nine days later. Four days after that, it rained two inches,
which tickled him to death. Just perfect for a new cotton seed.

He didn't know a second great farming collapse was coming,
almost as bad as 1920.

Just up the road past the barn his cousin Sidney Shurden's name
started to appear in the newspaper's tax sale advertisements in 1981.
That's always the first sign of a crumbling empire. He owed money
on his land in Township 22 North, Range 4 West, the paper reported, tracts in Section 1, Section 2 near the barn, and Section 11.
An academic paper I read called 1981–1986 the worst era in American agriculture since the collapse of 1929. In 1981 one agricultural
bank failed. In 1985 sixty-two did. The first Farm Aid relief concert happened in 1985 as a direct response by Bob Dylan and Willie
Nelson to the agricultural collapse.

Sunflower County kept emptying out, more people leaving every year. Between 1940 and 1980 the Black population of Sunflower
County fell from 43,000 to 21,000. The main force driving this
depopulation was mechanization and the displacement of cotton

atop the global economy. A 1978 headline in *The New York Times* read COTTON NO LONGER RULES IN SOUTH.

Interest rates hit 21.5 percent in 1981 and stayed in the 20 percent range for several years. Farmland values dropped as much as 60 percent. The suicide rate among farmers jumped 400 percent. Small farms got sucked up by bigger farms, which got sucked up by Wall Street investors. In 1935 there had been 6.8 million farms in America. By 1990 that number would be 2.1 million.

Sidney Shurden's name kept appearing in the tax sale rolls, land all over that first bend in the Drew-Ruleville Road, in Sections 1, 2, and 11. Many of Shurden's neighbors in Township 22 North lost land in tax sales. He wasn't alone. But his family had anchored this road for generations and that was ending on his watch. It ate at him. He lost his dad's plantation piece by piece. He lost the little strip of land where Willie Reed lived in 1955. The 1986 harvest did him in. Prices were low and a drought diminished yields. By the end of the year his name stopped appearing in the tax sale listings in the Indianola paper. His family farm was gone. At almost the same time Juliet Louis found out her husband Willie had once witnessed a famous murder, back when he had a different name. Willie Reed outlived the Shurden Plantation, where he worked for the last time in the summer of 1955.

J. W. Milam died in 1980.

Muddy Waters died in 1983. Mamie Till-Mobley retired that year from a career in the Chicago public schools, where she taught fifth grade.

Son House died in 1988.

Matthew Carter, Gloria's father, died in 1988, too.

The last commercial-scale cotton textile mill in Manchester closed in 1989.

The following year, 1990, Jeff Andrews opened a dental practice in Drew.

IN SECTION 36 OF TOWNSHIP 22 North an old farmhouse held the treasures collected over a lifetime in Hollywood by a local son made good named Luster Bayless. Bayless grew up across the street from his homestead as the poor kid of a white sharecropper. He hitchhiked from Ruleville to Hollywood, California, to join a friend who'd found a job as a costumer. It took him four years of grinding to get his big break. The man who changed his life was western star John Wayne. Bayless had gotten a job as the set costumer on *McLintock!* John Wayne loved him and they made thirteen more films together, including *True Grit*, *Rio Lobo*, and *The Shootist*. Bayless's credits include *Mary Poppins* and *Apocalypse Now*. His company, United American Costume, has grown to include 125,000 square feet of wardrobes. Until the day he died in 2022, Bayless could recite from memory Wayne's measurements: chest 49, hat 7⅜, shoe 10½D.

In the mid-1980s Bayless got obsessed with the Emmett Till murder. Bayless had a personal connection to the case. He lived on the same road where Emmett died, down where it dead-ended into Highway 8. Bayless convinced Roy Bryant, who lived nearby, to take a researcher on a tour of the murder. Bayless's researcher, a woman, ran a recorder the whole time.

She took Polaroids of Roy standing in front of the barn. They'd stay hidden for decades. When I first learned about the barn, Bayless was in assisted living and his daughter, Diana, ran the family business out in California. She told me she had the pictures and the recordings in one of their warehouses. The only people to listen to the tapes since they had been made were the FBI agents who discovered them during a reopening of the case twenty years ago.

Bayless paid Cecelia Lusk, a Ruleville native who worked at the state prison in Parchman, to do more research. She interviewed locals, including people who'd never talked before and would never talk again. She went to Delta State in Cleveland and Ole Miss in Oxford. She found that the stories had been torn out of the *Look* and *Life* magazines in the archives. In both courthouses in Tallahatchie County, she found the legal file folders for the case. They were empty. "Not one sheet of paper," she told me. "Someone had removed everything. There was absolutely not one piece of paper in those folders."

The fan was missing, the ring was missing, the trial transcript was missing, and most of the people who lived within eyesight of the barn had no idea what had happened there. It's almost as if a dome descended over the state and locked out anything that happened before 1970 when the schools finally integrated. People did truly horrible things to their fellow man. Yes, the violence, but also prosaic daily acts devoid of basic humanity. The image I can't shake is Elizabeth Wright running desperate and panicked in 1955 to her neighbor's house—the Bible makes clear the primacy of literal and spiritual neighbors—and begging the white woman there to use the phone, and her husband saying no.

LOCAL BLACK KNOWLEDGE about the barn faded, too, which also wasn't an accident. Jesse Gresham, a local pastor in Drew, says that a decade or so ago he went into a building owned by the county school board and found, in a locked room, sealed boxes of unused books that offered a detailed history of the civil rights movement.

"We found those books in one room," he says. "That was the first time I recognized that they're trying to hide the history. They don't want to think about what their own parents and grandparents did. They didn't want future generations to know they were snakes."

His wife, Delores Gresham, tells me she can feel the story of Emmett Till fading from Drew's collective memory.

"Most of the older generation has passed on," she says. "The younger generation, to tell you the honest truth, they probably couldn't care less. I do substitute teaching and I brought up Martin Luther King Jr. one time and they asked me, 'Who was that?' I stood there with my mouth wide open."

Delores Gresham has her own connection to the Till case. In December 1955, Elmer Kimbell, one of the men who at the very least helped clean up the Till murder, was drunk and driving Milam's pickup truck, the same one used to kidnap Emmett Till. He allegedly carried Milam's .45 with him, too, the same gun that had been used to kill Emmett Till. Kimbell got gas in Glendora and couldn't pay. Embarrassed, he shot and killed the station attendant. The attendant was Delores Gresham's father. A jury acquitted Elmer Kimbell, too. The next fifteen years would be full of violence and once it was over, nobody would admit that they or anyone they knew had anything to do with it.

A white Glendora resident said at the time, "There's open season on the Negroes now. They've got no protection, and any peckerwood who wants can go out and shoot himself one."

I sat with Delores in her living room one day. She likes floral prints. We talked about her parents and I asked how often she thinks about them.

"All the time," she said.

She looked over at a picture of her father. It's the only one she has. "He didn't even have a chance," she said softly.

THE OLD MILAM HOUSE sat empty overlooking the swamp and the road. High school kids found it out there. A party house. They'd build a fire in the yard or go inside to sit around and drink. At night it was dark in the front room. Big bay windows overlooked the cypress trees and the bayou. Sometimes the kids would go through Mrs. Buchanan's drawers. They found old farm bills and letters and leftover pieces of a life.

"It was like they left in a hurry," said Griff Cook, who was Sidney Shurden's stepson.

The high schoolers used it as a clubhouse. On the winter midmornings the ducks circled above a little pond nearby as they looked for a place to roost and wait out the day. At night the old cypress trees scared them. That was part of the fun. There's no light out in the country.

"Spooky as hell," Jason Shurden said.

The house looked like a set from a horror movie, everything in shambles. Vandals had left debris and graffiti. Someone had a gin fan out there.

"That thing had been so long abandoned," he said.

The kids explored the house. Inside they had a routine. Someone found Bob's old makeshift bedroom, which became the place to smoke weed. On the second story an enormous hole in the floor made walking around up there dangerous. The boys drank beer and whiskey. Sometimes they sat beneath the trees in the yard. They rolled joints. Jason Shurden made out with a few girls in the house.

The Buchanans had also left behind, with the house and the old bills, two pet peacocks. The birds strutted around the house with their huge green-and-purple plumes. One night Jason sat there in the woods down from the barn and he heard this noise in the darkness. Darkness and imagination amplify everything and he wondered if some wild animal, or a lost company of cavalry, was approaching in the night. Then a peacock came streaking through the trees.

ROY BRYANT WAS STILL ALIVE, barely, when Jeff Andrews bought the barn and built his home there on the bayou. Bryant lived 7.9 miles away. Tumors grew on his neck and in his throat. A few days before a big ice storm hit, Byron De La Beckwith got sentenced to life in prison for the murder of Medgar Evers. Bryant felt the world closing in. He feared he'd be next and didn't know where to turn. In desperation he went to the last people who'd been willing to help him.

John Whitten went to his office in Sumner that morning like he always did, a small-town southern lawyer who looked the part with his suit and country patrician accent. An elderly stranger came through the front door and stuck out his hand.

"I'm Roy Bryant," he said.

Whitten hadn't seen him since the trial. Roy's condition shocked him.

"I'm old," Bryant said.

Photos of Bryant in the last year of his life are hard to find. He'd been dead in the eyes of his peers for many decades by that point, just moving through the world, unwanted and mostly unseen. In this rejection of him, they—we—elevated him. He *was* the Delta, decaying and abandoned, wearing his sins on the outside, too. Standing in Whitten's office, Roy had less than a year to live.

"I'm sick," he said. "I can't work."

He asked Whitten for a favor. Maybe a few dollars or a lead on a job. The store had been closed for five years now and he struggled to make a living selling fruit and fireworks by the roadside. People rushing down Highway 49 in Ruleville who saw that dilapidated stand never knew that an American pariah stood blind and dying behind the counter. Whitten told him to get paid to write a book. Bryant turned and left. Whitten never saw him again.

The reporters never stopped coming to talk to him, motivated a little by hope of another confession, but mostly just to see a relic from a past that couldn't really be that distant if Roy Bryant was upright and walking around. The very fact of his existence put the lie to the erasure.

Immediately after Beckwith's conviction the New Orleans–based Till researcher Plater Robinson, the man whose house is full of filing cabinets, got in his car and headed north to Ruleville. He'd been driving the Delta for years talking to the rapidly dying cohort of people who held firsthand secrets about this famous killing.

"Every inch of ground is tortured," he told me.

Plater got to Ruleville and parked outside the Bryant home. Only two days had passed since Beckwith's conviction.

Robinson knocked on the door.

Roy's wife answered and ushered him inside. The house was dark. When Plater looked into the living room, he saw Roy Bryant lying on the couch. Bryant struggled to haul himself upright. He seemed genuinely excited to have company—until he realized what Robinson wanted to talk to him about.

"Let that goddamn stuff die," he said.

The news from Jackson worried him.

"What they're doing with Beckwith down there," he said.

"Well, they've already done it," Robinson said.

"And now they want to get me, so to hell with them," Roy said.

Bryant tried to stand up but couldn't. Robinson stared at him as afternoon light painted the ravages of time on his face. There was some cosmic justice. At the end of his life, Roy Bryant was small and scared.

"You can't help tell what they might do nowadays," Bryant said. "They might change the Constitution. NAACP do anything they want to. Money will change anything. Don't you believe that?"

"Well, I don't know that to be the truth."

"Shoot, I do," Bryant said.

"I can understand it's uncomfortable to talk about it," Robinson said, "but let me ask you another question."

"It's not uncomfortable for me to talk about anything," Bryant said. "I'm not talking about that particular case."

Roy, riddled with diabetes and cancer, sank back onto the couch and Robinson got in his car. People kept coming to Ruleville to see this dying old relic, like an oxidized bullet found on some battlefield. A college student at Mississippi Valley State, Michael Rosa, went to interview Bryant for a school project. He approached Bryant at his vegetable and fruit stand out on the highway. That day Bryant felt like talking. He treated Rosa politely and started to tell the story. Rosa said Bryant said "n——" at least one hundred times when describing the murder. Bryant said that after Carolyn told him about the whistle he planned on just beating Till but the boy made some comments that pushed him over the edge. He admitted to being drunk and said they already had the gin fan when they killed him in the barn. Bryant said they tied the fan around his neck right there on Leslie's farm. He told Rosa that Carolyn had been in the truck during the kidnapping, just like Moses Wright believed. He complained that the white folks in Ruleville wouldn't buy his watermelons and that his half brother, J.W., had made all the money from the *Look* magazine story.

Two weeks later, Roy Bryant died in a hospital in Jackson. His family brought his body back to the Delta and buried him just on the other side of Highway 8. His grave sits on the very edge of Township 22 North, Range 4 West, buried in the same thirty-six square miles of dirt he stained with Emmett Till's blood. After his death the southern preacher and social justice crusader Will Campbell sat down with Mamie Till-Mobley. Campbell had been run off from his job in 1956 as Ole Miss's campus spiritual adviser for his liberal views on race. His book *Providence*, about one piece of land in Mississippi, is a spiritual ancestor of this project.

He asked her if she felt anger that her son's killers had gotten away with murder.

"Didn't you hear? They got the death penalty," Till-Mobley replied.

"The death penalty?"

"Yes, the community ostracized them. Some of their family left them. Before long, cancer got both of them. They lost their lives for what they did to my boy."

THE YOUNG DOCUMENTARY FILMMAKER Keith Beauchamp, long on idealism and confidence if short then on experience, befriended Mamie Till-Mobley in the last years of her life. That sent him on a path of discovery in the Delta, looking for new information about the case. Somebody told him that the barn where Emmett Till had been killed was still standing. No outsiders knew the location.

"For a year I had been looking for the barn," he said.

Several people told him the barn was in Ruleville. He got lots of conflicting reports. The mistakes in the initial media reports that said the murder happened on Clint "Sheridan's" plantation made it harder for someone not plugged into Delta geography to locate. None of the three descriptions of the barn's ownership made in books and stories—Sheridan, Shurden, and Sturdivant—were accurate. Locals at the time called it the Milam barn. So mostly Beauchamp chased rumors. He felt like he couldn't go knocking on doors, at white homes or Black homes, and just start asking about the case.

"Because at the time people were forbidden to utter the words *Emmett Till*," he said. "People were still afraid to talk about Till publicly."

A series of introductions helped him close in. Beauchamp kept hearing that some of the killers had never been identified and were still alive. Everything felt new. He met the scholars Linda and David Beito, who introduced him to the Greshams in Drew: Jesse, who had found the hidden schoolbooks, and Delores, whose father had been lynched in 1955, too. They began to tell him all the things they knew. Nobody had ever asked them before.

Reverend Gresham told Beauchamp how to find the barn.

Keith drove around in the country but the directions didn't make sense. He went back to the Greshams to pick up Jesse. The preacher directed him turn by turn and when they got to the Dougherty Bayou south of town, he simply pointed. Keith drove Jesse back home and returned alone. He didn't know who owned the place or how receptive they might be to a stranger. He walked up to the door and knocked.

Jeff Andrews answered the door.

Keith asked the question. Jeff said yes.

He walked Keith around the property and took him to the barn.

Keith broke down in tears. Jeff and his wife, in that first meeting, shared a secret of their own. They both sensed the presence of spirits on the property. Jeff's wife even talked to a ghost when she got scared. She addressed the unseen spirit by name. She called him Emmett. Keith and Jeff stood together and talked and shared stories. The barn had taken its first step into the light.

KEITH'S DOCUMENTARY came out in 2005 and reintroduced the barn as part of the history. He was able to screen footage of the barn for Mamie Till-Mobley before she died in 2003. She asked him questions about what it felt like out there. A year later the FBI started sniffing around the case, wondering if it could indict Carolyn Bryant, who at the very least had identified Till to her husband and his half brother.

At the same time due west of Memphis, a birder named Gene Sparling paddled through a remote wetlands wildlife refuge when an enormous bird flew out of the woods and right in front of his eyes. He knew instantly that it was an ivory-billed woodpecker. He also knew that they were supposedly extinct. These were the birds that had ruled the skies above Township 22 North, double-knocking in the green swamp forests, whose home had been crushed by the rolling wheels of progress when the trees were cut down.

Two weeks after that initial sighting, the world's ivorybill experts converged on the swamp and two more men spotted the bird. Sixty years after its presumed extinction, the bird might have returned. Not all experts believed the sightings, and a war broke out among the few hundred people in the world who are obsessed with such data.

Three months later the FBI officially reopened the Till case.

Then the FBI searched Jeff Andrews's barn. Eventually the FBI exhumed the body of Emmett Till. One of the central pillars in the defense of Milam and Bryant was that the body Mamie Till took home to Chicago was not, in fact, her son. Prosecutors would have to deal with that at trial and so the Till family gave their permission. It was a somber day on the South Side of Chicago. The family held a small service and then the diggers went to work. They removed the vault and then the casket. As soon as the casket came out, the concrete vault crumbled to dust.

The assembled people gasped.

Emmett Till had been buried in a glass-top coffin. The glass hadn't broken. The fingerprint smudges of the mourners still showed. And the Tutwiler embalmer clearly had done his work carefully and with love. Emmett Till looked exactly as he had when they put him in the grave. The FBI photos taken in 2005 mirrored the famous *Jet* magazine pictures.

The law enforcement people took him to the morgue. The X-rays revealed that he'd been killed, as everyone believed, with a .45 automatic pistol firing 7.5 bird shot. A crowd of people gathered around and did the solemn work. A pathologist put X-rays up on the light box. The images of his skull showed all the missing pieces that never came out of the Tallahatchie. The DNA matched the family sample provided by Simeon Wright. The body taken and returned to the Chicago dirt was conclusively Emmett Louis Till.

Dale Killinger put the finishing touches on his report and three weeks later, the FBI presented it to the local prosecutor. The grand jury met and declined to bring charges against Carolyn Bryant. Killinger still blames Mississippi prosecutor Joyce Chiles for being gutless. He thought they could make a case against Carolyn Bryant, and Simeon Wright wanted the Black men who helped Milam to be held accountable, too.

As this was happening, another rush of ivory-billed woodpecker sightings occurred in a different swamp, this one on the border of Mississippi and Louisiana. A scientist at NASA's Stennis Space Center named Mike Collins saw the bird four more times. In late February he got the bird on videotape, although some in the ivory-bill universe were still unconvinced. Researchers found more birds at a swamp site in Florida. Then the sightings of the ivory-billed woodpecker almost completely stopped. The NASA man saw another bird in the spring of 2008 and that fall George W. Bush signed the Till Bill into law, making it easier for law enforcement agencies to collaborate on reopened civil rights cold cases. *The New York Times* ran a story about the search for ivory-billed woodpeckers ending. There hasn't been a confirmed sighting since.

The American Bird Conservancy does not presently list the bird as extinct. Rather, it's a species that's been "lost."

Jeff Andrews admitted to me, as he did to Beauchamp, that he and his family believe the spirit of Emmett Till haunts their barn. A paranormal expert returns time and again to the barn with the Andrewses' permission; she believes Emmett talks to her, too. Emmett always leaves her a sign, she says, and it always takes the same form. She says she finds big white feathers on the ground.

IN LATE 2017 the city of Memphis successfully outmaneuvered the state of Tennessee and found a loophole that would allow them to take down the statue of Nathan Bedford Forrest, the one that had been erected by his cronies as they were simultaneously buying the land where Emmett Till would eventually be killed. The state had passed a law that prohibited local cities from removing any historical statues or markers on public property, thinking that would keep liberal communities from tearing down Confederate monuments. But the city sold the park to a private nonprofit for one thousand dollars. The nonprofit, not bound by the law, swooped in one night and put the horse and rider in a big sling attached to a crane. A small crowd gathered to watch. Police milled around beneath the bright work lights. The statue was lifted off its base at exactly 9:01 p.m., a nod to Memphis's area code.

"Now drop it!" someone yelled.

That left the two bodies buried beneath the base. The nonprofit and the Forrest family disagreed about the definition of a headstone. The family believed the monument was a burial marker, since the Forrests had been buried beneath it. The family's attorney, Ed Phillips from Nashville, worked quietly with the city and the nonprofit to figure out what to do with the remains. In public Phillips made a lot of noises about having the statue put back up— he also represents the Forrest Chapter of the Sons of Confederate Veterans—but in private he just wanted closure for his clients, the six living great-great-grandchildren of Nathan and Mary Ann.

On a brutally hot and humid July afternoon in Nashville, Phillips met me in the parking lot of a suburban Starbucks. I got into his sedan and he headed out of town. He wanted to drive me to Forrest's childhood home in Chapel Hill.

"I understand people's feelings," he said as the skies darkened. "I understand the complexity of those feelings and nuances and all that. I get it. But at some point, you also have to recognize this: this man's been dead since 1877. I mean, he's dead. He's buried. At some point we keep wallowing in the past, or we just get past the past."

One of the six great-great-grandchildren died while he negotiated. Finally a deal seemed close. Neither side leaked anything. In the summer of 2021, four years after the statue came down, General Forrest and his wife were exhumed and moved. Undertakers carefully gathered the things left inside the crypt. They put his uniform buttons, the soles of his boots, and a little of his leather belt inside protective bags. Nothing else but bones remained. Nathan and Mary Ann got moved to their new burial place, where they will rest forever, or until Forrest comes back into favor and he gets exhumed again. When Phillips saw the new caskets for the first time both were draped in the first Confederate flag. When the funeral finished, they lowered the couple back into the ground and folded up the flags that had rested atop the caskets. Phillips took one home.

"That flag will go to my son," he said, "and hopefully his son."

Finally I spoke.

"Did you bury him in uniform?"

Ed turned to me and smiled.

"Yes."

"How do you get one?" I asked.

He said they called a tailor who makes high-end replicas for Confederate reenactors. All Forrest's exact measurements remained. This was the last Confederate uniform ever made. Maybe. Four rows of gold braid on the sleeves signified a general officer. The shoulder boards had stars. The sword knot was gold and came with a sword belt waist sash. That new wool uniform is down there right now, buried with old bones.

BY 2022, TWO YEARS AFTER George Floyd, Gloria Dickerson had found local traction in Sunflower County. On August 28, sixty-seven years after the murder in the barn, Dickerson's leadership and passion convinced the town of Drew to acknowledge for the first time that Emmett Till had died in their community. Another layer of erasure got stripped away. Hundreds of people gathered at an event space on Main Street near Gloria's office. The mayor, Melanie Ann Townsend, read the proclamation declaring it Emmett Louis Till Day and as she read, a church bell rang somewhere in the distance. People kept coming inside, finding the last empty chairs, lining the walls. The head of the Sunflower County NAACP reminded everybody to go and vote. "Emmett Till is on the ballot," he said. "Everything we've been fighting for the last sixty-seven years is on that ballot."

Everyone stepped out of the building on Main Street and into their cars. A procession formed and headed down toward South Street, which led out to the barn, where we parked. Dozens of cars snaked through the countryside. Lots of Delta plates. Coahoma County. Sunflower. Bolivar. Washington. More people parked on the gravel road and walked across the Dougherty Bayou toward Jeff Andrews's place. A big white tent with folding chairs waited beside the barn. The skies above our heads were blue.

Jeff Andrews stood outside the barn.

He pointed off at a bank of clouds on the horizon.

"It's raining across the field there," he said.

A preacher from Mound Bayou, Darryl Johnson, stalked around under the eaves of the barn waiting on his turn to speak. He's a fire-breather, people told me, and I looked forward to hearing him try to make sense of this place. I'd been many times by now, but always alone or with one or two other people. The barn always felt like a place that repelled people. Marvel Parker described it as "macabre" the first time we ever spoke about it. It was the site of violence, of shame, of depthless cruelty, a complicated site for historians to interpret or figure out an appropriate way to visit. All the other sites carry some note of redemption or tell the story of the societal decay that led to the killing, but this is a reminder of the opposite. There is no heroism to remember here. No defiance. Nobody burst through the door in the nick of time, or risked their life for another, nobody stood up to evil, no one stopped the torture. The only other space in twentieth-century American history with a similar absence of redemption is the 16th Street Baptist Church in Birmingham. But that's a site of pilgrimage. The barn remains a working barn. Now seeing all these people here made the barn's meaning feel different. It felt like a funeral, but this wasn't a burial so much as another exhumation.

"This is horrible ground you have made holy ground," an Episcopal priest said in welcome.

The rain started to fall, picking up speed until a downpour rolled water off the roof of the barn in a solid sheet. People huddled for shelter but nobody went inside. A soloist stepped to the front of the tent. He sang "Amazing Grace," but not as a dirge. He pushed the tempo and the crowd clapped and sang along. Then Reverend Johnson took the microphone. Rain dripped off the roof.

Johnson pointed at the barn and smiled.

"They thought they could cover it up!"

Everyone murmured approval.

"Call his name!" he preached.

"Emmett Till!" everyone responded.

The hair stood up on my arms. This was the first day of the barn's next act, as the preacher's energy and message supercharged the crowd. Nobody spoke except to say the dead child's name.

"What's his name?" Johnson roared.

"EMMETT TILL!" the crowd responded.

The preacher nodded.

"I was blind but now I see," he said.

The rain slowed down.

"This blood is calling from the ground!" the preacher said.

"Call his name," the preacher said.

"Emmett Till!"

"WHAT IS HIS NAME?"

"EMMETT TILL!"

"We are now his family. If you're from Mississippi, you're part of his family."

The rain had almost stopped and blue sky opened up. Johnson preached about the promise of America and got a call-and-response going.

"Emmett Till," the crowd said.

"And justice?"

"Emmett Till."

"For all!"

"Emmett Till!"

The choir director wiped away a tear. All the people lined up to scoop dirt from the barn floor and place it in a jar that would be sent to the lynching museum in Montgomery. Gloria Dickerson went first.

MEANWHILE THE WALLS OF SILENCE that had always protected Carolyn Bryant began to crack. Her fiercely loyal daughter-in-law, Marsha Bryant, filed for divorce against Carolyn's son Tom Bryant. Marsha agreed to talk to me and Mississippi investigative journalist Jerry Mitchell. We met in a suburban seafood joint with pastel accents and a beachy vibe.

"At one time his mother told me that Tom was just like Roy," Marsha said.

The waitress came around. Marsha ordered a soft-shell crab po' boy.

When she met Tom Bryant she didn't know any of his family history. She knew Roy and Carolyn before she learned about their lives in 1955.

"I had no idea," she said.

Finally Eula, Roy and J.W.'s mom, told Marsha that Roy had been on the cover of *Look* magazine. Marsha went and found a copy. That's how she learned.

Just before Roy died, they talked about the murder. He didn't confess, not exactly, but he seemed to be trying to tell her something. "I was asking him a little bit about the Till stuff," she said. "He never talked about it. And he told me, if there was one day he could change in his life, that would be the day."

We'd been sitting there for a while. The other lunch customers had mostly slipped out. Marsha told us that one of the main reasons for the divorce was how her husband watched nothing but Fox News in the aftermath of George Floyd and got more and more radicalized with every passing day.

"The older Tom got," she said, "he became more and more and more prejudiced."

"You've got to stop watching the news," she told him.

He watched more and more.

"All the George Floyd stuff was just making him crazy," she said, "and making him nastier and uglier."

———

THE SECRETARY OF THE INTERIOR, Deb Haaland, flew down to the Delta to review specific sites for a national monument. Momentum had been building. Congressman Bennie Thompson took her to Glendora, where she was told many details from the Huie account, which was written to protect Leslie Milam and to erase his barn. She was told that Till died in Glendora, which of course isn't true. She was told he was thrown from the Black Bayou Bridge, a claim that no evidence beyond simple proximity exists to support and plenty exists to disprove. She was told the cotton gin fan came from Glendora, which might be true but cannot be proved. The next stop after Glendora was the courthouse in Sumner.

Somewhere in the planning the barn had been dropped from the secretary's schedule. Nobody in the ETIC could really figure out why but they suspected. There were behind-the-scenes political battles with federal money at stake. Different people offered opinions and arguments. The barn seemed in danger of slipping out of the historical record once more because people wanted to fudge the history to get more money for certain towns in the Delta. In Sumner the government officials with the power to rewrite history all sat in the same place where the jury had sat before acquitting the killers of Emmett Till. The old courtroom had been faithfully restored to its exact look from 1955. The air felt heavy and then Gloria Dickerson stood to speak for the town of Drew.

"This story has haunted me ever since I was a child," she began.

She told the secretary about her parents, how they'd lived their adult lives in a tight square of Sunflower County, and how the ghosts of 1955 lived alongside them.

"When I was growing up, my family lived about a mile from the scene," she told the secretary. "And my mom would talk to us about that. Every day we came into Drew we would pass that barn, she would say, 'That's where Emmett Till was killed.' And we kept saying, 'Momma, who was Emmett Till?'"

She told her story of going out into the world and being called home.

"The story brought me back to Drew," she said. "I thought the barn could be a place where you talk about healing."

A few hours later the secretary of the interior's staff made an unscheduled visit to the Drew-Ruleville Road.

THE EMMETT TILL INTERPRETIVE Center needed money to save the barn. The National Park Service took over only fully restored sites and that meant the River Site and the courthouse were the only serious candidates. That left the preservation of the barn to private donors and activists. The issue all along with acquiring and preserving the sites was finding the money to buy them. Jeff Andrews had been as warm and gracious as the Tribbles had been rude and evasive but the issue still came down to money. It's hard to find money in the Delta. Then Patrick Weems got a call from a number he didn't recognize. A Beverly Hills number. The woman on the other end ran the philanthropic efforts of the star Hollywood producer Shonda Rhimes, the Black creative force behind shows like *Grey's Anatomy* and *Bridgerton*. She swore Patrick to secrecy. In all her years working for Rhimes, the woman said, this was the first project her boss had ever called *her* about supporting. Usually it worked the other way around. But this time the producer said she wanted to donate the money to buy the barn. To save it.

The ETIC board was thrilled but others, particularly Marvel

Parker, did not want to pay a white man what felt like blood money for a site that held the memory of extreme Black suffering. She talked privately in meetings about invoking eminent domain and just taking the barn, a political nonstarter in a state where land rights trump any other legal theory. I believe she understood how the barn could help economic and civic development in Drew, how it could supercharge Gloria Dickerson's efforts to save her hometown, and she also understood how the barn could attract attention and dollars to her organization and its sacred mission. But it still made her uncomfortable, so the board set about finding a price low enough for her and high enough for Andrews. Robert Raben, a lobbyist consulting for the ETIC, talked about the issue with his friend Barack Obama. They went through the public relations issues of a white man profiting from Black trauma.

"Nobody in the family is for it," Marvel told me.

Former president Obama said to buy it no matter the price, understanding that owning land is the only way to tell the truth about it. Eventually Marvel agreed to not oppose the purchase. She understood intellectually its value even as she struggled emotionally with the transaction. When the purchase was announced, via a *Good Morning America* exclusive that inaccurately said that the Parkers drove the buying of the barn, she raged in private but in public continued to tell people about the redemptive power of Roberts Temple. She wouldn't support the acquisition but she wouldn't exactly oppose it either. All this felt so fresh, not like ancient history at all. Sixty-eight years like one long night.

CAROLYN BRYANT DIED IN 2023 in a little town on the border between Louisiana and Texas. She spent the last year of her life as she spent the years after 1955: running from her past, still defiant. She died without ever coming clean. Wheeler Parker dreamed his whole adult life of sitting down with her and hearing the truth. At the end that's what he wanted. The truth. Other Till activists who never knew Emmett or Mamie pushed hard for an arrest on the kidnapping warrant from 1955. A grand jury even convened in Greenwood. The district attorney invited Wheeler and Marvel down to hear the news in person. There would be no charges, as all legal experts had predicted, because there was nobody left to testify against Carolyn except herself. She was the last one standing. The folks closest to Wheeler were annoyed at the family members pushing so hard for a legal process that could only end in exoneration. It seemed in Chicago like they were ignorant of the law, or just wanted the news cycles to raise awareness of the issue, or of themselves, which was worse. Those family members even accused Wheeler of being soft and old and tired.

THE BIDEN ADMINISTRATION let Wheeler and Marvel Parker know the National Park Service announcement would be made on Emmett's birthday at the White House. They asked Wheeler to introduce the president. Wheeler wouldn't fly anymore since a health scare in January, so Chris Benson, Dave Tell, Patrick Weems, and I rented a big van and picked him up the morning before the event. Wheeler came outside carrying his worn maroon leather hanging bag and Marvel handed us a bag of sandwiches she'd made for the drive. We pulled out of Argo, past Mamie Till-Mobley's high school, cutting through the suburbs toward the highway. Fields of swaying corn grew here when Wheeler first arrived in Chicago. Once his big dream was to travel around the world, he said a little wistfully. He did find time to drive with his brothers to Los Angeles and New York and to take a bus across the country. To him, traveling is about experiencing how other people live. I drove and listened to the conversations behind me.

Wheeler said he never believed he'd live to see a day like this. He received it as another sign that change comes slowly, and yet it comes. "Stay hopeful," he said.

When we stopped for gas the first time, he told me he was nervous about the speech. He laughed and, holding the door to the truck stop, told me the story about Winston Churchill giving the world's shortest speech.

"Never, ever, ever," he said.

Wheeler said he did a version of that once in Detroit and laughed.

Inside he browsed the aisles and then headed back out to the van.

Wheeler looked out the window of the car and announced that it was noon. We looked at our clocks to find it 11:52. The rhythms of his old sharecropping life remain hardwired. He only needs to see how light moves across the sky. We shook our heads and he laughed. He didn't grow up with clocks telling him when to break for lunch.

"When you step on your shadow," he said, "come out of the cotton field."

NBC called. Reuters called.

"You must think a lot about your cousin?" a reporter asked.

"For sixty-eight years," Wheeler said, his voice quiet. "Every day."

I WAITED OUTSIDE THE ENTRANCE to the West Wing, as the skies darkened and thunder boomed above the city. Today Emmett Till would have been eighty-two years old. He died alone in a barn in the absolute middle of nowhere, a godless place where his cries for his mother went unheeded, in a man-made landscape of profit margins and control, and for decades his name got whispered as a kind of code, pushed aside for those who couldn't stand the mirror his body held up, and now his name would be spoken and preserved forever in the most visible place in the world.

A White House staffer led us into the Indian Treaty Room.

The first familiar faces I saw were young people who'd traveled from Tallahatchie County. I found a seat behind Reverend Willie Williams from Sumner and Patrick Weems and Chris Benson. Backstage President Biden kissed Wheeler's hand, an Irish Catholic boy's act of respect and reverence. They walked out together. Everyone leaped to their feet. Three people stood at the podium. The vice president of the United States. The president of the United States. Reverend Wheeler Parker Jr.

Wheeler Parker, born at the intersection of 442 and the Quiver River, stepped up to the podium. The room got still. Joe and Wheeler whispered to each other and laughed. Kamala Harris leaned in to the microphone and said Parker "shared with me that he and his wife will be celebrating their fifty . . ."

Harris turned to Parker for a little help.

"Sixth," Wheeler said.

"Anniversary of marriage," Kamala Harris finished.

Everyone laughed and clapped.

Wheeler steadied himself and looked out at the packed room. His nerves faded away. He made a joke.

"In fact," he said, "we were married fifty-six years on Sunday."

He paused and smiled.

"My wife says, 'When we get to heaven, I'm gonna say, "Lord, not up here, too."'"

The room erupted in laughter. Parker looked out and laughed, too.

"I see we have a whole lot of *amen*s to that."

His friends in the crowd started to cry as he spoke.

"You see, I was born in Mississippi," he said. "I spent my early years as a sharecropper and was focused upon filling up a nine-foot sack."

The sun and shadow announced work and rest in his old world. He looked up. The crowd leaned in.

"From the outhouse to the White House," he said.

THE INDIAN TREATY ROOM was silent except for the sound of clicking cameras. One journalist, used to the gamesmanship and theater of this soulless town, said afterward that for one brief hour, Washington, DC, was a place where a man said what he meant. Where everyone within the sound of his voice understood they might live five more lifetimes and never see something so intimate and powerful. That honest man was Wheeler Parker.

"This is what America means to me," he said. "Promises made, promises kept. It has been quite a journey for me from the darkness to the light. Back then I could never imagine a moment like this: standing in the light of wisdom, grace, and deliverance."

He looked back at the man standing next to him. They're about the same age.

"Ladies and gentlemen, please join me in recognizing President Joe Biden."

Biden thought about 1955.

"I was twelve years old," he said softly.

Nobody moved.

"No matter how much time has passed, how many birthdays, how many events, how many anniversaries . . . ," he said, then stopped for just a moment and made eye contact with Wheeler in the front row. The two old men understood something about each other. "It's hard to relive this." Biden nodded again at Wheeler. "We were talking, Rev, about as if it happened yesterday. The images in your head. Things you remember."

The past three years have been a time for Weems and the Parkers to preserve the lessons and the life of Emmett Till. They have also been years of censorship and a renewed campaign to erase America's past, to protect students from whatever the truth might make them feel.

"At a time when there are those who seek to ban books, bury history," Biden said as he made his own closing argument, "we're making it clear—crystal, crystal clear"—the crowd's applause stopped him for a beat—"while darkness and denialism can hide much, they erase nothing. They can hide, but they erase nothing."

THE ENERGY OF THE PLANNING meetings changed when everyone got home, especially in Drew, where Gloria Dickerson could see a previously impossible path opening for her community and, especially, her students. She loves to praise them in public and if she doesn't think the crowd's applause is properly effusive, she'll rouse the crowd with comments like "Those are my students, y'all" and "Aren't my students so impressive?" and people will cheer again.

The purchase of the barn, and the footprint of a federally funded national park in nearby Sumner and Glendora, offered a path forward, to bring visitors to the area who wanted to look honestly into the soul of America. The public story of the Delta, whether the legend of the soil or even the recent blues renaissance, has always been driven by people who look like me. Now Gloria Dickerson in Drew, Willie Williams and Jessie Jaynes-Diming in Sumner, and Mayor Johnny B. Thomas in Glendora had the power to shape what the Delta means to locals and the rest of the world. They all hoped there was a future in it.

Patrick Weems and Jay Rushing, upon their return from Washington, met in Gloria's conference room on Main Street in Drew to discuss the coming events. Gloria runs a tight meeting. She gets an agenda written down and methodically goes through it. I love watching her mind work. She brings a quiet relentlessness to everything she does. Her mother, I think in moments like that, must have been a force of nature. They talked about the goals of all this work.

The Delta kept alive by the barn, or reborn by the saving of it, is mostly a place of memory. Jay Rushing sat at the end of the table. In the two years since he went with us wide-eyed to Chicago, he's become his own force of nature. He told Gloria and Patrick that the barn existed to him as the Rosetta Stone of the Delta, which could bring other erased histories into the light. He thought about his hometown of Cleveland and how nobody growing up taught him the history that happened just a few blocks away, much less the big tentpole moments like Emmett Till and Rosa Parks.

He brought up Bennie Thompson, who didn't know until a year or so ago that Till had been tortured to death in Sunflower County. All his life he'd learned the Huie version written by Milam and Bryant's defense lawyers. Gloria Dickerson had to tell him the truth. A politician who has dedicated his life to serving the Delta, particularly the most vulnerable Black citizens, had his essential Black history taught to him by a team of craven white defense attorneys from Sumner.

"We all have some connection," Rushing said. "Imagine how much history actually exists. In that sense we get to see how forgotten places are raised up from the darkness. We have essentially turned the light switch on."

FOR TWO DAYS in August 2023, the sixty-eighth anniversary of Emmett's death, the Delta stopped to remember. The ceremonies began on a Sunday. That morning I drove from my home in the Hills back to the flatlands, the same drive I'd made three years before to see the barn for the first time. Gloria Dickerson had organized the second annual ceremony celebrating Emmett's life and martyrdom at the barn. This year she worked with Patrick Weems to combine her event with a celebration for the new national park. I pulled into a country store in Tutwiler, where Highway 3 intersected with Highway 49, and ran into Jay Rushing. He, too, was stopping for a bite to eat. I followed him into Sumner and smiled at the National Park Service logo on the Emmett Till Interpretive Center.

We went into the courtroom where Milam and Bryant had been acquitted.

The Mississippi Valley State choir hummed "Bridge over Troubled Water" in an ethereal collective voice. A soloist stepped up to the microphone.

"Welcome to the Delta," she said.

The room became quiet as she began to sing.

From the cross to the grave.
From the grave to the sky.

She sang the last glassy note and sat down. The crowd waited. Outside the master of ceremonies, Von Gordon, and the high-ranking

Department of the Interior official sat in their cars parked behind a train passing through town. I sat in the courthouse beneath the slow-moving fans. A speaker vamped for time. The pastor from Antioch Baptist Church sat in front of me, next to an old friend of Jerome Little, a groundbreaking Black politician and the founder of Patrick's organization. Jerome, who died in 2011, had started all this remembering. Everyone felt his presence in the room and wished he could walk through the door with his big smile and bigger cowboy hat. People shuffled the program in their hands.

The front said "Welcome to a Day of Unforgettable Courage."

I looked around at the room and teared up. Myrlie Evers-Williams said once that yes, Mississippi was, but Mississippi is. The state deserved a chance to break free from its history. We spend so much time in the past here and yet so little time learning who we are and how we got here. These memorials offered a fresh start. A way to go into the past, to finally confront, to address, to apologize and make amends, and then to walk into the future together. It is not in vogue right now to talk of racial reconciliation, and that kind of hard line might work in some places but not in a place as broken as Mississippi. Writing this book taught me clearly that our only hope is to create a new, unified tribe—all of us Mississippians, who share the history and future of our home—and no matter what we all might think about each other, or what scars or grudges we hold, we need to lay down those grievances and engage in a united act of defiant survival. Either that or generation by generation watch nature take this Delta back and hold it safe until the next group of people come to try to extract its bounty.

Gloria Dickerson walked in wearing silver-toed shoes. The ghosts of Matthew and Mae Bertha Carter walked with her through the room. Planters and former sharecroppers sat side by side with an undersecretary of the interior, and the president of the local levee board—a diverse crowd in a place where life remains mostly segregated. A man and his wife from Chicago walked in. He had been a pallbearer for Mamie and wanted to pay his respects today. His wife stopped to talk to me and asked the best way to get in touch with Willie Reed's widow, Juliet, because they knew Willie before he died and knew I kept in touch with her. ETIC board member and tour guide Jessie Jaynes-Diming walked to the jury box with Sykes Sturdivant, whose grandfather once owned the land where Emmett was killed. The Episcopal minister from Vicksburg sat in the jury box, too. The room was full of preachers. Five men and women came in wearing Park Service uniforms. Finally, the train passed through town and the last few cars drove into the Sumner courthouse square and found a place to park.

VON GORDON, who runs a reconciliation-based nonprofit called the Alluvial Collective, stepped up to the lectern. His roots are in Sunflower County. He stood in the spot where Whitten had urged the jury to do their duty as "Anglo-Saxons" and protect their ancestors in the ground. A hush settled over the room.

"I'm a Delta boy," he said.

The crowd murmured its approval.

Gordon pulled out his dog-eared copy of Mamie Till-Mobley and Chris Benson's book and he began to read Mamie's words.

"Milam boasts about killing Emmett to teach him a lesson and also send a message to others."

The crowd murmured again.

"Milam saw it as his duty as a white man to send that message."

It felt like Mamie herself had come to talk to the crowd. She'd been called a n—— by Sheriff Strider in this very room, mocked by jurors for her tears in this very room. Now it was her spirit that owned this space and not theirs.

"Sending a message to Black folks is one of the key factors that separates a lynching from a murder," Gordon read. "In a lynching it is not just the killers who are guilty, it is the dominant culture."

I own a sizable share of that rich, valuable soil.

When I sit down in a Delta country club and sink into the green leather of a well-worn club chair, I feel at home.

"The entire society that permits such a thing."

We bought our farm in 1913.

"That encourages it."

The fifth generation of owners has already been born.

"Bryant and Milam were not the only guilty parties in the lynching of my son."

Mamie wrote that thousands of people created the dominant culture that killed Emmett, and many thousands more benefited from it, and while there's no way to unravel the complicated financial web that stretched from Manchester to New Orleans and enriched generations of people in between, there is a way to stand up now and say, *I'm sorry. It was wrong. We were wrong.*

Von put down the book and started talking.

"People who were responsible . . . ," he said, "powerful and influential people who could have chosen to lead and chose instead to incite."

A murmur rose from the crowd.

"People who could have condemned hate crimes . . . chose instead to condone."

He invoked Carolyn Bryant and then the dominant culture again.

"People who could have come clean . . . and chose instead to live the rest of their lives with blood on their hands."

The crowd murmured a little louder.

"This day every year I think it is really important to gather here and remember not just the tragedy of Emmett Till's death but all who were responsible for it and how we as stakeholders have to choose a different future."

People nodded and leaned in.

"I think she's describing a choice we have as citizens," he said.

He turned to his left and, full of anticipation, introduced the next speaker.

"Gloria Dickerson from Drew, Mississippi," he said.

Gloria walked over and took the microphone. Her voice sounded soothing, like a second-grade teacher. She asked everyone to stand, which we did with a shuffle of wood and shoes.

"Take a moment to breathe in and out."

"Okay."

"Just breathe in . . . and out."

The collective exhale made a sigh of a noise in the room.

"In."

"And out."

"In."

"And out."

The exhale sounded like a light summer sheet landing on your arm.

"Now you may be seated," she said.

The same shuffle of wood and shoes, and chairs and walking sticks, happened in reverse. Gloria waited until everyone got still.

"That felt good but you're not quite done," she said. "We want to take some time to reflect on why we're here. I know right now your mind has a lot of things going through it. I'm gonna ask you to let it all go and let your mind be free. I want to ask you in a minute to close your eyes and just sit in silence. Do that, and as you do that, continue to breathe in and out."

I could hear the compressors of the air-conditioning system.

"Silently reflect on what you're doing here today."

The room became as quiet as it had been all day.

"And now," she said, "on the count of three we're gonna open our eyes. Let's be present in the moment while you're here. One . . . two . . . three."

I DID NOT KNOW WHAT a lynching was until I was almost seventeen years old.

My parents sent me to a fancy boarding school. Lots of big farming and ranching families sent their kids there. The Sturdivants from Glendora went there. A Denton from Shelby. One of my classmates was an heir to the King Ranch in Texas. Another was heir to the Jim Beam bourbon empire. His last name was Beam. I failed spectacularly there, the first big thing I'd ever failed at in my life, and only with time can I now understand why. I had no sense of myself. My dad's politics, in hindsight, created a distance between me and my peers. My mom's farming empire felt like it belonged to my uncle only, and I developed zero connection with its history and no interest in its future. My most frequent companion was my own imagination and interior monologue. So when I got to the boarding school, I was a sketch of a person. To find myself I wore what I now can see as costumes. I would be the guy from the Deep South, surrounded by the mid-Atlantic southerners from Georgia, North Carolina, and Virginia. I leaned in to those Confederate roots. I ordered Confederate flags and hung them on the wall. Other students invented reasons to knock on my door at the end of the hall to see them. I imagined then these visitors thought the flags were cool but now I think they were just making fun of me, this lost boy a long way from home. As you might imagine, I was kicked out of that school. My mother is the only one who ever said out loud what we all knew: I'd gotten myself expelled on purpose and secretly felt nothing but relief. My parents came to get me around Easter to bring me back home. I tried to return to the script I believed had been written for me and started a new boarding school in the fall. I hated it immediately and felt lost there, too. At the time I'd been listening to nothing but Hank Williams Jr. and Charlie Daniels. All the music helped me articulate how uneasy I felt with these urbane, fancy people. Charlie had a song out called "Simple Man," about stopping crime with a tall tree and a short rope. I didn't know that was a lynching reference. I'd never once heard the name *Emmett Till*. So I hung one of the leftover Confederate flags and tied a noose and let it hang over the middle of the flag, mimicking a Hank Jr. flag I'd seen for sale in a rural Tennessee truck stop. It was my tribute to the Charlie Daniels song. It felt rebellious and dangerous. Inside I felt insecure and bitter.

My music teacher pulled me into his office immediately.

He laid into me but, mercifully, sensing I clearly had no idea what I'd done, explained step-by-step the history of racial violence in the South generally and in my home state specifically. I felt the floor drop out from beneath me, frantic and full of sorrow, and when I got to my room I immediately removed the flag. In some ways I've never shaken that feeling. That boarding school lasted a semester. When I got home, miserable and empty, I started reading all the books in our house. A veil slipped from my eyes. I read Willie Morris's critique of the South, *North Toward Home*, which showed me that it was possible both to love and hate a place. It taught me to be suspicious of those who did only one of the two. These were the first roots of my identity, and the first I'd ever heard that writing magazine stories and nonfiction books could be a job.

That reading marathon gave me the life I have now. I carried, somewhere inside, unacknowledged regret. Regret over the act, of course, but more about the ignorance. I'd brought shame on my family, and blasphemed the racially progressive work of my great-grandfather in Shelby, and my father in the modern Delta. But over the years I forgot about the flag, and the music teacher. I honestly hadn't thought about it in a long, long time. Then Gloria Dickerson asked us to sit quietly in this courtroom with our eyes closed. The flag, to my surprise, was the first thing I thought about. That old regret passed through my body. Von Gordon's charge echoed in my mind and right then, with my eyes closed, I finally understood. I almost cried in my chair. This book is for that ignorant boy and for all the ignorant boys like him. Like me. It's for the white kid in the Delta of Mississippi, or in the bedroom suburb of Birmingham, or Charlotte, or Atlanta, everywhere the poison of the Lost Cause has spread.

And to Wheeler and Marvel, reading this, I am sorry.

INSIDE THE COURTROOM, on August 27, 2023, the choir sang Sunday-morning harmonies. A hymn fit for a funeral, melancholy with thick chords for support and structure. "Give me Jesus." The crowd erupted into applause after the last note. Von Gordon stepped back to the microphone. Then the crowd sang "Lift Every Voice and Sing," the Black national anthem. The program printed the words for the white folks in the crowd. Reverend Willie Williams led the crowd in clapping the rhythm. I'd never been to an integrated church service in Mississippi. Not really. Maybe a random Black person at a white church, or the other way around. But never this. It felt hopeful. Jessie Jaynes-Diming, who'd been giving a tour of the barn just the day before, took her turn at the microphone.

"There are many other angels in this room," she said.

She opened her phone to find her notes. She wore a beautiful blue dress with a big silver brooch that evoked the wings of a bird.

"It's been a twenty-years journey to see this day," she said.

Then she began to read.

"Today as we stand here memories of Emmett echo around us. Memories that have become emblematic of a national struggle with racial justice. But it is essential that we remember Emmett was not just a symbol. He was a boy."

She paused, letting her emotions settle, and letting the emotions of the murmuring crowd do the same. Everyone thought about a child beaten to death for whistling. When she finished, a soloist from the Mississippi Valley State choir, an earthshaking musical outfit, stepped to the microphone.

"I was born by the river . . ."

Sam Cooke lived his first years 21.1 miles northwest of this room. He's singing about the Sunflower River, which runs through Township 22 North, Range 4 West. To get there from his childhood home turn right on Indiana, right on State Street, which is

Highway 61, drive through the intersection with Desoto, which is Highway 49, and you're there.

"Just like the river, I've been running . . ."

Sixty-one goes south to Rosedale, Greenville, Vicksburg, and north to Tunica and Memphis, where it turns into Third Street at the state line. Forty-nine goes south to Tutwiler, where it splits into two roads, 49E and 49W, the former headed to Drew and the barn, the latter headed to Greenwood and the store.

Cooke grew up by the Sunflower River. Emmett Till died by the Sunflower River.

"I've been running . . . ever since."

Protest music. A line of history stretching from Dockery and Charley Patton's first-person romps to Public Enemy's *It Takes a Nation of Millions to Hold Us Back*. Just 21.1 miles away, Sam Cooke was born in Clarksdale, Mississippi, and died in Los Angeles, where he's buried among so many other stars. His father outlived him by decades, staying a suburb or two over from Wheeler Parker and his family. He died in 1996 and is buried in the same cemetery as Emmett Till.

REVEREND WILLIE WILLIAMS SPOKE LAST.

The out-of-towners didn't know what was about to happen. Williams grew up going to school in Money. He's the cochair of the ETIC but most of all, he's the pastor at Raleigh United Methodist. The crowd applauded as he stood before them. He looked out at the crowd and glowed.

"Young man was just saying, it's been a long time but a change gonna come," he began. "I don't know about you but I do want to encourage you to think about your own change."

The crowd made a noise of approval.

"Think about the silence," he said.

Standing at the podium, which felt more and more like a pulpit as he started to stalk the stage and use his voice as an instrument, he looked in control.

"I was born in Tallahatchie County and grew up in Leflore County and heard bits and pieces about Emmett Till," he said. "His uncle, Crosby Smith, was a friend of my grandmother."

Nobody talked about it. Not white folks. Not Black folks. In other places it got studied in school, and discussed as a cautionary tale, but in the Delta, in the places where it happened, a curtain descended. Black folks whispered about it, maybe, and most white folks didn't know the story.

"We are broken," he said.

He fumbled for words and analogies. This was supposed to be a secular ceremony. Government folks get nervous when the preachers start firing on all cylinders.

"I'm a man of faith," Williams said. "I don't want to preach to you. I already preached this morning."

Everybody laughed.

"I do want to say this," he said.

He grinned. A preacher can't help himself.

"What happened to Emmett Till is a part of our brokenness," he said. "Whatever we want to say about injustice, before Emmett, after Emmett, what do you do with it? Do you allow it to destroy you?"

He looked around at the room. The brown paint on the railings and window frames. The slow-turning fans. Days like today, he said, are a time to reflect. To measure. "There is a scripture in the Bible in Acts 17," he said. "In one man God made all nations."

The crowd murmured.

"Some translations say 'one blood,'" he said.

"Listen at this," he said.

People looked around and saw their neighbors. As a white Del-tan, it is my sense that most Black people have been willing to for-give the unforgivable and give all of us a second and third and fourth chance. The issue all along has been our unwillingness to accept it. The barrier of silence has been too high to scale, and the forces keeping us from starting new on a fresh foundation of hon-esty are the same forces that tried to silence the story of the barn.

The Delta has always stored its sacred tablets and ancient texts in the land itself. Or, rather, the tablets and texts *are* the land. That's always been the prism. Listen to the dirt and it will sing its sagas of deep time. Human beings cleared vast forests and drained massive swamps to make these fields. To make the world that revolved around the planting and harvesting of these fields. It was made by man. Which means it can be unmade. Power has always been measured by the ability to alter and dominate the land. These mon-uments at the river in Glendora, at the courthouse in Sumner, and at the barn outside Drew. They are the beginning of a new clearing. Of another reshaping. Willie Williams spoke life into these ideas and then took his seat. Von Gordon stepped back to the microphone and explained that everyone would form a procession from the courthouse to the barn.

THE NEXT DAY A CROWD of dignitaries and invited guests gath-ered at the River Site. There was only one member of the Till fam-ily present and she had slipped off by herself. Moses Wright's great-niece, Sharon Wright, crossed her arms in grief. Her body language telegraphed her pain. She looked down into the brown water of the Tallahatchie River and a strange thought came immediately to her mind, as if some higher power had planted it there.

Emmett got out, she thought.

She thought about how many countless other Emmetts never escaped that water. His death and civic resurrection are remarkable because he did come back into the light, and because of that he became a symbol for all those unnamed dead who rest uneasily in the singing river. Sharon stood for a long time alone at the bank.

She came back and took her seat in the crowd and the dignitaries gave their speeches. I sat next to Sykes Sturdivant, whose family had both owned the barn *and* donated this land to the government for this park. They farm across the gravel road that leads to the landing from the main road. It was August 28, a holy day in Black America, which I did not realize until one of the speakers connected the dots for me. The anniversary of Till's death, and of Martin Luther King Jr.'s "I Have a Dream" speech, given on August 28, 1963, in tribute, and of the day Barack Obama accepted the Democratic nomination for president. Shannon Estenoz from the Department of the Interior gave a rousing speech, getting nods from civil rights icon David Jordan. Many people will visit this site, she said, and a few will leave forever transformed. This national monument was designed to create patriots, to unlock the hidden history buried in the dirt. Her voice caught with emotion as she spoke. She thanked the river for giving up its dead.

At the end the organizers asked Till family members to stand.

Sharon stayed seated for a beat and then reluctantly rose.

She was the only one.

A wreath sat beneath the podium made of the state flower of Mississippi and the official flower of Chicago, magnolias and chrysanthemums. A park ranger quietly asked Sharon to accompany the dignitaries and the wreath back to the river. They laid it down in memory of Emmett Till and then linked arms and walked away.

Willie Reed's friends Mike and Tina Small sat in front of me.

A park ranger pulled me aside to get more information on Reed, whose memory and courage will be celebrated in these new monuments. Medgar Evers's daughter sat in the second row. A friend rubbed her back when a speaker mentioned her father. Mayor Thomas sat a few rows behind her. He beamed. Patrick and Anna Booth Weems held their son Sam in the back.

Gloria Dickerson stood next to me and smiled.

WHEELER PARKER WENT INTO the hospital and stayed for a few days. I thought about our last drive. The ETIC has been developing a tour for people to travel these long, empty Delta roads between the barn and the national park sites. They asked me to drive and interview him so his words could form the foundation of that narration. I met him at a hotel. We drove all over the Delta. We talked about Bobo and about the passage of time. I realized as we rode that Wheeler Parker was going to die and not only was he not scared, he even seemed to welcome the glory to come. As we turned away from the store in Money and headed toward the courthouse in Sumner, I asked him what he thought happens to us in the first moments after we die. He said he'd been thinking about that a lot since his scare. In my truck he said he didn't cry at Bobo's funeral because he told himself that they would meet again. But that was just some abstraction then. In the last few years that idea has become real. Parker went through all the conversations he had, or heard anyone else having, about Emmett's relationship with Jesus Christ. He believes his friend was saved, so he is in heaven, right now, waiting. Parker thinks when he dies he will see Emmett again and they will embrace. He hopes his friend is happy with the work he's done in his name.

He rested between sites. I looked over every so often at him and found myself wanting whatever world he wanted, and searching for the grace he carried inside. When he's gone, Emmett will be a symbol, but as long as Wheeler lives and tells his story, Emmett remains a boy who loved jokes and his mom.

We took Highway 8 to the outskirts of Ruleville, in the shadow of the two water towers, and cut north toward Drew. This was the route the killers took in 1955 with Emmett scared to death in the back of the truck. The barn hid out of sight a few miles away. We passed Carl Watson's home. Old Black men sat in rusted metal chairs beneath little patches of pecan-tree shade. I looked over at Wheeler as the truck jumped and spun in the ruts. He was sleeping peacefully. Here was an old man who had been through terrible trauma, and been handed a heavy burden, and near the end of carrying both, he floated above everything, free and safe. As we drove the Drew-Ruleville Road, bulldozers scurried in geocoded patterns, turning a rice field back into a soybean field after just a season. New owners perhaps, or just stubborn old ones, not learning the lessons of the past. Patrick and Marvel rode in the car behind me. They wanted to see the plans in the works for the barn. Wheeler awoke just long enough to lean his seat back and then quickly dozed off again. He snored a little. I got to the Dougherty Bayou and drove up the hill and circled the truck around to face the barn.

Shadows fell across the gravel drive. Jeff Andrews was out of town, so we were alone. Marvel got out and stared back at the cypress brake. Patrick pointed toward the road as he described how the monument would look. Wheeler Parker awoke for a moment. He looked around to get his bearings and then closed his eyes again. A smile crossed his face, as if he'd been pulled from a beautiful dream and wanted to return.

Acknowledgments

I did hundreds of interviews and spent many hours with people from Mississippi and Chicago, especially Juliet Louis, Gloria Dickerson, Wheeler Parker, Marvel Parker, Annie Wright, Patrick Weems, Jeff Andrews, Willie Williams, Stafford Shurden, and many, many others. I've lived in archives in Florida, Chicago, Mississippi, Missouri, Seville, and others, as well as courthouses all over the Delta. The interviews and documents formed two of this book's three main pillars. The other, of course, came from previously published work.

There are a few books that are essential reading when retelling the Till story and those books often disagree slightly about the history of those few weeks in 1955. I deferred in those instances to accounts of the eyewitnesses like Wheeler Parker, Simeon Wright, and Mamie Till-Mobley. These books have been my constant companions of the past several years. Simeon Wright and Herb Boyd's *Simeon's Story*. Wheeler Parker and Christopher Benson's *A Few Days Full of Trouble*. Mamie Till-Mobley and Christopher Benson's *Death of Innocence*. Benson is a decorated journalist and thought

ACKNOWLEDGMENTS

leader and a journalism professor at Northwestern's famous Medill School. He's also a great person, a devoted son to his late, beloved mother, a loyal friend who regularly puts the needs of the important people in his life above his own.

The most comprehensive book written about the murder is *Emmett Till* by Devery Anderson and the book that most shaped my own thinking was *Remembering Emmett Till* by Dave Tell, where he introduces his idea about the ecology of memory. Tell's book, along with Will Campbell's *Providence* and William Least Heat-Moon's *PrairyErth*, gave me the spiritual north stars for this project. I took valuable information and inspiration from Mikko Saikku's *This Delta, This Land*.

In addition, I read books about cotton, manufacturing, Mississippi, blues, the Civil War, Reconstruction, Jim Crow, and many other adjacent topics. Six or seven of those dog-eared books emerged as critical companions on this journey. I want to start with Sven Beckert's book *Empire of Cotton*, which I read so many times I actually had to buy a second copy. This is a masterpiece and should be part of your library if it is not. Gene Dattel's *Cotton and Race in the Making of America* was an essential resource. Robert Palmer's book *Deep Blues* provided the best portrait of life in the sharecropper South and the research of blues scholar David Evans played an invaluable role in re-creating life in Township 22 North. Evans's *Big Road Blues* is a masterpiece, too. There are at least a hundred other books that contributed to this story. This murder will be written about many more times in the centuries to come so I hope that future authors will take my reporting further and correct any mistakes I made. I feel like a tiny cog in a huge machine that will, collectively, bring this terrible crime all the way into the light.

ACKNOWLEDGMENTS

I want to thank Mike and Tina Small.

I want to thank Therese and Dallis Anderson.

THIS BOOK WOULD NOT EXIST were it not for Katie Carter King and Eric Neel.

Katie King is a researcher based in San Francisco and she worked with me on this project every step of the way, helping me organize reporting, helping to find reporting and archives that I missed, chasing down impossible documents and histories. She worked hundreds of hours, with a huge amount of responsibility on her shoulders, and I am grateful both for her time, her work ethic, her expertise, and ultimately her friendship. There is no title that accurately sums up her role in this project. She is one of a kind.

Eric Neel is my editor at ESPN and nothing I put into the world, whether a work project or a personal one, is completed without his insight. He is a creative genius and a blood, blood brother. I would not be a professional writer today without him. His curiosities and values are on every page, of this work, of my ESPN stories, of the television shows and documentaries I produce. Everything.

I WANT TO THANK TIM HORGAN, the director of my television show *TrueSouth*, and our host, John T. Edge. This book got researched and written in many places over three or four years and so that meant they were around for every step of this process. With that in mind, I want to thank Mickey Hart, drummer, writer, thinker—rhythm master. I've been working on a film with him for most of the time I was writing this book and his philosophy for life and art and storytelling came into my life at the exact right time. I worry a lot about what people think, about how something is received and, to be frank, about how it sells. Seeing how he approaches the art of making new music, even today after his six decades of success, made me see the folly in those anxieties and made me learn the essentialness of putting the creative process first and everything else that comes along with it second. I am forever grateful to him, to his family, Caryl and Reya, to Rose, Tom, Jerome, and Jon.

I am forever indebted to Patrick Weems. His trust and friendship are gifts I treasure. I am similarly indebted to Gloria Dickerson, who emerges as a real hero of this story.

I want to thank my ESPN colleagues, especially Chris Buckle, Burke Magnus, and Jimmy Pitaro. My former editor, Paul Kix, did an early read of the book and made great suggestions; he is now a talented author in his own right and is a true inspiration. I want to thank my former boss, John A. Walsh, whose close read of the first draft led to some essential and powerful changes. His belief in me kickstarted my career and to have him still here riding shotgun with me means more than I could express. Thank you, John A. And thank you, John Skipper, who has provided constant encouragement since he first heard about this project. To Russ Dinallo and Torey Champagne, both ESPN filmmakers, thank you for listening to me talk about this book so much while we were making movies about other things.

I want to thank Seth Wickersham. We spoke every single day while this book was reported and written. I want to thank Tom Junod, who is the greatest magazine writer who ever lived. He talked through this story with me constantly and did an invaluable manuscript read that elevated the book. I want to thank Kevin Van

Valkenburg from No Laying Up. His kindness and generosity of spirit, and his deep belief in America's ability to evolve and improve and live up to our founding creeds, helped me never lose sight of this book's purpose and power.

A group of dedicated scholars and journalists did fact-check reads for me. I need to thank Davis Houck at Florida State for that read and for access to his archives, for his friendship and help. I need to thank Devery Anderson, again. Instead of being competitive—he wrote the encyclopedia of the Till murder—he came with a collaborative, collegial energy that I will never forget. I want to thank Jerry Mitchell, who is the greatest Mississippi journalist ever. I want to thank Ralph Eubanks for his read. I want to thank Dave Tell, again. I want to thank Chris Benson, again.

I want to thank John Cox, a Delta lawyer like his dad, and my dad, who helped me navigate private land records and Mississippi courthouse basements filled with unorganized boxes of files.

A book like this only gets written after the story has been thought about over and over, so although they likely didn't realize it, I want to thank my friends Webb, Tate, Josh, and Brokke because we were all together in the Smoky Mountains the first time I ever really said the whole sweeping arc of the book out loud. That conversation was an essential part of the process so I am grateful for their patience and friendship.

ONE FINAL NOTE ABOUT Wheeler and Marvel Parker. The weekend before I wrote these words of gratitude, my wife, Sonia, and I went to Chicago for Wheeler's eighty-fifth birthday party. Marvel organized every last detail and as people stood up and gave beautiful toasts to Wheeler, and to the Parker family, I was reminded, once again, that the Till murder happened to a nation, and a people, but most of all it happened to a family. A family that still exists, a family that lives across the street and next door to one another, still, a family that still feels the freshness of that wound, a family that remembers a young child named Bobo. An aunt who was present at his birth is still alive. So while this is a story that historians, journalists, and activists claim as their own, please don't ever forget there are people in Argo, Illinois, for whom this death remains not symbolic but deeply, painfully personal. I adore the Parkers, and if you are moved to action by this book, please look up the Till Institute in Chicago and ask them how you can help. As Wheeler says, anyone with a fire in their belly for justice is a friend and an ally.

THIS BOOK WOULD NOT HAVE HAPPENED without David Black, Scott Moyers, and Mia Council. I owe the three of them a lot more than a sentence or two in an acknowledgment. David is an agent but that does not accurately explain the role he plays in my life and the lives of countless other writers. I think all his clients secretly believe they are his favorite. That is his gift. Put it this way. Two people have the ability to unlock my Apple account if I died. My wife and David Black. Mia is a brilliant woman whose empathy and smarts allow her to see the cosmos and help you see it, too. And Scott is a legend. The GOAT. This is my third book with him and I hope we have a dozen more. Thank you, brother. I owe you.

The team at Penguin Press (and Penguin Random House) is indispensable: Hilary Roberts, Christine Johnson, Lauren Lauzon, Katie Hurley, Christina Nguyen, Amanda Dewey, Claire Vaccaro, Yuki Hirose, William Jeffries, and Sharon Gonzalez.

ACKNOWLEDGMENTS

This book would not have happened without Jeff Goldberg and Denise Wills at *The Atlantic* magazine. They were the first two people to see this story and believe in its revelatory and redemptive power. Denise's edits on the magazine story that became this book were incredibly important in the shaping of the story that is now between these covers.

I want to thank all my mentors, especially Rick Telander.

Without my mother, Mary, and her brother, Rives, there would be no book: your ethical and progressive worldview allowed me to be the kind of person capable of writing a story like this one. I owe the two of you everything and love you both immensely.

Someone else who I admire greatly is my Uncle Michael, who is the last living Thompson brother: thank you for being the patriarch of our family and for representing the hopes and dreams of Will, Daddy, and Frazier.

Last, and most of all, I want to thank my wife, Sonia, who kept our lives running while this book took over more and more of my time, and therefore our time. She is the center of everything good that happens to our family. I want to thank my two smart beautiful girls, Wallace and Louise, who make any of this worth doing. It is my hope that my honesty about where we come from will help the two of you understand your past and forge a better future. Whenever I felt like pulling a punch, I imagined the two of you and knew that only the truth would suffice. There is not a prouder daddy in the world and I adore you both completely.

Notes

I: The Barn

3 **Patterson's country store**: Testimony of Willie Reed, September 22, 1955, *State of Mississippi v. J.W. Milam and Roy Bryant*, Second District of Tallahatchie County, Seventeenth Judicial District, FBI Case File No. 62D-JN-30045-FD302, 212; Mamie Till-Mobley and Chris Benson, *Death of Innocence: The Story of the Hate Crime That Changed America* (New York: One World, 2003), 182; Dale Killinger, in conversation with the author; Steve Shurden, in conversation with the author; 1950 U.S. Census, Sunflower County, Mississippi, Beat 5, Enumeration District 67-84, April 12, 1950, 13.

3 **His girlfriend, Ella Mae**: Devery S. Anderson, *Emmett Till: The Murder That Shocked the World and Propelled the Civil Rights Movement* (Jackson: University Press of Mississippi, 2015), 175; "Ella Mae Shuns Willie," *Jackson Daily News*, September 30, 1955, 1.

4 **the whim of the landlord**: Willie (Reed) Louis discussed this dynamic at length when interviewed by Stanley Nelson for *American Experience* (Boston: WGBH Educational Foundation, 2003).

4 **worked for Clint Shurden**: Beginning with the trial transcript and filtering into the press, there was name confusion regarding Sheriden/Shurden, which persists. However, any misconceptions were rectified when the FBI investigation was made public in 2006. FBI Case File No. 62D-JN-30045-FD302.

4 **renting to own**: Contract and agreement dated December 22, 1952, regarding "West Half of Section 2, Township 22, North; Southwest Quarter, South Half of Northwest Quarter and West Half of Southeast Quarter, of Section 35, Township 23, North; All in Range 4, West, Sunflower County, Mississippi, and Containing 657 Acres, More or Less," Sunflower County Magistrate Court, Book Y-12, 23–31.

4 **They'd also learned to recognize**: Testimony of Willie Reed, 226–27; George F. Brown, "Willie's Up North, but He's Scared," *The Pittsburgh Courier*, October 8, 1955, 1, 8.

4   **local sharecropper kids:** Testimony of Willie Reed, 241; James, Eunice, and Ruthie Reed, in conversation with the author.

5   **Forrest Trail, they called:** Susie V. Powell, ed., "Source Material for Mississippi History: Preliminary Manuscript, Sunflower County," vol. 67, Works Progress Administration for Mississippi, Series 447: Historical Research Material, 1935–1942, Mississippi Department of Archives and History; Elizabeth Ann Wilson, *Promised Land or Sandy Bayou: A Compendium of Early History of the Town of Drew and Its Immediate Vicinity* (self-published, 1976); Marie M. Hemphill, *Fevers, Floods, and Faith: A History of Sunflower County, Mississippi, 1844–1976* (Indianola, MS: Sunflower County Historical Society, 1980), 63–64, 78; Andrew Nelson Lytle, *Bedford Forrest and His Critter Company* (Nashville: J.S. Sanders, 1931), 382–83.

6   **called the Cotton Curtain:** In fact, it was not only expats in Chicago but Black migrants from the South generally, as can often be witnessed in midcentury Black periodicals. See "'Cotton Curtain' Rises on Rape of Simple Mississippi Justice," *The Afro-American*, November 5, 1955, 2, and others.

6   **heard the pickup truck:** Testimony of Willie Reed, 214–15.

6   **In the back, three Black men:** You will find differing numbers of Black field hands who were in the pickup truck, in texts from both 1955 and today—some offer three, others two. The trial transcript reads as three, however, and this number is supported by FBI findings. Federal Bureau of Investigation, "Prosecutive Report of Investigation Concerning Emmett Louis Till," February 9, 2016, FBI Case File No. 62D-JN-30045-FD302, 89.

7   **the Singing River:** Susan Klopfer, *Who Killed Emmett Till?* (self-published, Lulu, 2010), 33.

10   **progressive white boys:** Patrick Weems, in conversation with the author.

10   **Charles Merrill of Merrill Lynch:** Patrick Weems, digital communication with the author.

10   **all the cotton mansions:** Reverend Wheeler Parker Jr. and Christopher Benson, *A Few Days Full of Trouble: Revelations on the Journey to Justice for My Cousin and Best Friend, Emmett Till* (New York: One World Ballantine, 2024), 87.

13   **cold fried chicken:** Curtis Wilkie, in conversation with the author.

13   **Bill Gates is the third-largest:** Rives Neblett, in conversation with the author; Gwin Smith, in conversation with the author.

14   **also painted green:** Testimony of Willie Reed, 216; Louis, interviewed by Nelson.

14   **Amanda Bradley lived there:** Testimony of Willie Reed, 222; Testimony of Amanda Bradley, September 22, 1955, *State of Mississippi v. J.W. Milam and Roy Bryant*, Second District of Tallahatchie County, Seventeenth Judicial District, FBI Case File 62D-JN-30045-FD302, 253; Michael Joseph Miller, *Murder in the Delta: The Emmett Till Story* (Bellwood, IL: MGM, 2016), 66.

14   **"Mandy," Reed asked:** Till-Mobley and Benson, *Death of Innocence*, 183; Reed, interviewed by Nelson; "Dr. Howard: Situation in Mississippi Extremely Serious," *Pittsburgh Courier*, October 8, 1955, 1, 4.

14   **She looked out the window:** Testimony of Amanda Bradley, 254, 255.

14   **sharecropper named Frank Young:** David T. Beito and Linda Royster Beito, *Black Maverick: T.R.M. Howard's Fight for Civil Rights and Economic Power*, The New Black Studies Series (Urbana: University of Illinois Press, 2009), 120–21; Clark Porteous, "Officers Work All Night on Searches," *Memphis Press-Scimitar*, September 21,

1955, 1, 7; Olive Arnold Adams, *Time Bomb: Mississippi Exposed, and the Full Story of Emmett Till* (Mound Bayou: The Mississippi Regional Council of Negro Leadership, 1956), 11–21; 1950 U.S. Census, Sunflower County, Mississippi, Beat 5, Enumeration District 67–89, April 13, 1950, 14; Testimony of Willie Reed, 220–23.

14 **the nearby Zama plantation:** Anderson, *Emmett Till*, 105–6.

14 **"you Black bastard":** "Dr. Howard: Situation in Mississippi."

14 **presented like a pistol-whipping:** Summarized in Federal Bureau of Investigation, "Prosecutive Report," 99–110; Dale Killinger, in conversation with the author.

14 **"Mama, save me!":** Emmett's cries were described by Dr. T.R.M Howard, as told to him by Willie (Reed) Louis. "500 in Los Angeles Rally, 1,600 in Boston Assail Lynching of Child," *Daily Worker*, October 13, 1955, 3.

15 **came out to the pump:** Till-Mobley and Benson, *Death of Innocence*, 183; Testimony of Willie Reed, 220–24; Adams, *Time Bomb*, 11–21; Federal Bureau of Investigation, "Prosecutive Report," 108; "Dr. Howard: Situation in Mississippi."

15 **sounds stopped entirely:** Beito and Beito, *Black Maverick*, 121.

15 **back with a tarp:** Federal Bureau of Investigation, "Prosecutive Report," 89; Testimony of Willie Reed, 227; Testimony of Amanda Bradley, 257; "Dr. Howard: Situation in Mississippi"; Porteous, "Officers Work All Night," 9.

15 **covered in cottonseed:** Federal Bureau of Investigation, "Prosecutive Report," 91; Porteous, "Officers Work All Night," 7.

15 **a high school classmate:** Christy Grayson, "Wreck Kills Pedestrian," *The Clarksdale Press-Register*, June 10, 1996, 1.

16 **the latest historical marker:** Aimee Ortiz, "Emmett Till Memorial Has a New Sign. This Time, It's Bulletproof," *The New York Times*, October 22, 2019, A13; Smithsonian National Museum of American History, Behring Center, "Reckoning with Remembrance: Explore Online," n.d.; Dave Tell, *Remembering Emmett Till* (Chicago: University of Chicago Press, 2019), 242.

16 **three Ole Miss frat boys:** Jerry Mitchell, "A Year after an Instagram Photo of Ole Miss Frats Hoisting Guns in Front of a Bullet-Riddled Emmett Till Sign Went Viral, Questions Remain," Mississippi Center for Investigative Reporting, August 28, 2020.

16 **group of white nationalists:** Vanessa Swales, "White Supremacists Flee from Emmett Till Memorial While Filming Video," *The New York Times*, November 6, 2019, A13.

17 **called Emmett "Bobo":** Simeon Wright and Herb Boyd, *Simeon's Story: An Eyewitness Account of the Kidnapping of Emmett Till* (Chicago: Lawrence Hill Books, 2011), 37; Till-Mobley and Benson, *Death of Innocence*, 12, 119.

17 **horror and fear:** Wright and Boyd, *Simeon's Story*, 51.

17 **heard the rumors:** Ruthie Mae Crawford, interviewed in *The Untold Story of Emmett Louis Till*, directed by Keith Beauchamp (Till Freedom Come Productions, 2005).

17 **standing over the bed:** Wright and Boyd, *Simeon's Story*, 57–60; Wheeler Parker Jr., interviewed in *The Untold Story of Emmett Louis Till*, directed by Keith Beauchamp.

17 **in that house another night:** Wright and Boyd, *Simeon's Story*, 60.

18 **measure the exact distance:** Wheeler Parker Jr. and Simeon Wright, interviewed by Devery Anderson, February 7, 2007, Devery Anderson Papers, Florida State University Special Collections, Tallahassee, Florida.

18 **in the trunk of his car:** Wheeler Parker Jr., in conversation with the author; Annie Wright, in conversation with the author.

18 **willingness to absorb pain:** Davis Houck, in conversation with the author.

18 **all white people:** Patrick Weems, in conversation with the author.

19 **about the jury verdict:** Richard Rubin, "The Ghosts of Emmett Till," *The New York Times Magazine*, July 31, 2005, 30.

21 **442 and the Quiver River:** Parker and Wright, interviewed by Anderson; Wheeler Parker Jr., in conversation with the author.

22 **people would come looking for him:** Louis, interviewed by Nelson; Naomi Nix, "Willie Louis Dies at 76; Witness to 1955 Murder of Emmett Till," *Los Angeles Times*, July 24, 2013; "Dr. Howard: Situation in Mississippi," 1, 4; Testimony of Willie Reed, 216–17, 233.

22 **Frank Young, who'd helped:** Beito and Beito, *Black Maverick*, 120–21.

23 **sent him into a rage:** Porteous, "Officers Work All Night," 9; Beito and Beito, *Black Maverick*, 115, 118.

23 **found a war room:** Beito and Beito, *Black Maverick*, 120; Louis, interviewed by Nelson.

23 **could trust, Clark Porteous:** Anderson, *Emmett Till*, 102; Booker, "A Negro Reporter at the Till Trial," *Nieman Reports*, January 1956.

23 **Dr. Howard set up a meeting:** James L. Hicks, "White Reporters Doublecrossed Probers Seeking Lost Witnesses," *Cleveland Call and Post*, October 15, 1955; Christopher Metress, ed., *The Lynching of Emmett Till: A Documentary Narrative*, The American South Series (Charlottesville: University of Virginia Press, 2002), 161; James L. Hicks, "Unbelievable! Jimmy Hicks' Inside Story of a Miss. Lynch Trial," *Baltimore Afro-American*, October 25, 1955, 1, 4; Booker, "Negro Reporter at the Till Trial."

23 **"some white men":** Booker, "Negro Reporter at the Till Trial."

23 **intimidating witnesses into silence:** Hicks, "Unbelievable! Jimmy Hicks' Inside Story"; Beito and Beito, *Black Maverick*, 124.

24 **later, a graduate student:** Hugh Stephen Whitaker, "A Case Study in Southern Justice: The Emmett Till Case" (master's thesis, Florida State University, 1963). According to this thesis, a special prosecuting attorney in Ripley, Mississippi, admitted to Whitaker that the Black accomplices were in fact in a nearby jail, although he claimed not to have known this truth at the time of prosecution. However, the Black press reported their correct locale, even as the prosecutorial team repeatedly told journalists this was a false lead.

24 **Inside was Frank Young:** Hicks, "Unbelievable! Jimmy Hicks' Inside Story"; Anderson, *Emmett Till*, 105–6.

24 **a child of Italian immigrants:** 1950 U.S. Census, Sunflower County, Mississippi, Beat 5, Enumeration District 67-84, April 12, 1950, 13; Augustus Van Zama World War I Service Card, accessed through Ancestry.com; Augustus Van Zama Military Veteran Application for Headstone or Marker, accessed through Ancestry.com; Augustus Van Zama World War I Draft Registration Card, May 24, 1917, accessed through Ancestry.com.

24 **led the search:** Hicks, "Unbelievable! Jimmy Hicks' Inside Story"; Booker, "Negro Reporter at the Till Trial"; "George Smith was a Dedicated Lawman," *The Greenwood Commonwealth*, October 10, 1974, 4.

24 **cartoonishly racist:** Hugh Whitaker described Sheriff Strider as "the personification of the type of law enforcement that had caused so many Negroes to 'go North'";

Whitaker, "Case Study in Southern Justice." In a late-in-life interview with Timothy B. Tyson, Carolyn Bryant stated that Strider "was kind of like the Godfather in Mississippi at the time. Whatever he said was what you [did]." See also David Halberstam, *The Fifties* (New York: Random House, 1994), 439.

24 **claim jurisdiction over the case:** "Muddy River Gives Up Body of Slain Negro Boy," *The Commercial Appeal*, September 1, 1955, 1, 4.

25 **"These witnesses have a story":** Booker, "Negro Reporter at the Till Trial."

25 **Clark Porteous, the white reporter:** Hicks, "Unbelievable! Jimmy Hicks' Inside Story."

26 **seventy miles an hour:** Hicks, "Unbelievable! Jimmy Hicks' Inside Story."

26 **Smith promised not to issue:** Booker, "Negro Reporter at the Till Trial."

27 **simple clothes of the sharecroppers:** According to Jimmy Hicks, who was on the scene, "Ruby [Hurley of the NAACP] and [Moses] Newsome disguised themselves as sharecroppers. Mose, who was 130 pounds, went away wearing a size 46 pair overalls, and Ruby wearing a Mother Hubbard dress and a bandana and actually looked for a moment like a sharecropper"; Hicks, "White Reporters Doublecrossed."

27 **local Black pastor:** Hicks, "Unbelievable! Jimmy Hicks' Inside Story"; Anderson, *Emmett Till*, 106.

27 **they found Willie Reed:** Anderson, *Emmett Till*, 106; Louis, interviewed by Nelson.

28 **Easter Sunday, 1994:** Jeff Andrews, in conversation with the author; 2023 Tax Property Records, Sunflower County, parcel ID no. 141-02-00-004.01.

29 **Reed into his chambers:** Till-Mobley and Benson, *Death of Innocence*, 176–77.

30 **Mamie Till testified first:** Testimony of Mamie Bradley, September 22, 1955, *State of Mississippi v. J. W. Milam and Roy Bryant*, Second District of Tallahatchie County, Seventeenth Judicial District, FBI Case File 62D-JN-30045-FD302, 183–212; "Congressman Diggs, Till's Mother in Attendance at Sumner Trial," *Jackson Advocate*, September 24, 1955, 1.

30 **Willie Reed went next:** Testimony of Willie Reed, 213–48; Louis, interviewed by Nelson.

30 **stared back at him and smiled:** Till-Mobley and Benson, *Death of Innocence*, 183.

30 **Willie Reed rode home:** Lynn Shurden, in conversation with the author.

30 **They'd come from Ireland:** Unless otherwise noted, the Shurden family history discussed in this section derives from a self-published family memoir: W. O. Shurden, *Cotton: Always "King" with Me! An Autobiography by W. O. Shurden, as Told to Wilbur Jones* (1985).

31 **the aristocratic Sturdivants:** Chasing the power and reach these high-class families held was done more directly than one might first assume. In 1939 Otha Shurden, Clint's brother, made his first land purchase of 415 acres from M. P. Sturdivant Sr. for $22,000, paying off his loan within three years. This was not a rhetorical ascension but rather a quite literal one. Shurden, *Cotton*, 18.

31 **On August 9, 1968, a Friday:** Otha Shurden incorrectly states in his memoir that this trip took place in April 1968, but the president's daily diary clarifies the exact day and time. Otherwise, the details of his story mirror the official documentation, and this tale is discussed at length. Shurden, *Cotton*, 28–32; "President's Daily Diary entry, 08/09/1968," President's Daily Diary Series, LBJ Presidential Library, Austin, Texas.

33 **Architects who have examined it:** Belinda Stewart, in conversation with the author.

36 **long-out-of-print history book:** Wilson, *Promised Land or Sandy Bayou*.

37 **nighttime run from Friars Point:** Powell, "Sunflower County," 122, 284, 297; Wilson, *Promised Land or Sandy Bayou.*

37 **the Forrest Place was owned:** Although many of the early deeds to Sunflower County were lost when the then–county seat of McNutt was absorbed into Leflore County in 1871, Aaron Forrest's recorded landownership survives through two publicly recorded land transactions in Leflore: September 1862, deed book D, Leflore County courthouse, 530–31, and November 1863, deed book D, Leflore County courthouse, 544–45; "The Forrest Place," *Delta Democrat-Times* (Greenville, MS), September 15, 1940, 32.

37 **Andrew Jackson Daniel:** Hemphill, *Fevers, Faith, and Floods*, 185, 189.

39 **job with the Roy Clark plantation:** Anderson, *Emmett Till*, 175; "Ella Mae Shuns Willie," 1.

41 **Land Ordinance of 1785:** C. Albert White, *A History of the Rectangular Survey System* (Washington, DC: Bureau of Land Management, 1991), 11.

42 **sold to yeoman farmers:** This failed historical impulse toward yeomanry and its implications in Southern slaveholding states is well documented in Walter Johnson, *River of Dark Dreams: Slavery and Empire in the Cotton Kingdom* (Cambridge, MA: Belknap Press, 2017).

42 **On May 3, 1785:** J. S. Higgins, *Subdivisions of the Public Lands: Described and Illustrated with Diagrams and Maps* (Higgins, 1887), 79.

42 **was simply too high:** The price that the average American farmer would be able to pay for land was routinely discussed on the congressional floor while debating these laws. See *Annals of the Congress of the United States*, 4th Cong., 1st Sess. (1796), 860.

43 **Land Law of 1800:** Higgins, *Subdivisions of the Public Lands*, 81–84.

43 **grandson of a white man:** David Evans, "Charley Patton: The Conscience of the Delta," in *Charley Patton: Voice of the Mississippi Delta*, ed. Robert Sacré, American Made Music Series (Jackson: University Press of Mississippi, 2018), 34, 133–34.

43 **place of rage:** Ted Gioia, *Delta Blues: The Life and Times of the Mississippi Masters Who Revolutionized American Music* (New York: W. W. Norton, 2008), 49; Robert Palmer, *Deep Blues* (New York: Penguin Books, 1982), 57; Evans, "Charley Patton," 38.

43 **the poet Caroline Randall Williams:** Caroline Randall Williams, "You Want a Confederate Monument? My Body Is a Confederate Monument," *The New York Times*, June, 26, 2020.

44 **Her mother especially:** Keith Somerville Dockery McLean and Deborah C. Fort, *Wanderer from the Delta* (Philadelphia, MS: K.S.D. McLean, 2002), 119.

45 **In his arms he carried:** Till-Mobley and Benson, *Death of Innocence*, 184; Anderson, *Emmett Till*, 164; Louis, interviewed by Nelson; "Diggs Flies Till Witness to Chicago!," *The Pittsburgh Courier*, October 1, 1955, 5.

46 **tell her goodbye:** "Ella Mae Shuns Willie," 1.

46 **at the end of the road:** Anderson, *Emmett Till*, 163–64; Ted Poston, "Mose Wright Left Everything to Flee for Life," *New York Post*, October 3, 1955, 28; Lee Blackwell, "2 Who Fled Mississippi Tell Stories," *The Chicago Defender*, October 1, 1955, 2.

46 **steering wheel was Medgar Evers:** Till-Mobley and Benson, *Death of Innocence*, 196–97; Jerry Mitchell, digital correspondence with the author.

46 **Evers's Oldsmobile 88:** Jerry Mitchell, "Did Medgar Evers' Killer Go Free Because of Jury Tampering?" *Literary Hub*, February 24, 2020.

46 **Two strangers approached them**: Till-Mobley and Benson, *Death of Innocence*, 197; Louis, interviewed by Nelson; AP Wire photo and caption, *Tampa Bay Times*, October 1, 1955, 13.

47 **apartment at 2103 South Michigan**: "Ella Mae Shuns Willie," 1.

47 **Reporters met Reed**: "Willie Reed, Till Witness, Starting Life Anew, Chicago," *Delta Democrat-Times* (Greenville, MS), September 29, 1955, 2.

47 **charitable strangers offered**: "Daily News Readers Offer to Send Willie Reed's Girl Friend to Chicago," *Jackson Daily News*, September 29, 1955, 1; "Ella Mae Shuns Willie."

47 **reporter, Bill Spell**: "State Negroes Held 'Captive' in Chicago," *Jackson Daily News*, October 5, 1955, 1; "Woman Witness Told to Keep Silent," *Jackson Daily News*, October 6, 1955, 1; "How the NAACP Network Operates," *Jackson Daily News*, October 7, 1955, 1; "Till Trial Figures Deny They Are NAACP's 'Captives'" *York Daily Record*, October 8, 1955.

47 **described as a nervous breakdown**: "State Negroes Held 'Captive'"; "Willie Reed Won't Return as Till Witness," *Sun Herald* (Biloxi, MS), October 10, 1955, 2.

48 **his father's last name**: Juliet Louis, in conversation with the author.

49 **blast radius of shame**: When I first began reporting this book in the summer of 2020, the publicly traded company FPI Colorado, LLC, owned much of the land in "the blast radius of shame." Over the last four years, their footprint around the barn has been shrinking; however, local tax records indicate that as of 2023, FPI Colorado still owned 1917.80 acres in Sunflower County, including a parcel of 323.40 acres that directly abuts the barn.

50 **people vandalize the headstone**: Dave Tell, in conversation with the author.

50 **W. D. III, "Dee"**: Unless otherwise noted, exchanges between the Marlow family and the Hamers come from Fannie Lou Hamer's oral history interview in Howell Raines, *My Soul Is Rested* (New York: Penguin Books, 1977); J. Todd Moye, *Let the People Decide: Black Freedom and White Resistance Movements in Sunflower County, Mississippi, 1945–1986* (Chapel Hill: University of North Carolina Press, 2004), 99–101, 232–33; and Kate Clifford Larson, *Walk with Me: A Biography of Fannie Lou Hamer* (New York, Oxford University Press, 2021).

51 **Dee Marlow appeared**: Fannie Lou Hamer, "Hearing before a Select Panel on Mississippi and Civil Rights, Testimony of Fannie Lou Hamer," *Congressional Record*, 88th Cong., 2nd Sess., June 4, 1964.

51 **Roy Bryant lived out**: Anderson, *Emmett Till*, 277; Vera Joe Bryant obituary, *Bolivar Commercial* (Cleveland, MS), May 3, 2012, 3.

52 **used to be the Sunflower Plantation**: Jane Adams and D. Gordan, "This Land Ain't My Land: The Eviction of Sharecroppers by the Farm Security Administration," *Agricultural History* 83, no. 3 (2009): 323–51; Horace F. Taylor, "Sunflower Plantation, Part 1: A History" (pamphlet).

52 **next to Mae Bertha Carter**: Constance Curry, "Silver Rights: One Family's Struggle for Justice in America," *Virginia Quarterly Review* 68, no. 1 (1992): 24–34; Constance Curry, *Silver Rights* (San Diego: Harcourt Brace, 1996), 54.

52 **The Carter family lived**: Curry, "Silver Rights."; Gloria Dickerson, in conversation with the author.

52 **The Birch plantation**: Connie Curry, "Son Ham's Hat," *Southern Changes* 14, no. 2 (1992): 15–17; Curry, *Silver Rights*, 87.

52 The Pemble place: J. Todd Moye, *Let the People Decide: Black Freedom and White Resistance Movements in Sunflower County, Mississippi, 1945–1986* (Chapel Hill: University of North Carolina Press, 2004), 174; Curry, *Silver Rights*, 6.

53 the manager, Ramsey Thornton: Curry, "Silver Rights"; "Mid-Delta Obituaries: Ramsey Thornton," *The Delta Democrat-Times* (Greenville, MS), September 21, 1973, 12.

53 Thornton honked his horn: Curry, "Silver Rights"; Curry, *Silver Rights*, 35.

53 somebody would shoot up: Curry, "Silver Rights"; Curry, *Silver Rights*, 7–8, 9–10, 23.

53 Thornton explained that: Curry, "Silver Rights."

54 stood in the doorway: Curry, "Silver Rights"; Curry, *Silver Rights*, 36–37.

60 filmmaker Stanley Nelson: Stanley Nelson, in conversation with the author.

61 thought he'd been killed: Wheeler Parker Jr., in conversation with the author.

61 open something up in Willie: Juliet Louis, in conversation with the author; James, Eunice, and Ruthie Reed, in conversation with the author.

61 first time in fifty years: Dale Killinger, in conversation with the author; Juliet Louis, in conversation with the author.

65 clay pigeons or Coke cans: Patrick Weems, in conversation with the author; Jessie Jaynes-Diming, in conversation with the author.

66 It still fires: Federal Bureau of Investigation, "Prosecutive Report," 96.

66 Sidney, moved into the house: Lynn Shurden, in conversation with the author; Jason Shurden, in conversation with the author; "Sidney George Shurden," *Orlando Sentinel*, May 16, 2010, B7.

II: Destinies

80 founded until 1899: Marie M. Hemphill, *Fevers, Floods, and Faith: A History of Sunflower County, Mississippi, 1844–1976* (Indianola, MS: Sunflower County Historical Society, 1980), 183.

81 towered above the river: The natural history in this section was derived from a variety of different sources, including: Margaret Devall, "What Delta Looked Like before Europeans Settlers Came," *Delta Wildlife*, Spring 2010, 8–9; Mikko Saikku, *This Delta, This Land: An Environmental History of the Yazoo-Mississippi Delta* (Athens: University of Georgia Press, 2005); James W. Swinnich, *Living and Playing the Blues . . . on Dockery Plantation-Farms* (self-published, Outskirts Press, 2021), 114; U.S. Department of Agriculture Soil Conservation Service in cooperation with the Mississippi Agricultural Experiment Station, "Soil Survey: Sunflower County, Mississippi," series 1952, no. 5, February 1959; Evan Peacock, *Mississippi Archaeology Q & A* (Jackson: University Press of Mississippi, 2005), 49–68.

81 deeper than two hundred feet: Robert W. Harrison, *Alluvial Empire* (Washington, DC: The Delta Fund in cooperation with Economic Research Service, U.S. Department of Agriculture, 1961), 33.

82 forests were the songbirds: Saikku, *This Delta, This Land*, 234.

82 found measurable erosion: Peacock, *Mississippi Archaeology*, 58; Saikku, *This Delta, This Land*, 68–69.

82 Scientists still call the ruins: 17-N-2, Walford Survey Notes, November 28, 1940, Lower Mississippi Survey, Peabody Museum of Archaeology and Ethnology, Harvard University.

82 life at Walford: Kimberly Nicole Harrison, "Temper, Mounds, and Palisades: The Walford Site (22Su501) of Sunflower County, Mississippi" (master's thesis, University of Mississippi, 2015). See also Patricia Kay Galloway, *Choctaw Genesis, 1500–1700*, Indians of the Southeast (Lincoln: University of Nebraska Press, 1995), 28–34, 347; R. Barry Lewis and Charles B. Stout, eds., *Mississippian Towns and Sacred Spaces: Searching for an Architectural Grammar* (Tuscaloosa: University of Alabama Press, 1998), xi; James F. Barnett, *Mississippi's American Indians*, Heritage of Mississippi Series, vol. 6 (Jackson: University Press of Mississippi, 2012), 42–44; John Connoway, in conversation with the author; Jessica Crawford, in conversation with the author.

82 sharecropper South centuries later: Galloway, *Choctaw Genesis*, 33, 34; Saikku, *This Delta, This Land*, 61.

82 main mounds and public squares: Lewis and Stout, *Mississippian Towns and Sacred Spaces*, 11–19, 40; Harrison, "Temper, Mounds, and Palisades," 24–28.

83 mapping of this land: Alison Sandman, "Spanish Nautical Cartography in the Renaissance," in *The History of Cartography: Cartography in the European Renaissance* (Chicago: University of Chicago Press, 2009); Or Hasson, "Between Clinical Writing and Storytelling: Alfonso de Santa Cruz and the Peculiar Case of the Man Who Thought He Was Made of Glass," *Hispanic Review* 85, no. 2 (Spring 2017): 155–72; Renate Burri, "The Rediscovery of Ptolemy's Geography," *Imago Mundi* 61, no. 1 (2009): 124–27. For a fuller understanding of the breadth of Spanish mapmaking, see *The Luso-Hispanic World in Maps: A Selective Guide to Manuscript Maps to 1900 in the Collections of the Library of Congress*. It is an excellent place to start.

84 the de Soto map: Galloway, *Choctaw Genesis*, 210–15.

86 his horse bolted: Social pages, *The Enterprise Tocsin*, October 19, 1916, 5.

86 girlfriend was Luvenia Slaughter: Connie Curry, "Son Ham's Hat," *Southern Changes* 14, no. 2 (1992): 15–17; Constance Curry, *Silver Rights* (San Diego: Harcourt Brace, 1996), 75–81, 95–97, 100–101.

88 The French followed: Galloway, *Choctaw Genesis*, 165, 223–24.

88 that way until 1954: 1954 photos of Prentiss, Mississippi, exposed when the Mississippi River fell so low as to expose the old town, M117, Prentiss, Mississippi, Photos Collection, Delta State University, Cleveland, Mississippi; Bill Crider, "Mississippi River Uncovering Community It Buried Years Ago," *St. Joseph News-Press*, July 11, 1954, 12; Mary Thompson, in conversation with the author.

88 Jolliet and Marquette found: Galloway, *Choctaw Genesis*, 165–66.

89 Choctaws' matrilineal society: James Taylor Carson, *Searching for the Bright Path: The Mississippi Choctaws from Prehistory to Removal*, Indians of the Southeast (Lincoln: University of Nebraska Press, 1999), 15.

89 credit and debt: Daniel H. Usner Jr., *American Indians in the Lower Mississippi Valley: Social and Economic Histories*, Indians of the Southeast (Lincoln: University of Nebraska Press, 1998), 66.

89 Panton, Leslie & Company: "The English firm of Panton, Leslie and Company, with Spanish authorization, began to monopolize trade with Indian villages east of the Mississippi." Usner, *American Indians*, 70.

89 Tribes reorganized their daily: Barnett, *Mississippi's American Indians*, 107.

89 Some made salt: Henry Watterson Heggie, *Indians and Pioneers of Old Eliot* (Grenada, MS: Tuscahoma Press, 1989), 4; Carson, *Searching for the Bright Path*, 122.

89 English was deerskin: Barnett, *Mississippi's American Indians*, 107.

90 agreed on set prices: Usner, *American Indians*, 68.

90 looking for game: Carson, *Searching for the Bright Path*, 64; Usner, *American Indians*, 72; Barnett, *Mississippi's American Indians*, 161.

90 Natchez tribal leaders: Barnett, *Mississippi's American Indians*, 123–27; Marcel Giraud, "The Natchez Drama and Its Consequences," in *A History of French Louisiana*, vol. 5, trans. Joseph C. Lambert and Brian Pearce (Baton Rouge: Louisiana State University Press, 1974), 388–439; Le Page Du Pratz, *The History of Louisiana*, book 1, Project Gutenberg.

90 French at Fort Rosalie: Barnett, *Mississippi's American Indians*, 124–25; James F. Barnett, *The Natchez Indians: A History to 1735* (Jackson: University Press of Mississippi, 2007), 115–27.

90 only four hundred free: Barnett, *Mississippi's American Indians*, 126; Giraud, "Natchez Drama," in *A History of French Louisiana*, 426.

90 sold into slavery: Saikku, *This Delta, This Land*, 74; Barnett, *Mississippi's American Indians*, 126–27.

91 most ended up: Dunbar Rowland and A. G. Sanders, *Mississippi Provincial Archives . . . French Dominion*, vol. 3 (Jackson: Press of the Mississippi Department of Archives and History, 1927), 580–81; Noel Edward Smyth, "'The End of the Natchez?' A Genealogy of Historical, Literacy, and Anthropological Thought about the Natchez Indians since the Eighteenth Century" (working paper, University of California, Santa Cruz, 2013).

91 named John Law: Unless otherwise noted, the biographical information about John Law in this section comes from Adolphe Thiers, *The Mississippi Bubble: A Memoir of John Law*, trans. Frank S. Fiske (New York: W. A. Townsend, 1859); Janet Gleeson, *Millionaire: The Philanderer, Gambler, and Duelist Who Invented Modern France* (New York: Simon & Schuster, 2000); and James Buchan, *John Law: A Scottish Adventurer of the Eighteenth Century* (London: MacLehose Press, 2018).

92 first private bank: John K. Bettersworth, *Mississippi: A History* (Austin, TX: Steck Company, 1959), 71–72.

92 known in France as Mississippians: Bettersworth, *Mississippi*, 73.

92 on the prowl in Paris: Thiers, *Mississippi Bubble*, 135.

92 Law's company founded: Barnett, *Mississippi's American Indians*, 111; Mira Wilkins, *The History of Foreign Investment in the United States to 1914*, Harvard Studies in Business History, vol. 41 (Cambridge, MA: Harvard University Press, 1989), 11–12.

92 national bank of France: Franklin D. Riley, *School History of Mississippi* (Richmond, VA: B. F. Johnson, 1915), 40.

92 John Law fled: Wilkins, *History of Foreign Investment*, 12.

93 died in Venice: Bettersworth, *Mississippi*, 73.

93 ownership of the millions of acres: Richard D. Younger, "The Yazoo Land Frauds" (master's thesis, Marquette University, June 1950); Edward E. Baptist, *The Half Has Never Been Told: Slavery and the Making of American Capitalism*, paperback ed. (New York: Basic Books, 2016), 18–20.

94 U.S. senator James Gunn: Younger, "Yazoo Land Frauds," 29–30; George R. Lamplugh, "James Gunn: Georgia Federalist, 1789–1801," *The Georgia Historical Quarterly* 94, no. 3 (Fall 2010): 313–41.

94 "eight to ten" slaves: Younger, "Yazoo Land Frauds," 26.

94 **Eli Whitney, inventor:** Brenden Edward Kennedy, "The Yazoo Land Sales: Slavery, Speculation, and Capitalism in the Early American Republic" (PhD diss., University of Florida, 2015), 24.

94 **James Gunn's Georgia Company:** Baptist, *Half Has Never Been Told*, 20–21; Kennedy, "Yazoo Land Sales," 106; George R. Lamplugh, *Politics on the Periphery: Factions and Parties in Georgia, 1783–1806* (Newark: University of Delaware Press, 1986), 113.

94 **1795 to James Greenleaf:** Younger, "Yazoo Land Frauds," 37; "Evidences of Title Derived from Georgia," *American State Papers, 1789–1838*, Public Lands, vol. 1, 1789–1809, 218–19.

94 **Nathaniel Prime dominated:** Kennedy, "Yazoo Land Sales," 138–39.

95 **every major city:** Jane Elsmere, "The Notorious Yazoo Land Fraud Case," *Georgia Historical Quarterly* 51, no. 4 (December 1967): 425–42; Kennedy, "Yazoo Land Sales," 135.

95 **Alexander Hamilton weighed in:** Elsmere, "Notorious Yazoo"; Younger, "Yazoo Land Frauds," 35.

95 **annulled the sales:** The Rescinding Act, passed February 13, 1796 (Georgia state legislature).

95 **state senator from Hancock County:** Kennedy, "Yazoo Land Sales," 110–11; "Augusta, September 26," *Augusta Chronicle and Gazette of the State*, September 26, 1795, 3.

95 **Gunn went into hiding:** Younger, "Yazoo Land Frauds," 33; Joel Chandler Harris, *Stories of Georgia* (New York: American Book Company, 1896), 130.

95 **His wife killed herself:** Lamplugh, "James Gunn."

95 **other senator, James Jackson:** Younger, "Yazoo Land Frauds," 33.

95 **Jackson wrote beautiful:** Kennedy, "Yazoo Land Sales," 127. See also James Jackson, *The Letters of Sicilus, to the Citizens of the State of Georgia* (Augusta, GA: [John E. Smith?], 1795).

95 **scripted and ritualized ceremony:** Younger, "Yazoo Land Frauds," 35; Kennedy, "Yazoo Land Sales," 142–43.

96 **commodity in the mechanizing world:** Eugene R. Dattel, *Cotton and Race in the Making of America: The Human Costs of Economic Power*, paperback ed. (Lanham, MD: Ivan R. Dee, 2011), 30–38.

96 **Slave narratives report:** F. E. Sanderson, "Liverpool and the Slave Trade: A Guide to Sources," *Transactions of the Historic Society of Lancashire and Cheshire* 124 (1972): 154–76; Sven Beckert, *Empire of Cotton: A Global History* (New York: Vintage Books, 2015), 88–97. For a fuller look at the connections between cotton, England, and the American South, see Jim Powell, "Cotton, Liverpool, and the American Civil War" (PhD thesis, University of Liverpool, October 2018).

96 **a thousand-year tradition:** Dattel, *Cotton and Race*; Beckert, *Empire of Cotton*; E. L. Jones, *The European Miracle: Environments, Economies, and Geopolitics in the History of Europe and Asia*, 3rd ed. (New York: Cambridge University Press, 2003).

97 **didn't know who had purchased:** Younger, "Yazoo Land Frauds," 32–39.

100 **correspondence is full of his fear:** George Washington, letter dated February 17, 1795, in *A Compilation of the Messages and Papers of the Presidents, 1789–1922* (New York: Bureau of National Literature and Art, 1897), 167.

100 **his friend Henry Knox:** Henry Knox to George Washington, July 7, 1789, Gilder Lehrman Institute of American History, GLC02437.04272.

101 **he'd fought side by side:** Clara Sue Kidwell, *Choctaws and Missionaries in Mississippi, 1818–1918* (Norman: University of Oklahoma Press, 1995), 22.

101 **fall of 1805:** Barnett, *Mississippi's American Indians*, 172; Arthur H. DeRosier, *The Removal of the Choctaw Indians* (Knoxville: University of Tennessee Press, 1989), 32; Gideon Lincecum, "Life of Apushaimataha," in *Pushmataha: A Choctaw Leader and His People, A History of the Choctaw Nation and Her Greatest Leader* (Tuscaloosa: University of Alabama Press, 2004), 26–103.

102 **Yazoo securities flooded:** Kennedy, "Yazoo Land Sales," 37, 244; Brenden Edward Kennedy, "Mississippi Stocks and the 1795 Yazoo Land Sale: Slavery, Securities Markets, Native American Dispossession, and the Panic of 1819 in Alabama," *The Alabama Review* 74, no. 3 (July 2021): 203–39.

103 **old indigo and tobacco lands:** Dattel, *Cotton and Race*, 9; Baptist, *Half Has Never Been Told*, 12; Beckert, *Empire of Cotton*, 103.

103 **Virginia politicians began:** Baptist, *Half Has Never Been Told*, 29; *Encyclopedia Virginia*, s.v. "The Virginia Slavery Debate of 1831–1832," encyclopediavirginia.org /entries/virginia-slavery-debate-of-1831-1832-the/.

103 **cotton gin was invented:** Kennedy, "Yazoo Land Sales," 24.

103 **historian Ira Berlin:** Ira Berlin, *The Making of African America: The Four Great Migrations* (New York: Viking, 2010), 100.

103 **slave trader named Walker:** William Wells Brown, *Narrative of William W. Brown, an American Slave, Written by Himself* (London: Charles Gilpin, 1849), available at University of North Carolina at Chapel Hill Libraries.

103 **"seasoning" as people acclimated:** Theodore D. Weld, *American Slavery as It Is: Testimony of a Thousand Witnesses* (New York: The American Anti-Slavery Society, 1839), available at University of North Carolina at Chapel Hill Libraries.

104 **half the nation's cotton:** Kennedy, "Yazoo Land Sales," 258.

104 **volcanic eruption in modern Indonesia:** John J. Post, "The Economic Crisis of 1816–1817 and Its Social and Political Consequences," *The Journal of Economic History* 30, no. 1 (March 1970): 248–50; Bernice de Jong Boers, "Mount Tambora in 1815: A Volcanic Eruption in Indonesia and Its Aftermath," *Indonesia* 60 (1995): 37–60.

105 **Panic of 1819 would build:** Usner, *American Indians*, 91–92; Kennedy, "Mississippi Stocks."

105 **called him Big Boy:** Carolyn Bryant, interviewed by Timothy B. Tyson.

105 **His father was William:** *Bryan Book: Genealogy Collection*, preserved by Brent R. Brian, obtained through the Internet Archive; Charlie Brady, "Descendants of F. Anderson and Washington Bryan," South Carolina's Information Highway.

105 **Doc Forts, as his:** *Bryan Book: Genealogy Collection*, preserved by Brent R. Brian and obtained through the Internet Archive; "Died," *Spectator*, July 14, 1821. The nickname specifically permeates family genealogical lore, but it is witnessed in documentation such as his listing on the 1820 federal census.

105 **Bryan married Elizabeth DuPont:** "Marriage and Death Notices from the City Gazette," *South Carolina Historical and Genealogical Magazine* 28, no. 4 (October 1927): 242; Henry A. M. Smith, "The Ashley River: Its Seats and Settlements," *South Carolina Historical and Genealogical Magazine* 20, no. 2 (April 1919): 112–13.

105 **Greek Revival mansion:** Batavia Plantation plat map images courtesy of the South Carolina Historical Society.

106 **got sick and died**: "Marriage and Death Notices"; The will of F. Bryan and probate documents, including the names of some of the people he owned, from the Petition Analysis Record of Anne Bryan, C. D. Bryan Anderson, Joseph [Josiah] D. Bryan, Accession no. 21382911, Series 2 County Court Petitions, Barnwell District, South Carolina, Race and Slavery Petitions Project, University of North Carolina at Greensboro. In his will, written directly before his death, he wrote of being "diseased of body but of sound mind."

106 **Bryan boys migrated**: 1830 U.S. Census, St. Luke's Parish, Beaufort District, South Carolina, n.d., 307; 1840 U.S. Census, Lindsey, Coosa County, Alabama, n.d., 299.

106 **had four girls**: 1850 U.S. Census, Barnwell District, South Carolina, July 31, 1850, 328.

106 **pushed to the edge**: After marrying his wife in Alabama, Henry remained stalwart on following in his father's footsteps and pressing farther west. The 1870 census shows him with his wife, three children, and housekeeper, "Young Mattie," all living in Kemper County, Mississippi, on the Alabama state line. This is also the first time you see his name written as "Bryant," with a *t*. It appears he changed his name as he crossed the state border. The family eventually moved to Tallahatchie County, Mississippi, where he is buried. 1860 U.S. Census, Townships 9, 10, 11, & 12, Choctaw County, Alabama, August 3, 1860, 91; 1870 U.S. Census, Dekalb, Kemper County, Mississippi, August 15, 1870, 168.

107 **lived two doors down**: 1880 U.S. Census, Tallahatchie County, Mississippi, Beat 3, Enumeration District 108, July 2, 1880, 49.

107 **Ed Devaney, the oldest juror**: Devery S. Anderson, *Emmett Till: The Murder That Shocked the World and Propelled the Civil Rights Movement* (Jackson: University Press of Mississippi, 2015), 92.

108 **road built from New Hope**: Public Notices, *Tallahatchie Messenger*, September 5, 1980, 4.

108 **Dave Milam, the grandfather**: This affair was well documented in the local newspapers. "Frightful Tragedy," *The Democratic-Herald* (Charleston, MS), May 20, 1897; "The Trial Continued," *The Democratic-Herald* (Charleston, MS), May 27, 1897; "Joe Coleman Is Free," *The Democratic-Herald* (Charleston, MS), July 15, 1897.

109 **Pushmataha came north**: Barnett, *Mississippi's American Indians*, 187–88; Carson, *Searching for the Bright Path*, 92; DeRosier, *Removal of the Choctaw*, 66.

110 **"The paper is untrue"**: Kidwell, *Choctaws and Missionaries*, 184–85; Lincecum, *Pushmataha*, 74–87; Thomas L. Wiley, *Pushmataha: The Forgotten Warrior* (Jackson, MS: Monarch, 2023).

110 **rooms at Tennison's Hotel**: DeRosier, *Removal of the Choctaw*, 79–80; "Died," *Washington Gazette*, December 24, 1824, 2.

110 **Pushmataha addressed his men**: "Pushmatahaw," *Appleton's Journal of Popular Science, Literature and Art*, August 6, 1870, 155–68.

111 **one last request**: DeRosier, *Removal of the Choctaw*, 82–83; "Pushmatahaw."

112 **congressman Edward Everett**: Edward Everett, "A Member of Congress Speaks Out against the Removal Policy," in *Speeches on the Passage of the Bill for the Removal of the Indians Delivered in the Congress of the United States*, ed. Jeremiah Evarts (Boston, 1830), 299.

112 **the best possible terms**: DeRosier, *Removal of the Choctaw*, 104–6, 113; Kidwell, *Choctaws and Missionaries*, 132–33.

112 **forks of Dancing Rabbit Creek**: Barnett, *Mississippi's American Indians*, 195–96; Kidwell, *Choctaws and Missionaries*, 134–36; Carson, *Searching for the Bright Path*, 120–24; DeRosier, *Removal of the Choctaw*, 122–125.

112 **regathered the remaining chiefs**: DeRosier, *Removal of the Choctaw*, 122–25.

112 **more than "Choctaw children"**: DeRosier, *Removal of the Choctaw*, 66.

113 **Treaty of Dancing Rabbit Creek**: Barnett, *Mississippi's American Indians*, 196–97, 201; Tim Tingle, *Walking the Choctaw Road* (El Paso, TX: Cinco Puntos Press, 2005), 38–51; Dunbar Rowland, *History of Mississippi: The Heart of the South*, vol. 1 (Chicago: S.J. Publishing, 1925), 556.

113 **blacksmith named William Forrest**: Andrew Nelson Lytle, *Bedford Forrest and His Critter Company*, Southern Classics Series (Nashville: J. S. Sanders, 1931), 16; Jack Hurst, *Nathan Bedford Forrest: A Biography*, reprint ed. (New York: Vintage, 1994), 14–15; General Thomas Jordan and J. P. Pryor, *The Campaigns of Lieut.-Gen. N. B. Forrest and of Forrest's Cavalry* (Dayton, OH: Press of Morningside Bookshop, 1977), 19; Captain J. Harvey Mathes, *Great Commanders: General Forrest*, The Great Commanders Series (New York: D. Appleton, 1902), 3–4.

113 **"a good many years"**: Lytle, *Bedford Forrest*, 9.

113 **ten miles from any neighbor**: John A. Wyeth, *That Devil Forrest: Life of General Nathan Bedford Forrest* (1908; repr., Mount Pleasant, SC: Arcadia Press, 2017), 12–13.

113 **William Forrest died suddenly**: Jordan and Pryor, *Campaigns of Lieut.-Gen. N. B. Forrest*, 5.

113 **have an outpost**: "The Forrest Place," *Delta Democrat-Times* (Greenville, MS), September 15, 1940, 32.

114 **named Hugh Stewart**: H. C. Stewart, "T22 R4W Choctaw Cession of 1830," Bureau of Land Management, 388, 403–4; Lola Cazier, *Surveys and Surveyors of the Public Domain, 1785–1975* (Washington, DC: U.S. Government Printing Office, Superintendent of Documents, 1978).

114 **Dense thickets covered**: Stewart, "T22 R4W Choctaw Cession of 1830."

115 **ad he placed**: Brian Steel Wills, *The River Was Dyed Red with Blood: Nathan Bedford Forrest & Fort Pillow* (Norman: University of Oklahoma Press, 2014), 35.

115 **won and lost many battles**: Mathes, *Great Commanders*, 358; Captain Eric William Sheppard, *Bedford Forrest: The Confederacy's Greatest Cavalryman* (New York: Dial Press, 1930), 296–97; Harry Abernathy, "Famous General Retired to Coahoma County Plantation," *The Clarksdale Press Register*, July 21, 1984.

115 **Colonel Jeffrey Forrest**: Wills, *River Was Dyed Red*, 62; Lytle, *Bedford Forrest*, 267; Jordan and Pryor, *Campaigns of Lieut.-Gen. N. B. Forrest*, 396; Wyeth, *That Devil Forrest*, 318.

116 **Civil War ever got to**: Yazoo County Convention & Visitors Bureau, "The Civil War Comes to Yazoo: 1862–1864" (pamphlet), 1–8.

116 **edges of the Delta brimmed**: John C. Hudson, "The Yazoo-Mississippi Delta as Plantation Country," *Tall Timbers* 16 (1979): 66–87.

116 **export of cotton**: Dattel, *Cotton and Race*, 170–75, 186; Beckert, *Empire of Cotton*, 248.

117 **streets of Memphis**: Lytle, *Bedford Forrest*, 386; Abernathy, "Famous General Retired."

117 **A year after the war veterans**: J. Michael Martinez, "'A Brotherhood of Property-Holders, the Peaceable, Law-Abiding Citizens of the State,'"in *Carpetbaggers, Cavalry, and the Ku Klux Klan: Exposing the Invisible Empire During Reconstruction* (New York: Rowman & Littlefield, 2007), 8–25.

117 "I want to join": Lytle, *Bedford Forrest*, 382–83.

117 a man called: Lytle, *Bedford Forrest*, 383.

118 themselves Heggie's Scouts: Hugh Stephen Whitaker, "A Case Study in Southern Justice: The Emmett Till Case" (master's thesis, Florida State University, 1963), 32–35.

118 inside the county courthouse: Whitaker, "Case Study in Southern Justice," 46–47; Riley, *School History of Mississippi*, 317–18.

118 "a type of racialized": Niambi M. Carter, "Intimacy without Consent: Lynching as Sexual Violence," *Politics & Gender* 8, no. 3 (2012): 414–21.

118 Vicksburg voters elected: Riley, *School History of Mississippi*, 314–15; Whitaker, "Case Study in Southern Justice," 46–47.

119 a fellow old soldier: Lytle, *Bedford Forrest*, 386.

120 Sven Beckert wrote: Beckert, *Empire of Cotton*, 279.

120 first cotton future: Dattel, *Cotton and Race*, 294–95.

120 New York Cotton Exchange opened: Beckert, *Empire of Cotton*, 320.

121 no functioning banking system: Dattel, *Cotton and Race*, 303–5.

121 plantation owners experimented: Beckert, *Empire of Cotton*, 282, 285–88; Saikku, *This Delta, This Land*, 110–11, 121; Stephen V. Ash, *A Massacre in Memphis: The Race Riot That Shook the Nation One Year after the Civil War* (New York: Hill and Wang, 2013), 72; Dattel, *Cotton and Race*, 329–30.

121 Future governor James Vardaman: Jerry Mitchell, "On This Day in 1890," *Mississippi Today*, November 1, 2023.

121 just around 1,300: Dattel, *Cotton and Race*, 271; Whitaker, "Case Study in Southern Justice," 39.

121 passed textbook laws: Riley, *School History of Mississippi*, 356.

122 citizens in our textbooks: Riley, *School History of Mississippi*; Bettersworth, *Mississippi*.

122 a similar obsession in Japan: Robert Kramm, "Haunted by Defeat: Imperial Sexualities, Prostitution, and the Emergence of Postwar Japan," *Journal of World History* 28, no. 3/4 (December 2017): 587–614.

122 Poor white farmers: Bettersworth, *Mississippi*, 334.

123 billowing engine smoke: Mia Bay, *Traveling Black: A Story of Race and Resistance* (Cambridge, MA: Harvard University Press), 85.

123 Lloyd Binford, the infamous: Whitney Strub, "Black and White and Banned All Over: Race, Censorship and Obscenity in Postwar Memphis," *Journal of Social History* 40, no. 3 (Spring 2007): 685–715.

124 the Taliaferro family: Just as the Milam ancestors spelled Milam in a variety of ways from "Mylan" to "Maylem" and the Bryant ancestral lineage doesn't always employ the "*t*" in their last name, you'll find many different spellings of Taliaferro in the historical record.

124 Spring Hill, Somerset, and Lucky Hit: LindaRe, "Three Intersecting Plantations," map courtesy of Beverley Ballantine, *Between the Gate Posts* (blog), November 3, 2011.

124 Emmett Till's kin: LindaRe, "Left the Plantation to Join Federal Army," research notes courtesy of Beverly Ballantine, *Between the Gate Posts* (blog), April 16, 2013.

124 Smith Brown, one of Till's: 1870 U.S. Census, Copiah County, Mississippi, Townships 9 & 10 West of R.R., Linden, August 2, 1870, 115–16; 1880 U.S. Census, Copiah

County Mississippi, Rose Hill District, Enumeration District 16, June 22, 1880, 27; 1900 U.S. Census, Copiah County, Mississippi, Mount Hope Voting Precinct, Enumeration District 41, June 11, 1900, 6; 1910 U.S. Census, Copiah County, Mississippi, Mayharris Township, Beat 4, Enumeration District 53, April 20–21, 1910, 3.

125 **owned by P. H. Brooks:** Beverly Morgan, in conversation with the author; Valerie Grim, "Black Farm Families in the Yazoo-Mississippi Delta: A Study of the Brooks Family Farm Community, 1920–1970" (PhD diss., Iowa State University, 1990).

125 **like his white Confederate father:** Beverly Morgan, in conversation with the author.

126 **man named Oliver Carter:** 1870 U.S. Census, Wilkes County, Georgia, Militia District 174, Washington Post Office, August 15, 1870, 144; 1880 U.S. Census, Wilkes County, Georgia, Militia District 175, Enumeration District 134, June 14, 1880, 37; 1900 U.S. Census, Wilkes County, Georgia, Upton Township, Enumeration District 116, June 1, 1900, 26; Return of Qualified Voters, Wilkes County, Georgia, Election District 29, August 6, 1867, 25.

127 **called a scalawag:** Dattel, *Cotton and Race*, 315.

127 **This crash is what ruined:** Mathes, *Great Commanders*, 363; Sheppard, *Bedford Forrest*, 296–97; "The Panic of 1873," Business Research Guides, This Month in Business History: September, Library of Congress.

127 **Black elected officials:** Riley, *School History of Mississippi*, 312.

128 **Baring Brothers in London:** Beckert, *Empire of Cotton*, 287.

128 **In 1880 cotton prices:** Katherine M. B. Osburn, *Choctaw Resurgence in Mississippi: Race, Class, and Nation Building in the Jim Crow South, 1830–1977*, Indians of the Southeast (Lincoln: University of Nebraska Press, 2014), 28–29.

128 **16 percent of farmers were sharecroppers:** John C. Willis, *Forgotten Time: The Yazoo-Mississippi Delta after the Civil War* (Charlottesville: University Press of Virginia, 2000), 188.

128 **The same year the rivers:** John Solomon Otto, *The Final Frontiers, 1880–1930: Settling the Southern Bottomlands*, Contributions in American History, no. 183 (Westport, CT: Greenwood Press, 1999), 26.

128 **first railroad project:** Otto, *Final Frontiers*, 21–22; Dattel, *Cotton and Race*, 316.

129 **Frank and Mary Hamilton:** Unless otherwise noted, this section comes directly from Mary Mann Hamilton, *Trials of the Earth* (Boston: Back Bay Books, 2017).

129 **blues lyrics as the Yellow Dog:** Hemphill, *Fevers, Floods, and Faith*, 260–63; Robert Palmer, *Deep Blues* (New York: Penguin Books, 1982), 45.

129 **brought the railroad:** James Oliver, Patrick R. Shepard, and Carol Heathman Polasini, *The Oliver Family: Mississippi Delta Legacy* (n.p.: James Oliver, 2020), 27–28; Saikku, *This Delta, This Land*, 191.

129 **southern lumber grew:** Saikku, *This Delta, This Land*, 171.

129 **Little towns appeared:** Hemphill, *Fevers, Floods, and Faith*, 114–82; Saikku, *This Delta, This Land*, 193.

130 **Settlers followed close:** Palmer, *Deep Blues*, 90.

132 **$1.25 an acre:** Saikku, *This Delta, This Land*, 173.

132 **225,000 acres in Bolivar County:** Florence Warfield Sillers, *History of Bolivar County, Mississippi* (Jackson, MS: Daughters of the American Revolution, Mississippi Delta Chapter, 1948), 225.

132 **more than a million acres:** Saikku, *This Delta, This Land*, 173.

132 **holding company Delta & Pine Land:** *Evers v. Watson*, 156 U.S. 527 (1895); Saikku, *This Delta, This Land*, 173–74; Otto, *Final Frontiers*, 21, 50–51.

132 **called the Sunflower Land & Manufacturing Company:** Oliver, Shepard, and Polasini, *Oliver Family*, 83; "The Charter of Incorporation of the Sunflower Land and Manufacturing Company," *DeSoto Times* (Hernando, MS), January 16, 1890, 2.

133 **Will Dockery bought a lot:** Saikku, *This Delta, This Land*, 129; Palmer, *Deep Blues*, 49–50.

133 **Buffalo-based lumber corporation:** Taylor, "Sunflower Plantation, Part 1," 1–7.

133 **working through vast stands:** Oliver, Shepard, and Polasini, *Oliver Family*, 43.

133 **950-foot artesian well:** Taylor, "Sunflower Plantation, Part 1," 2.

133 **five dollars an acre:** Taylor, "Sunflower Plantation, Part 1," 2.

133 **170 Black families:** Taylor, "Sunflower Plantation, Part 1," 2.

133 **Will Dockery rode horses:** Swinnich, *Living and Playing the Blues*, 24, 73, 104–16.

133 **He raged against:** Swinnich, *Living and Playing the Blues*, 73, 114.

134 **Dockery bought huge tracts:** Saikku, *This Delta, This Land*, 129; Sillers, *History of Bolivar County*, 170–73.

134 **He liked to listen:** Blues historians have long argued over whether or not Will Dockery enjoyed listening to the music being played on his plantation, but this 1898 letter to his wife, Hughla, states his feelings clearly: "The Negroes are having a dance back of the store about 450 yards into the cane and it is an interesting sight to me for I don't know if I have enjoyed anything so much." Swinnich, *Living and Playing the Blues*, 66, 116; Ted Gioia, *Delta Blues: The Life and Times of the Mississippi Masters Who Revolutionized American Music* (New York: W. W. Norton, 2008), 46.

134 **"craps à la negro":** Swinnich, *Living and Playing the Blues*, 117.

134 **His store burned:** Swinnich, *Living and Playing the Blues*, 107–12.

134 **hired a night watchman:** Swinnich, *Living and Playing the Blues*, 73.

134 **"The free n—— is a failure":** Swinnich, *Living and Playing the Blues*, 111.

134 **cleared, burned, and drained:** Chris Myers Asch, *The Senator and the Sharecropper: The Freedom Struggles of James O. Eastland and Fannie Lou Hamer* (New York: New Press, 2008), 68; Otto, *Final Frontiers*, 38, 59; Hemphill, *Fevers, Floods, and Faith*, 654; Saikku, *This Delta, This Land*, 170.

135 **no more bears to kill:** Saikku, *This Delta, This Land*, 233.

135 **called it the Peavine:** Swinnich, *Living and Playing the Blues*, 19–20; Norm Cohen and David Cohen, *Long Steel Rail: The Railroad in American Folk Song* (Urbana: University of Illinois Press, 2000), 410; Florence Warfield Sillers, *History of Bolivar County, Mississippi* (Jackson, Mississippi: Daughters of the American Revolution, Mississippi Delta Chapter, 1948), 225; Bill Lester, interviewed by Amy C. Evans, August 9, 2012, Dockery Farms Oral History Project; Keith Wood, "Peavine Railroad," *Bolivar Bullet*, January 6, 2021.

135 **The first railroads:** Dattel, *Cotton and Race*, 316.

135 **only seventy miles:** Otto, *Final Frontiers*, 27.

135 **route got cleared by:** Sillers, *History of Bolivar County*, 225.

135 **Every morning before sunrise:** Palmer, *Deep Blues*, 53; Hemphill, *Fevers, Floods, and Faith*, 404.

136 **rode for free:** Swinnich, *Living and Playing the Blues*, 19.

136 **hooks in the Delta:** Otto, *Final Frontiers*, 27–28; Dattel, *Cotton and Race*, 317; Saikku, *This Delta, This Land*, 192; Sillers, *History of Bolivar County*, 225.

136 **fifteen dollars an acre:** Sillers, *History of Bolivar County*, 225.

136 **known as deadenings:** Oliver, Shepard, and Polasini, *Oliver Family*, 27–30; Saikku, *This Delta, This Land*, 179–80, 188.

136 **that number would grow:** Otto, *Final Frontiers*, 27, 60.

137 **Stuyvesant Fish, bought:** Dattel, *Cotton and Race*, 318; John M. Barry, *Rising Tide: The Great Flood of 1927 and How It Changed America* (New York: Simon & Schuster, 1997), 108; "For Model Plantation in South," *The New York Times*, April 5, 1902.

137 **A gingko tree:** Horace F. Taylor, "Sunflower Plantation, Part 1: A History" (pamphlet); "Teddy Roosevelt's Ginkgo Tree Still Standing in Bolivar County," *The Clarksdale Press Register*, October 28, 2002, 7.

137 **Stephen D. Lee spoke:** "Ends All Ill Will," *Chicago Tribune*, May 31, 1995, 9; "Let There Be Peace," *The Chicago Chronicle*, May 31, 1895, 1–2; Jarrett Shapiro, "Chicago's 'Harmonious Forgetfulness': John Cox Underwood and the Meaning of Reconciliation at Confederate Mound, 1885–1896," *Chicago Studies* 10 (2020), 221–73.

137 **The blues historians:** See David Evans, *Big Road Blues: Tradition and Creativity in the Folk Blues* (New York: Da Capo Press, 1987); Palmer, *Deep Blues*; Gioia, *Delta Blues*; Swinnich, *Living and Playing the Blues*; Clyde Adrian Woods and Ruth Wilson Gilmore, *Development Arrested: The Blues and Plantation Power in the Mississippi Delta*, paperback ed. (London: Verso, 2017); David Evans, "Charley Patton: The Conscience of the Delta," in *Charley Patton: Voice of the Mississippi Delta*, ed. Robert Sacré, American Made Music Series (Jackson: University Press of Mississippi, 2018); and others.

138 **word spread of a man:** Swinnich, *Living and Playing the Blues*, 105.

138 **"I am master":** Swinnich, *Living and Playing the Blues*, 6.

138 **Sunflower County alone:** Swinnich, *Living and Playing the Blues*, 110.

138 **His commissary accepted:** Palmer, *Deep Blues*, 54.

138 **became regular visitors:** Swinnich, *Living and Playing the Blues*, 23.

138 **called Dockery & Donelson:** Swinnich, *Living and Playing the Blues*, 118–19.

139 **The flood of 1897:** Otto, *Final Frontiers*, 36–37; Dunbar Rowland, *History of Mississippi: The Heart of the South*, vol. 2 (Chicago: S. J. Clarke, 1925), 537; Saikku, *This Delta, This Land*, 152.

139 **new drainage projects:** Otto, *Final Frontiers*, 36–37, 50; Rowland, *History of Mississippi*, 537.

140 **Deutsche Bank began:** Beckert, *Empire of Cotton*, 316.

140 **many of the men:** "News of Bygone Days from the Commercial Appeal Files," *The Commercial Appeal* (Memphis), August 4, 1974, 1–2; "Scheme to Raise the Funds," *The Commercial Appeal*, June 2, 1895, 1.

141 **Nathan Bedford Forrest statue in Memphis:** "Don't Forget It: Meeting of the Forrest Monument Association," *The Memphis Appeal-Avalanche*, November 25, 1891; "Veil Is Drawn from the Bronze Statue of Forrest," *The Commercial Appeal* (Memphis), May 17, 1905, 1, 3–4.

141 **tried to sort out:** "They Are Here," *The Memphis Appeal-Avalanche*, October 13, 1891.

141 **"great leader of this secret clan":** "Veil Is Drawn."

141 **"Forrest loved children":** "Small Talk," *The Commercial Appeal* (Memphis), April 23, 1905, 6.

142 **Iowa-based timber company:** "Cedar Rapids' Wealthiest Man," *The Gazette* (Cedar Rapids, IA), 15.

NOTES

142 That winter, near the end: Otto, *Final Frontiers*, 36.

143 felt like a future: Swinnich, *Living and Playing the Blues*, 115.

143 Across the bayou Will Dockery: Swinnich, *Living and Playing the Blues*, 17.

143 saying that Guy Thomas: "Murphreesboro Dots," *The Democratic-Herald* (Charleston, MS), March 10, 1904, 1.

144 named Henry Sloan: Palmer, *Deep Blues*, 50; Evans, "Charley Patton," 43, 53–54; Swinnich, *Living and Playing the Blues*, 35–36.

144 No recordings of him exist: Swinnich, *Living and Playing the Blues*, 35; Palmer, *Deep Blues*, 99.

144 Patton's grandfather was: Evans, "Charley Patton," 34–36.

145 name-checked Will Dockery: Arnold Shaw, "The Mississippi Blues Tradition and the Origins of the Blues," in Sacré, ed., *Charley Patton*, 14; Evans, "Charley Patton," 25.

145 his throat slit: Evans, "Charley Patton," 50.

146 Howlin' Wolf, who learned: Palmer, *Deep Blues*, 48; Evans, "Charley Patton," 37; Jim O'Neal, "Modern Chicago Blues: Delta Retentions," in Sacré, ed., *Charley Patton*, 202.

146 Charley told him: Evans, "Charley Patton," 37.

146 grid couldn't handle the wattage: Vance Lauderdale, "The Lyceum," *Memphis Magazine*, May 4, 2011.

146 guest of honor was William Forrest: Unless otherwise noted, the following account comes directly from "Captain Forrest's Burial Today," *The Commercial Appeal* (Memphis), February 9, 1908, 1–2.

146 carried into combat: "In Honor of Capt. Forrest," *The Commercial Appeal* (Memphis), February 2, 1908, 7.

147 In Baltimore, when a young: "The Clansman Thrills," *The Baltimore Sun*, March 13, 1906, 12.

147 William to go on stage: "At the Theatres," *The Commercial Appeal* (Memphis), February 2, 1908, 20.

148 Something awoke inside him: "Captain Forrest's Burial Today."

148 Charley Patton played: Swinnich, *Living and Playing the Blues*, 32; Evans, *Big Road Blues*, 176.

149 Most of the new arrivals: J. Todd Moye, *Let the People Decide: Black Freedom and White Resistance Movements in Sunflower County, Mississippi, 1945–1986* (Chapel Hill: University of North Carolina Press, 2004), 28–29.

149 a culture evolved: Evans, "Charley Patton," 45.

149 no access to credit: Beckert, *Empire of Cotton*, 290.

150 British company wanted: This is described in detail in Otto, *Final Frontiers*, 51–52.

151 "soared," made "a wild leap": "New Cotton Record," *The New York Times*, March 5, 1918; "Wild Leap in Cotton," *The New York Times*, April 10, 1917.

151 "A riot of extravagance": Sillers, *History of Bolivar County*, 225.

151 in the Bank of Drew: Hemphill, *Fevers, Faith, and Floods*, 200.

152 bought his own farm: Evans, "Charley Patton," 45–46; Swinnich, *Living and Playing the Blues*, 32.

152 Southern Cotton Picker Company: Swinnich, *Living and Playing the Blues*, 113; "The Central South," *The Iron Age* 95, no. 17 (April 29, 1915): 982, digitized by the Internet Archive.

152 tried to close: Swinnich, *Living and Playing the Blues*, 21, 23.

152 first mass exodus: Asch, *Senator and the Sharecropper*, 48–49.

153 True Light Cemetery: Swinnich, *Living and Playing the Blues*, 81; Lester, interviewed by Evans.

153 Black soldiers returned: Swinnich, *Living and Playing the Blues*, 70.

153 "We return fighting": W.E.B. Du Bois, "Returning Soldiers," *The Crisis* 18 (May 1919): 13.

153 The Klan returned: "Some 18 million Americans were sufficiently disturbed by the wrenching changes in post–World War I America to join the ranks of the KKK." Bertram Wyatt-Brown, *The House of Percy: Honor, Melancholy, and Imagination in a Southern Family* (New York: Oxford University Press, 1994), 226; Swinnich, *Living and Playing the Blues*, 70; Vincent Mikkelsen, "Coming from Battle to Face a War: The Lynching of Black Soldiers in the World War I Era" (PhD diss., Florida State University, 2007).

153 The enemies of the poor: Wyatt-Brown, *House of Percy*, 232.

153 first returning Black veteran: Mikkelsen, "Coming from Battle," 40, 99–110, 121–29; NAACP, *Thirty Years of Lynching in the United States: 1889–1918* (New York: NAACP National Office, 1919); Cameron McWhirter, *Red Summer: The Summer of 1919 and the Awakening of Black America* (New York: St. Martin's Griffin, 2012), 51, 68–75, 96–113; Whitaker, "Case Study in Southern Justice," 64; Jason Morgan Ward, "The Infamous Lynching Site That Still Stands in Mississippi," *Time*, May 16, 2016.

154 "Go to hell": Whitaker, "Case Study in Southern Justice," 66.

154 exodus of blues musicians: Evans, *Big Road Blues*, 182, 261; Asch, *Senator and the Sharecropper*, 50; Swinnich, *Living and Playing the Blues*, 50.

155 David Evans wrote: Evans, *Big Road Blues*, 190, 197.

155 wealth in cotton country: Boyd Lee, "Wonders Wrought by 40-Cent Cotton," *The New York Times*, February 1, 1920, 80; "Cotton Prices Drop 50 to 69 Points," *The New York Times*, February 1, 1950, N5.

155 The next week brought: "India's Cotton Crop," *The New York Times*, February 1, 1920, N6; "British Message Sends Cotton Down," *The New York Times*, February 5, 1920, 21; *International Herald Tribune*, "1920: Cotton Prices Fall," *The New York Times*, November 30, 1995.

156 enough unspun cotton: "Interesting Statistics of Cotton Carry Over of 1920," *The Yazoo Herald*, December 31, 1920, 6.

156 Membership in the Klan rose: "Night Rider Raids Spread in South," *The New York Times*, October 11, 1920, 1.

156 replace cotton with synthetics: "Synthetics and the Cotton Textile Industry," *Monthly Review, Federal Reserve Bank of Atlanta* 30, no. 4 (April 30, 1945).

156 next door to her father-in-law: Curry, *Silver Rights*, 80, 84.

158 relative named Son Ham: Curry, "Son Ham's Hat," 15–17; Curry, *Silver Rights*, 87–88.

159 Friday, December 14, 1923: "Negro Runs Amuck, Four Killed and Six Wounded Near Drew," *Drew Leader*, December 21, 1923, available at Florida State University Special Collections; Evans, *Big Road Blues*, 190–93; Kay Mills, *This Little Light of Mine: The Life of Fannie Lou Hamer, Civil Rights and the Struggle for Black Equality in the Twentieth Century* (Lexington: University Press of Kentucky, 2007), 11–12;

Mike Manning, interviewed by Plater Robinson; Nan Elizabeth Woodruff, *American Congo: The African American Freedom Struggle in the Delta* (Chapel Hill: University of North Carolina Press, 2012), 138–39.

159 **manager, Tom Sanders:** "Adds Murder to Murder," *The Kansas City Times*, December 15, 1923, 3; "Burning Oil to Dislodge Fugitive Slayer of 3," *The Evening News* (Harrisburg, PA), December 15, 1923; "Four Killed in Battle with Negro Farmers," *The Dothan Eagle* (Dothan, AL), December 15, 1923; Evans, *Big Road Blues*, 190–92.

159 **the entire cotton season:** "Boll Weevil Less Active Than Expected," *The Commercial Appeal* (Memphis), August 27, 1923, 10.

161 **at the Wild Bill Bayou:** "Negro Runs Amuck"; "Mississippi Delta Town Waked by Volleys of Shots," *Sun Herald* (Biloxi, MS), December, 15, 1923, 1; "Four Killed in Battle with Negro Farmers."

161 **Pullum had killed:** "Fourth Victim of Negro Dies," *Sun Herald* (Biloxi, MS), December 17, 1923, 1; "Fourth Death Near in Attack on Desperado," *The Commercial Appeal* (Memphis), December 16, 1912, 19; "Death List Five in Drew Tragedy," *The Clarion-Ledger* (Jackson, MS), December 18, 1923; "Negro Tenant Shoots Three, Wounds Nine," *The Selma Times-Journal*, December 15, 1923, 1; "Battled Posse Mississippians Over 7 Hours," *The Journal and Tribune* (Knoxville, TN), December 15, 1923, 1, 12; "Three Killed by Desperate Negro Shooter," *The Chattanooga Daily Times*, December 15, 1923, 1; Manning, interviewed by Robinson; Susan Klopfer, *Who Killed Emmett Till?* (self-published, Lulu, 2010), 59–65.

162 **enforced a strict curfew:** Swinnich, *Living and Playing the Blues*, 86; Nick Salvatore, *Singing in a Strange Land: C. L. Franklin, the Black Church, and the Transformation of America* (New York: Little, Brown, 2005), 14.

162 **The Franklin family left:** Salvatore, *Singing in a Strange Land*, 14.

162 **a cloud of "pain and misery":** Davis Houck, in conversation with the author.

163 **"Eslie" Milam's house burned:** "Scobey, Route One," *The Sun-Sentinel* (Charleston, MS), October 9, 1924, 6.

163 **whole thing caved in:** "Two of Three Victims of Gravel Pit Accident Die of Their Injuries," *The Sun-Sentinel* (Charleston: MS), October 27, 1927, 1; "1 Killed, 3 Injured in Gravel Pit Cave-In on Highway to Charleston," *The Sun-Sentinel* (Charleston: MS), October 25, 2007, 6.

163 **little piece of land:** "Notice of Trustee's Sale: Sale of Lands," *The Sun-Sentinel* (Charleston, MS), December 22, 1927; "Notice of Trustee's Sale: Sale of Lands," *The Sun-Sentinel* (Charleston, MS), January 5, 1928.

163 **for the land, Turner-Farber-Love:** "Notice of Trustee's Sale: Sale of Lands," *The Sun-Sentinel* (Charleston, MS), December 22, 1927, 4.

164 **house on Dockery burned:** Joe Rice Dockery, interviewed by John Jones, December 13, 1979, Mississippi Department of Archives and History, AU 544 Dockery, 2.

164 **peaked in 1930:** In fact, in 1930, "Sunflower County was among the most densely populated areas in the entire South." Asch, *Senator and the Sharecropper*, 67.

164 **duck hunt in Louisiana:** Dockery, interviewed by Jones, 24–25; Wyatt-Brown, *House of Percy*, 178; Keith Somerville Dockery McLean and Deborah C. Fort, *Wanderer from the Delta* (Philadelphia, MS: K.S.D. McLean, 2002), 67; Stuart Omer Landry, *History of the Boston Club* (New Orleans: Pelican, 1938), 186–89, 196–97; Barry, *Rising Tide*, 217, 218.

NOTES

165 **Dockery had written:** Swinnich, *Living and Playing the Blues*, 105.

165 **"We had the richest":** Sillers, *History of Bolivar County*, 173.

165 **Joe Rice Dockery said:** Palmer, *Deep Blues*, 56.

166 **In *Deep Blues*:** Palmer, *Deep Blues*, 90.

166 **In 1929 Paramount Records':** Evans, "Charley Patton," 14, 67; Swinnich, *Living and Playing the Blues*, xii.

166 **his Stella guitar:** Palmer, *Deep Blues*, 83; Stephen Calt and Gayle Wardlow, *King of the Delta Blues: The Life and Music of Charlie Patton* (Newton, NJ: Rock Chapel Press, 1988), 182.

166 **in a northern studio:** Palmer, *Deep Blues*, 83–85; Swinnich, *Living and Playing the Blues*, 42.

167 **Willie Brown leaned:** Evans, "Charley Patton," 83.

167 **believed to exist:** Alex van der Tuuk, digital correspondence with the author.

168 **Delta collapsed outright:** Otto, *Final Frontiers*, 83–96; Hemphill, *Fevers, Floods, and Faith*, 155; Swinnich, *Living and Playing the Blues*, 22.

168 **John Otto wrote:** Otto, *Final Frontiers*, 91.

168 **made it to the Delta:** 1910 U.S. Census, Tallahatchie County, Mississippi, Beat 3, Enumeration District 74, May 19, 1910, 16B–17A; 1920 U.S. Census, Tallahatchie County, Mississippi, Beat 3, Enumeration District 132, February 17, 1920, 2B–3A; 1930 U.S. Census, Tallahatchie County, Mississippi, Beat 3, Enumeration District 68-8, April 10, 1930, 8A.

169 **Black man bled on the floor:** Bryant, interviewed by Tyson.

169 **read off the names:** Scott Blackwood, *The Rise and Fall of Paramount Records* (Baton Rouge: Louisiana State University Press), 1–3.

170 **liked to teach the children:** Swinnich, *Living and Playing the Blues*, 38; Lester, interviewed by Evans.

171 **"Time will tell":** "Arouses Usual Alarm," *Indianola Enterprise*, September 20, 1934, 6.

172 **shortness of breath:** Palmer, *Deep Blues*, 86; Evans, "Charley Patton," 83–87, 118–19; T. Dewayne Moore, "Charley Patton's Grave: More Than a Memorial in Holly Ridge," *Mississippi Folklife*, Spring 2018.

172 **They sang over his body:** Palmer, *Deep Blues*, 89; Moore, "Charley Patton's Grave."

173 **timber concern Taylor & Crate:** Jane Adams and D. Gordan, "This Land Ain't My Land: The Eviction of Sharecroppers by the Farm Security Administration," *Agricultural History* 83, no. 3 (2009): 323–51; Taylor, "Sunflower Plantation, Part 1."

174 **called the Farm Security Administration:** James Donald Holley, "The New Deal and Farm Tenancy: Rural Resettlement in Arkansas, Louisiana, and Mississippi" (PhD thesis, Louisiana State University and Agricultural and Mechanical College, August 1969).

174 **remove the Black families:** Adams and Gordan, "This Land Ain't My Land"; Holley, "New Deal and Farm Tenancy."

174 **At the plantation's peak:** Adams and Gordan, "This Land Ain't My Land"; Taylor, "Sunflower Plantation, Part 1," 2.

175 **J. W. Riddell, who'd been:** Adams and Gordan, "This Land Ain't My Land," 334.

175 **houses got torn down:** Adams and Gordan, "This Land Ain't My Land"; Taylor, "Sunflower Plantation, Part 1," 3.

176 **her pregnant daughter:** Mamie Till-Mobley and Chris Benson, *Death of Innocence: The Story of the Hate Crime That Changed America* (New York: One World, 2003), 3–6.

176 **The father, Louis Till:** Till-Mobley and Benson, *Death of Innocence*, 3–6.

176 **"like a government office":** Till-Mobley and Benson, *Death of Innocence*, 4.

177 **The Peavine shut down:** Sillers, *History of Bolivar County*, 230.

177 **reign over the family empire:** Swinnich, *Living and Playing the Blues*, 132; McLean and Fort, *Wanderer from the Delta*, 23, 61, 64–65, 73, 76, 80, 113.

177 **world beyond cotton:** Swinnich, *Living and Playing the Blues*, 130.

178 **the Ithaca Gun Company:** Rachel Hendricks, "A Site's History: Ithaca Gun Company" (honors thesis, College of Agriculture and Life Sciences, Landscape Studies, of Cornell University, January 2011); "Colt M1911A1 & Ithaca 1911A1 (Colt type)," catalog no. FIR 11517, Imperial War Museums, London.

179 **In 1943 Luvenia Slaughter:** Curry, *Silver Rights* 104.

179 **at the Hopson Plantation:** Dockery, interviewed by Jones, 10.

180 **oldest daughter, Mae Bertha:** Curry, *Silver Rights* 103–4.

180 **last confirmed sighting:** Saikku, *This Delta, This Land*, 227–28.

180 **Chicago Mill and Lumber:** Saikku, *This Delta, This Land*, 227–28.

180 **"We are just money grubbers":** Saikku, *This Delta, This Land*, 228.

180 **animals had vanished:** Saikku, *This Delta, This Land*, 226.

181 **Don Eckelberry, just twenty-three:** Saikku, *This Delta, This Land*, 228.

181 **J. W. Milam served:** Dale Killinger, digital correspondence with the author, April 3, 2023; 289th Infantry After Action Report, February 1945, Army Heritage Center Foundation, Carlisle, Pennsylvania, 18, 23.

181 **Milam's company attacked:** Unless otherwise noted, the information in this section comes from the following primary documentation: 289th Infantry Morning Reports, Regiment Company C and E, November 1944–March 1945, National Personnel Records Center, National Archives, St. Louis; "The Battle in the Ardennes 23 Dec 1944–27 Jan 1945; The Colmar Pocket Battle 30 Jan 1945–9 Feb 1945; The Battle for the Ruhr 31 Mar 1945–15 Apr 1945," *The 75th Infantry Division in Combat*, 75th Infantry Division Office of the Commanding General, June 4, 1945, Ike Skelton Combined Arms Research Library Digital Library; 289th Infantry S-3 Periodic Reports, February 1945, National Personnel Records Center, National Archives, St. Louis; 289th Infantry Extracts from S-3 Journal, February 1945, Narrative Report to Accompany Appendix 1, National Personnel Records Center, National Archives, St. Louis; Captain Archie R. Hyle, Infantry, "The Operations of the 3rd Battalion 291st Infantry (75th Infantry Division) North of Aldringen, Belgium, January 22, 1945," The Infantry School, Advanced Infantry Officers Course No. II, Fort Benning, Georgia, 1949; Captain Willoughby B. Tyler, Infantry, "The Operations of the 289th Infantry Regiment (76th Infantry Division) at Appenwihr, France, 31 January–5 February 1945 (Rhineland Campaign) (Personal Experience of a Battalion Adjutant)," Advanced Infantry Officers Course No. I, The Infantry School, Fort Benning, Georgia, 1948.

182 **Shrapnel tore through:** John W. Milam in the U.S. World War II Hospital Admission Card Files, 1942–1954, National Archives and Records Administration; "Mississippi Casualties from All Fronts," *Delta Democrat-Times* (Greenville, MS), March 16, 1945.

183 **summer of 1947:** Till-Mobley and Benson, *Death of Innocence*, 34–35, 104.

183 **called it Dark Fear:** Federal Bureau of Investigation, "Prosecutive Report of Investigation Concerning Emmett Louis Till," February 9, 2016, FBI Case File No.

62D-JN-30045-FD302, 21–23; Simeon Wright and Herb Boyd, *Simeon's Story: An Eyewitness Account of the Kidnapping of Emmett Till* (Chicago: Lawrence Hill Books, 2011), 25; Reverend Wheeler Parker Jr. and Christopher Benson, *A Few Days Full of Trouble: Revelations on the Journey to Justice for My Cousin and Best Friend, Emmett Till* (New York: One World Ballantine, 2024), 84.

183 **Moses Wright, the child:** Anderson, *Emmett Till*, 23; Wright and Boyd, *Simeon's Story*, 5–9, 13, 34; Parker and Benson, *A Few Days Full of Trouble*, 84.

184 **"He was German":** Wheeler Parker Jr. and Simeon Wright, interviewed by Devery Anderson, February 7, 2007, Devery Anderson Papers, Florida State University Special Collections, Tallahassee, Florida.

184 **The family made money:** "Determined to Harvest Bumper Crop," *Tri-State Defender* (Memphis), September 17, 1955, 1.

185 **pastored a church:** Wright and Boyd, *Simeon's Story*, 34.

185 **two hundred pounds of cotton:** "Determined to Harvest Bumper Crop."

185 **Emmett didn't understand:** Till-Mobley and Benson, *Death of Innocence*, 108; Anderson, *Emmett Till*, 26.

186 **"Let's go back," he'd shout:** Wright and Boyd, *Simeon's Story*, 43.

186 **alone on the ocean:** Wheeler Parker Jr., "Wheeler Parker Jr. Interview, 5-23-11," interview by Joseph Mosiner, Civil Rights History Project, Southern Oral History Program under contract to the Smithsonian Institution's National Museum of African American History & Culture and the Library of Congress, May 23, 2011; Wright and Boyd, *Simeon's Story*, 26.

186 **Emmett borrowed a hammer:** Till-Mobley and Benson, *Death of Innocence*, 35.

186 **Everybody hated him:** Kenneth L. Bowers, letter to the editor, *Los Angeles Times*, November 2, 1985, A2.

186 **Carolyn Holloway were dating:** Carolyn Bryant and Marsha Bryant, "I Am More Than a Wolf Whistle" (unpublished manuscript), 2008, 19.

186 **houses on Heathman Frazier Road:** 1950 U.S. Census, unincorporated Sunflower County, Enumeration District 67-34, April 7, 1950, 6; 1950 U.S. Census Map, Batch 45, Sunflower County, Mississippi, ED MS 67-1 to 95, NAID 20739889.

188 **loose network of stores:** Anderson, *Emmett Till*, 24; Whitaker, "Case Study in Southern Justice"; Federal Bureau of Investigation, "Prosecutive Report," 23.

188 **A fire burned down:** "No Plea for Help Arrived Firemen Say," *Enterprise-Journal* (McComb, MS), February 25, 1953, 1.

188 **burned down again:** "Glendora Hard Hit by Damaging Fire," *The Greenwood Commonwealth*, February 7, 1955, 1.

188 **moonshine and bootlegging operation:** Plater Robinson, in conversation with the author; Whitaker, "Case Study in Southern Justice, 161.

188 **"white trash" and "peckerwoods":** The derogatory class-based term *peckerwoods* exploded into the national consciousness after the Till trial and acquittal. See David Halberstam, "Tallahatchie County Acquits a Peckerwood," *The Reporter* (New York), April 19, 1956, 26–30.

188 **"he's not paying":** Bryant, interviewed by Tyson.

188 **Ed and Bud Milam:** State v. Milam, 210 Miss. 13 (1950), 48 So. 2d 594.

188 **man named A. C. Love:** Anderson, *Emmett Till*, 271.

189 **That brother, Benjamin Love:** Anderson, *Emmett Till*, 271.

189 "On a vacation," Milam told them: Anderson, *Emmett Till*, 271.

189 telling his wife: Bryant and Bryant, "I Am More Than a Wolf Whistle."

190 old Dockery Commissary: McLean and Fort, *Wanderer from the Delta*, 109–10.

190 Delta & Pine started: Pete Daniel, *Lost Revolutions: The South in the 1950s* (Chapel Hill: University of North Carolina Press, 2000), 44; Early C. Ewing Jr., interviewed by Roberta Miller, Oral History Project: Greenville and Vicinity, Mississippi Department of Archives and History and the Washington County Library System, June 5, 1978.

190 first-ever refrigerator: Wright and Boyd, *Simeon's Story*, 9–10, 31.

190 parts of his life: Wright and Boyd, *Simeon's Story*, 31.

191 followed the presidential elections: Wright and Boyd, *Simeon's Story*, 9–10.

191 Black shoe store: Gloria Dickerson, in conversation with the author.

192 White Mississippi reacted: Whitaker, "Case Study in Southern Justice."

192 named Robert "Tut" Patterson: Moye, *Let the People Decide*, 56–58; Hemphill, *Fevers, Floods, and Faith*, 748; Neil R. McMillen, *The Citizens' Council: Organized Resistance to the Second Reconstruction, 1954–1964* (Urbana: University of Illinois Press, 1971), 16, 36.

192 "If we white Southerners submit": Bryan Hardin Thrift, "Robert 'Tut' Patterson," *Mississippi Encylopedia*, n.d.

193 a Yazoo County planter: "Woman Solon in Defense of State Citizens' Councils," *The Clarion-Ledger* (Jackson, MS), September 14, 1954, 1.

193 Patterson made his views clear: William A. Caldwell, "Simeon Stylites: The Champion from Far Away," *The Record* (Hackensack, NJ), 60.

193 on South St. Lawrence Avenue: "Parents and Relatives Keep Silent in Case of Boy Charged with Ugly Remarks to Storekeeper's Wife," *Jackson Advocate*, September, 3, 1955, 1.

193 In this holiday glow: Till-Mobley and Benson, *Death of Innocence*, 84–87, 90.

III: 1955

197 On January 1, 1955: Mamie Till-Mobley and Chris Benson, *Death of Innocence: The Story of the Hate Crime That Changed America* (New York, One World, 2003), 86–87.

197 "turkey dinners," Ollie says: Ollie Gordon, in conversation with the author.

198 turned out to be a photographer: Till-Mobley and Benson, *Death of Innocence*, 87.

200 alone into downtown Chicago: Till-Mobley and Benson, *Death of Innocence*, 88–89.

201 like superheroes to him: Till-Mobley and Benson, *Death of Innocence*, 61, 79.

202 "before dark," he wrote: Till-Mobley and Benson, *Death of Innocence*, 88–89.

203 Harold Wilson make a plea: Unless otherwise noted, the entirety of this section comes from 538 Parl. Deb. H.C. (5th ser.) (1955), cols. 447–576.

206 leader Sir Raymond Streat: Sir Raymond Streat, *Lancashire and Whitehall: The Diary of Sir Raymond Streat*, vol. 2, ed. Marguerite Dupree (Manchester: Manchester University Press, 1987), 755–64.

207 started passing laws: Hugh Stephen Whitaker, "A Case Study in Southern Justice: The Emmett Till Case" (master's thesis, Florida State University, 1963), 74–79.

208 "A kangaroo court": Charles M. Hills, "Affairs of State: Warren Doesn't Know South," *The Clarion-Ledger* (Jackson, MS), April 17, 1955, 39.

208 about the achievement gap: Brown v. Board of Education, 349 U.S. 294 (1955); "'Attitude' Gets Challenge in Desegregation Argument," *Cincinnati Enquirer*, April 13, 1955, 2.

208 Democratic gubernatorial: Whitaker, "Case Study in Southern Justice," 81–82.

209 "A hot summer away": Sam Johnson, "Mississippi Has 5 Candidates Making Bid for Governor," *The Greenwood Commonwealth*, May 7, 1955, 1.

209 The talk in the cafés: Whitaker, "Case Study in Southern Justice," 61–101.

209 "a few killings": William A. Caldwell, "Simeon Stylites: The Champion from Far Away," *The Record* (Hackensack, NJ), December 8, 1955, 120.

209 "the gun and the torch": "Bar Association President Tells Rotarians of Segregation Fight," *Delta Democrat-Times* (Greenville, MS), August 11, 1955, 11.

209 "There will be bloodshed": "Journalists Debate Desegregation Story," *The Clarion-Ledger* (Jackson, MS), April 23, 1955, 4.

209 preacher in Belzoni: David Halberstam, *The Fifties* (New York: Random House, 1994), 430–31.

209 His print shop: Jack Mendelsohn, "A Man Who Was Somebody: The Rev. George W. Lee, May 7, 1955," in *The Martyrs: 16 Who Gave Their Lives for Racial Justice* (New York: Harper & Row, 1966), 1–11.

210 The threats intensified: Halberstam, *Fifties*, 430.

210 focused on Lee: Mendelsohn, "Man Who Was Somebody," 4.

210 told the FBI: "George Lee: Notice to Close File," Department of Justice, Civil Rights Division, File No. 144-40-2154, July 12, 2011.

210 Belzoni chief of police: Halberstam addresses this pervasive dynamic eloquently: "In Belzoni, as in many other Mississippi towns, the most violent racists frequently led dual lives: They were men who broke the law even though they were often officers of the law. No one knew this better than Lee." Halberstam, *Fifties*, 430; "George Lee: Notice to Close File."

210 The FBI believes Ray: "George Lee: Notice to Close File."

210 number 3 buckshot: "George Lee: Notice to Close File."

211 Mississippi since 1951: "Urge Ike to Seek Justice," *Tri-State Defender* (Memphis), September 10, 1955, 1.

211 DIES IN ODD ACCIDENT: "Negro Leader Dies in Odd Accident," *The Clarion-Ledger* (Jackson, MS), May 9, 1955, 16.

211 "A ladies' man," he told reporters: As Halberstam reports, this case did not make it past the Mississippi media and had zero national coverage at the time. "This is what Mississippi white men had always done, and therefore it was not news." Halberstam, *Fifties*, 431; "Justice Department Asks FBI to Probe Delta Negro Death," *The Clarion-Ledger* (Jackson, MS), May 22, 1955, 1.

211 after the shooting, the FBI found: "George Lee: Notice to Close File."

212 didn't arrest anyone: Halberstam, *Fifties*, 431.

212 casket lid open: David T. Beito and Linda Royster Beito, *Black Maverick: T.R.M. Howard's Fight for Civil Rights and Economic Power*, The New Black Studies Series (Urbana: University of Illinois Press, 2009), 118.

212 Ellis Wright's role: American Friends Service Committee (Southeastern Office), National Council of the Churches of Christ in the United States of America (Department of Racial and Cultural Relations), and Southern Regional Council,

"Intimidation Reprisal and Violence in the South's Racial Crisis," n.d., 13. His correspondence regarding the Citizens' Councils can also be found in the University of Mississippi's Special Collections in the Citizens' Council Collection, Correspondence.

213 **On the same page:** "Millsaps Board Says Free Inquiry by Its Students Encouraged," *Delta Democrat-Times* (Greenville, MS), March 15, 1958, 1; "Group Is Determined Negroes Will Vote," *Delta Democrat-Times* (Greenville, MS), March 15, 1958, 1.

213 **"threat to our community":** "Citizens' Council Alerted about Bi-racial Threat," *The Clarion-Ledger* (Jackson, MS), May 5, 1962, 8.

213 **mocked my great-grandfather in print:** Hoddington Carter, "Ellis Wright & Bill of Rights," *Delta Democrat-Times* (Greenville, MS), March 11, 1958, 4.

215 **every Monday morning:** Whitaker, "Case Study in Southern Justice," 21–60.

216 **"All deliberate speed":** Brown v. Board of Education.

216 **All five candidates tried:** Sam Johnson, "Mississippi Has 5 Candidates," 1; Whitaker, "Case Study in Southern Justice", 81–82.

216 **Emmett Till was on the edge:** Till-Mobley and Benson, *Death of Innocence*, 91–93.

217 **back to South St. Lawrence Avenue:** "Parents and Relatives Keep Silent."

218 **a birthday party:** Till-Mobley and Benson, *Death of Innocence*, 94–97.

219 **who would pull the fire alarm:** Wheeler Parker and Simeon Wright, interviewed by Devery Anderson, February 7, 2007, Devery Anderson Papers, Florida State University Special Collections, Tallahassee, Florida.

222 **United Daughters of the Confederacy luncheon:** "Great Forrest Was Born 134 Years Ago Today," *Memphis Press-Scimitar*, July 13, 1955, 29; "Tribute Paid to 'Old Bedford,' as UDC Honors His Birthday," *The Commercial Appeal* (Memphis), July 14, 1955.

222 **Mississippi history book I studied:** Jesse O. McKee, *Mississippi: A Portrait of an American State* (Montgomery, AL: Clairmont Press, 1995); Rebecca Miller Davis, "The Three R's—Reading, 'Riting, and Race: The Evolution of Race in Mississippi History Textbooks, 1900–1995," *Journal of Mississippi History* 72 (2010): 1–45.

224 **house of Gloria Dickerson's parents:** Gloria Dickerson, in conversation with the author; Constance Curry, *Silver Rights* (San Diego: Harcourt Brace, 1996), 44–45.

224 **Amzie Moore, who organized:** *The Mississippi Encyclopedia*, ed. Ted Ownby, Charles Reagan Wilson, and University of Mississippi (Jackson: University Press of Mississippi, 2017), s.v. "Amzie Moore"; Amzie Moore, interviewed by Judy Richardson, March 22, 1980, for *America, They Loved You Madly*, available at Washington University in St. Louis University Libraries.

225 **Black informers in Township 22:** Curry, *Silver Rights*, 48.

225 **schoolteacher named Dola Walters:** Whitaker, "Case Study in Southern Justice," 88–95; Board 'Files' NAACP Petition," *The Greenwood Commonwealth*, August 13, 1955, 1; "Leading White Citizens Grow Weary Defending Negroes as School Petitions Increase Tension in State," *Jackson Advocate*, August 13, 1955, 7.

226 **signed in Yazoo City:** Halberstam, *Fifties*, 430; "'Non-discriminatory Basis,' NAACP Asks School Board: Letter to Board Is Signed by 53 Negroes," *The Yazoo Herald*, 1–2; Mary Aickin Rothschild, "The Volunteers and the Freedom Schools: Education for Social Change in Mississippi," *History of Education Quarterly* 22, no. 4 (Winter 1982): 405.

226 **scheduled to leave Chicago:** Till-Mobley and Benson, *Death of Innocence*, 98–100.

228 "worse than that": Till-Mobley and Benson, *Death of Innocence*, 100–101.

228 years earlier, in 1941: Robert T. Palmer, *Deep Blues* (New York: Penguin Books, 1982), 3–4.

228 followed his mentor north: Palmer, *Deep Blues*, 7; Pete Daniel, *Lost Revolutions: The South in the 1950s* (Chapel Hill: University of North Carolina Press, 2000), 10; Wayne E. Goins, *Blues All Day Long: The Jimmy Rogers Story*, Music in American Life (Urbana: University of Illinois Press, 2014), 29.

228 at 3652 Calumet Avenue: Goins, *Blues All Day Long*, 29.

229 in 1952, Howlin' Wolf: Peter Guralnick, *Searching for Robert Johnson* (New York: Plume, 1998), 26; Ted Gioia, *Delta Blues: The Life and Times of the Mississippi Masters Who Revolutionized American Music* (New York: W. W. Norton, 2008), 289.

232 "Wow," Benson said: Reverend Wheeler Parker Jr. and Christopher Benson, *A Few Days Full of Trouble: Revelations on the Journey to Justice for My Cousin and Best Friend, Emmett Till* (New York: One World Ballantine, 2024), 253–54, 259.

232 Mamie handed him: Till-Mobley and Benson, *Death of Innocence*, 104; Parker and Benson, *Few Days Full of Trouble*, 101; "Till Nearly Missed His Fatal Journey to Land of Cotton," *The Clarion-Ledger* (Jackson, MS), September 19, 1955, 1.

233 saw the train: Till-Mobley and Benson, *Death of Innocence*, 104–5.

233 judge Tom Brady: Judge Tom P. Brady, "A Review of Black Monday" (address to the Indianola Citizens' Council, October 28, 1954).

233 More than two thousand: Whitaker, "Case Study in Southern Justice," 6–7.

234 Senator Eastland took the stage: "Citizens Council Plans Community Meetings in Tate," *Tate County Democrat*, August 18, 1955.

234 veteran named Lamar Smith: Whitaker, "Case Study in Southern Justice," 177–78; Simeon Wright and Herb Boyd, *Simeon's Story: An Eyewitness Account of the Kidnapping of Emmett Till* (Chicago: Lawrence Hill Books, 2011), 10–11.

234 heard Smith's last words: "Not One Witness," *St. Louis Post-Dispatch*, June 28, 1956, 23.

235 sound of the train died away: Till-Mobley and Benson, *Death of Innocence*, 105.

235 She knew that by two: Till-Mobley and Benson, *Death of Innocence*, 105–6.

236 outside to meet them: Wright and Boyd, *Simeon's Story*, 41.

236 handful of mud as proof: Parker and Wright, interviewed by Anderson.

236 listen to radio programs: Wright and Boyd, *Simeon's Story*, 33–34, 41–42; Till-Mobley and Benson, *Death of Innocence*, 113–14.

236 out on the front porch: Wright and Boyd, *Simeon's Story*, 42–43; Parker and Benson, *Few Days Full of Trouble*, 12–13.

237 hot before sunrise: Wright and Boyd, *Simeon's Story*, 43–46.

238 home and help Elizabeth: Wright and Boyd, *Simeon's Story*, 41; Till-Mobley and Benson, *Death of Innocence*, 112.

238 state and national elections: Wright and Boyd, *Simeon's Story*, 9; Parker and Wright, interviewed by Anderson.

238 raided a watermelon patch: Wheeler Parker Jr., "Wheeler Parker Jr. Interview, 5-23-11," interview by Joseph Mosiner, Civil Rights History Project, Southern Oral History Program under contract to the Smithsonian Institution's National Museum of African American History & Culture and the Library of Congress, May 23, 2011; Wright and Boyd, *Simeon's Story*, 49.

239 Doris Jean Mosely: *The Chicago Defender*, August 27, 1955.

NOTES

239 **The kids got out:** Like so many other parts of this encounter, the exact number of kids in the car that Wednesday night—and who exactly they were—has been debated and argued over, even by the witnesses who were there.

239 **supposed to be in Money:** Parker and Benson, *Few Days Full of Trouble*, 12; Till-Mobley and Benson, *Death of Innocence*, 100.

240 **the story he'd heard:** Mattie Smith Colin, "Mother's Tears Greet Son Who Died a Martyr," *The Chicago Defender*, September 10, 1955.

240 **cousin Curtis Jones:** Adding confusion to the case in the national press, the cousin who rode down from Chicago with Emmett was sometimes misidentified as Curtis Jones. See Halberstam, *Fifties* 431; Parker and Benson, *Few Days Full of Trouble*, 116.

241 **had the same reaction:** Wright and Boyd, *Simeon's Story*, 101; Parker and Wright, interviewed by Anderson.

241 **local man, Albert Johnson:** Devery S. Anderson, *Emmett Till: The Murder That Shocked the World and Propelled the Civil Rights Movement* (Jackson: University Press of Mississippi, 2015), 29.

242 **clocked their exit:** Parker and Benson, *Few Days Full of Trouble*, 13–15.

242 *years ago in Chicago:* Everything in italics here and on the next few pages the author was present for, and comes directly from his notes, recordings, and recollections.

242 **Ruthie Mae Crawford watched:** Ruth Crawford interview with Keith Beauchamp, seen in *The Untold Story of Emmett Louis Till* (2005).

242 **wasn't there at the store:** Parker and Wright, interviewed by Anderson.

243 **He did not say "ma'am":** Anderson, *Emmett Till*, 31; Parker and Wright, interviewed by Anderson.

243 **get her gun:** Carolyn Bryant and Marsha Bryant, "I Am More Than a Wolf Whistle" (unpublished manuscript), 2008.

243 **"better than that," Maurice said:** "Warned by Cousin," *The News Journal* (Wilmington, DE), September 10, 1955, 1.

243 **Others believe his whistle:** Parker and Benson, *Few Days Full of Trouble*, 14; Anderson, *Emmett Till*, 28–29.

244 **refused to shop there:** Whitaker, "Case Study in Southern Justice," 159–60; Anderson, *Emmett Till*, 201; Dave Tell, *Remembering Emmett Till* (Chicago: University of Chicago Press, 2019), 164–65; Joe Atkins and Tom Brennan, "Bryant Wants the Past to 'Stay Dead,'" *The Clarion-Ledger* (Jackson, MS), August 25, 1985.

244 **Then the family:** Jerry Mitchell, "'They Just Want History to Die': Owners Demand $4 Million for Crumbling Emmett Till Store," *The Clarion-Ledger* (Jackson, MS), August 29, 2018.

245 **Ben Roy gas station:** Dave Tell, *Remembering Emmett Till* (Chicago: University of Chicago Press, 2019), 164, 184–88; "Money, Mississippi Historic Storefront Restoration: Phase 1, Ben Roy's Service Station," For Consideration of the Mississippi Civil Rights Historical Sites Grant, Submitted to the Mississippi Department of Archives and History, May 2011; Patrick Weems, in conversation with the author.

245 **to the table for the grocery:** Tell, *Remembering Emmett Till*, 184–88.

246 **As Dave Tell wrote:** Tell, *Remembering Emmett Till*, 189.

247 **rides into Greenwood:** Wright and Boyd, *Simeon's Story*, 53–55; Parker and Wright, interviewed by Anderson.

248 **He loved dogs:** Till-Mobley and Benson, *Death of Innocence*, 115–16.

251 embargoed and unpublished memoir: Bryant and Bryant, "I Am More Than a Wolf Whistle."

253 on Friday morning: "Till Releases, 1955–1956," William Bradford Huie Papers, Series 17, The Emmett Till Story, 1945–1969, box 39, folder 353b, The Ohio State University Special Collections, Columbus, OH; "Related Correspondence 1955," William Bradford Huie Papers, Series 17, The Emmett Till Story, 1945–1969, box 39, folder 353a, The Ohio State University Special Collections, Columbus, OH.

253 tour of the Delta: Marvel and Wheeler Parker Jr., in conversation with the author.

254 returned home on Friday: Bryant and Bryant, "I Am More Than a Wolf Whistle."

255 Johnny Washington left Money: Parker and Benson, Few Days Full of Trouble; Federal Bureau of Investigation, "Prosecutive Report of Investigation Concerning Emmett Louis Till," February 9, 2016, FBI Case File No. 62D-JN-30045-FD302.

256 "'deal with the Chicago boy'": Whitaker, "Case Study in Southern Justice," 106.

256 hounded, for the rest of her life: Bryant and Bryant, "I Am More Than a Wolf Whistle."

258 men most commonly identified: Tell, Remembering Emmett Till, 44–45; Anderson, Emmett Till, 82.

260 where Simeon and Emmett shared: Wright and Boyd, Simeon's Story, 57.

261 "get to be sixty-five": Anderson, Emmett Till, 37.

261 white neighbors' phone: Wright and Boyd, Simeon's Story, 61.

261 "It was horrible," he said: Parker, interviewed by Anderson.

262 Marvel's dad left Mississippi: Marvel Parker, in conversation with the author.

262 tornado destroyed it: Wright and Boyd, Simeon's Story, 83.

263 Carolyn Bryant's voice: Parker, "Wheeler Parker Jr. Interview"; Anderson, Emmett Till, 37.

263 cried for his mama: Bonnie Blue, Emmett Till's Secret Witness: FBI Confidential Source Speaks (Park Forest, IL: BL Richey, 2013), 174.

264 The crepe-soled shoes: Whitaker, "Case Study in Southern Justice," 110; Anderson, Emmett Till, 235.

264 Hugh Clark was there: Federal Bureau of Investigation, "Prosecutive Report."

266 banks of rivers and bayous: Parker, Few Days Full of Trouble, 106.

266 at first was his name: Till-Mobley and Benson, Death of Innocence, 117.

267 know his full name: Till-Mobley and Benson, Death of Innocence, 119–20.

268 in the Delta, Crosby Smith: Anderson, Emmett Till, 38–40; David A. Shostak, "Crosby Smith: A Forgotten Witness to a Mississippi Nightmare," Negro History Bulletin 38, no. 1 (December 1974–January 1975): 320–25.

268 her mother rallied support: Till-Mobley and Benson, Death of Innocence, 119–23; Anderson, Emmett Till, 40.

268 Crosby said later: Shostak, "Crosby Smith."

268 "no laughter in our house": Wright and Boyd, Simeon's Story, 62.

269 guard the house alone: Wright and Boyd, Simeon's Story, 62.

269 But the guilt remained: Parker and Wright, interviewed by Anderson.

269 "to buy cotton pickers": Wright, interviewed by Anderson.

270 put on a train home: Anderson, Emmett Till, 44.

270 late in the afternoon: Wheeler Parker Jr., in conversation with the author; Joy Parker, in conversation with the author; Parker and Benson, Few Days Full of Trouble, 256; Parker, "Wheeler Parker Jr. Interview."

273 "Go hug your mother": Till-Mobley and Benson, *Death of Innocence*, 121.

273 with Marvel in 1968: Marvel and Wheeler Parker Jr., in conversation with the author.

276 Moses's twenty-five acres: Anderson, *Emmett Till*, 44.

276 drove him toward Glendora: Anderson, *Emmett Till*, 45–47.

276 identified the body: Anderson, *Emmett Till*, 46; Wright and Boyd, *Simeon's Story*, 63–64.

278 She broke the news: Ollie Gordon, in conversation with the author; Till-Mobley and Benson, *Death of Innocence*, 126–27; Anderson, *Emmett Till*, 47.

278 telegram to President Eisenhower: "Telegram from Mamie Bradley (mother of Emmett Till) to President Eisenhower," September 2, 1955, DDE's Records as President, Alphabetical File, box 3113, Emmett Till, NAID 12196780, The Eisenhower Foundation, Abilene, KS.

279 body buried immediately: Anderson, *Emmett Till*, 48–49.

279 under one condition: Anderson, *Emmett Till*, 52, 55.

280 "when you died," she cried: Anderson, *Emmett Till*, 54.

283 got presented, even locally: Christopher Metress, ed., "Discovery and Indictment," in *The Lynching of Emmett Till: A Documentary Narrative*, The American South Series (Charlottesville: University of Virginia Press, 2002), 14–43; Whitaker, "Case Study in Southern Justice," 120–21.

283 had her stashed: Bryant and Bryant, "I Am More Than a Wolf Whistle."

285 story about 1974: Federal Bureau of Investigation, "Prosecutive Report."

287 worst of them: Dale Killinger, in conversation with the author.

288 with their shirts off: James Gunter, "Wives Serious, Children Romp as Trial Begins," in Metress, *Lynching of Emmett Till*, 50–53.

288 *New York Post* wrote: Murray Kempton, "The Baby Sitter," in Metress, *Lynching of Emmett Till*, 54.

288 morning of opening arguments: Whitaker, "Case Study in Southern Justice," 154; Tell, *Remembering Emmett Till*, 158; John Herbers, "Cross Burning at Sumner Went Almost Unnoticed Yesterday," *Delta Democrat-Times* (Greenville, MS), September 22, 1955, 11.

290 Kempton would describe the grilling: Murray Kempton, "He Went All the Way," in Metress, *Lynching of Emmett Till*, 66.

291 "Sambo, Sambo, Sambo": Till-Mobley and Benson, *Death of Innocence*, 175.

291 Moses Wright lived until eighty-six: Moses Wright's exact birthday is, unfortunately, disputed. As Devery Anderson succinctly explains, "Wright was not always sure about the year of his birth. Discrepancies about age were not uncommon at the time, especially among those raised in rural areas. He stated on his World War I draft registration in 1917 that he did not know his exact birth date, but believed he was then twenty-seven years old. If he was right, then his birth would have occurred around 1890. In 1930 he said he was then forty, which also indicated a birth year of 1890. By the summer of 1955, however, he had come to believe that he was born in 1891. The 1900 US Census lists his birth as April 1892, and when that record became available after 1970, he came to accept this date himself. If correct, this meant that in August 1955, he was sixty-three, not sixty-four as he told reporters a week after returning from Chicago." To alleviate any confusion on the part of the reader, I chose to rely on 1891 as his birth year, so that it would line-up with the age he purported to be in his testimony. Anderson, *Emmett Till*, 23.

291 "scared to death": Moses J. Newson, "Death Threat to Till's Uncle: Minister Says He'll Leave Dixie," *The Chicago Defender*, September 17, 1955.

292 was named Dallas: Wright and Boyd, *Simeon's Story*, 81–82; Anderson, *Emmett Till*, 196; Paul Burton, "'Ole Man Mose' Sells Out, He'll Move to New York," *The Clarion-Ledger* (Jackson, MS), September 26, 1955, 1; Ted Poston, "Mose Wright Left Everything to Flee for Life," *New York Post*, October 3, 1955, 5; Newson, "Death Threat to Till's Uncle."

292 "After the speaking tour": Wright and Parker, interviewed by Anderson; Anderson, *Emmett Till*, 258.

292 "Not even to me": Wright and Parker, interviewed by Anderson.

292 housing project on Sixty-Third Place: Anderson, *Emmett Till*, 259.

295 destroyed, lost, or hidden: Metress, *Lynching of Emmett Till*, 45.

296 "roll over in their graves": Anderson, *Emmett Till*, 151.

296 "mountain out of a molehill!": Anderson, *Emmett Till*, 78.

296 he preached to this jury: Anderson, *Emmett Till*, 152.

300 "This is one": Anderson, *Emmett Till*, 154.

301 He mocked Mamie: Anderson, *Emmett Till*, 157.

301 blood and tissue: John W. Milam VA Claims File 427162014, Department of Veterans Affairs, St. Louis, Missouri.

302 standing in a bread line: "What Happened to the Key Figures in the Emmett Till Case?" *The Clarion-Ledger* (Jackson, MS), September 13, 2018.

303 "does something like that": Whitaker, "Case Study in Southern Justice," 161.

304 "salt in a raw, open wound": Wright and Boyd, *Simeon's Story*, 89.

IV: Tomorrow

309 Rosa Parks got the 1955: Unless otherwise noted, the entirety of this section is derived from Jeanne Theoharis, *The Rebellious Life of Mrs. Rosa Parks* (Boston: Beacon Press, 2013).

309 Dexter Avenue Baptist Church: David T. Beito and Linda Royster Beito, *Black Maverick: T.R.M. Howard's Fight for Civil Rights and Economic Power*, The New Black Studies Series (Urbana: University of Illinois Press, 2009), 138–39.

309 Her husband was cooking: Transcript of interview of Rosa Parks by Judith Vecchione for *Eyes on the Prize*, November 14, 1985, Henry Hampton Collection, Film and Media Archive, University Libraries, Washington University in St. Louis.

310 said later she thought: Beito and Beito, *Black Maverick*, 139.

310 by the Sumner courthouse: Dave Tell, *Remembering Emmett Till* (Chicago: University of Chicago Press, 2019), 49–51.

310 store on the market: Devery S. Anderson, *Emmett Till: The Murder That Shocked the World and Propelled the Civil Rights Movement* (Jackson: University Press of Mississippi, 2015), 275.

311 This meeting would birth: Transcript of interview of William Bradford Huie by Blackside, Inc., for *Eyes on the Prize*, August 30, 1979, Henry Hampton Collection, Film and Media Archive, University Libraries, Washington University in St. Louis.

311 the local Blacks: Anderson, *Emmett Till*, 231–34.

312 **"just like prohibition"**: William Bradford Huie to Mr. Walters and Lee Hills, October 18, 1955, William Bradford Huie Papers, CMS 84, Series 17: The Emmett Till Story, 1945–1969, The Ohio State University Special Collections, Columbus, OH.

312 **His work would study**: Huie to Walters and Hills.

312 **"got to have our Milams"**: William Bradford Huie to Roy Wilkins, October 12, 1955, William Bradford Huie Papers, CMS 84, Series 17: The Emmett Till Story, 1945–1969, The Ohio State University Special Collections, Columbus, OH.

312 **"let the chips fall"**: Huie to Walters and Hills.

312 **"ain't gonna be no integration"**: Huie to Wilkins.

313 **"moonshine likker and violence"**: Bill Huie to Dan Mich, October 21, 1955, William Bradford Huie Papers, CMS 84, Series 17: The Emmett Till Story, 1945–1969, The Ohio State University Special Collections, Columbus, OH.

313 **"if your man is the liberal type"**: Huie to Mich.

313 **"hot" in Hollywood**: Huie to Walters and Hills.

314 **"speak to him on the street"**: Huie to Mich; transcript of interview of William Bradford Huie.

314 **disappeared from history**: Tell, *Remembering Emmett Till*, 47.

315 **the man told him**: Bob Buchanan, in conversation with the author; Charlotte Buchanan, in conversation with the author.

316 **he told the Memphis *Commercial Appeal***: John Varlas, "Archie Knows His Role," *The Commercial Appeal* (Memphis), April 23, 2017, 28.

316 **he told the New Orleans *Times-Picayune***: Peter Finney, "A Quiet Cheerleader; Archie Manning, Patriarch of New Orleans' First Football Family, Watches His Son Peyton Play in Super Bowl XLI Today," *The Times-Picayune* (New Orleans), February 4, 2007, 1.

316 **he told the Indianola *Enterprise-Tocsin***: Jamie Scrivener, "Small-Town Life Shaped Football Hero's Character," *The Enterprise-Tocsin* (Indianola, MS), November 12, 2015, B4.

316 **elderly Black man**: Daniel Beaumont, "The Second Coming of the Son," in *Preachin' the Blues: The Life and Times of Son House* (New York: Oxford University Press, 2011), 3–26; Ted Gioia, *Delta Blues: The Life and Times of the Mississippi Masters Who Revolutionized American Music* (New York: W. W. Norton, 2008), 372–74.

319 **"how to play like Son House"**: Kyle Crockett, "A Study of the Life and Legacy of Son House on the Identity and Character of Blues Culture" (undergraduate thesis, University of Mississippi, 2014), 42, https://egrove.olemiss.edu/hon_thesis/558/.

319 **all a "publicity stunt"**: Chris Myers Asch, *The Senator and the Sharecropper: The Freedom Struggles of James O. Eastland and Fannie Lou Hamer* (New York: The New Press, 2008), 207; Michael R. Beschloss, *Taking Charge: The Johnson White House Tapes 1963–1964* (New York: Simon & Schuster, 1998), 442–43.

319 **saw the red Volkswagen**: Gioia, *Delta Blues*, 372–74; Beaumont, "Second Coming of the Son," 3–26.

320 **to the ground in 1965**: Keith Somerville Dockery McLean and Deborah C. Fort, *Wanderer from the Delta* (Philadelphia, MS: K.S.D. McLean, 2002), 81.

320 **Steve Shurden stepped in**: Stafford Shurden, in conversation with the author; Steve Shurden, in conversation with the author.

321 **Keith Dockery looked back**: McLean and Fort, *Wanderer from the Delta*, 119.

321 "comes out pretty strong": McLean and Fort, *Wanderer from the Delta*, 118.

321 trial transcript disappeared: Christopher Metress, ed., *The Lynching of Emmett Till: A Documentary Narrative*, The American South Series (Charlottesville: University of Virginia Press, 2002), 45.

322 woman named Joetha Collier: Fannie Lou Hamer, Maegan Parker Brooks, and Davis W. Houck, *The Speeches of Fannie Lou Hamer: To Tell It like It Is*, Margaret Walker Alexander Series in African American Studies (Jackson: University Press of Mississippi, 2011), 133; Keisha N. Blain, "They Called Her 'Black Jet,'" *The Atlantic*, April 28, 2022.

322 six days apart: "Hubert Clark Rites Friday," *The Sumner Sentinel*, November 23, 1972, 1; "Melvin Campbell," *Delta Democrat-Times* (Greenville, MS), November 11, 1972, 6.

322 military histories burned: Walter W. Stender and Evans Walker, "The National Personnel Records Center Fire: A Study in Disaster," *The American Archivist* 37, no. 4 (October 1974): 521–49.

323 Roy Bryant ran a little: Anderson, *Emmett Till*, 276–77.

323 Bryant walked his wooden: Mary Perry, in conversation with the author.

324 called Lee Academy: Michael W. Fuquay, "Civil Rights and the Private School Movement in Mississippi, 1964–1971," *History of Education Quarterly* 42, no. 2 (Summer 2002): 159–80.

326 Reg Shurden walked: Lynn Shurden, in conversation with the author; Stafford Shurden, in conversation with the author.

326 the worst era in American agriculture: Jerome M. Stam and Bruce L. Dixon, "Farmer Bankruptcies and Farm Exits in the United States, 1899–2002," *Agricultural Information Bulletin*, no. 788 (Economic Research Service, U.S. Department of Agriculture), 11; Willard W. Cochrane, *The Development of American Agriculture: A History Analysis*, 2nd ed. (University of Minnesota Press, 1993) 151.

326 kept emptying out: Gilles Vandal, review of *Let the People Decide: Black Freedom and White Resistance Movement in Sunflower County, Mississippi, 1945–1986*, by J. Todd Moye, *Journal of Social History* 40, no. 2 (Winter 2006): 533–34.

328 named Luster Bayless: Dale Killinger, in conversation with the author; Plater Robinson, in conversation with the author; "Luster Bayless," *The Clarksdale Press Register*, March 30, 2020, A3.

329 offered a detailed history: Jesse Gresham, in conversation with the author; Delores Gresham, in conversation with the author.

330 "open season on the Negroes now": W. Ralph Eubanks, *Ever Is a Long Time: A Journey into Mississippi's Dark Past* (New York: Basic Books, 2005), 68.

331 Sidney Shurden's stepson: Griff Cook, in conversation with the author.

331 "Spooky as hell": Jason Shurden, in conversation with the author.

332 Roy's condition shocked him: Anderson, *Emmett Till*, 281; Paul Hendrickson, *Sons of Mississippi: A Story of Race and Its Legacy* (New York: Vintage Books, 2004), 11.

333 "Every inch of ground": Plater Robinson, in conversation with the author; Plater Robinson, "The Murder of Emmett Till," Soundprint Media, n.d.

334 when describing the murder: Susan Klopfer, *Who Killed Emmett Till?* (self-published, Lulu, 2010), 153–55.

335 "They got the death penalty": Jerry Mitchell, digital communication with the author.

335 "looking for the barn": Keith Beauchamp, in conversation with the author.

337 Keith's documentary came out in 2005: *The Untold Story of Emmett Louis Till*, directed by Keith Beauchamp.

337 birder named Gene Sparling: Bill Bowden, "Ivory-Billed Woodpecker Last Seen in East Arkansas Extinct, Federal Agency Says; Ornithologists Outraged," *Arkansas Democrat Gazette*, September 30, 2021.

338 crumbled to dust: Wheeler Parker Jr. and Marvel Parker, in conversation with the author.

338 revealed that he'd been killed: Dale Killinger, in conversation with the author.

338 the FBI presented it: Dale Killinger, in conversation with the author.

339 named Mike Collins: Michelle Donahue, "Possible Ivory-Billed Woodpecker Footage Breathes Life into Extinction Debate," *National Audubon Society*, January 25, 2017; Catrin Einhorn, "Experts Strive to Prove 'This Bird Actually Does Exist,'" *New York Times*, May 19, 2023, A21.

339 signed the Till Bill into law: The Emmett Till Unsolved Civil Rights Crime Act of 2007.

339 haunts their barn: Jeff Andrews, in conversation with the author.

340 he said as the skies darkened: Ed Phillips, in conversation with the author.

342 died in their community: Gloria Dickerson, in conversation with the author.

344 Her fiercely loyal: So much so that Marsha Bryant is listed as the coauthor of Carolyn Bryant's unpublished memoir, "I Am More Than a Wolf Whistle."

345 "At one time his mother": Marsha Bryant, in conversation with the author.

Index

INDEX